Cultures of Infancy

Cultures of Infancy

Heidi Keller
University of Osnabrück

Psychology Press
Taylor & Francis Group

New York London

Psychology Press
Taylor & Francis Group
270 Madison Avenue
New York, NY 10016

Published in Great Britain by
Psychology Press
Taylor & Francis Group
27 Church Road
Hove, East Sussex BN3 2FA

© 2007 by Taylor & Francis Group, LLC
Psychology Press is an imprint of Taylor & Francis Group
Originally published by Lawrence Erlbaum Associates
Reprinted in 2009 by Psychology Press

Cover design by Tomai Maridou

Printed in the United States of America on acid-free paper
10 9 8 7 6 5 4 3
International Standard Book Number-13: 978-0-8058-6315-4 (Softcover)
International Standard Book Number - 978-0-8058-4895-3 (Hardbound)

Library of Congress Cataloging-in-Publication Data

Keller, Heidi, 1945-
  Cultures of infancy / Heidi Keller
      p. cm.
  Includes bibliographical references and index.
  ISBN 978-0-8058-4895-3 (cloth) ISBN 978-0-8058-6315-4 (pbk.)
    1. Infants—Care—Cross-cultural studies. 2. Infants—Development—Cross-cultural studies.
    3. Parenting—Cross-cultural studies. I. Title.
GN482.1.C85   2007
305.232—dc22   2006022184

Visit the Taylor & Francis Web site at
http://www.taylorandfrancis.com

and the Psychology Press Web site at
http://www.psypress.com

Contents

Foreword

Robert LeVine

This book opens a new window on a world of human experience long acknowledged in developmental psychology but only now being systematically explored: the world of cultural variation in parenting and infant development. Heidi Keller asserts that culture is not incidental or marginal to child development but an essential ingredient in the plans of parents, the kinds of care they provide, and the developmental pathways they establish for their infants. The wealth of evidence presented herein, based on the most extensive program of cross-cultural research on parenting and infancy conducted to date, leaves little doubt that the understanding of cultural differences—not in the abstract but in the particular ways that cultural agendas structure parental behavior and activate different potentials for behavioral development beginning in infancy—is fundamental to any science of child development. With findings from Africa, Asia, and Latin America, as well as Europe and North America, the authors show what different pathways of development are found in their diverse samples and how parental theories and infant care vary by cultural traditions, educational attainment, and generation. Their presentation is fascinating for anyone who has wondered how parenting practices differ and what difference it makes to child development. Keller has also set a new standard for empirical research in this field and created a new reference point for future theory, research, and scientific debate.

Recent texts and even expert panels (Shonkoff & Phillips, 1999) have not hesitated to generalize about early childhood development without considering the 90% of human offspring who grow up in the economically less developed countries of the world or even those growing up in affluent but non-Western countries such as Japan.

They seem to assume that cultural variation, although significant in principle for developmental theory, has not yet been studied with sound enough methods to be taken seriously in a review of the child development research literature. That assumption has long been manifestly fictitious, and this book renders it completely untenable. Yet the child development field has been so resistant to taking cross-cultural evidence seriously that it may not be amiss to consider once again the centrality of cross-cultural research in the science of human child development.

On the theoretical side, cross-cultural research derives its importance from the *plasticity* of human development. The plasticity concept is usually attributed to Virchow, known as the founder of cellular pathology in biomedical research, who was also the leader of German physical anthropology during the last decades of the 19th century. Boas, later to be a major figure in American anthropology, went to Virchow's laboratory in Berlin in 1884 for anthropometric training, and he became a great admirer of Virchow. When Virchow died in 1902, Boas wrote an appreciation of him in *Science,* expounding the plasticity concept:

> Cells, in the course of their lives, may change their forms according to age and according to the influences to which they are subjected. Such changes take place both in the healthy and the sick organism, and often it is impossible to draw a sharp line between normal physiological, and abnormal or pathological, changes … . [I]n reality there is no distinct line of demarcation between physiological and pathological processes, that the latter are only physiological processes which take place under difficult conditions …
>
> [H]is position rests on the general scientific principle that it is dangerous to classify data that are imperfectly known under the point of view of general theories, and that the sound progress of science requires us to be clear at every moment, what elements in the system of science are hypothetical and what are the limits of that knowledge which is obtained by exact observation. (Boas, 1902, reprinted in Stocking, 1974, pp. 38–40)

Thus human bodies change in response to differing environmental conditions, variations appearing to be pathological may be normal responses to differing conditions, and scientists should distinguish what they knows from what they guess. Boas saw Virchow's concept of plasticity or mutability as a basic biological principle that was directly applicable to the physical growth of humans, and his exposition of Virchow's ideas is virtually a charter for his own research on child growth among immigrants in New York. By the time he wrote this passage, Boas had taught in G. Stanley Hall's psychology department at Clark University (1889–1892) and was well acquainted with American and German psychology. He did not do psychological research himself, but his students Edward Sapir, Margaret Mead, and Ruth Benedict were undoubtedly exposed to his views on plasticity, and particularly on the dangers of mistaking an adaptive response to environmental change for a pathological one. In exploring a human domain characterized by plasticity—language, child development, and psychological attitudes—they argued, the scientific observer must avoid jumping to the hasty conclusion that an unfamiliar variant is pathological (or otherwise inadequate). Intensive research can expose the conditions in which differing forms and practices of speaking, rearing children, thinking, and feeling are normal and possibly adaptive. The difference between the ordinary person and the scientist is the latter's systematic examination of those conditions, the better to avoid misdiagnosing difference as pathology or inferiority.

This is precisely what Keller does for the parenting of infants in this book. Nso mothers of Cameroon view the practices of German mothers as inadequate and vice versa, but Keller examines the conditions in which each set of practices is meaningful and makes adaptive sense in its local habitat. Plasticity in the developmental pathways of human children requires this ecological (or ecocultural) research strategy to advance scientific understanding and avoid fallacies of interpretation.

This brings us to the methodological point. Developmental psychology has adopted the laboratory experiment as its model of scientific research, notwithstanding the fact that most developmental variations cannot be produced in the laboratory. Although it is widely acknowledged that Brunswick was right to point out a half-century ago that many psychological experiments are not ecologically valid, neither psychology as a discipline nor its developmental part has legitimized the collection and full publication of the contextual data that could enable interpretations of experimental and other quantitative evidence to achieve validity. Thus the major journals in developmental psychology do not permit publication of extensive ethnographic data even when they are needed to draw credible conclusions from quantitative data.

This adherence to the ideals of the laboratory experiment in the field of child development is particularly strange given the Darwinian ancestry of the field and of the life sciences as a whole. Darwin was a field researcher who explored and recorded diversity in nature, thus providing a credible basis for the most powerful theory of living things we have yet had. Following his lead, field workers in biology and population biologists made great advances in the 20th century, through ecological explorations and the theoretical contributions of the population sciences. In this book, Keller shows us how child development researchers could make such contributions if they, too, followed the Darwinian model for exploring diversity rather than research ideals derived exclusively from experimental science.

Thus this book can be read as a primer for a new kind of child development research, one firmly grounded in principles and methods of the life sciences, exploring variations afforded by the plasticity of human development through methods that are ecological and cultural as well as psychometric, and qualitative as well as quantitative. The research designs used in this book exploit the variability of parenting practices and developmental pathways across far-flung cultures, across the generations of a single community, and within cohorts of mothers at a point in time, to gain a deeper understanding of parenting and child development as human phenomena.

We are all indebted to Bronfenbrenner (1979) for his early and important efforts to free developmental psychology from the limitations of the experimental model and point the way toward ecological research in this field. However, Bronfenbrenner's model of the child's environment put culture at the outside, along with other peripheral factors. With this book, it should be evident to all that culture is an intimate and unavoidable part of the child's environment, involved in all interactive experiences. By reaching around the world for the included research, Keller has led the way to a new level of understanding of children and their parents. Let others follow; there is much to be done.

Preface

This book deals with developmental pathways as cultural solutions for universal developmental tasks. Evolutionary theories assume that developmental tasks evolved to solve adaptation problems that occurred during human phylogeny. To become a competent adult, people must acquire abilities and skills during ontogeny that help the individual to survive and thrive in a particular environment. We address the first integrative developmental task: relationship formation with significant others. We assume that early social experiences with primary caregivers are represented in a primary structure of the self that has developmental consequences for solving the next integrative developmental tasks of self-development during toddlerhood, self-recognition, and self-regulation. This conceptualization implies structural continuity of developmental pathways in a nondeterministic way.

We have proposed that environments should be defined along prevailing sociodemographic characteristics, especially age and education of the parents and sibling status of the target child. These environmental parameters are reflected in practices and ideas that people who live in the particular environment share. We have defined two prototypical environments: urban, educated, middle-class families of Western societies and traditional, subsistence-based, rural farming families with little formal education. Western, urban, middle-class couples start reproduction and family formation in their late 20s and early 30s, with husbands being 2 to 4 years older than their wives, and they raise one or two children. Husbands and wives in rural families may differ substantially in age. However, women bear their first child usually in their late teens and have many children. Both environments emphasize different conceptions of the self and different psychologies. Western, urban, middle-class families embody the cultural model of independence with the self being autonomous and separate. The rural village families embody the cultural model of interdependence with the self being intrinsically interconnected with others and joint or corporate agency.

The research program that is presented in this book systematically analyzes the early socialization experiences, as conceptualized in the cultural model of parenting (comprising socialization goals, parenting ethnotheories, and parenting practices during interactional situations) of 3-month-old babies. Middle-class mothers from Berlin (Germany), Los Angeles (United States), and Athens (Greece) represent the independent model, whereas rural farming families from the ethnic tribe of the Nso in Cameroon and Rajput families from Gujarat (India) represent the interdependent model. The results of different studies reveal unanimously that the two groups of families do indeed have distinct models of parenting with almost no overlap. The independent model focuses on the mental model of the child and cognitive stimulation, whereas the interdependent model focuses on the social environment and moral standards and motor stimulation. In longitudinal analyses it can be demonstrated that the early experiences have developmental consequences in that the independent model supports early self-recognition, whereas the interdependent model supports early self-regulation.

Autonomy and relatedness, however, represent independent dimensions, which allow multiple combinations and therefore also multiple psychologies. Using our research program we analyzed cultural models of parenting in different groups of families, representing these possible combinations: urban, educated, middle-class families from traditionally interdependent societies, like middle-class families from San José (Costa Rica), Beijing (China), and Delhi (India); rural and urban families from the same cultural background, like rural and urban Cameroonian Nso families and Indian rural and urban Hindu families; historical comparisons of sociodemographically comparable families during different historical epochs in Germany, Cameroon, and Costa Rica; and generational comparisons of grandmothers' and mothers' views on early child care in a multicultural study. The results of these studies reveal that there are more models than the cultural models of independence and interdependence, but that there is no third prototype. The different dimensions of parenting are not as consistent as the two prototypical models with a trend toward something in between.

These topics are presented theoretically and empirically in the following nine chapters. Chapter 1 introduces the developmental phase of infancy. Chapter 2 presents the state of the art of infant psychobiology, specifically detailing the evolutionary design for relationship formation. The component model of parenting conceptualizes parenting systems and interactional mechanisms as universal components that can form multiple combinations. Chapter 3 goes into this volume's concept of culture as defined as shared practices and shared meaning systems that are based on sociodemographically defined environments. The two prototypical models of independence and interdependence are introduced and the selected research sites are described that represent the two models. Chapter 4 summarizes the research methodology of the infancy assessments in detail, so that the methods on which the results are based are transparent. Chapter 5 presents an empirical analysis of the dimensions of the parenting model, socialization goals, parenting ethnotheories, and parenting practices. Chapter 6 summarizes the different studies done on combinations of models of independence and interdependence. Chapter 7 reports the interrelations among the different dimensions of parenting for the different cultural environments. Chapter 8 presents a longitudinal analysis of three cultural environments, focusing on the developmental tasks of self-recognition and self-regulation. There is an outlook on following developmental tasks, the development of an autobiographical memory and the theory of mind. Chapter 9, the last chapter, synthesizes the results and presents a reconceptualization of the models of the self.

This volume presents the first systematic analysis of culturally informed developmental pathways, utilizing ethnographic reports and quantitative and qualitative analysis. With the distinct patterns of results that the studies have revealed, it should help to redefine developmental psychology as part of a culturally informed science based on evolutionary groundwork.

ACKNOWLEDGMENTS

Each book represents a universe of meaning as well as of relationships. One would not be possible without the other. Whereas I am solely responsible for any accidental errors, the development of ideas conceptualized here and the linked empirical study program have been profoundly influenced by significant persons who have accompanied me through my career. The beginning of my scientific career was nourished by an admiration for my academic mentor Albert Wellek, one of the last traditional German full professors (*Professor Ordinarius*) at the University of Mainz. Despite being a child of the 1968 student movement in Germany, I was deeply impressed by this world of traditional humanities. Although my career took a different route, this early impression made by liberal thinking within a conventional social world has lasted a lifetime and I am grateful for having experienced the old model of the *Universitas*.

The seminal book by Norbert Bischof, *Das Rätsel Ödipus* (The Enigma of Oedipus), deeply influenced my thinking and I regret the fact that this explosion of interdisciplinary brilliance has never been translated into English. With this preparation and an intrinsic enthusiasm for doing research, I first became acquainted with evolutionary theory through the late Christian Vogel during our yearly meetings of the research program on behavioral ontogeny and behavioral genetics, an early interdisciplinary program of the German Research Council. My first longitudinal study was supported for the duration of the 10-year program by the council. This completely new universe of meaning transformed my theoretical perspective and became one of the cornerstones of the theory presented in this volume.

At the same time, my interest in cross-cultural psychology emerged, mainly with respect to the identification of behavioral universals. My first participation in a cross-cultural study was with the late John Williams and Deborah Best, with whom I still try to promote the development of the field of cross-cultural psychology. During that time, my research began to focus on early parenting and its developmental consequences. Together I and my former students and current esteemed colleagues, Axel Schölmerich and Athanasios Chasiotis, started conducting our first cross-cultural comparisons of early parenting. We had the chance to reanalyze clips from films that Irenäus Eibl-Eibesfeld had produced in remote areas such as Papua New Guinea and Yanomami Indian reserves in South America. Ype Poortinga became a reliable, challenging discussion partner during that time. Although we were able to identify similar parenting patterns across these diverse environments, we found tremendous quantitative differences. My reading of cultural psychologists and cultural anthropologists at that time was another turning point. The oeuvres of Robert LeVine and Patricia Greenfield were particularly impressive. I realized that the shared ideas had to be added to the analysis of behavioral regulation to be able to understand parenting completely. The positive response to my work that Bob and Patricia later expressed and their encouraging support has meant, and still means, an awful lot to me. I had finally found my soul mates. Also Fred Rothbaum's and Robin Harwood's works were and still are an ongoing source of inspiration.

The 1991 article by Markus and Kitayama was another important landmark because it convinced me of the fruitfulness of their cultural self-construals approach as a way to systematize cultural variability, especially because the dichotomous, bipolar concept of individualism–collectivism had continued to be unsatisfactory for my developmental analyses. Together with Çigdem Kağitçibaşi's reconceptualization, the cultural side of my approach became deeply influenced by their thinking.

Having assembled a theoretical toolbox, I felt ready for an empirical research program. Together with my wonderful friends and colleagues from different parts of the world, I developed culturally sensitive assessments of early socialization experiences.

My oldest collaborative arrangement is with the Instituto de Investigationes of the Universidad de Costa Rica in San José. Using a connection initially established by my former student Delia Miranda Fricke, Professor Henning Jensen, the present vice president of research of the Universidad de Costa Rica, and I have collaborated successfully for many years, accompanied by a regular exchange of students. Several stints as a visiting professor at the Universidad de Costa Rica helped me to gain more insight into the wonderful culture and nature of Costa Rica.

Professor T. S. Saraswathi substantially helped me to learn about Indian culture and Hinduism and introduced me to the Department of Human Development and Family Studies at the M. S. University in Baroda, where I was able to complete my first studies in India with the help of Professor Prerana Mohite and her devoted collaborators and students. Professor Parul Dave from the same department introduced me to Aruna Lakhani, former director of the Deepak Foundation, without whose help and support we would never have been able to do research in the Nandesari villages in Gujarat. I was lucky to be invited several times to be a visiting professor at the M. S. University, including being given the honorable Nehru Chair professorship and being a fellow at the department's Advanced Study Institute. It was during a conference at the M. S. University in Baroda that I first met Professor Nandita Chaudhary from Delhi University, who has since then been a wonderful and inspirational collaborator. I am very thankful to have had these glimpses of the Hindu way of life.

I became interested in the Nso culture through Professor Bame Nsamenang, who I first met at the laboratory of Professor Michael Lamb (then at the National Institutes of Health, Bethesda, MD), who had invited me to spend a sabbatical at his institute, and where Professor Nsamenang had recently become a postdoctoral fellow. The inspiring atmosphere that Michael was able to create helped all of us to learn from each other. My interest in West Africa was further piqued by meeting wonderful Professor Therese Tchombe, at that time at Yaounde University, during a conference that Professor Nsamenang had organized. However, our Cameroonian studies would never have been possible without Dr. Relindis Dzeaye Yovsi, who came as a doctoral student to my lab and who has not only changed our lab's direction toward one of relatedness, but who also has taught us a lot about her own culture of relatedness. Nobody else could have conducted all this wonderful research with as much scientific vigor, devotion, and incredible commitment.

The friendship and support of Professor Patricia Greenfield, who invited me to be a visiting professor at UCLA, helped me to collect further components of my research program. In the context of a worldwide multicultural research program, there is nothing like getting permission from the institutional review board—in other words, meeting the board's ethical standards—to conduct a study in the United States! I was lucky to work with a wonderful group of students, in particular Janet Tomiyama who coordinated the Los Angeles study and helped to get through the administrative jungle. It was my UCLA student Wingshan Lo who went to Beijing University for an internship. With the support of Professor Yanjie Su and her student Yifang Wang, she was able to collect data on the Chinese families who are now also in the longitudinal program. Several conference visits to China have made me curious about learning more about the Chinese family culture in the future.

The study in Greece, an important second European research site along with Germany, where the first studies were conducted, was conducted in collaboration with Professor Zaira Papaligoura (now at the University of Thessaloniki), to whom my longtime friend Professor James Georgas from Athens University had introduced me years ago. Zaira has been a wonderful and reliable collaborator since then.

There are also two German colleagues to whom I am extremely grateful for their long-term, fruitful collaboration: Professor Arnold Lohaus, now at the University of Bielefeld, with whom I have conducted most of the German studies; and the linguist Professor Elke Hentschel, now at the University of Berne, Switzerland, whose linguistic competence has added a new perspective to the analysis of the verbal material.

In addition to the invaluable and inspiring collaboration with all these wonderful colleagues, the research program would never have been conducted and this volume could never have been completed without the group of extraordinary students in my research laboratory at the University of Osnabrück. Without Monika Abels, the rural Gujarati assessments could never have been made. She devoted all of her formidable intellectual powers to the work in the Nandesari villages, learned Gujarati, and solved all kinds of foreseeable and unforeseeable problems. She also helped collect data in Berlin and Los Angeles, where Verena Min from Regensburg University (who now lives in Los Angeles) also participated. Monika's doctoral thesis expanded our study program with respect to the warmth dimension of parenting, especially in India. Research students Bettina Lamm, Jörn Borke, and Andreas Eickhorst walked into my office one day and told me that they wanted to expand our research program to include studies of fathers. They conducted the father studies and wrote their master's theses about fathering. Andreas got his PhD on a longitudinal father study and has since left our lab. Jörn has switched to our graduate program and is now writing his doctoral dissertation on the development of regulatory problems in infancy, including those involving fathers. Bettina has collected data in Cameroon together with Relindis. Her doctoral thesis expands our study program to include the analysis of Cameroonian Nso children's and German children's ethnotheories of parenting. Joscha Kärtner joined our team only 3 years ago and has developed an enthusiasm for the study of mirror recognition, among other things, for which he has designed a short-term longitudinal study program. His doctoral thesis expands our study program to include a cross-cultural study of empathy. Astrid Kleis joined us at the same time as Joscha. She collected the 19 months of data from the Berlin sample and is in charge of the analysis of autobiographical memory. Her doctoral dissertation deals with socialization goals and parenting ideas of bicultural West African-German couples. Florian Kießling from the young researcher group in our department collaborates with us on the theory of mind assessments, for which he has developed a battery of tasks. His training and supervision of those doing the assessments in Germany and Cameroon was crucial. Graduate students Carolin Demuth and Hiltrud Otto have also contributed to the study program. Hiltrud has focused on the analysis of verbal–vocal synchrony and Carolin on the qualitative analysis of mother–infant conversations and interviews. Finally, Petra Kuensemueller helped reanalyze the 1977 Mainz longitudinal study.

All these collaborators and students are reliable, multitalented members of the lab who have contributed in numerous ways to the study program starting with its conceptualization, to data assessment, data analysis including training and supervising research students, computation, and finally to preparing papers and conference presentations. They all create a wonderful working atmosphere with occasional unparalleled cross-cultural dinner parties.

Although everybody mentioned contributed in the one or other way to this volume, there are some I want to single out for thanks for their contributions. Without their support, this book would literally not have been written. Athanasios

Chasiotis reviewed several of the chapters. His suggestions were crucial for the organization of the volume. Bettina Lamm, Joscha Kärtner, and Monika Abels reviewed the chapters, made last-minute computations, and revised several of the chapters. Their suggestions and recommendations were also crucial.

Uwe Nerger prepared all the figures and tables as well as the photos. Marita Bojang prepared the complete manuscript and copyedited the text, compiled the list of references, and put it all together. Both have prepared book manuscripts with me before. They are among the people without whose assistance this volume would not have been possible.

Nandita Chaudhary's network helped me finding a professional native English copyeditor who also speaks German. Abigail Clay has been very reliable and very timely.

Last but not least I want to mention the sources of funding and the institutional support that I received for my research and preparation of the volume. The research was mainly supported by the German Research Council. The German Academic Exchange Service also contributed, as did the Carl-Duisberg Foundation, the Samourkas Foundation, the Sievert Group, and the collaborating universities. The development of the outline of the volume and the first draft of the initial chapters were prepared when I was a scholar-in-residence at the Netherlands Institute for Advanced Study in the Humanities and Social Sciences. The final writing was supported with a sabbatical from my university. Lori Stone from Lawrence Erlbaum Associates was patient with all my questions during the final process of writing.

The families who participated in our studies merit our profound gratitude. They let us participate in their lives and shared their ideas with us. Their hospitality, sincerity, and openness have made this journey a most pleasurable experience.

1
The Conception of Infancy

THE DEVELOPMENTAL PHASE OF INFANCY

Infancy constitutes a separate life stage in all primates. However, in other mammals, infancy ends with the cessation of weaning and is followed by the juvenile period, in which the young are no longer dependent on the parents for survival but are not yet sexually mature (Bogin, 1999a). Humans are the only species that has a biologically and behaviorally distinct phase of childhood forming a stable interval between infancy and the juvenile period (Bogin, 1990, 1999b). Infancy in humans constitutes the life span between birth and about 2 years of age and, as such, is a small percentage of the average person's life expectancy (Lamb, Bornstein, & Teti, 2002). However, a 2-year-old child is still dependent on its parents for survival and development. Infancy does not last longer in humans than in some of the other primates, but the quality is different because the greater care required by the human infant is accompanied by more intense social stimulation (Locke & Bogin, in press). Humans need this preparatory period to be able to adapt to the complex social environment that constitutes their niche. The extreme helplessness (altriciality) of the human infant has been interpreted as a consequence of a physiological preterm birth (Prechtl, 1984) or the obstetrical dilemma (Washburn, 1960) presented by hominid brain growth. Two months before birth, the human brain is already more developed than the brain of a newborn macaque (Clancy, Darlington, & Finlay, 2001). Unlike for other primates' brains, human neonatal brain growth continues in a rapid, fetal-like trajectory for the next year (R. D. Martin, 1983). From an evolutionary perspective, the altriciality is also part of a repro-

1

ductive strategy to become a better adult (Alexander, 1979; better adult hypothesis), as it allows the baby to invest all available resources in growth and development. Helplessness can therefore be regarded as a socially and cognitively beneficial state. Infants are dependent on the caregiving environment that shapes the early developmental trajectory, and this environment is determined by the investment that parents make in the child. This investment, in turn, is contingent on the ecosocial resources available to the parents. On the other hand, infants have remarkable cognitive and social abilities (Rochat, 2004) that allow them to interact with their environment. Thus, early social experiences form the basis of psychological development where infants construct and co-construct internal representations of social relations and a primary conception of the self (Keller, 2001, 2003b). In fact, an infant's construction of a sense of self as the result of experiences commences in the early weeks of life. It originates in the processes of sensory perception (Neisser, 1993) and imitation (Meltzoff, 1990), emphasizing the primacy of perceptual, social, and affective factors in the structuring of the presymbolic self during the first months of life (Kopp & Brownell, 1991; Neisser, 1993).

The brief period of infancy has attracted the interest and the attention not only of biologists, but also of philosophers, physicians, psychologists, and anthropologists, from Plato's time (about 350 B.C.), or perhaps even earlier. Infants are attractive social partners for everybody; they elicit positive emotions, the motivation to care and protect, and the desire to interact. The beginning of infancy research is usually dated to Tiedemann's diary descriptions of his little son from the year 1787. Nevertheless, since then, the psychological reality of the infant has been underestimated for a long time, from scholars with various theoretical backgrounds. James (1890) made an often cited statement that "the baby, assailed by eyes, ears, nose, skin and entrails at once, feels it all as one blooming, buzzing confusion" (p. 488). W. Stern (1914/1923) also thought of infants as reflexive beings in a general state of basic sensibility that is uniform and unpatterned as fog. Similarly, Stern described the state of infancy as if we were lying dreaming on the sofa with eyes closed, merging the perceptions of brightness, the noises from the street, the pressure of our clothes, the temperature of the room into one general perceptual state—only much more vague and dull, this is how we should think of the sensibility of a small child.

The psychoanalyst Spitz felt that we do not have concepts, not even words to describe this no man's land of human beginnings. We still do not know how to talk about the psyche of the newborn, the first impulses of the mind in the twilight world before sunrise (Spitz, 1992, cited in Koehler, 1986).

Even Piaget (1953) underestimated infants' ability as simple reflexive reactions to light:

> Perception of light exists from birth and consequently the reflexes which insure the adaptation of this perception (the papillary and palpebral reflexes, both to light). All the rest (perception of forms, sizes, positions, distances, prominence, etc.) is acquired through the combination of reflex activity with higher activities. (p. 62)

Since the 1950s this picture has dramatically changed. In particular, ethologists with the patience for long-term observations have vividly documented that the blooming and buzzing confusion has been more of a historical misconception than a reflection of the behavioral organization and the social competencies of infants. Baby biographies and the belief in the importance of individual infants made the historically unprecedented documentation of infancy during the 20th century possible. The competent infant was discovered (Bell, 1968; Rochat, 2004): a human being with needs, preferences, desires, emotions, and even a free will (Ainsworth, 1973; Rothbaum, Pott, Azuma, Miyake, & Weisz, 2000; Rothbaum, Weisz, Pott, Miyake, & Morelli, 2000), a human being that not only receives care, but also one that exerts a substantial influence on the caregiving environment. The first handbook of infancy was published in 1973 (Stone, Smith, & Murphy, 1973). This new scientific discipline developed rapidly.

THE SCIENTIFIC STUDY OF INFANCY

The interest in the scientific study of infancy has been driven primarily by two sets of questions that are compelling for the study of behavioral development in general: questions concerning the roles of heredity and experience and questions concerning the roles of continuity and plasticity across the life span. For a long time these discussions were as ambitious as they were controversial. In the tradition of a stimulus response psychology there was no place for encompassing interactions between organism and environment. Behavior was regarded as almost infinitely pliable, which preempted the need to even consider such interactions (Keller, Poortinga, & Schölmerich, 2002). During this period views on the relation between culture and biology were primed by both implicit and often explicit views of mutual exclusivity of the physical and the mental or social domain, as if they were separate entities. In this process, much of culture and much of biology disappeared in favor of a trait-oriented understanding of human psychological functioning. Biologically oriented views focused on physiological and neurological mechanisms as the hardware correlates of mental processes. Both perspectives implied the ignorance of the biological embeddedness and the evolutionary history of human behavior; selection pressures and (biological) adaptation processes were seen as applying to other species but not humans (Keller, 2003b). If culture was of concern it was mainly in the form of an independent variable rather than being perceived as complex contexts comprising ecological, social, and psychological processes. Moreover, a developmental perspective was not acknowledged as an essential ingredient in broader frameworks of behavior and culture. However, we can only start understanding human functioning if we consider how cross-cultural invariance and variation emerge from the common biological origins in interaction with the ecocultural environment during the course of ontogenetic development (Keller, Poortinga, & Schölmerich, 2002).

Scientific advances during the last decades with respect to brain development, neurophysiology, cultural psychology, and evolutionary theory have helped us to develop a better understanding of the intrinsic interplay between heredity and experience as well as continuity and change. It has been convincingly demonstrated that culture and biology cannot be separated from each other. Humans are biologically cultural (Bussab & Ribeiro, 1998; Rogoff, 2003).

Bischof (1996) proposed the seemingly paradoxical concept of the *inborn environment* to emphasize that an organism defines his or her environment in a nontrivial sense. The inborn environment represents the features of the context that evolved during phylogeny into individual genetic traits that allowed for optimal adaptation. The inborn environment is equivalent to the "environment of evolutionary adaptedness" (Tooby & Cosmides, 1990, p. 386). Therefore there are no pure genetic effects, nor pure environmental effects, with the consequence that only environmental openness can be tested and not genetic determinism.

The genotype defines a phenotypical reaction norm describing the epigenetic landscape of potential developmental pathways. This implies that the environmentally mediated relation between genotype and phenotype is crucial and not the relation between gene and environment. Complex physical and psychological characteristics are the result of epigenetic processes with the behavioral and developmental plasticity of humans representing the genetically defined adaptive potential for change. This hereditary endowment enables the individual to acquire knowledge and to flexibly organize and reorganize it over the life span. The early experiences lay the foundation for structural continuity across developmental tasks.

2 The Psychobiology of Infancy

INFANT PREPAREDNESS FOR SOCIAL LEARNING: BRAIN DEVELOPMENT DURING INFANCY

The rapid pace of human brain development begins prenatally and continues through the second year of postnatal life (Gould, 1977). By 6 months the human brain weighs 50% of what it will in adulthood, at 2 years 75%, and at 10 years 95% (Tanner, 1978). Enormous postnatal brain development is necessary be-cause—due to evolutionary pressures that resulted in an enlarged brain as com-pared to other primates—gestation can only be extended to the point where the infant's skull will fit through the birth canal. The birth canal is limited in width be-cause of the constraints of bipedality, causing the "obstetrical dilemma" (Washburn, 1960). Thus human babies are born physically immature (physiologi-cal preterm birth; Prechtl, 1984). This prolonged period of immaturity and de-pendency is one of the most important aspects of human development (Bjorklund & Pellegrini, 2002). Brain size in primates is not only related to the length of the ju-venile period but also to sociality (Dunbar, 1995). It is assumed that dealing with the challenges of cooperating and competing with other members of the social group was the driving force of the evolution of intelligence and cognition (Alexan-der, 1979; Geary & Flinn, 2001).

Two processes in particular describe the factors typical of the species and the individual in brain development. Experience-expectant processes are common to all members of the species and evolved as neural preparation for incorporating general information from the environment. The overproduction and trimming of synaptic connections between the nerve cells illustrate experience-expectant information storage. Experience-dependent information storage reflects learning and brain change unique to the individual. The neural basis of experience-dependent processes appears to involve the active formation of synaptic connections as a product of experience (Greenough, Black, & Wallace, 1987). Thus, experience is the product of an ongoing reciprocal interaction between the environment and the brain (C. A. Nelson, 2005).

Large brains and long juvenile periods may afford greater plasticity of the brain (Gottlieb, 1992). Most of the brain growth appears to be due to increases in the size of neurons. Synapse formation (connections among neurons) continues throughout life, and thus ensures plasticity. Although synapse formation must be under genetic influence to some degree, research has indicated that experience is the primary factor in synaptogenesis (Gottlieb, 1992; Greenough et al., 1987). Experience changes the brain, which in turn affects what new information is learned (neural constructivism; Quartz & Sejnowski, 1997). Thus, the brain is organized by the electrical and chemical activity of developing neurons and by information received through the senses as much or even more than by the unfolding of a genetic "blueprint." Neurophysiological research has thus indicated that the newborn period can be characterized as the brain imprint period. Accordingly, the neonatal environment has major and lasting consequences for development (Storfer, 1999).

Two kinds of plasticity are common in the nervous system: modifiability and compensation. Modifiability means that although cells are predesigned for specific functions, those functions may be attuned to other functions. Lamb et al. (2002) argued that specificity exists at the cellular level, that there is initial equipotentiality of sensitivity, that cells are susceptible to experience and that this susceptibility is restricted to infancy; that is, it functions only during a very early sensitive period. This implies that infants are born not only with a brain ready to respond to critical features of the environment, but that the brain can react to particular features of the particular, individual environment. Compensation involves the ability of some cells to substitute for others, indicating that local cellular defects may be compensated for by neighboring cells.

Many features of childhood serve as preparations for adulthood, yet there are also adaptive aspects of childhood that evolved to serve an adaptive purpose for that specific time in development (Bjorklund, 1997). For example, under the appropriate conditions, newborn infants will imitate a range of facial gestures, although imitation of facial expression decreases to chance levels by about 2 months (Fontaine, 1984). It has been speculated that neonatal imitation does not support the acquisition of new behaviors, but has a specific function for the neonate, like for nursing, establishing prelinguistic conversation (Legerstee, 1991) and facilitating infant–mother social interaction (Bjorklund, 1987) at a time when the infant cannot yet control its gaze and head movements in response to social stimulation (Bjorklund & Pellegrini, 2002). These examples highlight the importance of early social interaction.

It can be concluded that environmental experience is critical to the differentiation of the brain tissue itself (Cicchetti & Tucker, 1994). A large body of evidence supports the principle that cortical and subcortical networks are generated by genetically programmed, initially overabundant production of synaptic connections, which is then followed by an environmentally driven process of competitive interaction to select those connections that are most effectively maintained by environmental information. The infant brain is designed to be molded by the environments it encounters (Thomas et al., 1997). Learning, therefore, is the driving force of human development.

LEARNING AS THE HUMAN MODE OF DEVELOPMENT

Genes exert their effects in fixed programs that are invariably coded in the DNA of the genotype, and in open programs that are environmentally labile and prepared to acquire information through learning (Mayr, 1988). Most macromorphological changes are tightly controlled by fixed genetic scripts (cf. C. A. Nelson, 1999), detailing that the environment is needed but does not exert major differential effects (experience-expectant processes). Open genetic programs set the stage for differential effects of environmental influences (experience-dependent processes). Proponents of interpersonal neurobiology (Schore, 1994; Siegel, 1999) argue that the structure and function of the developing brain are determined by how experiences, especially within interpersonal relationships, shape the genetically programmed maturation of the nervous system. The caregiver provides experiences, which shape genetic potential by acting as a psychobiological regulator of hormones that directly influence gene transcription. Psychoneuroendocrinological changes during critical periods initiate lasting effects at the genomic level, which are expressed in the imprinting of evolving brain circuitry (Schore, 2000).

The modes in which open programs influence and direct behavior are "legion" (Mayr, 1988, p. 68; MacDonald, 1988), indicating that these interactions occur at a variety of neurophysiological and behavioral levels and are domain specific (Darwinian algorithms; Cosmides & Tooby, 1987).

Therefore, learning based on open genetic programs cannot be understood as a general mechanism with universal properties: "The more we have studied learning abilities, the more impressed we have become with their specificity" (Trivers, 1985, p. 102). However, the different modes of learning show biases that may reflect selective forces. Thus, learning has to be specified with respect to the content that is to be learned and the timing of when it is learned. The interplay of content specificity and timing of learning is regarded as specifying epigenetic rules (E. O. Wilson, 1975) or central tendencies (MacDonald, 1988) that direct attention to specific (environmental) cues at specific times. Such effects may be weaker or stronger, the classical ethological conception of the sensitive period for imprinting being the strongest case. The acquisition of specific information during specific time windows enables easy learning (Boyd & Richerson, 1985; Draper &

Harpending, 1988). The specification of content and timing of learning draws on the implicit notion that the genotype needs specific information from the environment to develop its phenotypic appearance (evolved codesigns; Rochat, 1997; inborn environment; Bischof, 1996). Because many aspects of development are activity dependent, a broad range of individual differences results.

Meanwhile the discovery of mirror neurons has opened another exciting avenue for the understanding of gene–environment interaction. Mirror neurons are brain cells that respond equally when an actor performs an action and when the actor witnesses somebody else performing the same action. First, individual mirror neurons were identified in the brains of macaque monkeys (Rizzolatti, Luppino, & Matelli, 1998). In humans, the same activities in single neurons could not be identified but the existence of a specific area or a mirror network could be (Iacoboni, 2005; Rizzolatti, Fogassi, & Gallese, 2001). Imitative learning, which is extremely important for ontogenetic development, could therefore be founded in genetic processes.

In summary, it can be concluded that human infants are predisposed with genetic programs for the acquisition of environmental information, which is of primordial significance for shaping their neurophysiological and psychological development. However, it can be assumed that the complexity of the human nervous system and the multiple facets of context and environment make it impossible to formulate a single adaptive relation between context and behavior (cf. Belsky, Steinberg, & Draper, 1991; Chisholm, 1992; Greenfield & Suzuki, 1998; Keller, 2000a, 2000b; Keller & Greenfield, 2000; Keller, Lohaus, Völker, Cappenberg, & Chasiotis, 1999; Lerner & De Stefanis, 1999; Rothbaum, Pott, et al., 2000; Rothbaum, Weisz, et al., 2000).

LEARNING RELATIONSHIPS: THE ACQUISITION OF A SOCIAL MATRIX

The first overarching developmental task that infants the world over have to master is to develop relationships with their primary caregivers. Mastery of this task supports the survival, growth, and development of the altricial infant. Developmental tasks have evolved as universal themes of humankind. The way they are solved must be adapted to the particular environment into which the baby is born. Earlier solutions prepare pathways for solving later developmental tasks. However, these pathways of structural continuity are not deterministic in the sense that the early pattern allows one single later consequence. It is obvious that along developmental pathways a multiplicity of influences shape developmental outcomes. Human plasticity allows for modification, compensation, and restructuring at any point in development. Nevertheless the development of continuity is easier than that of discontinuity and most individuals experience coherence and consistency throughout their biographies (Keller, 1991).

The learning of relationships is based on infants' inherent curiosity and motivation to learn. Learning biases direct their attention to their social partners. In these interpersonal and interactional contexts infants acquire the parameters that define relationships and, with this, the definition of the contextual foundation of the self. The bonding processes of the caregivers to the infant are determined in multiple ways by neurophysiological and psychological processes. These bonding processes result in the caregiver being motivated to protect, care for, and stimulate the infant. Caretaking can be understood as practices that are situated in the cultural model of the particular environment. A first developmental result can be assumed at about 3 months of age. The 3-month age range is regarded as a developmental transition in different parts of the world. In the Western literature it demarcates the first bio(social)-behavioral shift (M. Cole & Cole, 1989; Emde, 1984), with a first developmental result being the processes of relationship formation (Keller, 1992) when a sense of an emergent self is formed (D. N. Stern, 1985). Infants show the first signs of intentional exploration and a sense of their own power over their physical and social environment. During the second month of life, the myelinization of the occipital cortex that is connected to face perception begins, marking a milestone in brain development that prepares a qualitative change in social interactions and emotional regulation. From about 3 months of age on, infants categorize stimuli on the basis of perceptual similarity (Eimas & Quinn, 1994; Hayne, Rovee-Collier, & Perris, 1987) and become sensitive to spatial location (Baillargeon, Bistline, & Sonnet, 1989; Huttenlocher, Newcombe, & Sandberg, 1994).

In a longitudinal study of German middle-class families during the first years of the children's lives, we found that the amount and the quality of eye contact is an expression of an infant's primary relational conception at about 3 months of age. The amount of eye contact in dyadic free-play interactions peaks at that age and decreases afterward to virtually zero. At 3 months there are also the largest interindividual differences. The percentage of time infants look into their parents' eyes ranges from 0% to 100% (Keller, 1992; Keller, Gauda, Miranda, & Schölmerich, 1985). Moreover, there is a particular interactional phenomenon that can only be observed during the focal time of 3 months: gaze aversion. Gaze aversion is an active behavior of the child to avoid eye contact with mother, father, or both. Gaze aversion, as well as the amount of eye contact, is directly related to the preceding interactional experiences; for example, in terms of parental contingent responsiveness, acceptance of infant's state and signals (Keller & Gauda, 1987). The amount of eye contact and gaze aversion is also related to developmental consequences, for example, exploratory behavior at 2 years of age (Keller, 1979, 1992) and the development of developmental delays and behavioral problems (Keller & Gauda, 1987).

This developmental transition is also expressed in German parents' and pediatricians' expectation that infants should sleep independently and through the night from about 3 months on. In India, there are ceremonies at about the same time where the infant is exposed for the first time to the sun and the moon (Saraswathi & Pai, 1997), thus also opening new developmental contexts. However, so far not much longitudinal research has been published about non-Western contexts.

Infants' Predispositions to Relationship Learning

Despite a tremendous array of interindividual differences among infants with respect to height and weight, skin color, activity, and responsiveness (Brazelton, 1977; Greenfield & Childs, 1991), infants are nevertheless similar to each other to a large extent. This similarity concerns endowment and predispositions, especially toward social interactions (Keller & Greenfield, 2000; Keller, Poortinga, & Schölmerich, 2002). Because infants are helpless, they need to attract and maintain the attention and the motivation of their social environment to care for them. Morphologically they enact the *babyness* (*Kindchenschema*), that Lorenz (1969) first described. Babyness refers to a relatively large head as compared to the rest of the body, a round face, big eyes, and a prominent forehead. It has been demonstrated in different species that these features block aggression and elicit positive emotions and protective motivation. Infants express attachment behaviors from birth on. They communicate distress and cry and they also communicate positive emotions when they gaze, smile, and vocalize.

They can express differential preferences and attention for visual and auditory stimuli (Fantz, 1961, 1963; Keller, 1979) and they prefer the human face over other perceptual displays (Bushnell, 1998; Mondloch et al., 1999; Morton & Johnson, 1991; Simion, Valenza, & Umilta, 1998). Morton and Johnson (1991) argued for the existence of an innate face-detecting device they called "Conspec" (conspecifics), which "perhaps comprises just three dark patches in a triangle, corresponding to eyes and mouth" (Pascalis, de Schonen, Morton, Deruelle, & Fabre-Grenet, 1995, p. 80), which serves to direct the newborn infant's visual attention to faces (see also Slater, 2004). Indeed, infants scan the eye region of the face first and include the mouth at about 2 months of age (Salapatek, 1975). However, their competencies are more detailed. Newborns imitate a variety of facial gestures that an adult model performs (Meltzoff & Moore, 1977, 1984, 1992, 1994, 1997). Meltzoff (1995) suggested that "newborns begin life with some grasp of people" (p. 43). Infants can see the adult's face, but they cannot see their own. Nevertheless there must be some representation of their own body because they match their own unseen but felt facial movements with the seen but unfelt facial movements of adult models. Meltzoff and Moore (1997) proposed that they do this by a process of active intermodal matching. Part of the repertoire of perceiving and processing information from the environment is an analytical mechanism that detects contingencies (M. W. Watson, 1994). *Contingency* refers to the temporal pattern between two events that potentially reflects a causal dependency. M. W. Watson (1994) conceived of contingency as an inborn module that applies to two independent mechanisms. *Responsiveness* is looking forward in time and it registers an upcoming stimulus event as a function of an emitted response. *Dependency* is looking backward in time and it monitors the relative likelihood that a given stimulus event was preceded by a particular behavior. Until about 3 months of age, infants seek the highest level of contingency they can detect (M. W. Watson, 1994). After 3 months of age, infants are motivated to explore high but imperfect degrees of stimulus–response contingencies (J. S. Watson, 1985).

Based on prenatal experiences, newborns prefer their mothers' voices to the voice of another woman in a conditioning procedure where they learned to adjust their sucking response in different ways to produce the different voices (DeCasper & Fifer, 1980). There is no preference for the fathers' voices in newborns. These findings also demonstrate that the fetus already has some kind of abstract memory for the constellation of features that distinguished the mother's voice from other similar voices. The fetus is also already able to analyze speech along various dimensions, not only encoding auditory information that identifies the mother but also attending to acoustic patterns related to linguistic structure. Infants distinguish between verses that they had heard in utero and unheard ones even if both are read by the mother (DeCasper & Spence, 1986). Infants are able to discriminate phonetic units before they have much listening experience (Jusczyk, 1997). They begin life with the potential to make the wider range of phonetic distinctions of many different languages. Over the first few months of life, fast perceptual learning occurs as a result of hearing a particular language. At 6 to 8 months infants can still discriminate among diverse contrasts, an ability that disappears almost completely between 10 and 12 months (Fernald, 2004).

For a long time, the first years of life have been regarded as being governed by infantile amnesia. This view has now changed dramatically. Empirical evidence shows that the fundamental components of the information processing system, including implicit and explicit memory, are present and functioning in the human neonate (Rovee-Collier, 1997). From their earliest days on, infants can encode, store, and retrieve varied information about the stimuli to which they are exposed and the events they experience. Furthermore, infants encode contextual information into their memories (Rovee-Collier, 1997). The seeming discontinuity in the recall of personally experienced events originates not in the memory "hardware" per se, but in other areas of memory "software," namely the emergence of the cognitive self. The emergence of the cognitive self during the second year of life provides a new framework around which memories can be organized (Howe & Courage, 1993, 1997).

Infants and young children process information more slowly than adults (Kail, 1997). Therefore, repetition and pervasiveness of stimulation is important for learning. Also, memory fades quickly and must be reinstated by repetitive and pervasive experiences (Rovee-Collier & Shye, 1992). Accordingly, those experiences will become manifest in the self-structure that the infant repeatedly experiences. Support for this notion has come from different sources. Frequent repetition of trials facilitates learning and the development of expectations (Knopf, 2003). Children who are rarely touched have 20% to 30% lower brain weights than infants who are frequently touched (Nash, 1997). The frequency of particular parental verbal input related to the speed and quality of children's language acquisition (Tamis Le Monda, Bornstein, Cyphers, Toda, & Ogino, 1992; Tomasello, Kruger, & Ratner, 1993). The amount of eye contact during the early months of life is predictive for socioemotional regulation during childhood (Keller, 1992). The number of aversive experiences is related to the development of psychopathology

(Schore, 2000; Sroufe, 1988). It can be assumed that the prevalent social experiences are represented in perceptual and motor schemas, which form the earliest memory structure of the self.

Parenting can be regarded as exposure to particular stimuli in particular contexts. Thus, the earliest experiences are supposed to prime developmental pathways by providing the child with a knowledge structure that can be used as a lens to interpret and organize incoming information and to store and retrieve it (Bjorklund, 1987; Howe & Courage, 1997).

The Parental Codesign

Humans are also predisposed to be parents and therefore equipped with a parenting repertoire complementary to the child's care-eliciting repertoire. Accordingly, the study of parenting during children's early developmental stages is largely characterized by assumptions about universal parental propensities and practices. The intuitive parenting program, as proposed by H. Papoušek and M. Papoušek (1987, 1991) is based on the assumption of a phylogenetically evolved, culture-, gender-, and age-independent and, therefore, universal system of parenting (cf. M. Papoušek, Papoušek, & Bornstein, 1985). The intuitive parenting program focuses on behavior, like eye contact, infant vocalizations, and baby talk (motherese); metacommunicative elements like understanding, playing, stimulating, and modulating; and stylistic variables like empathic (i.e., warm and signal-guided) responsivity (M. Papoušek, 1994). The intuitive parenting program is considered to activate and support consequent developmental achievements, for example, social competence and language acquisition. Empirical support for cross-cultural validity has been presented with respect to baby talk (motherese) as an intuitive adaptation to infants' communicative and information-processing capacities, manifested by higher pitch, frequent repetitions, simple sentence structure, and exaggerated and slow expressions (H. Papoušek & M. Papoušek, 1987; see Figure 2.1).

Another significant mechanism is contingency during face-to-face interactions (Keller, Chasiotis, & Runde, 1992; Keller, Lohaus, et al., 1999; Keller, Schölmerich, & Eibl-Eibesfeldt, 1988). Contingency indicates that there is a pan-cultural tendency of caregivers to respond to infants' signals within 200 to 800 milliseconds. This short reaction time qualifies these responses as being intuitive reactions and not cognitively mediated, intentional acts.

Also, attachment researchers have proposed that parental (maternal) sensitivity is a normative behavioral quality that consists of attentive, prompt, consistent, and adequate behavioral responses to infants' cues (Ainsworth, Bell, & Stayton, 1974; Ainsworth, Blehar, Waters, & Wall, 1978). The mixture of these components in a unitary organization of sensitivity, expressed in one bipolar dimension ranging from not-at-all sensitive to very sensitive, has been identified as the central feature of parental sensitivity (J. A. Martin, 1989). Especially the combination of prompt behavioral reactions in terms of contingency and the adequate and emotionally tuned behavior in terms of warmth is regarded as centrally linked to behavioral conse-

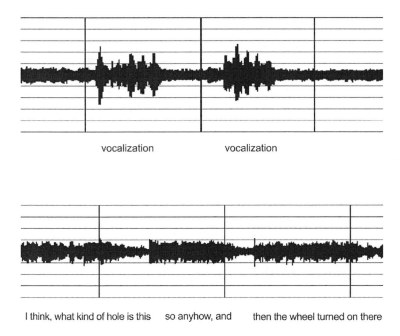

vocalization   vocalization

I think, what kind of hole is this   so anyhow, and   then the wheel turned on there

FIGURE 2.1.   Spectral analysis of maternal utterances in baby talk (top) and adult conversation (bottom).

quences (Dunham & Dunham, 1995; Russel, 1997; Wahler, 1994). Ainsworth and collaborators (1978) considered sensitivity to be the main parenting quality in the first year of life. Sensitivity is qualified as a culture-independent behavioral style that is causally linked to attachment security (the standard assumption of attachment research; Lamb, Thompson, Gardner, Charnov, & Estes, 1984; Posada et al., 2002; Rothbaum, Pott, et al., 2000; Rothbaum, Weisz, et al., 2000).

Besides these conceptions, a plethora of parental, mainly maternal, behaviors in interaction with infants during the first months of life have been described in the literature. In a comprehensive overview of 66 investigations, de Wolff and Van IJzendoorn (1997) identified as many as 55 ways to define parenting in studies that are based on the attachment paradigm. Moreover, there is a considerable body of literature on parent–infant interaction with a systemic background (Fivaz-Depeursinge & Corboz-Warnery, 2001) or a nativist orientation (Lamb & Easterbrooks, 1981; Yarrow, Pedersen, & Rubenstein, 1977).

On the other hand, tremendous cultural and contextual differences between the parenting behaviors and styles of caregivers with small infants have also been reported (e.g., Hewlett, Lamb, Leyendecker, & Schölmerich, 2000; Hoff-Ginsberg & Tardif, 1995; Konner, 1991; LeVine, 1990, 1994; Super & Harkness, 1996; Weisner, 2000; for summaries see Greenfield & Suzuki, 1998; Keller, Harwood, & Carlson, 2006; Shweder et al., 1998).

From an evolutionary perspective, parenting has evolved as part of an individual's reproductive strategies (Bjorklund, 2000; Keller, 2001). Evolutionary theorists have argued that it is highly unlikely that only one adaptive pattern of parent–child relationships evolved in the environment of evolutionary adaptedness (Belsky, 1999). Accordingly, there are alternative strategies to recurrent problems that our ancestors faced in the evolutionary past (Bjorklund, 1997). Therefore, we have proposed the *component model of parenting,* which specifies modules that capture universal propensities as well as cultural peculiarities of parenting in one model (Keller, 2000b; Keller, Lohaus, et al., 2004; Keller, Voelker, & Zach, 1997).

THE COMPONENT MODEL OF PARENTING

The component model of parenting postulates a phylogenetically evolved universal repertoire of parenting systems that are individually modulated by interactional mechanisms. The parenting systems are defined by particular parenting behaviors; the interactional mechanisms shape the mode and style of these behaviors. Primary care, body contact, body stimulation, object stimulation, face-to-face exchange, and the narrative envelope are considered to each form systems of functionally related behaviors. Yet the expressions of these behaviors can differ substantially, because the interactional mechanisms modulate the interactional style. The interactional mechanisms comprise basically the mode of attention (exclusive or shared), contingency in terms of prompt reactivity, and emotional warmth. The interactional mechanisms can be addressed to positive or negative interactional cues within the different parenting systems, expressing individual, as well as cultural, priorities (Keller, 2002a).

The parenting systems and interactional mechanisms are considered to be basically independent from each other (Keller, 2003a) to allow alternative strategies through different combinations. Recent research in developmental neuroscience further supports the assumption of domain specificity. The research reveals that in 2-month-old infants a network of areas, which matches the core system for face perception that has been identified in adults, is activated. This activation refers to the relatively specialized functional activity of the visual associative cortex (Tzourio-Mazoyer et al., 2002). Parenting systems can occur in multiple combinations; the mechanisms can be effective within all systems of parenting. This does not mean that the various systems do not promote specific mechanisms differently. Parenting behaviors have been documented in children as young as 3 years of age, parents and nonparents of either gender (M. Papoušek & Papoušek, 1991). The parenting systems together with the interactional mechanisms can be considered as exhaustively descriptive of the experiential array of infants during the first months of life. They represent contexts of parental investment that differ with respect to energy, time, attention, and emotional tone that are devoted to the infant. Therefore, the component model of parenting makes possible evolutionary-based functional analysis of parenting behaviors (Buss, Haselton, Shackelford, Bleske, & Wakefield, 1998).

The Parenting Systems

In the following section the parenting systems are briefly described and their psychological functions are elaborated from the existing literature.

Parenting System 1: Primary Care.   Providing primary care for infants in terms of food, shelter, and hygiene characterizes any parenting effort and clearly represents the oldest phylogenetic part of the parenting systems. The expenditures of primary care, however, may vary tremendously. Under extreme circumstances of poverty and environmental stress, nursing may form the main maternal investment that a woman can offer. Hitchcock and Minturn (1963) described the childrearing environment for Indian Rajput babies during the 1950s as adults not paying much attention to them. They were nursed only when they cried in some cases with remarkable time delays. Similarly, De Vries (1984) also documented that Masai babies who had difficult and irritable temperaments had a greater chance of surviving, because quiet infants were not able to catch their mothers' attention in the context of extreme scarcity and poverty. Figure 2.2 demonstrates some examples of primary care situations.

FIGURE 2.2.   Primary care from a rural Gujarat, an urban Nso, and a Euro-American mother. Photo from Culture and Development Lab, University of Osnabrück.

The psychological function of the parenting effort as expressed in the primary care system can be regarded as reducing distress (Hitchcock & Minturn, 1963), rather than initiating positive behavioral states. With the promptness of response that an infant receives and, thus, experiences relief from pain and distress, security and trust in protection and the availability and reliability of the social surrounding are developed as a primary dimension of the emerging self (Bischof, 1985; Bowlby, 1969; Erikson, 1950). In some cultural environments, nursing in anticipation of distress promotes closeness and interpersonal fusion (Keller, Voelker, & Yovsi, 2005; Rothbaum, Pott, et al., 2000; Rothbaum, Weisz, et al., 2000; Yovsi, 2001).

Parenting System 2: Body Cohntact. A second system of parenting is constituted by body contact and extensive carrying. In many different ecocultural contexts, infants are carried on the bodies of their mothers or other caregivers for a substantial part of the day, in LeVine's (1990) terminology "back and hip cultures." For example, Aka Pygmy mothers carry their infants for about 8 hours a day (Hewlett, 1991a, 1991b; cf. for the !Kung, Barr, Konner, Bakeman, & Adamson, 1991), and South American Ache infants spend about 93% of their daylight time in tactile contact with mainly the mother (Hill & Hurtado, 1996). Cosleeping maintains close body contact during the night as well. Body contact in primates, especially grooming, has been qualified as fostering group coherence. Different primate societies spend up to 30% of their waking hours with reciprocal grooming, which affects the release of endorphins, helping to sooth the groomed partner and hence allowing the development of trust (Dunbar, 1996). Figure 2.3 demonstrates some examples of body contact situations.

FIGURE 2.3.   Body contact of a German and an Indian urban middle-class mother and a rural Nso mother. Photo from Culture and Development Lab, University of Osnabrück.

The psychological function of body contact mainly consists of the experience of emotional warmth, which is associated with social cohesion (MacDonald, 1992), and feelings of relatedness and belongingness (e.g., Mize & Pettit, 1997). These feelings seem to be associated with the acceptance of norms and values of the elder generation (Bandura, Ross, & Ross, 1963; Hetherington & Frankie, 1967). Warmth contributes to the child's willingness to embrace parental messages and values (Kochanska & Thompson, 1997; Maccoby, 1984), preparing the individual for a life that is based on harmony and respect for hierarchy among family members or the primary social group (cf. Keller, Lohaus, et al., 1999). Parental care in terms of body contact allows continued participation in subsistence labor, for example, through farming, fetching water, cooking, and so forth, although carrying a child might compete for a mother's time with other resource-producing activities (Hill & Hurtado, 1996).

Parenting System 3: Body Stimulation.   The third system of parenting is also based on body communication. Mothers, but also fathers (like the South American Yanomani; Keller et al., 1988), stimulate their infants by providing them with motorically challenging experiences through touch and movement. The array ranges from West African caregivers lifting the whole baby up and down in an upright position to German caregivers gently exercising arms or legs of the infant (Keller, Yovsi, & Voelker, 2002). Figure 2.4 demonstrates some examples of body stimulation.

Body stimulation, which is not usually done for long periods, can be related functionally to motor development. The motor precocity of the African infant (Geber & Dean, 1959; Super, 1976) has been interpreted as a consequence of these early stimulation patterns (Bril, 1989). The specific African body stimulation pattern is based on ethnotheories, like the Nigerian Yoruba concept of mobility and the Nso concept of proper developmental stimulation, expressing an appreciation for increasing the speed of development, because children who walk early can start training for household responsibilities early, like running errands (Ogunnaike & Houser, 2002). Indian baby bathing and massaging as a different mode of body stimulation has also been demonstrated as accelerating developmental progress (Landers, 1989; Walsh Escarce, 1989).

The psychological function of body stimulation might generally consist of intensifying body perception and, thus, the discovery of the baby's own physical effectiveness in relation to resources of the environment. The body is experienced as an "agent" situated in the environment (Rochat, 1997, p. 99) and, thus, the emergence of a body self is promoted.

FIGURE 2.4.   Body stimulation of an urban German mother and rural Nso and Gujarati mothers. Photo from Culture and Development Lab, University of Osnabrück.

Parenting System 4: Object Stimulation.   The object stimulation system is aimed at linking the infant to the nonpersonal world of objects and the physical environment in general. Early object stimulation is pervasive in Western industrialized societies where the objects may replace the caregiving person (Keller & Greenfield, 2000). Object stimulation is also popular in urban contexts of non-Western societies and is more and more recognized in traditional communities as well, with the explicit expectation of fostering cognitive growth (Keller, Voelker, & Yovsi, 2005; Yovsi, 2001). It focuses on shared extradyadic attentional processes and thus initiates and supports the development of metacognitions. Object stimulation is closely related to exploratory activities (Keller, 1992). Figure 2.5 demonstrates some examples of object stimulation.

However, not all parents worldwide value exploration as much as Western parents do during this early life stage. For example, Rothbaum, Pott, et al. (2000) and Rothbaum, Weisz, et al. (2000) proposed replacing exploration with accommodation as related to attachment for Japanese developmental trajectories. The psychological function of early object stimulation consists in nurturing the cognitive system and disengaging the infant from the dependency of social relationships at the same time.

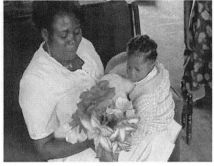

FIGURE 2.5.   Object stimulation of urban German and urban Nso mothers and a rural Gujarati mother. Photo from Culture and Development Lab, University of Osnabrück.

Parenting System 5: Face-to-Face Contact.   The fifth parenting system consists of face-to-face exchange, which is characterized especially by mutual eye contact. The parental investment in the face-to-face system consists mainly in the exclusive devotion of time and attention to dyadic behavioral exchange. Face-to-face interactions are highly arousing, affect-laden, short interactional events that expose infants to high levels of cognitive and social information (Schore, 2001). In a study to assess the social experiences in first- and later-born German 3-month-old infants, we found situations totaling 75 minutes (firstborn) and 66 minutes (later-born) that allowed face-to-face contact with all available caregiving persons over a 10-hour observation period. The episodes were dispersed over the day and sometimes interrupted other activities, such as diaper changing (Keller & Zach, 2002). Face-to-face exchange follows the rules of pseudo-dialogues, allowing the infant to perceive contingencies. Through the prompt answers toward communicative signals, infants can perceive themselves as the cause of the parental action. Figure 2.6 demonstrates some examples of the face-to-face context.

Thus the infant is informed about his or her uniqueness and self-efficacy. The synchronization during face-to-face exchange facilitates the development of verbal dialogue and promotes the infant's capacity for self-regulation (Feldman,

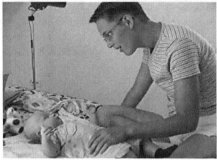

FIGURE 2.6.   Face-to-face context of urban German, Indian, and Nso mothers.
Photo from Culture and Development Lab, University of Osnabrück.

Greenbaum, & Yirmiya, 1999). Warmth can also be communicated in face-to-face situations (Keller, Lohaus, et al., 1999; Lohaus et al., 2005), mainly through sharing (positive) emotions. The prevalence of the face-to-face parenting system is especially salient in contexts where a separated agency has to meet the demands of self-contained and competitive social relationships.

Parenting System 6: The Narrative Envelope.   In recent years, there has been an increased focus on the role of language in the construction of the self (e.g., Budwig, 1995). Two approaches can be differentiated: language as grammar (e.g., Mülhäusler & Harré, 1990; Shotter, 1989) and language as discursive action (e.g., Potter & Wetherell, 1987; for a further discussion see Budwig, 1995). Harré (1992) argued that concepts such as the self are created discursively and are to be understood as attributes of conversations rather than as mental entities. The threefold analytical scheme of *language, langue,* and *parole,* introduced by de Saussure, makes it possible to demonstrate the relation between the macrogenetic level of cultural beliefs (language) and the individual or microgenetic level (unity of *langue* and *parole*). The authors suggested that signs are collective models taken over from language by persons and stored in memory, and which become the basis for construction of thought through verbal means.

In developmental psychology, language has traditionally been used as a way to help researchers uncover children's emerging conceptions of self and other throughout development (Budwig, 1995; Joerchel & Valsiner, 2004). It has been argued, however, that language itself plays a fundamental role in the child becoming able to construct notions of self and other from birth on, and even before parents talk to their babies and thus teach them cultural lessons. A middle-class Los Angeles mother interacts in a free-play situation with her 3-month-old firstborn son:

Okay, you're the tallest boy in the world huh?

Look how tall you are. Look at those strong legs ....

Look, how big that boy is ....

Super, baby, super baby. Look at that,

Look at that big boy, look at that big boy!

This middle-class Beijing mother interacting with her 3-month-old daughter conveys a different message:

Niu Niu is so small ...

Shake the small legs, the small legs. The small legs.

Language serves as a tool for the child to gain access to culturally appropriate notions of self, especially in maternal narrative styles. It has been demonstrated that the style in which caregivers talk to their children is reflective of the cultural models of the self and the relation of self to others (Fung, 1994; Keller, Hentschel, et al., 2004; Leichtman, Wang, & Pillemer, 2003; P. J. Miller, Potts, Fung, Hoogstra, & Mintz, 1990; Minami, 2002; K. Nelson, 2003; Ochs, 1988; Rabain-Jamin, 1979; Wang, 2004). Based on this evidence we conceptualize parental conversational practices and narrations as an extra parenting system.

Summary.   It can be concluded that infants and caregivers are predisposed with an evolved and universal behavioral program. Parents transmit contextually relevant information that is adaptive for the particular environment through contexts they create and interactional exchanges. Infants acquire this information and co-construct their conceptions of the self and of relationships. The universal repertoire becomes context sensitive and context specific during ontogeny. The early experiences lay the foundation for individual developmental pathways.

Empirical Evidence for the Parenting Systems

In several cross-cultural studies we have demonstrated that all six parenting systems can in fact be found in diverse cultural environments, as well as during different historical epochs (Keller, Borke, Yovsi, Lohaus, & Jensen, 2005; Keller & Demuth, in press; Keller, Hentschel, et al., 2004; Keller & Lamm, 2005; Keller,

Lohaus, et al., 2004; Yovsi & Keller, 2003). Figure 2.7 demonstrates the occurrences of body contact, body stimulation, object stimulation, and face-to-face contact in free-play interactional situations in five sociocultural environments. The occurrence is computed in 10-second intervals out of about 15 minutes of videotaped interactional time (Keller, Lohaus, et al., 2004). For details of the assessment, coding, and analysis see chapter 4.

Figure 2.7 demonstrates that members of diverse cultural environments engage in the same parenting systems while interacting with their 3-month-old babies. Rural Cameroonian Nso and Indian Gujarati villagers, as well as urban middle-class mothers in Germany and Greece, and urban lower class mothers from Costa Rica, all demonstrate body contact, body stimulation, object stimulation, and face-to-face context. It is evident that parents also all care for their infants in terms of nursing, cleaning, and talking to them. We were likewise able to identify these parenting systems in long-term historical comparisons of German middle-class families over 30 years, as well as in short-term historical comparisons in German and Costa Rican middle-class families and Nso farmer families (Keller, Borke, et al., 2005). Nevertheless, the caretaking profiles as expressed by the amounts of the different behavioral systems vary substantially across cultural en-

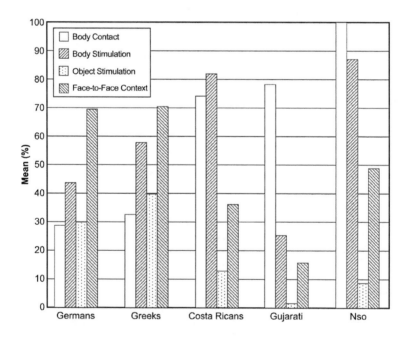

FIGURE 2.7 The occurrence of body contact, body stimulation, object stimulation, and face-to-face context parenting systems in five sociocultural environments.

vironments, as well as across historical epochs. These differences form the basis of cultural styles of parenting that are outlined in chapters 5 and 6.

Our second assumption is that the parenting systems are independent of each other and can form multiple combinations. In multicultural analyses, we tested the occurrence of the four parenting systems—body contact, body stimulation, face-to-face context, and object stimulation—systematically with 214 families from nine different cultural communities (Keller, Borke, et al., 2006). Again, mothers and their 3-month-old infants were analyzed with respect to the occurrence of parenting systems during free-play interactions (Keller, Borke, et al., 2006). The combination of face-to-face contact and body stimulation is the most frequent combination and occurs in 37.5% of the 10-second intervals, followed by the combination of body contact and body stimulation that occurs in 34.9% of the intervals; the combination of face-to-face contact and object stimulation occurs in 24.6% of the intervals; body contact and face-to-face contact occur in 16.8% of the intervals; only face-to-face contact in 21.1%; and the combination of face-to-face contact, body stimulation, and object stimulation in 10.1% of the intervals. These figures indicate that multiple combinations are possible and, in fact, do occur.

To test the general relationships among the parenting systems, Pearson product–moment correlations were calculated among the four parenting systems. Table 2.1 shows the correlations for the total sample. There are negative correlations between body contact and face-to-face exchange, as well as object stimulation. There are also negative correlations between object stimulation and body stimulation. There is a positive correlation between body contact and body stimulation.

These correlations indicate the existence of different parenting strategies: face-to-face contact and object stimulation on the one hand and body contact and body stimulation on the other.

Moreover, we assume that body contact and the face-to-face context can be regarded as alternative parenting systems in that when the expression in one is high, the expression in the other is low although both are physically possible at the same time. We base this assumption on findings that high amounts of body contact are consistently associated with low amounts of mutual visual engagement and vice versa

TABLE 2.1
Correlations Between Parenting Systems

	Body Stimulation	Object Stimulation	Face-to-face Context
Body contact	.28*	–.46*	–.22*
Body stimulation	—	–.39*	.13
Object stimulation		—	.02
Face-to-face context			—

Note. N = 214.
*p < .01.

(Keller, Lohaus, et al., 2004; LeVine, 2004). At an individual level it has also been demonstrated that mutual visual engagement increases when 2- and 3-month-old infants are placed out of contact compared to when they are being held by their mothers (Lavelli & Fogel, 2002). This association has also been shown in chimpanzees. Bard et al. (2005) demonstrated that in chimpanzees mutual gaze was inversely related to maternal cradling. When mother and infant are in constant physical contact there is little mutual gaze. These researchers further argued that mutual engagement can be primarily tactile, which is the most basic evolutionary pattern, found in most nonhuman primates and humans in rural ecocultural environments (Bard, 2002; Stack, 2004). When physical contact is reduced, mutual engagement shifts to the visual mode. These different strategies are examined in more detail in chapters 5 and 6.

The Interactional Mechanisms

Interactional mechanisms are thought to modulate and individualize the parenting systems and their psychological consequences. They are conceived of as basically independent of the parenting systems and from each other. Interactional mechanisms can be further specified with respect to their reference to positive or negative infant cues. It has been demonstrated that caregivers within and across cultures differ with respect to their individual orientation toward positive and negative emotionality. As neurophysiological studies and research on personality functioning have demonstrated, positive and negative emotionality have to be regarded as independent functional systems, which are located in different areas of the brain (Dawson & Fisher, 1994; Fox, 1991; Kuhl, 2001). These assumptions are also supported by medium correlations (.31) between maternal contingency toward positive and negative signals of 5.5-month-old babies.

The interactional mechanisms of attention, warmth, and contingency are outlined in the following paragraphs.

Attention.   Cultures differ with respect to the attentional patterns that are prevalent in child care. In Western urban middle-class families, where most of the interactional studies reported in the literature were conducted, an exclusive dyadic attentional focus of the caregiver, usually the mother, toward the infant is assumed to represent adequate parenting (Ainsworth et al., 1978). Yet exclusive attention is a precious resource that caretakers in most of the childrearing contexts cannot afford to allocate extensively. The more commonly found attentional pattern of caregiving in the majority world (Kağitçibaşi, 1996b) is shared attention (Rogoff, 2003; Rogoff, Mistry, Göncü, & Mosier, 1993), conceptualizing caregiving as a cooccurring activity (Saraswathi & Pai, 1997). In these cases, the caretaker, also usually the mother, attends to extradyadic activities like daily chores as well as to the baby who is in close proximity at the same time. Cooccurring caretaking is considered the culturally appropriate way in many environments where women's economic contribution to the maintenance of the family is crucial and mother–infant separation is considered inadequate parenting. Figure 2.8 demonstrates the different modes of attention.

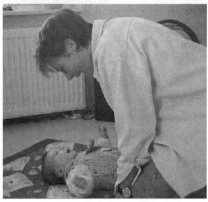

FIGURE 2.8.   Exclusive and shared attention (German, rural and urban Nso mothers). Photo from Culture and Development Lab, University of Osnabrück.

West Cameroonian Nso women watching videotapes of Nso mother–infant interactions emphasized that the infant should be carried on the left side; carrying the infant on the right arm is not good, because it does not allow the mother to carry out other chores effectively (Keller, Voelker, & Yovsi, 2005). Cooccurring attention is focused mainly on negative infant signals, whereas exclusive dyadic attention is mainly directed toward the infant's positive interactional cues.

Children experiencing cooccurring attention seldom experience being the center of attention, but they are also never alone. The cultural practice of cooccurring care during day and night (cosleeping) supports closeness and thus the development of strong and loyal family bonds with which every member accepts the place that is assigned to him or her by cultural customs (Nsamenang & Lamb, 1994, for the Cameroonian Nso; Greenfield, 1999, for Zinacantecan Mayan; Rabinovich, 1998, for Brazilians; Rothbaum, Pott, et al., 2000, and Rothbaum, Weisz, et al., 2000, for Japanese). The shared attentional pattern informs children that they are a coagent in a communicative system. On the other hand, the exclusive attention that is awarded to a child has consequences for the development of the concept of self as an individually distinct and unique agent.

Warmth. Warmth has been recognized as an important ingredient of parenting across many different cultures (Rohner, 1986) since the early parenting style studies during the 1950s and 1960s (Becker, 1964; Schaefer, 1959). Warmth is mainly seen as opposed to parental control (e.g., Kağitçibaşi, 1997). Warmth is described as giving and expressing affection and positive affective exchange (Mac-Donald, 1992), openness and accessibility (Baumrind, 1971), nurturance, understanding, and empathy (Hetherington & Frankie, 1967). MacDonald (1992) conceptualized warmth as an independent parental quality with consequences for the development of early social relationships.

Warmth generally seems to play an important role for the development of social and emotional competence (Maccoby & Martin, 1983; Mize & Pettit, 1997); for example, it is considered to be a significant condition for the development of altruism and sharing (Radke-Yarrow, Zahn-Waxler, & Chapman, 1983; Staub, 1979). Besides fostering social coherence, warmth seems to be related to the development of social imitation and role-taking. Within the context of social learning theory (Bandura & Huston, 1961), it has been demonstrated that children imitate adult role models more when these role models display warm and affectionate behavior (as well as powerful models; Bandura et al., 1963) as compared with cold and distant behavioral models. Maternal nurturance increases imitation from daughters (Mussen & Parker, 1965) and parental warmth predicts identification with parents (Hetherington & Frankie, 1967). Warm, positive, and affectionate parent–child relationships "are expected to result in the acceptance of adult values by the child, identifying with the parent, and a generally higher level of compliance" (MacDonald, 1992, p. 761).

Contingency. In interactions with babies, parents (as well as caretakers in general) display a propensity for prompt responsiveness to infant cues. Accordingly, prompt reactivity is part of different conceptions of parenting, such as Ainsworth's sensitivity rating (Ainsworth et al., 1978), intuitive parenting (H. Papoušek & Papoušek, 1991), and behaviorally based evaluations of parenting (Leyendecker, Lamb, Fracasso, Schölmerich, & Larson, 1997). There are different time spans reported in the literature that are considered prompt, ranging from 2 seconds (Millar, 1972) to between 5 and 7 seconds (Perrez, Achermann, & Diethelm, 1983), mainly as responses toward distress signals. There is evidence that parents in fact respond much faster to a substantial portion of infants' nondistress signals—within a latency window of 200 to 800 milliseconds (Keller, Lohaus, et al., 1999; Lohaus et al., 2005; Lohaus, Keller, Voelker, Cappenberg, & Chasiotis, 1997; H. Papoušek & Papoušek, 1991). With this short time frame, the intuitive character of parental responses is further emphasized, because shorter behavioral latencies would be reflexive and longer ones cognitively mediated (Lohaus et al., 1997; Lohaus, Völker, Keller, Cappenberg, & Chasiotis, 1998; H. Papoušek & Papoušek, 1991). The necessity of the short time span seems to be related to infants' restricted memory capacity, because habituation studies have demonstrated that infants do not learn that events belong together if the time lag between them exceeds 1 second (Stang, 1989; cf. van Egeren, Barratt, & Roach, 2001). Parental contingency matches infants' contingency detection mechanisms, which are present from birth (Gewirtz & Pelàez-Nogueras, 1992). The perception of temporal relationships is discussed as constituting a general mechanism of information processing that includes social as well as nonsocial events (Tarabulsy, Tessier, & Kappas, 1996). With this capacity, infants can relate events to their own actions (cf. J. S. Watson, 1967, 1971). Contingency perception does not seem to be dependent on specific affective displays, although infants enjoy matched affect (Meltzoff, 1990). However, infants experiencing any environmental or behavior-based contingencies result in positive affect, whereas the violation of contingency expectations—for example, during still-face situations, in which mothers are instructed not to react physically to the infant, but to keep their faces still (Ellsworth, Muir, & Hains, 1993)—is accompanied by negative affect and distress. Thus, contingency detection seems to be self-rewarding. Contingent responses cause infants to smile and may be innately pleasurable (J. S. Watson, 1972, 2001). Contingency constitutes a dyadic system over which the infant already has control (Chisholm, 2003).

The function of the contingency experience based on nondistress face-to-face interaction is considered to promote the acquisition of early perceptually based self-knowledge (cf. Neisser, 1993) by learning that behaviors have consequences (Lewis & Goldberg, 1969) and by seeing their actions reflected in others (Bigelow, 1998). Consequently, contingency experience has been related to the development of beliefs about personal effectiveness (Skinner, 1985; cf. Seligman, 1975) and the predictability of the behavior of others (Lamb, 1981). Thus, contingency experiences partially determine personal socialization experiences (Lamb & Easterbrooks, 1981). Hunt (1963) maintained that environmental changes as a response to infant's behavior may affect the infant's rudimentary sense of mastery (cf. Ainsworth, 1979; Ainsworth et al., 1974; Ainsworth et al., 1978). The developmental consequence of the contingency experience during early interactions can, thus, be linked to the development of control beliefs that determine a conception of the self as a causal agent.

Empirical Evidence for the Interactional Mechanisms

We were also able to demonstrate empirically that the interactional mechanisms occur across the diverse cultural contexts mentioned earlier (Keller, Kuensemueller, et al., 2005). Figure 2.9 demonstrates warmth and contingency toward positive and negative infant stimuli. The data are z standardized, so that the columns indicate whether the expression of these variables is below or above the mean in all cultural samples. Contingency toward positive infant signals (looking, positive vocalizations, and smiling) is expressed as the relative frequency of maternal responses that are occurring within a latency window of 1 second. Contingency toward negative signals is expressed as the prompt regulatory activity to the infant's distress and crying. Regulatory activity can be as diverse as breastfeeding and distracting the baby with a toy. Warmth toward positive signals is restricted to

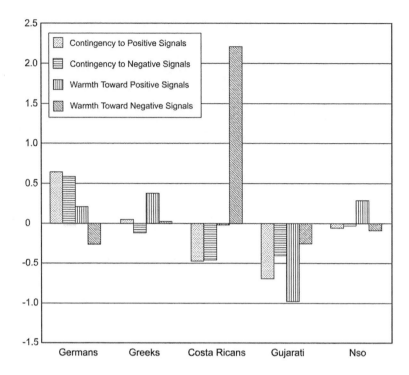

FIGURE 2.9. The occurrence of the interaction mechanisms of contingency and warmth toward positive and negative infant signals in five sociocultural environments.

the face-to-face context with smiling and baby talk. Warmth is of course also expressed in the amount of body contact (see Figure 2.7). Warmth toward negative signals is defined as empathic response toward infant distress and crying (for more details, see Keller, Kuensemueller, et al., 2005; chap. 4, this volume). This analysis also demonstrates the frequent occurrence of these interactional mechanisms, although they occur to varying degrees in the different cultural contexts (see Figure 2.9). The analysis of these differences is also addressed later in chapters 5 and 6.

There were no systematic relations among the parenting systems, the interactional mechanisms, and between parenting systems and interactional mechanisms. It is particularly interesting that warmth and contingency do not form a unitary conception of parenting, as has often been claimed (e.g., Ainsworth et al., 1978). Our data confirm MacDonald's (1992) argument that warmth and contingency form independent components of parenting. There is no statistical relation in any cultural community between contingency toward positive infant signals and contingency toward negative infant signals in this study (Keller, Kuensemueller, et al., 2005). These data confirm earlier studies. In a factor analysis of different interactional measures assessed in videotaped free-play situations in two German samples of mothers and their 3-month-old infants ($N1 = 14$, $N2 = 31$) and one

Euro-American sample ($N = 12$) with a comparable socioeconomic background, we identified a three-factor solution consisting of a nonverbal contingency factor, a verbal contingency factor, and a sensitivity and warmth factor. This exploratory analysis provided the first evidence for the independence of behavioral contingency and warmth (Keller, Schneider, & Henderson, 1994; Keller, Zach, et al., 1994).

To further explore the interactional structure of parenting behavior, we conducted a longitudinal study of 63 middle-class northern German mothers and their 3-month-old infants. Data analysis was based on videotaped parent–infant interactions in free-play home situations each about 15 minutes long. Trained observers assessed contingency on the basis of face-to-face interactional exchanges, using a microanalytical computer-based procedure (cf. Keller, Lohaus, et al., 1999). Two chance-corrected indexes of contingency were computed (cf. J. S. Watson, 1979, 1985; for methodological details see chap. 4, this volume). Different trained raters assessed sensitivity, focusing specifically on affectionate, warm parenting (Ainsworth et al., 1974), for the same video sequences. Results did not reveal associations between maternal sensitivity and warmth and the contingency indexes, thus supporting the evaluation of independent components.

Summary

We were able to demonstrate empirically that the theoretical system of components of parenting, consisting of behavioral systems and interactional mechanisms, could be identified in diverse cultural environments. The co-occurrence of systems and mechanisms creates behavioral styles, which we discuss in chapters 5 and 6. Body contact and face-to-face context can be understood to be two alternative parenting strategies, inducing different psychological consequences, for example, with respect to family cohesion (see Figure 2.10).

FIGURE 2.10.   German (right) and Cameroonian Nso (left) children's drawings of their families.

3 The Concept of Culture

Our conceptualization of culture implies a dynamic and socially interactive process with two main components: the creation of shared activity leading to cultural practices and the creation of shared meaning leading to cultural interpretations (Greenfield, 1997; Greenfield & Keller; 2004; Rogoff, 2003). Shared activities (cultural practices) constitute the material side of culture. Shared meanings (cultural interpretation) represent the symbolic side of culture and the interpretation and evaluation of the world. Thus, culture is inside as well as outside the individual.

As a species, humans are biologically primed to acquire, create, and transmit culture. Cultural differences are variations on themes of universal importance and differential emphases put on particular practices (Rogoff, 2003). As such, culture is the primary mode of human adaptation (Greenfield & Keller, 2004; Rogoff, 2003). Therefore, development consists of the construction and co-construction of cultural contents within the framework of biological predispositions (Keller, 2002a, 2002b, 2002c; Keller & Chasiotis, 2005). As development represents a process of change, culture likewise represents ontogenetic and historical processes of change (Greenfield, 1996; Keller & Lamm, 2005).

We draw on conceptions that suggest that culture and human psychology reflect the demands of ecocultural environments (Berry, 1976; Hewlett & Lamb, 2002; LeVine, 1974, 1988; Weisner, 1987; B. B. Whiting, 1963), the socioeconomic structure of a society (Morelli & Tronick, 1991), human ecology (Lamb & Sternberg, 1992), and types of communities (Levy, 1984). Based on the conceptualizations of the "Whiting model for psycho-cultural research" (J. W. M. Whiting, 1981), we have based our study program on the diagram shown in Figure 3.1.

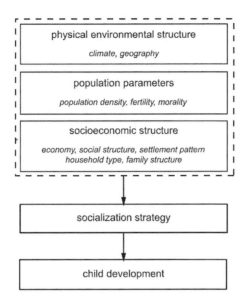

FIGURE 3.1.   The ecocultural model of child development.

Figure 3.1 depicts a hierarchical model for which the physical structure of an environment is the basis for developing population parameters, and for which fertility and mortality form a functional unit (Chisholm, 1999; Voland, Dunbar, Engel, & Stephan, 1997; M. Wilson & Daly, 1997). The socioeconomic structure, including the economic base of the family as well as its social patterning, defines the framework for the socialization strategies consisting of ideas and practices, which directly influences children's development and, therefore, adult psychology. As already assumed by J. W. M. Whiting (1981), the customary methods by which infants (and children) are cared for have enduring psychological and physiological effects on the members of the respective society. In line with a cultural-historical perspective, we take into account socialization strategies as expressed in people's everyday activities, which form the natural laboratory for studying the role of culture in human development (M. Cole, 2005).

We now want to address two ecosocial environments that can be regarded as representing extremes with respect to sociodemographic characteristics, and that, as a consequence, generate two extremely different types of psychology. The first ecocultural context is the dense social network of traditional village communities. The economy is usually subsistence based with little economic diversity among families and clans. The population is small scale with person-to-person interactions as the familiar social mode. Formal education, if available at all, is basic. Lifestyle is characterized by hierarchical family systems based on age and gender and communal work. Reproduction starts early and is based on a more quantitative strategy with more children and less individualized parental investment (Belsky, 1999; Belsky et al., 1991; Keller, 2003c). The value of children to the family is psychological and economical (Kağitçibaşi, 1996b).

The second ecocultural context refers to the anonymous, large-scale social life of Western postindustrialized knowledge societies (Keller, 2003c; Keller, Zach, & Abels, 2005). The economy is money based and incomes vary from individual to individual due to societal and individual factors. Formal education levels are usually high. Lifestyles are based on personal achievement and late reproduction with few children and a more individualized parental investment (Keller & Chasiotis, 2005). The value of children to the individual parent is psychological but not economical (Kağitçibaşi, 1996b). On the contrary, the elderly generation often economically supports their grandchildren's education.

These two types of communities and their respective psychologies form prototypes that can be regarded as extreme patterns from which varieties may arise. With this approach we do not address countries or societies as units of cultural and cross-cultural analysis; rather, we define particular sociocultural communities within societies as the basis for comparison. To understand the exact nature of a prototype, it is crucial to analyze more than one cultural community with comparable sociodemographic characteristics. We study West African Nso and Indian Gujarati Rajput villagers as prototypical for the rural agrarian context and German, Greek, and Euro-American middle-class families as prototypical for the urban, educated context. The German families live in Berlin, Muenster, Marburg, and Mainz; the Greek families in Athens; and the Euro-American families in Los Angeles.

It is assumed that the prototypical psychology that is adapted to the rural, agrarian socioeconomic environment can be described as the interdependent self (Kağitçibaşi, 1996a; Keller, 2003b; Markus & Kitayama, 1991). The interdependent self-construal denotes an individual who defines himself or herself as part of a social system (mainly the family), seeks harmonious relationships, accepts hierarchy (mainly age and gender based), values cooperation and conformity, and is identified with his or her role in the social environment. The interdependent self-construal prioritizes the perception of a fluidly defined and contextually based individual as an interrelated coagent with others (Greenfield, Keller, Fuligni, & Maynard, 2003; Keller, 2003a). Changes in self-domains over time are acknowledged (Flores, Teuchner, & Chandler, 2004). Kağitçibaşi (1996a, 2005) defined interdependence as embodying heteronomy and relatedness. Heteronomy involves being subject to another's law, the state of being governed from the outside, or having to depend on another person for action. Relatedness means including others within the boundaries of the self. The relationship with others becomes the central feature of the self-concept.

The prototypical psychology that is assumed to be adapted to the urban educated socioeconomic environment can be described as the independent self (Kağitçibaşi, 1996a; Keller, 2003a; Markus & Kitayama, 1991). The conception of the independent (or individualistic, autonomous) self-construal denotes an individual who is self-contained, competitive, separate, unique, and self-reliant; has an inner sense of owning opinions; and is assertive (Markus & Kitayama, 1994). The model of independence focuses on mental states and personal qualities supporting self-enhance-ment, self-expression, and self-maximization. The self is defined as "essentialist," which means having a timeless core identity that also does not change across situa-tions (Flores et al., 2004). The essence of independence in Kağitçibaşi's model (1996a) is autonomy and separateness. Chirkov, Ryan, Kim, and Kaplan (2003) de-fined a person to be autonomous "when his or her behavior is experienced as will-ingly enacted and when he or she fully endorses the actions in which he or she is engaged and/or the values expressed by them" (p. 98). To be experienced as an au-tonomous entity, the self does not depend on the other (Markus & Kitayama, 1991).

Although the two prototypical environments are assumed to be associated with different psychologies, it is important to keep in mind the universal fact of human existence: We are all both individual persons (agency) and members of collectivi-ties (communion; Bakan, 1966; Erikson, 1968; Guisinger & Blatt, 1994; Killen & Wainryb, 2000). However, the form that individual characteristics and collective membership take and their relative importance differ along the dimensions consti-tuting the two kinds of environments; the phenotypical synthesis emerging in a particular sociocultural environment prioritizes one or the other dimension (Keller, Lohaus, et al., 1999; Poortinga, 1992). This is not a binary conception, as it conceives of independence and interdependence as two independent dimen-sions. There are infinite combinations along these dimensions that also generate an infinite number of intermediate psychologies, which we discuss in chapter 6. Because we do not assume a bipolar and dichotomous nature of these conceptions, we are not simplifying cultural complexities (Killen, McGlothlin, & Lee-Kim, 2002) and do not subscribe to a grand-divide theory with a reductionistic stance (Branco, 2003; Chirkov et al., 2003; Hollos & Leis, 2002; Mascolo & Li, 2004; Neff, 2003; Pirttilä-Backman, Kassea, & Ikonen, 2004; Realo, 2003; Saraswathi, 2004; Shimizu, 2001). The following sections introduce these sociodemographic contexts with individual portraits for the different study communities that are ad-dressed in this book, emphasizing both similarities and differences. The portraits are based on existing literature and ethnographic reports.

THE SOCIODEMOGRAPHIC PORTRAIT OF TRADITIONAL RURAL VILLAGE LIFE

The West Cameroonian Nso Farmers

The Nso originate from the Tikar people of the Adamawa province of Cameroon. The Tikar was a family made up of two brothers and a sister by the name Ngonso. Due to the warrior environment, a conflict erupted among the three siblings on where to migrate. The dispute separated the three siblings, who then took their people in different directions. Ngonso, the eldest sibling, migrated with her Nso people. After fighting a series of battles, they finally settled in their present site in Kumbo in the Northwest province of Cameroon, which is in the English-speaking part of the country (see Figure 3.2).

a.

b.

FIGURE 3.2. (a) A view of Kumbo; (b) Entrance to Kumbo market. Photos by Joscha Kärtner.

The Nso are one of the largest ethnic groups in the Western grass fields of the Republic of Cameroon with a population of about 217,000 inhabitants (Goheen, 1996; Sub-Divisional Office Mbvem, 1998). The average life expectancy at birth is 47.04 years for men and 48.67 years for women. The age structure in Cameroon is 41.7% between 0 and 10 years, 55% between 15 and 64 years, and 3.3% 65 years and over (The World Factbook, 2005). The infant mortality rate is 72.14 deaths per

1,000 live births for boys and 64.27 for girls (UNICEF, 2000). However, mortality varies with environmental factors like source of drinking water and distance to health services in different regions (see Figure 3.3). The fertility rate in Cameroon is 4.47 children per woman (The World Factbook, 2005). There are no special statistics available for the Nso. The number of children per woman and other sociodemographic characteristics of our Nso samples are reported in Table 3.1.

Although there is still a large number of illiterate people, especially in the older generation, basic education in the Nso villages is mandatory, with a large variety of public and church-based nursery and primary schools such as government-run, Catholic, Baptist, Presbyterian, and Muslim schools (see Figure 3.4). Secondary schools are distant and only located around the town of Kumbo.

The Nso are sedentary farmers. Subsistence is a combination of communal efforts and endeavors of family members, children included. Apart from farm products (see Figure 3.5), coffee is commonly produced and sold to the local cooperative. Timber is an investment that brings income to owners especially when trees have grown to gigantic sizes. Raffia palm stems are tapped at least twice a day and the wine and the kola nuts are sold for local consumption, rituals, and sacrifices. Men should be in possession of *keng* (wealth) in the form of raffia palms, coffee plantations, forest lands and, most of all, children.

The Nso villages are composed of compounds—extensions of several clustered houses without sheaths where each courtyard merges with another (see Figure 3.6)—and each is headed by a lineage head (Goheen, 1996). An average Nso

FIGURE 3.3. Women waiting in the health center. Photo by Bettina Lamm.

TABLE 3.1

Sociodemographic Profiles of the Samples With an Interdependent Model of Parenting

	N	Mean Age of Mothers	Mean Age at Birth of the First Child	Mean Years of School Attendance	Mean Number of Children	Percentage of First Born Infants	Percentage of Female Infants	Percentage of Married Mothers	Mean Number of Persons Per Household
Rural Nso (1998/99), Cameroon	28	26.7	—[a]	7.6	3.2	10.7%	53.6%	67.9%	7.1
Rural Nso (2000), Cameroon	13	25.8	—[a]	6.8	2.7	46.2%	53.8%	69.7%	5.6
Rural Nso (2002), Cameroon	30	29.2	21.4	6.7	3.3	36.7%	63.3%	62.1%	7.5
Rural Gujarati (1998), India	23	26.8	18.6	—[a]	2.4	34.8%	34.8%	100.0%	7.4
Rural Gujarati (1999), India	24	22.4	18.4	4.4	2.3	29.2%	50.0%	100.0%	6.7
Rural Gujarati (2003), India	16	22.7	18.7	2.8	2.1	43.8%	56.3%	100.0%	6.0

[a] No information available.

a.

b.

FIGURE 3.4.   (a) Schoolchildren waiting for school to start; (b) Schoolchildren during the morning welcome ceremony. Photos by Bettina Lamm.

household (i.e., the father, mother, unmarried children and kin) is composed of 6.7 persons (Yovsi, 2003).

The houses are usually constructed of red mud bricks and roofed with zinc. Windows are made from planks or bamboo. Wealthier households have homes built from concrete blocks with cement floors. The kitchen is usually a separate structure and consists of a fire pit made of three stones and shelves where food and

FIGURE 3.5.   Fruits and vegetables being sold on roadside markets. Photo by Heidi Keller.

utensils are stored (see Figure 3.7). Foods to be preserved are dried and stored in a granary in the rafters above the kitchen (see Figure 3.8).

In the big house there is a sitting room with chairs, family and religious pictures on the wall, posters of advertisements, calendars, the head of the family's traditional belongings, and other important family possessions. There are other significant houses in the compound such as a *njangi,* or meeting house, and mourning and religious sites. Small portable radios are common and most households use bush lamps because very few can afford electricity. There is a community water project that provides water to the population for free. There are very few shops that sell the necessary items such as salt, palm oil, kerosene, matches, soap, and sugar. Other items are bought in the town, which has a daily market (see Figure 3.9).

Because the settlement pattern is patrilocal, children settle at their father's homestead. Every male child owns land within the lineage territory where he builds his own house. The share belonging to a female child who leaves the parents and marries is given to one of the sons. The average marriage age for Nso women is 19.8 years (Yovsi, 2003). The woman usually marries a man who is older than her and is expected to give birth to several children. Girls are married off for a bride price.

a.

b.

FIGURE 3.6. Life happens mainly outside the house. Photos from Culture and Development Lab, University of Osnabrück.

FIGURE 3.7. A kitchen with a fireplace. Photo by Bettina Lamm.

FIGURE 3.8. Corn is one of the most popular staples and is hung on the wall to dry. Photo from Culture and Development Lab, University of Osnabrück.

FIGURE 3.9. The hilly landscape is very fertile. Photo by Bettina Lamm.

The Indian Gujarati Rajputs

The Gujarati Rajputs living in the villages of the Nandesari area (see Figure 3.10) are a warrior caste from Saurashtra who migrated to this area approximately four centuries ago. They belonged to a few families who were all related to each other and came from Gohelwad (therefore: Rajput, Gohel). Today about 13,000 to 14,000 families live in 30 villages. The Nandesari area is located approximately 20 kilometes north of Baroda (Vadodara), a rather densely populated region in the state of Gujarat, India (Bruesseler, 1992; Singh, 1971).

The average life expectancy in Gujarat at birth is 61.5 years for men and 62.8 years for women. The age structure is as follows: 34.6% between 0 and 14 years of age, 59.7% between 15 and 59, and 5.7% are at least 60 years old (Chauhan, 1991). In the Nandesari area, the infant mortality rate has been reduced in recent years, decreasing from 107 per 1,000 to 32 per 1,000 (Deepak Medical Foundation, Deepak Charitable Trust, 2000). On average, women marry at the age of 16 years in the Nandesari area. A woman is expected to give birth to two sons and a common ideal is to have two sons and one daughter. Of all births, 94% are live births, of which 82.5% survive. In the Nandesari area approximately 53% of the women are illiterate (Lakhani, Ganju, & Mahale, 1997), whereas female illiteracy in rural Gujarat is generally 60.1% and male illiteracy 39.9%. The sociodemographic statistics for our Gujarati Rajput samples are reported in Table 3.1. Some children go to local kindergartens (see Figure 3.11).

Approximately 50% to 60% of the men living in and around Nandesari work in the chemical factories in the area. The rest are to a great extent occupied with farming and raising cattle—either on their own land or as hired farm hands. Women's main occupations are housework, farming, and raising cattle (Lakhani et al., 1997). The majority of the people (74%) have a medium economic level. They live in semi-*pucca* houses (some of the structure is made of concrete, the rest of clay) and own a fan, a radio, a bicycle, and a gas stove or the like. A bicycle is a precious possession (see Figure 3.12).

a.

b.

FIGURE 3.10. (a) Typical landscape in the Nandesari area; (b) Langurs watching the area. Photos by (a) Monika Abels, and (b) Heidi Keller.

The 16% who belong to the lower socioeconomic level live in *kuccha* houses (constructed mainly of clay, with a handmade floor made of mud and cow dung that has to be renewed at least once a year) and only a *chullah* (traditional stove made from clay or supported with a few bricks—usually dried cow dung is the primary fuel) is used (see Figure 3.13).

FIGURE 3.11. A local village kindergarten, where the slide is the main attraction. Photo by Monika Abels.

FIGURE 3.12. A bicycle is precious possession. Photo by Monika Abels.

a.

b.

FIGURE 3.13.   (a) Food is stored inside the house; (b) Fireplaces are often outside. Photos from Culture and Development Lab, University of Osnabrück.

The villages in the Nandesari area range in size from 400 to 10,000 inhabitants. Villages usually consist of a cluster of houses including shops with basic goods, and possibly a school. In a few villages, where there are different castes, there are separate areas for these castes.

The joint family is considered to be the prototype of the Indian rural family and constitutes the normative household pattern (see Figure 3.14).

FIGURE 3.14.   Joint family in Gujarat. Photo from Culture and Development Lab, University of Osnabrück.

In this pattern the sons stay with their parents and the woman marries into her husband's (parents') household, where the couple lives with their children. The family has a hierarchical structure and the eldest male member of the family is usually the head of the family (Deka, 1993). According to Deka (1993), not only residence, but also property and income are shared, and there is a common code of conduct within the family. However statistics demonstrate that the nuclear family is the predominant family type (see Figure 3.15).

In the Nandesari area, according to Lakhani et al. (1997), approximately 64% of the families are nuclear and 36% are joint. The average family consists of 5.4 members. Yet these statistics do not contradict the idea of the extended family, as families do not live isolated from one another (Abels, 2002). Many of them live in a constant exchange with and close linkage to their neighboring relatives, with whom they exchange favors and share chores (a sister-in-law might cook when the woman is menstruating or a cousin might look after the baby while the mother is fetching water).

Summary: The Rural Village Context

The two types of communities represent similar socioeconomic surroundings. Both areas are tropical with dry and rainy seasons. Temperatures range from 20°C to 45°C depending on the season. The vegetation in the Nso land is predominantly savanna with patches of natural forest or primary vegetation. The natural vegetation in the Nandesari area consists mainly of dry, thorny forest. The infant mortality rate is

FIGURE 3.15.   A nuclear family in Gujarat. Photo from Culture and Development Lab, University of Osnabrück.

high, although it is decreasing with the improvement of health services. Education levels, although increasing, are still low, especially for women. The families in both areas live mainly off farming and occasionally have some cattle. Families are patrilocal and hierarchically organized with the oldest male member being the head of family, deciding on all social and economic matters. Households are large, with about six to seven members on the average. Even if families are nuclear, relatives live next door or close by, so that family life is still embedded into an extended social network. Women marry early and also start their reproductive lives early. They have three to five children on average. Table 3.1 summarizes the sociodemographic characteristics of the samples that we studied within these communities.

The sample characteristics confirm the sociodemographic profile that we outlined earlier. Children in the Cameroonian samples attend school for about 7 years, which is the amount of formal schooling offered in the villages. The Indian women's level of formal school experience is even lower, with 3 to 4 years on the average. Women's age at the first birth is around 18 to 20. The mean number of children is lower than the national averages, with about three children per woman in the Nso samples and between two and three children in the Gujarati samples. However, many women have experienced the death of a child. In line with Hindu tradition, all of the Gujarati mothers are married, whereas only two thirds of the Nso women are married. The mean number of persons living in the households is between six and seven for both settings. The samples thus represent the contexts for what they were selected.

THE SOCIODEMOGRAPHIC PORTRAIT OF WESTERN URBAN MIDDLE-CLASS FAMILIES

Greek Urban Middle-Class Families

Our study site is Athens, a Greek metropolis with 729,137 inhabitants. Average life expectancy in Greece is 76.59 years for men and 81.76 years for women. The age structure of the population in Greece is 14.4% between 0 and 14 years, 66.8% between 15 and 64 years, and 18.8% 65 years and older. The infant mortality rate is 5.53 deaths per 1,000 live births. Since the middle of the 1970s, fertility rates in Greece have declined mainly due to social and economical changes (as in all industrially developed societies) with a present mean of 1.3 children per woman (National Statistical Service of Greece, 1998; The World Factbook, 2005). The vast majority of births are within wedlock; unmarried couples with children are still an unusual phenomenon in Greek society (Maratou-Alipranti, 1999). Ninety-eight percent of the population belong to the Greek Orthodox Church. In the Athens area, the nuclear family structure represents 89.4% of the families. However, close relatives, especially parents, usually live in the same neighborhood and assist the spousal family in childrearing. Thirty-eight percent of older people live with their children in the Athens area. Georgas et al. (1997) demonstrated that the difference in family relationships among Greece, the Netherlands, Britain, and Germany lies mainly in the relationships between the extended family members. Moreover, in northern and western Europe, the family bonds are mainly limited to the intergenerational network, whereas in Greece the kinship involves grandparents, uncles, aunts, and cousins. Because the fathers are away from home the greatest part of the day, and thus are not involved in childrearing, the mothers hold themselves solely responsible for the goodness of the child (Doumanis, 1983). Figure 3.16 presents a Greek mother with her children at Christmas.

FIGURE 3.16.   A Greek mother and her child. Photo by Zaira Papaligoura.

German Urban Middle-Class Families

Our German study sites are the country's capital of Berlin, with about 3.5 million citizens; the North Rhine-Westphalia city of Muenster with about 267,000 citizens; and the more southern university cities of Marburg in Hesse with about 71,000 citizens and Mainz, the capital of Rhineland-Palatinate, with about 192,000 citizens. Life expectancy in Germany is 75.66 years for men and 81.81 years for women. The age structure of the population is 14.4% between 0 and 14 years, 66.7% between 15 and 64 years, and 18.9% 65 years and older. The infant mortality rate is 4.16 deaths per 1,000 live births. The fertility rate in Germany has declined continuously in recent decades to 9.4 (world average: 25.5), reflecting a total fertility rate of 1.3 (The World Factbook, 2005). The mean age of primiparous mothers is about 29 years and that of first-time fathers approximately 30 years. Women have 14 weeks maternity leave and are paid 100% of their salaries. Three years of parental childrearing leave is compensated with an income-corrected flat rate for 2 years and is unpaid for the third year. Families who want a second child often prefer a dense spacing.

Germans receive high levels of education. In 2003, 1,168 schools operated in Berlin with various areas of specialization (*Statistisches Landesamt Berlin, 2004*).

The stereotypic German family is a "complete" family: a married couple with one or two children. Germans marry at the end of their 20s and expect the husband to be 2 to 3 years older than the wife. Official marriage ceremonies are performed at the civil registry office. The majority of couples also have church weddings. Protestant and Roman Catholic churches cover 34% of the population each, 3.7% are Muslim and unaffiliated, and 28.3% are "other."

Only 9% of people between 70 and 85 years of age who have at least one living child live together with the child in the same household (Kohli, 1999; Kohli, Kuenemund, Motel, & Szydlik, 1997). However, 90% of the elderly have a child living within a 2-hour drive. These data indicate that in Germany, family members tend to live in close proximity as well.

In recent decades, magazines have often declared the death of the classical nuclear family: More couples are deciding to live together outside the context of marriage, a first pregnancy more frequently precedes rather than follows marriage, dual-career families increase in number, women decide to be single mothers by choice, and gay or lesbian parents claim equal rights as "traditional" families (cf. Blossfeld, 1995).

Yet, the concept of the family is based on the institution of marriage as specifying emotional bonds between husband and wife with the clear perspective of raising children. Accordingly, German mothers and fathers view children as fulfilling their life's purpose (Gauda & Keller, 1987; Jagenow & Mittag, 1984). However, irrespective of a changing public attitude and the increasing presence of women in the labor force, the role distribution in the majority of German families is still more or less traditional in the described sense (Vaskovics, 1999), at least during the so-called family phase when children are small, especially until they enter school at age 6. Only 1.6% of the fathers take paternity leave. Johanna's father is one of the rare exceptions (see Figure 3.17).

FIGURE 3.17.   A German couple with their young daughter Johanna. Photo by Bettina Lamm.

Middle-Class Euro-American Families

Our Euro-American study site is the southern Californian urban center of Los Angeles, which is located in Los Angeles County and has about 10 million inhabitants. Life expectancy in the United States is 74.89 years for men and 80.67 years for women. The age structure of the population in Los Angeles County is 7.4% below 5 years, 20.3% between 6 and 18 years, 54.6% between 19 and 63 years, and 9.7% 65 years and older (*U.S. Census Bureau, 2005*). The infant mortality rate is

6.5 deaths per 1,000 live births. The national fertility rate is 2.08 children per woman (The World Factbook, 2005). The age at first birth increased from 24.6 to 27.2 between 1970 and 2000 and is referred to as the maturing of motherhood. Because paid maternity leave is not readily available from most employers, women usually use a combination of short-term disability, sick leave, vacation, and personal days to have some portion of their maternity leave paid. Among the women who take maternity leave, about 80% take 12 weeks or less (U.S. Department of Health and Human Services, 2005).

There are 2.98 persons per household in Los Angeles County, with an average household income of $42,189. There is a high level of education with about 25% of the population age 25 and older holding a bachelor's degree or higher. Declining marriage rates and increasing divorce rates have characterized formal relationships among U.S. couples in recent decades (Teachman, Tedrow, & Crowder, 2000). About one third of all births in 1999 in the United States were to unmarried women, with this trend increasing (B. C. Miller, Leavitt, Merrill, & Park, 2005). Nevertheless, father, mother, and children are still the cultural family norm in the United States. Men are marrying first at about 26 years of age, which is nearly the same as 100 years ago, whereas women are marrying first at 25 years of age as compared to 20 years of age in the 1950s (B. C. Miller et al., 2005). Marriage and family patterns are based on the Judeo-Christian context (B. C. Miller et al., 2005). About 9 out of 10 people in the United States acknowledge having a religious affiliation, which has not changed more than 4% over the last two decades (B. C. Miller et al., 2005). Figure 3.18 presents a Euro-American family in Los Angeles at the beach.

FIGURE 3.18.   A Euro-American family on the beach. Photo by Lauren Greenfield/VII.

Summary: The Western Urban Middle-Class Context.

The three urban research sites also represent similar sociodemographic surroundings. Both husband and wife in urban middle-class families in Western societies have a high degree of formal education, which is grossly underestimated by the national means. The actual sociodemographic characteristics of our study communities are reported in Table 3.2. Life expectancy is high and infant mortality is low. A cash economy is the economic base of the urban middle-class families. Families are nuclear (the couple and their children), although other family members often live close by. However, the primary responsibility for childrearing lies with the parents. Men and women have equal rights. Nevertheless, during the family phase when children are small, there is a traditional division of labor with women being on maternity leave and staying at home, whereas husbands are the breadwinners and work outside the home. Women marry in their late 20s, which is also when they start their reproductive lives. They have one or two children on average.

The mothers in all the selected samples had a high level of formal education (between 14 and 17 years of schooling). They were all between 30 and 35 years of age when they had their first child. With respect to marital status, the German samples in particular reflect the national trend of more couples living together without being formally married. The household sizes are between three and four persons, reflecting the nuclear character of the middle-class Western families. Thus, these samples also reflect the sociodemographic profiles of the contexts for which they were selected.

CONCLUSION: TWO CULTURAL PROTOTYPES

In line with the existing literature (e.g., Hauser & Schnore, 1965), we have demonstrated that our prototypical sociodemographic communities differ in systematic ways from each other. The sociodemographic characteristics incorporate the rural–urban distinction with different levels of technological development and different organizations for the social environment. Urban communities are large and anonymous, whereas rural communities are small and populated by familiar actors. Also the pace of environmental and contextual change differs vastly across these two environments. Urban environments change quickly and different generations face different contextual demands. Therefore, socialization strategies are negotiated horizontally among peers and influenced by popularization of scientific results. Changes in rural contexts are slow so that vertical, intergenerational transmission is an adaptive socialization avenue. Thus the two environments represent different challenges for which parents want to prepare their offspring based on different caretaker psychologies. Chapter 4 presents the cultural models of parenting as related to the two prototypes and based on empirical studies within the study communities described. Although we tried to assess the complete research program within all the study communities, it was not possible in all respects, so some data are not available for some study communities.

TABLE 3.2

Sociodemographic Profiles of the Samples With an Independent Model of Parenting

	N	Mean Age of Mothers	Mean Years of School Attendance	Mean Number of Children	Percentage of First Born Infants	Percentage of Female Infants	Percentage of Married Mothers (Living Together in an Unmarried Partnership)	Mean Number of Persons Per Household
Berlin, Germany (2002)	40	33.8	15.3	1.4	70.0%	46.2%	42.1% (50.0%)	3.4
Marburg, Germany (2000)	60	29.6	13.9	1.0	100.0%	45.0%	65.0%	3.1
Muenster, Germany (1993)	20	30.7	14.3	1.0	100.0%	45.0%	80.0% (20.0%)	—[a]
Mainz, Germany (1977/78)	37	26.6	13.9	1.0	100.0%	48.4%	100.0%	3.2
Los Angeles, USA (2002)	21	35.0	17.1	1.4	68.2%	63.6%	95.0%	3.5
Athens, Greece	50	30.3	13.5	1.4	64.0%	50.0%	—[a]	—[a]

[a] No information available.

4 The Research Methodology: Infancy Assessment

Most of our infancy studies focus on infants who are about 3 months old, which we have determined to be a key age during early infancy. The first developmental stage in terms of relationship formation culminates at about 3 months of age. Children's development at the age of 3 months has also been proven to be significant in the prediction of their later developmental achievements (Keller, Loewer, & Runde, 1990; see chap. 8, this volume). In the following sections I summarize the assessment and analysis procedures for the different research questions. More details about these procedures can be found in the articles that are referred to in the particular paragraphs. In chapter 8, where I report the developmental consequences of early social experiences, I describe the particular follow-up methodologies with the individual studies.

RECRUITMENT OF STUDY PARTICIPANTS

The selection of study sites was based on the sociodemographic profiles of particular environments. The recruitment procedures therefore had to be adapted to the conventional standards of these environments. In rural communities, personal contacts with persons who held official positions with respect to community life (like chiefs [traditional title holder] in Cameroon or *dais* [traditional midwives] in Gujarat) were our basis for further admission. In urban communities, newspaper advertisements or information provided by hospitals, birth preparation, and baby classes were the basis of recruitment. The first contact in rural communities was always face to face, and in urban settings generally by telephone.

The field researchers were members of the cultural community under study. Only in the case of the rural Indian assessments did German research assistants conduct the studies with the help of local interpreters, as it was not possible to find local collaborators for the assessments. The German students were prepared intensively for their work and the German coordinator of the rural Indian assessment (Monika Abels) learned the local language, Gujarati (Abels, in press).

Information about the study was provided to prospective participants during the first contact. Families with a 3-month-old infant were eligible to participate and an appointment was made for an interview at their home. The home visit started with an informal meeting during which the family was informed about the purpose of the study. We stressed that we consider parents and mothers in particular to be experts in child care and socialization and that we wanted to learn about child care in different cultures. Depending on the local culture we emphasized the important role of grandmothers in childrearing and introduced our focus on mothers in this study with the comparability across cultural samples. We explained that we would like to make videotapes with mothers and their babies in their home environment and then analyze them later. The verbalization of the instruction was adapted to the local communication style. After the informal opening conversation, demographic information was recorded and observations and interviews were done. After the home visit the families were given a small gift in appreciation for their participation. The following specific recruiting procedures were used for the individual samples.

For the Nso samples, assessments were made by a native Nso researcher and local assistants. The subdivisional officer first contacted the *fon,* or traditional king, of Mbiame to inform him about the study and solicit his assistance (see Figure 4.1).

FIGURE 4.1.   Parts of a *fon* palace in northwest Cameroon. Photo by Heidi Keller.

The families were contacted through announcements in the Catholic and Protestant churches, social gatherings and women's groups, as well as personal contacts of the research team. After the first contact, many women willing to participate in the study were registered, but only those with infants between 2.5 and 3 months of age were actually included. Additionally, we were able to access the birth register of the local health center to obtain exact birth dates. Subsequently, the team used the registration details to locate the mothers to make appointments for the home visits. The mothers were contacted individually at their homes and an appointment for the assessment was made. All conversations were in Lamnso, which is the local language. Lamnso (native name: *Lám nso*) belongs to the Niger-Congo language family and is a Southern Bantoid language.

For the Indian Gujarati Rajput samples, the German study coordinator, together with four German field workers and local assistants, supported by the nongovernmental organization (NGO) Deepak Foundation, collected the data. The NGO provided lists of babies that had been born 2 months before in Gujarati Rajput villages. The research assistants contacted the families of these babies with the help of a local *dai* (traditional birth attendant) or Deepak Charitable Trust child-care worker (see Figure 4.2).

The local helper was present during the first visit, during which the family members were informed about the details of the project and asked for their consent. One researcher accompanied by a local interpreter of the Gujarati language visited the families. During the first visit, information about family members was

FIGURE 4.2.   Health workers from the Deepak Foundation with our research team. Photo by Monika Abels.

recorded and the family was asked when it would be convenient to be visited at home.

For the Greek sample, local research assistants from the University of Athens initiated contact with the mothers of young babies with the cooperation of hospitals in Athens. Mothers recuperating in the hospital after delivery were asked to participate. After consent was given, the mother's address and birth date of the infant were registered. The families were contacted again, by telephone, when the infant was between 2.2 and 3.0 months old to schedule an appointment for the assessment. One researcher visited the families at home.

For the German sample, three local research assistants from the University of Marburg, University of Muenster, and University of Osnabrück approached the mothers of young babies with the help of local hospitals and placed newspaper advertisements to which the mothers responded and volunteered to participate in the study. After the consent of the mother, the birth date of the infant was registered, the address noted, and an appointment was made for the assessment. Families were visited in their homes by a single researcher.

Recruiting Euro-American families posed the most problems due to privacy policies that did not allow mothers in baby classes or hospitals to be approached. Students from UCLA and two bilingual German students (one living in Los Angeles) recruited participants through advertisements in community journals. Some participants were approached after they had left baby classes and some were recruited using the snowball technique. The mothers were provided with information that was approved by the UCLA Institutional Review Board for Research Ethics. Those who consented to participate were later contacted by phone to set up an appointment for the home visit.

For the Costa Rican samples, local research assistants from the University of Costa Rica in San José (Instituto de Investigaciones Psicológicas) collected the data. The research assistants recruited families who were introduced to them through friends, neighbors, and relatives. However, relatives of the research assistants did not participate. Participating families recommended other families they knew (snowball technique). In an initial telephone call mothers were informed about the study and asked to participate. After consent was given, the birth date of the infant was registered, the address noted, and an appointment was made for the assessment. Mothers of 3-month-old infants were visited at home, informed about the study, and asked to participate. All communication was in Spanish.

Families in Delhi were located with the help of a pediatrician. The pediatrician provided contacts with mothers who were his patients and visited him regularly. These mothers had babies who were about 3 months old. The mothers were then contacted by the research assistants from Lady Irwin College, University of Delhi, by phone; the ones who agreed to take part in the study were visited at home. Further contacts were provided by these mothers, as they introduced us to their friends and family members who had children in the required age group. Communication was in Hindi or in English or a mixture of both languages, whatever the mothers preferred.

Mothers in Vadodara, Gujarat, were contacted through friends and families of the local research assistants from the Maharaja Sayajirao University of Baroda and recruited using the snowball technique. The mothers were first contacted by phone or visited at home and an appointment was set. Communication was done in the local language, Gujarati.

The families in Beijing were recruited through hospitals, pediatricians, and birth preparation and baby classes in collaboration with research assistants from the University of Beijing and a bilingual Chinese American student from UCLA. Mothers were informed that we were interested in their ideas and beliefs about good parenting and their behaviors toward their infants. Informed consent was attained on a completely voluntary basis. Families were contacted by phone and an appointment was set up when the infant was 3 months old. The families were visited in their homes. A trained female research assistant visited the families. Communication was in Mandarin.

The recruitment of the urban Nso families was very difficult because urban educated families from the Nso ethnic community are rare. Local researchers started identifying eligible families through community-based neighborhood work in the town of Kumbo. Participating families identified related families and friends living in the cities of Douala, Bamenda, Buea, and Yaounde. Local research assistants contacted these families by phone and traveled to their homes for the assessments. Communication was in Lamnso or a mixture of Lamnso and English.

PROCEDURES

We tried to assess all dimensions of the cultural model of parenting with multiple methods. Our multicultural study program utilizes method triangulation; that is, different methodologies are used to assess the different dimensions, especially interviews and questionnaires, videotaped and in situ spot observations. Moreover we use quantitative as well as qualitative methodology (Greenfield, 1997; van de Vijver & Leung, 1997). Quantitative analysis was based on coding systems that were computed with analyses of variance (ANOVAs), multivariate analyses of variance (MANOVAs), cluster, discriminant, or regression analyses. The qualitative research methodology is mainly applied to the verbal material. It is not to be understood as a strict set of analytical procedures but rather as a "broad theoretical framework, which focuses on the constructive and functional dimensions of discourse, coupled with the reader's skill in identifying significant patterns of consistency and variation" (Potter & Wetherell, 1987, p. 169).

It can be described as the inductive and recursive procedure of coding and interpreting data. Coding has a pragmatic rather than analytical goal of gathering together instances for examination and therefore is done as inclusively as possible (see also Mey, 2000; Seidel, 1998). The qualitative methodology is used to substantiate and differentiate the quantitative results (Keller & Demuth 2005; Keller, Demuth, & Yovsi, 2006; Keller, Hentschel, et al., 2004).

The Assessment of the Social Context

Daytime Experiences.   The social context of infants was analyzed using the method of spot observations. Spot observations allowed us to portray the social experiences of a baby in the context of everyday activities. The method of spot observations was developed to characterize the activities of groups and individuals within particular societies. The fieldwork of Munroe and Munroe (1971) used spot observations for cross-cultural comparisons. Spot observations as described by Rogoff (1978) are a modified time-sampling method of observation in which the observer is relatively unobtrusive, taking a "mental snapshot" of the activity that is going on at the moment when he or she enters the observation site (cf. Draper, 1975; LeVine et al., 1994; Munroe & Munroe, 1971; for a summary see Gross, 1984). Spot observations must be done over an extended period at different times of the day and on different days of the week to ensure that differences reflect variations between populations and not merely random fluctuation due to the variability in people's activities. In our studies we assessed 20 spot observations that were distributed evenly between 8 a.m. and 6 p.m. over a period of 1 week. We restricted the observations to 1 week due to the fast developmental progress of infants during the early months of life.

Spot observations do not provide information about the temporal extension of situations and activities. We therefore modified the method of spot observations by complementing it with brief time-sampling observation periods. The unannounced visits to the families across the daylight hours correspond to the idea of spot observations, but each observation unit lasted 15 minutes. During the 15 minutes, defined behavioral codes were assessed within 10-second intervals, which enabled us not only to assess the persons involved with the baby, but also the activities. The ongoing activities were observed for 10 seconds and then the appropriate codes were recorded on a prepared observation sheet during the next 20 seconds. Time intervals were indicated by an automatic device into the ear of the observer. A total of 5 minutes of actual observation resulted from each unit. For the 20 home visits, the net observation time per family equaled 100 minutes. This method was applied in the Nso and Gujarati villages. One team of either observer and guide (Nso) or observer and translator (Gujarati) visited one family for all 20 observational units.

The spot methodology was also used for German middle-class families, for whom the method had to be adapted. Because it was not possible to visit middle-class families unannounced multiple times we used extensive video material that had been assessed in an earlier study (Keller & Zach, 2002). For the coding of video sequences, 20 sequences, each 15 minutes long, were randomly selected for coding from the 10-hour video recording before the videotaped material was viewed by the coders. This was done to match the unannounced appearance of the observer in the other two populations. Coding was done for each of the chosen 15-minute units in accordance with the procedure for the real-life spot observations (Keller, Abels, et al., 2005).

The infants' social contexts were assessed by coding each present person's behaviors simultaneously with the infant's state. The analysis of the state of the infant was essential because the infant's state creates a context of interaction. Depending on the interactional context the same behavior can be interpreted very differently (Schölmerich & Weßels, 1998). We were especially interested in behaviors that can be assumed to promote relatedness (nursing, body contact, and body stimulation) as compared to those promoting autonomy (object stimulation, face-to-face or eye contact). Codes were applied only when the corresponding behavior lasted for at least 5 seconds during the interval. The codes are defined as follows:

- *Infant states.*
  - *Sleep.* The infant is sleeping or is about to fall asleep. Signs of falling asleep are yawning, closed or closing eyes, and relaxed muscle tone.
  - *Attentive.* All signs of sleep and sleepiness are absent and the infant does not fuss or cry.
  - *Fuss or cry.* The infant is awake and cries or manifests signs of being upset by moaning, whining, or whimpering.
- *Persons' presence.* Each individual person with the infant (a) within reach (straight arm length or closer), or (b) within viewing distance (the person can see the infant, but the infant does not necessarily have to be able to see the person) was coded separately. Parenting behaviors were coded for each person as the category applied usually with the infant being within reach.
- *Responses to crying.*
  - *Nursing.* The caregiver (usually the mother) nurses the infant.
- *Body contact.* Body contact comprises more contact between the caregiver and the infant than just the caregiver's hands touching infant's body. The baby is carried or held on the caregiver's arms, hip, or back; or the baby is held on the caregiver's lap or legs. The caregiver and baby may also lie close to each other on a bed or the caregiver may be sitting with bodily contact to a lying baby.
- *Caressing.* The caregiver caresses the infant with her or his own face or parts of the face (mouth, nose).
- *Body stimulation.*
  - *Holding.* The baby is held with hands in front of the caregiver without body contact. The baby can also stand on caregiver's upper legs.
  - *Vestibular stimulation.* The infant is rocked with the whole body or upper trunk. The infant can have body contact or can be lying in a cradle or sling.
- *Object stimulation.* The caregiver introduces an object or toy into the interaction and tries to direct the infant's attention to the object.
- *Face-to-face.* The infant's and caregiver's bodies are positioned so that they can look into each other's faces. The occurrence of eye contact during the 10-second interval is recorded separately if it occurs.

All scores for parenting categories were calculated as percentages of the specific states.

Coders were trained intensively in the coding of spot observations with the help of videotapes before the fieldwork started. We used tapes of Nso, Gujarati, and German mothers' daily routines that were recorded for other studies conducted by Keller and Zach (2002), Keller, Kuensemueller, et al. (2005), and Yovsi (2001). We calculated Cohen's kappa for the assessment of eight different 20-minute tapes from Nso, Rajput, and German families for each pair of coders. Coders were considered reliable as soon as they reached kappa values for all coding categories above .70. Additionally, the first five home visits in the rural Gujarati families were done by pairs of coders to prove they were in agreement during fieldwork. Kappa values remained above .70 for all coded categories.

Sleeping Arrangements.   Sleeping arrangements for the Nso children were assessed with interviews. Nso natives conducted the structured interviews in Lamnso. The mothers who consented were interviewed in their homes, with the father, grandmother, other children, or relatives included in the session at times. Information was collected on sleeping patterns and practices; breastfeeding and nocturnal care provisions; the child's behavior and development; and the demographic variables of parents, family, and housing structure. Interviews lasted for about 30 to 90 minutes. The mother's responses to the interviews were subsequently coded by two independent coders. All disagreements were discussed and codes thus agreed on were used in the data analysis (Yovsi & Keller, 2006). Moreover, in questionnaire studies with multiple samples, developmental timetables were assessed with respect to the age at which a baby is expected to sleep alone and sleep through the night.

Because the results of the interview and the observational studies revealed that the mother is the single most important caregiver in the diverse contexts, our further studies mainly address the mother as the caregiver. One set of studies also addresses the father as a caregiver. For these analyses, sociocultural orientations, socialization goals, parenting ethnotheories, and interactional behaviors are assessed. One study assesses grandmaternal views on early child care.

The Assessment of the Sociocultural Orientation

To assess the sociocultural orientation of familism we used the family allocentrism scale (Lay et al., 1998). The family allocentrism scale measures the orientation and attitude toward the family of origin with 21 items, including 6 inverted items. The items are presented in Figure 4.3.

Mothers were asked to evaluate how much they agreed with the statements using a 5-point Likert scale ranging from 1 (*not at all*) to 5 (*completely*). The measurement was generated by recoding the inverted items and summing the values of all items. Cronbach's alpha was .89 over 204 participants from different ecocultural environments (Keller, Lamm, et al., 2006).

		I agree			
	1 not at all	**2**	**3**	**4**	**5** completely
1. I resemble my parents very much.					
2. My family likes me to work very hard.					
3. I follow my own feelings even if it makes my parents very unhappy.					
4. My family's achievements honour me.					
5. The ability to obtain good family relations is a sign of maturity.					
6. After marriage parents should keep out of vital decisions of their children.					
7. My family's opinion is important to me.					
8. To know I can rely on my family makes me happy.					
9. I would look after my parents in their old age.					
10. If a family member has a problem I feel responsible.					
11. Even when I am not at home I consider the opinions of my parents.					
12. I would be ashamed to refuse a favour to my parents.					
13. My happiness depends on the happiness of my family.					
14. I have obligations and responsibilities in my family.					
15. There are a lot of differences between me and other members of my family.					
16. It is important to get along with the family at any cost.					
17. One should keep thoughts that could annoy the family to oneself.					
18. My needs are different from that of my family.					
19. When I leave my parents' home they cannot count on me any more.					
20. I respect the wishes of my parents even if they are not my own.					
21. It is important to feel independent from your family.					

FIGURE 4.3.　The family allocentrism scale.

The Assessment of Socialization Goals

Socialization goals were assessed with quantitative methodology using a questionnaire, and with qualitative methodology based on interviews. The questionnaire consisted of a list of 10 statements concerning qualities that a child should learn or develop during the first 3 years of life that were derived from descriptions of independent and interdependent self-construals in the literature. The mothers were asked to evaluate their agreement with these statements using a 5-point Likert scale ranging from 1 (*not at all*) to 5 (*completely*). A principal component analysis produced two dimensions that can be labeled as representing autonomous (five items) or relational (five items) socialization goals. The autonomous socialization goals subscale includes the following items:

- Develop self-confidence.
- Develop competitiveness.
- Develop a sense of self-esteem.
- Develop independence.
- Develop a sense of self.

The relational socialization goals subscale comprises the following items:

- Learn to obey elderly people.
- Learn to obey parents.
- Learn to care for the well-being of others.
- Learn to cheer up others.
- Learn to control emotions.

The scores of the autonomous and relational socialization goals were defined as the mean of the respective five items for each dimension.

These subscales showed very good reliabilities (Cronbach's $\alpha = .93$ for the autonomous socialization goals over 204 participants from diverse ecocultural environments and Cronbach's $\alpha = .89$ for the relational socialization goals). The measures did not correlate with each other ($r = .01$, $p = .904$; Keller, Lamm, et al., 2006).

Because the questionnaire methodology, especially the rating scale format, is differentially familiar to participants from diverse ecocultural environments, we also assessed these socialization goals with the method of pairwise comparison. Therefore we printed each socialization goal on a separate card and presented them pairwise in a random order. The mothers were asked to select the item out of the two that they valued most. To test whether a mother had a preference for autonomous or relational socialization goals, we computed a ratio score by dividing the autonomy score by the relatedness score. A score greater than 1 indicates a preference for autonomous socialization goals and a score lower than 1 is indicative of a preference for relational socialization goals (Kärtner, Keller, Yovsi, Abels, & Lamm, 2006).

In addition, socialization goals were analyzed qualitatively from interviews. The following excerpt from a picture-based interview (see chap. 5, this volume) with a Los Angeles mother (37 years old, 3-month-old daughter, teacher) illustrates this methodology. Indicators of socialization goals are in bold:

(M = mother, I = interviewer)

M: So, you know, you wanted help them **develop their independence**, but you know, you also want to make sure **the baby knows that you are there for them**.

[This mother articulates that developing independence is important, but so is trust, in that the baby knows there is somebody there for them. The interviewer asks then:]

I: So, what's important about developing their independence or …

M: What's important about it? Uh, well, it.'s this apparently third month they are able you know, to feel and process, I guess it's in their brains somehow, the textures. The more different textures they feel the better it is **for their brain development, sensory development**. And that I also think, you know, in a safe environment little by little it is good. As a teacher, I think children are **happier when they are also independent** not always needing somebody there, you know, they just get fussy and they don't feel, you know—a baby—a kid should be **confident and happy** to be—to play by themselves sometime. I think that's okay. [laughter] But you know when they are little, you don't wanna leave them, but yeah, little by little I think it's healthy to let them play alone.

In this discussion, the mother adds brain development, sensory development, confidence, and happiness as desirable socialization goals.

The Assessment of Parenting Ethnotheories

We analyzed parenting ethnotheories at different levels: content, discourse style, and verbal structure. The content refers more to explicit and conscious ideas about parenting. Style and structure refer to the narrative and linguistic embodiment of the parenting ideas, which can be considered more intuitive and less conscious in nature (Hentschel & Keller, 2006; Keller, Hentschel, et al., 2004; Keller, Kärtner, Borke, Yovsi, & Kleis, 2005).

The Content of Parenting Ethnotheories.   To assess the content of parenting ethnotheories, we used three different methodologies that are all grounded in the component model of parenting described earlier (see chap. 2, this volume).

First, we constructed a parenting ethnotheory scale that described different parenting practices with infants. This scale consists of 10 statements that were assigned to an autonomous (five items) or a relational (five items) parenting model based on earlier studies on cultural conceptions of parenting (Keller, 2003c; Keller, Voelker, & Yovsi, 2005; Keller, Yovsi, & Voelker, 2002), as well as cultural differences in parenting styles (Keller, 2003c; Keller, Lohaus, et al., 2004; Keller, Yovsi, et al., 2004). Mothers of 3-month-old babies were asked to express their agreement on a 5-point Likert scale ranging from 1 (*not agree at all*) to 5 (*agree completely*). Measurements were generated by calculating the mean of the items that were part of each respective scale. The independent scale included items that focus on early self-regulation of the infant, contingent reactions to positive infant signals, object stimulation, and face-to-face interaction. The interdependent scale consisted of items emphasizing body contact, motor stimulation, and prompt satisfaction of physical needs (see Figure 4.4).

The measures correlated negatively with each other ($r = -.25$, $p < .01$). The reliabilities of these scales were acceptable (Keller, Lamm, et al., 2006).

The questionnaire was developed in German. Translation and back translation into the other study languages was done by individuals who were bilingual with their native tongue and German or English.

Second, we developed an interview methodology that enabled us to analyze content (as well as style) of parenting ethnotheories on the basis of picture cards. We collected photos representing five parenting systems as defined by the component model of parenting—primary care, body contact, body stimulation, object

In the following, you will find a selection of statements which address the correct handling of a mother with her baby and her small child respectively. Again some statements will be familiar to you, others not. You will probably agree to some and not to others.

Please think again of a baby with about 3 months of age and express your agreement or disagreement with a number between 1 and 6.

Don't think much about each statement, but react **spontaneously!**

	I agree				
	1 not at all	2	3	4	5 completely
1. It is important to rock a crying baby on the arms in order to console him/her.					
2. Sleeping through the night should be trained as early as possible.					
3. It is not necessary to react immediately to a crying baby.					
4. You cannot start early enough to direct the infant's attention towards objects and toys.					
5. Gymnastics make a baby strong.					
6. If a baby is fussy, he/she should be immediately picked up.					
7. It is good for a baby to sleep alone.					
8. When a baby cries, he/she should be nursed immediately.					
9. Babies should be left crying for a moment in order to see whether they console themselves.					
10. A baby should be always in close proximity with his/her mother, so that she can react immediately to his/her signals.					

FIGURE 4.4. The parenting ethnotheory scale.

stimulation, and face-to-face contact—from the different cultural communities. So, we interviewed middle-class German mothers with the display of photos from middle-class German mothers and rural Cameroonian Nso mothers with the display of photos from rural Cameroonian Nso mothers. Figure 4.5 demonstrates the set of pictures for the rural Gujarati interviews.

In a validation study, Abels and Kärtner (2004) asked 22 German undergraduate students of psychology to describe the five picture cards representing the five parenting systems. After this task was completed, the conception of the five parenting systems was briefly introduced by the experimenters. The next task consisted of sorting 15 picture cards into the five parenting system categories. Chi^2 tests revealed that the five systems were recognized beyond chance level $\chi^2(4, N = 22) = 124.61$ to $226.42, p < .001$.

FIGURE 4.5.   The set of five pictures for the rural Gujarati ethnotheory interview. Photo from Culture and Development Lab, University of Osnabrück.

The recognition of the different systems did not differ for the sample pictures either: The parenting systems from German, Euro-American, and rural Cameroonian Nso mother–infant situations were equally well recognized. Of course, this does not guarantee the cultural validity of all the picture cards, but it is at least a hint at a broad understanding of the pictured parenting systems.

At the beginning of the picture card interview, the mothers were presented with the five picture cards representing the five parenting systems all at once. The mothers were asked to pick the card that represented the best parental care for a 3-month-old baby. Then they were asked probing questions about why they thought that this was the best way of caring for a small baby. The other cards were discussed in a similar manner. Again, mothers of 3-month-old babies were interviewed. In one of our studies we also interviewed the grandmothers of these babies (see chap. 6, this volume). An interview took approximately 30 minutes on average. All interviews were tape recorded and transcribed verbatim. The non-English and non-German interviews were translated word for word into German or English. Translations were done by native speakers of the respective language who were bilingual with German or English. Ten percent of all interviews were translated by at least two different people. Nevertheless, translation is a general problem for multilanguage research projects because not only may the translation be difficult, but concepts also differ across cultures as do styles of talking. The transcripts were coded with a system of categories derived from the component model of parenting. The codes comprise the parenting systems of primary care, body contact, body stimulation, face-to-face context, object stimulation, and verbal and vocal interaction, and the interactional mechanisms of attention, contingency, warmth, and reference to positive and negative emotions. Moreover, references to dialogue and communication were coded separately. Each occurrence of the following contents was coded:

- *Primary care (PC)*. All comments relating to nursing, diapering, bathing, washing, combing, and so forth, or ensuring the child's health were coded. Examples: I like this picture because she is feeding her baby. It is very important to change the child's diaper. She has covered the child so the child will not fall ill.
- *Body contact system (BC)*. Any comments relating to mode and extent of body contact were coded here. These included, for example, holding the baby, touching the baby, and closeness. Examples: The mother touches the baby a lot. Here the father is holding the child on his lap.
- *Body stimulation system (BS)*. Comments relating to motor exercises, motor handling, and massaging; rocking or swinging the child; lifting the child up and down; making the child lie on its belly, sit, or stand; or making the child exercise are also included in this category. Examples: She is exercising the child, moving her arms and legs. She is rocking the child.
- *Object stimulation system (OS)*. Comments relating to objects and object exploration. The object may be a toy but also any other object that is re-

ferred to as being used in a playful manner. Examples: It's nice how they play with the toys. The child can also look at the fan moving.

- *Face-to-face context (FF)*. Comments referring to the facial system and face-to-face facial behavior. Comments must refer to mother and infant. Referring to dialogues is also coded here. If the mother is looking at the baby but the baby is not described as being in communicative behavior with the mother, the remark is not coded. Examples: They look at each other. The mother is making a face and the child is imitating it.
- *Verbal and vocal interaction (VI)*. Comments referring to vocal stimulation by the caregiver (talking, singing, naming) and comments referring to infant and caregiver interacting vocally and verbally are coded as vocal interaction. Examples: She is singing to her baby. Mother and baby are talking to each other.

The interactional mechanisms were defined as follows:

- *Attention* (interactive engagement). This was coded separately for exclusive attention (AT+) and shared attention (AT−).

  - *AT+*. Comments relating to the exclusive attention and concentration of attention toward the baby are coded with the positive pole of attention. Example: I like how attentive the mom is with the baby.
  - *AT−*. Comments referring to a shared attention or a low concentration of attention toward the baby belong to the negative pole of this category. Example: And this one is the last just because she is watching TV while breastfeeding.

Distress regulation (DR). Comments referring to the behavior of the mother regulating infant distress states (including fussing and crying). The caregiver's behavior does not have to be specified. Distress regulation can include the following:

- Giving a pacifier.
- Body contact and tactile behavior, including carrying.
- Body stimulation.
- Object stimulation.

Examples: You have to breastfeed a baby when she cries. She is soothing the baby.

- *Distress prevention (DP)*. Comments referring to prevention of crying are coded here. Example: Children that are carried a lot cry less.
- *Contingency to positive signals (C)*. Comments referring to the temporal aspect of maternal behavior toward the infant's signals in the face-to-face context. Example: This mother always reacts promptly whenever the infant looks at her.

- *Warmth in positive states (W).* Comments referring to positive emotion or the emotional expression of maternal behavior toward the infant. Comments referring to affective sharing (laughing together, being on the same wavelength, etc.) are also coded as warmth. Example: Whenever the baby looks at the mom, her face brightens.
- *Body warmth (BW).* Comments referring to expressions of bodily warmth like caressing, patting, kissing. Example: A mother should cuddle her baby, caress her, just let her know she is there.
- *Negative signals (NS).* Comments referring explicitly to negative emotions and emotional states of the child without stating distress regulation or distress prevention. Example: The child is sad.
- *Positive signals (PS).* Comments referring explicitly to positive emotions and emotional states of the child, thereby emphasizing the importance of positive affect and emotionality. Example: The child looks happy in this photograph.
- *Dialogue (DIA).* Comments referring to communication in general. Example: She wants to have communication.

The following example from a Los Angeles mom (37 years old, teacher) illustrates the procedure. Categories described before are shown in bold:

M: Uh, it looks like she is probably burping the baby **primary care** [laughs] just comes right after feeding the baby **primary care**. It's very important because the baby gets rid of gas **primary care**, because if they don't they can feel falsely full **primary care** and not get enough nutrition **primary care**. Um, she could also be just holding the baby **body contact** and soothing the baby **distress regulation**, rubbing the baby's back which is important **body stimulation**—something that you do all day, makes the baby feel good **positive signals** …

I: OK. Now we got three more left.

M: OK. So, she fed the baby **primary care**, she burped the baby **primary care**, she held the baby **body contact**. [laugh] Let's see. Uh, next I would choose, um, I think I'll choose this one. And this is something especially I find I do in the morning; like right when my baby wakes up. She is very happy **positive signals** and she wants to talk a lot, to look at me—to have, you know, communication **dialogue**. So I think it's important that she is establishing that with the baby **dialogue**. You know, just mother and child who are talking **verbal interaction**, listening to the baby, looking at the baby **exclusive attention**.

The interviews were coded with the help of the software package Atlas.ti. Figure 4.6 gives an example of a screen shot.

The reliabilities for the codes were calculated on the basis of a sample of 15 interviews belonging to different cultural communities, analyzed by two different coders. Overall, Cohen's kappa was .84. The reliabilities for the different categories ranged from K = .58 (exclusive attention) to K = 1 (shared attention).

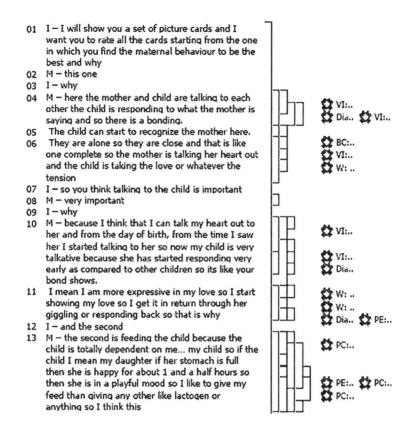

01 I – I will show you a set of picture cards and I want you to rate all the cards starting from the one in which you find the maternal behaviour to be the best and why
02 M – this one
03 I – why
04 M – here the mother and child are talking to each other the child is responding to what the mother is saying and so there is a bonding.
05 The child can start to recognize the mother here.
06 They are alone so they are close and that is like one complete so the mother is talking her heart out and the child is taking the love or whatever the tension
07 I – so you think talking to the child is important
08 M – very important
09 I – why
10 M – because I think that I can talk my heart out to her and from the day of birth, from the time I saw her I started talking to her so now my child is very talkative because she has started responding very early as compared to other children so its like your bond shows.
11 I mean I am more expressive in my love so I start showing my love so I get it in return through her giggling or responding back so that is why
12 I – and the second
13 M – the second is feeding the child because the child is totally dependent on me... my child so if the child I mean my daughter if her stomach is full then she is happy for about 1 and a half hours so then she is in a playful mood so I like to give my feed than giving any other like lactogen or anything so I think this

FIGURE 4.6.   Example of the computerized coding of the ethnotheory interviews with the Atlas.ti software.

The codes for the parenting systems and the interactional mechanisms categories were summarized per person and relativized individually, separately for parenting systems and interactional mechanisms; that is, the amount of body contact a mother mentioned was relativized to the amount of all mentioning for the six parenting systems. The interview data are not available for the Athens mothers (for more information, see Keller, Abels, et al., 2006).

Some further content categories, like mental state, are included in the analysis of the conversational styles, described in the next section. These categories are not described here, as the two domains of content are part of different research traditions.

The third method that we applied to assess the content of parental ethnotheories consisted of video-based focus group discussions with German and Indian middle-class and Nso farming women. Groups were recruited by respected women such as nurses, midwives, and women's group leaders. Groups of five to seven women met in private houses or public buildings such as schools or community centers. Two sessions of 2 to 3 hours each were scheduled for each group. At the beginning of each group session, the experimenters introduced the task and stressed that early child care is a matter of personal beliefs and that there are no right or wrong views. In the first session 10 video clips of their own culture were shown and discussed; in the second session 10 video clips of a foreign culture were presented and discussed (the German tapes for the Nso and the Gujarati women and the Nso tapes for the German women). Each video sequence lasted 6 minutes. After each sequence, the tape was stopped and the women were invited to give their subjective comments about what they felt was good or bad in the interaction session and why. The comments were audiotaped. The videotaped sequences were selected from observational studies of mother–child interactions with 3-month-old babies (Lohaus et al., 1997; Voelker, 2000; Yovsi, 2001). The video-taped German mothers all belonged to the middle class and were videotaped in their homes. The German infants were all firstborns. The videotaped Nso mothers were farmers, and the infants included firstborns and later-borns. The videotaped Indian mothers were rural farmers and the infants included firstborns and later-borns. The video sequences of the three cultural communities covered all parenting systems and interactional mechanisms. The transcripts of the audiotaped focus group discussions were analyzed with coding systems based on the component model of parenting (Keller, 2002b; Keller, Voelker, Yovsi, & Shastri, 2005; Lohaus et al., 2004; see Table 4.1).

A Nso and a German coder coded the transcripts independently from each other. Overall agreement for all categories was 80%. Discrepancies were jointly discussed. There was no case of disagreement that could not be resolved immediately. To obtain an independent measure of reliability a third coder was trained. This coder assessed 30 randomly selected statements without any information about the respondents' cultural origins. Cohen's kappa with the original categorizations was .82 (Keller, Voelker, & Yovsi, 2005; Keller, Yovsi, & Voelker, 2002).

The methods of the picture card interview and the focus group discussions are based on the assumption that the attentiveness and sensitivity for parenting practices correspond with the importance of the subjectively assigned relevance. This importance is assumed to be expressed in the amount of mentioning of particular categories. In the first run, we differentiated the statements with respect to positive and negative evaluations of the statement. Because the nature of the qualification did not influence the results, we skipped it for the sake of greater clarity. Moreover, the focus group discussions and the picture card interviews were analyzed using qualitative methodology.

The Discourse Analysis of Parenting Ethnotheories.   Based on studies reporting cultural differences in maternal narrating styles in line with the cultural models of independence and interdependence (e.g., P. J. Miller, Wiley, Fung, & Liang, 1997; Wang, 2001, 2004), we proposed assessing the narrative embodiment of parenting ethnotheories as a further avenue to understanding them (Kärtner et

TABLE 4.1
Codes Developed for the Analysis of the Focus Group Discussions

Category	Definition	Examples
Primary care	Comment evaluates maternal care for the infant's health and security.	• When the toy fell down, she wiped the dirt from it which is good. • It was not correct on the mother's part to leave the baby with the elder sister and go away though the elder sister is not so big to look after the baby well.
Distress regulation	Comment evaluates maternal regulations of negative infant signals.	• The baby is crying too much but the mother is not trying to sooth the baby. • The mother didn't become distressed when the infant was crying. She allows her to cry. • How can a woman keep the child laying and crying and she cannot pick him up.
Body contact	Comment evaluates body contact between mother and infant.	• I have seen that she is only holding the baby for holding sake. • When you have a small baby you should cuddle ("koyti") her to avoid air from touching him. • She continuously keeps the child in her lap because of which the child may feel tied up or bound. • I like the way the mother was sitting with the infant in her lap all the time.
Body stimulation	Comment evaluates motor stimulation and exercises.	• It is too early to make a baby stand or sit. • She lifts the child up and down, so that the "places" of the child become relaxed. • Constant rocking of child is not required.
Warmth with positive signals	Comment evaluates caressing and expression of positive affect.	• The child feels warm and fine as well as the mother. • She gives very much love to her infant. • She does not touch the infant tenderly.
Object stimulation	Comment evaluates object stimulation.	• She shows things to the child that he can learn and know which is good. • The infant was hold in a way that she could observe all the many things around her and she was very happy.
Vocal stimulation	Comment evaluates vocal behavior of the mother (talking, singing, naming).	• When the child woke up she was just holding her without calling her name. When you have a baby and he wakes up from sleep the first thing you do is to call her name before anything. • She does not talk to the child.
Attention	Comment evaluates the attention given to the infant.	• She is with the child and her head turns away from the child. She is not looking at the child as admiring as a mother does. • The mother gives all her attention to the child. • She should put the baby down and leave her to play independently.
Contingency with positive signals	Comment evaluates the promptness of maternal responses towards looking, smiling and vocalizing.	• She answered when the infants made sounds. • She didn't react when the infant looked at her face.
Face-to-face dialogue	Comment refers to eye-contact and face-to-face exchange.	• Then there was a nice episode of eye contact. • The facing out position is not good. If she is the only caretaker of a baby, she will recognize her only through speech and would not know her facial image.
Relationship	Comment evaluates the relationship in terms of abstract concepts.	• There was very much harmony. • No contact between mother and child.

Note. These codes were developed based on the component model of parenting.

al., 2006; Keller, Hentschel, et al., 2004). Additionally we analyzed some data with linguistic methods used for discourse analysis (Hentschel & Keller, 2006).

Language as a cultural code system that is relevant for socialization processes has been analyzed in the verbal interactions of caregivers with babies and small children (e.g., Ochs, 1988; Rabain-Jamin, Maynard, & Greenfield, 2003; Rabain-Jamin & Sabeau-Jouannet, 1997). Two narrative styles have been identified. First, the elaborative (Fivush & Fromhoff, 1988), also referred to as the high elaborative (Hudson, 1990; Reese, Haden, & Fivush, 1993) and the reminiscent (Engel, 1995), or conversation eliciting (Tulviste, 2003) style is characterized by frequent questions, elaborations, and the tendency to integrate the child's input so that an equal conversational pattern emerges. The narrations are rich, embellished, and detailed. The focus is on personal attributes, preferences, and judgments. Emotions are often regarded as a direct expression of the self and an affirmation of the importance of the individual (Markus & Kitayama, 1994). The elaborated style has been identified as being characteristic of a sociocultural orientation emphasizing autonomy (Fiske, Kitayama, Markus, & Nisbett, 1998; Markus & Kitayama, 1994). On the other hand, the repetitive (Fivush & Fromhoff, 1988; McCabe & Peterson, 1991), also referred to as the low elaborative (Hudson, 1990, Reese et al., 1993), practical (Engel, 1995), or directive (Chao, 1995) style is characterized by commands and instructions and the mother taking a leading role in conversations. A high value is placed on the social context, moral rectitude, and behavioral consequences (P. J. Miller, Jung, & Mintz, 1996; Mullen & Yi, 1995; Wang, Leichtman, & Davies, 2000). Emotions tend to be viewed as disruptive and are expected to be controlled (Wang, 2001; Wang et al., 2000; cf. Bond, 1991; Chao, 1995). The repetitive style has been identified as characteristic for a sociocultural orientation focusing on interpersonal relatedness (Fiske et al., 1998; Markus & Kitayama, 1994).

Because these different concepts and categories were developed for conversational analyses, their ability to adequately analyze the verbal statements of mothers talking about ethnotheories had to be proven. Not all categories apply equally well; for example, commands and instructions are specific to mother–child interactions and are not relevant to ethnotheoretical accounts. The verbal categories that we found indicative of autonomy were instances when mothers referred to a child having mental states like emotions, cognitions, needs, and preferences, when she centered on herself and the richness of maternal talk. The relational verbal categories were those instances where mothers contextualized their own or others' experiences and behavior by talking about the social context or referring to moral correctness, social regulations, and concern with authority (Kärtner et al., 2006). Quantitative and qualitative analyses were conducted with the transcribed or transcribed and translated versions of the picture card interviews. A coding scheme was developed based on past work on family conversational styles in different sociocultural environments (Fivush, 1994; Mullen & Yi, 1995; Reese et al., 1993; Wang, 2001, Wang et al., 2000). Two composite variables were constructed. Each composite variable was composed of several component variables. Each component variable was coded by counting the number of occurrences in each transcription. Because the coding categories were based on the occurrences of specific aspects, they were not mutually exclusive but overlapped among utterances.

The composite variable of amount was the number of words counted and relativized by the number of turns. This measure indicates how many words a mother spoke based on one prompt by the interviewer. For the composite variable of autonomy, two major component variables with various subcomponents were coded:

1. *Autonomy mother.* This variable indexes the mother's tendency to refer to the autonomous functioning of herself.

   a. *I-statement.* The mother explicitly refers to herself as the speaking person. Example: I think it's really important in the beginning.
   b. *Self-referral.* The mother refers to herself and her own child or her own experiences. Example: I have seen in the case of both my children, they have responded to me in [the] 2nd or 3rd month.

2. *Mental state of the baby.* This variable indexes the mother's tendency to refer to the autonomous functioning of a child. The mother refers to the baby as having or developing the following:

   a. *Cognitions.* Examples: He understands that these are the toys I will play with, or He will think that you are just playing.
   b. *Emotions.* Example: The child is happy.
   c. *Needs, volitions, and preferences.* Examples: She likes to be talked to and being held or Sometimes the babies want … to do their own thing.

The relatedness variable indexes the mother's tendency to contextualize her own and others' behavior. Two components were coded:

1. *Social context.* The mother talks about the social context or other persons. Examples: Children will never be aloof from the parents, or When she [the baby] looks at us then she also recognizes that this is my father, this is my mother, these are my siblings and she is able to recognize her own people, or The child will be seeing people around him and will no more be crying.
2. *Reference to authorities.* The mother refers to moral correctness, social regulations, and concern with authority. Examples: So this should be done, one should talk to the baby, or [The] baby should always be neat and clean. I have seen [it] like [this] in documentaries and all and I have read this also that it is good for the baby's development that you hug the baby and be in close proximity with the child. One has to hold the child like this. You are not supposed to leave the child … alone.

This coding was also conducted with the help of the Atlas.ti software.

All coding categories were weighted by the length of the transcription in words. The resulting scores for all component and composite variables were relative frequencies per 1,000 words.

Two trained coders independently coded the transcriptions of five randomly selected mothers from each cultural sample. Overall interrater agreement for all categories just described was 82%, ranging from 78% (rural Nso) to 84% (urban Nso). The coders' ratings were scored as the number of agreements divided by the number of agreements plus the number of disagreements (for more details, see Kärtner et al., 2006).

Children's Interactional Experiences

Because our intention was to examine a comparable setting in every culture, which makes it possible to assess similarities as well as differences in parenting, we decided to focus on free-play situations. Free-play situations require the infant to be awake and fed to be in an optimally attentive and interested mood. We did not define any further specifications with respect to content or duration. Although the studied cultural communities differ substantially in their definitions of adequate care of small babies (Keller, Lohaus, et al., 2004; Yovsi & Keller, 2003), they all had an understanding of playing with a baby, as we had tested in a pilot study. Because we are mainly interested in cultural (i.e., shared) definitions of parenting, we accept a potential bias with respect to social desirability. Socially desirable parenting presumably expresses what is valued in a particular cultural community. The analysis of primary care situations would have restricted the range of observable parenting systems and would have had systematic biases with respect to the prevalence of breastfeeding (Abels, 2002; Yovsi & Keller, 2003). To familiarize the families with the videotaping procedure, we recorded care and other routine situations prior to the actual recording of the free-play mother–infant interaction. These practice situations were not included in the video analysis. The home situations were videotaped with a portable camera. The mean recorded time of the free-play sequences ranged between 10 and 20 minutes.

The Analysis of the Parenting Systems and Interactional Mechanisms

Parenting Systems. The videotaped free-play interactions were analyzed with a computer-based video analysis system. A multicategory classification approach was implemented to facilitate assessment of the different parenting systems, as well as assessment of the interactional mechanisms of emotional warmth and contingency toward positive and negative infant signals. The assessments of the parenting systems and the interactional mechanisms were conducted by different coders who had no information about any of the other data sets. The category "mode of attention" was not included in the analysis, because the instruction to play with the infant inevitably has a bias toward exclusive attention. The behavioral categories of mother and infant were coded by microanalytical event sampling to analyze maternal contingency to positive infant signals and by a time-sampling method for all other categories. First, the whole free-play interaction sequence was divided into 10-second intervals. Then the interactional sequences of all mother–infant dyads were coded according to the occurrence of the different categories. Contextual categories that refer to the position of mother and child and to the infant's state were assessed. Intervals with an awake and positive versus an awake and negative (distressed) state of the infant were distinguished. Positive state intervals were analyzed concerning the activation of the four parenting systems (body contact, body stimulation, object stimulation, and face-to-face context). Only intervals where the position was favorable for a face-to-face exchange and the child was alert and not distressed were microanalyzed with respect to the registration of interactional mechanisms during positive state intervals (contingency and emotional warmth). If, during the face-to-face episodes, the mother or child could not be clearly seen on the video, these events were identified and coded as not visible for behavior assessment. This meant that measurements and reliabilities were based on episodes during which the relevant behavior was not obscured in any way. During negative state intervals, contingency and warmth to negative infant signals were assessed.

The parenting systems and the verbal and vocal contingency were assessed using Interact software (Mangold International Inc.). To perform this analysis, the videotapes were digitized; this software makes it possible to do online coding via shortcuts (see Figure 4.7). The individual codes are described next.

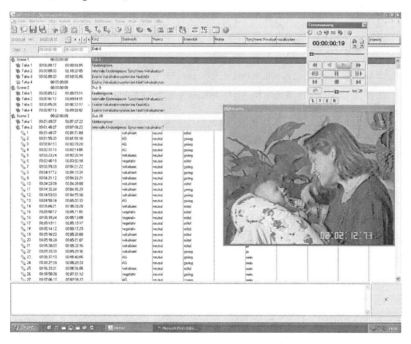

FIGURE 4.7. Example of the computerized analysis of the behavioral interactions with Interact software.

- *Body contact.* To measure the activation of this parenting system, the percentage of positive infant state intervals was registered in situations where body contact occurred in any of the following positions:

  - Holding (the mother is holding the child and both feet or parts of one leg of the child are in contact with the mother).
  - Sitting (the child is sitting on the mother's lap and both legs, but the torso of the child is not in contact with the mother).
  - Lap (both legs and parts of the torso of the child are in contact with the mother).
  - Close proximity (the child's entire body, or almost all of it, is in contact with the mother).

The percentage of time—in terms of number of intervals with body contact—was calculated.

- *Body stimulation.* All vestibular, kinesthetic, motor, or tactile stimulation and upright holding was coded per interval. The number of intervals in which at least one kind of body stimulation took place was calculated.
- *Object stimulation.* The activation of this parenting system was assessed by the mere occurrence of object play during the 10-second intervals. The indicator was the number of intervals during which the mother tried to attract the attention of the infant with an object that was touched by her, the child, or both of them.
- *Face-to-face context.* To assess this parenting system, we registered the number of intervals during which the mother positioned her body and head in relation to her infant in a way that optimizes face-to-face exchange for at least half of the time interval (5 seconds). The distance between their faces is neither too close nor too far for eye contact and the angle between the mother's face and body and the axis of the infant's shoulders was a maximum of 45 degrees. By producing these conditions, the mother encourages the baby to look into her face and to establish eye contact by simply looking straight ahead or not moving his or her head more than 45 degrees.

The reliabilities for body contact, body stimulation, object stimulation, and face-to-face context were calculated on the basis of a subsample of 20 video sequences from different cultural samples analyzed by the two different coders. To obtain a coefficient of agreement, Cohen's kappa was calculated and resulted in K = .91 for the body contact system, K = .74 for the body stimulation system, K = .91 for the object stimulation system, and K = .81 for the face-to-face system.

Interactional Mechanisms.   For the analysis of contingency and warmth, only face-to-face intervals during positive infant states were included.

To grasp the contingency of the mother-to-infant communicative signals, we analyzed the occurrence of defined discrete nonverbal behavioral events during face-to-face exchanges using microanalytical event sampling. Nonverbal categories of the infant's behavior consisted of the onset and cessation (measured in seconds) of looking at the mother's face and the onset of smiling. Maternal categories consisted of the onset and offset (measured in seconds) of looking at the infant's face, the onset of smiling, and the onsets of expressive eyebrow and mouth movements. Expressive eyebrow and mouth movements were not distinguished according to their emotional quality. The first maternal behavior following each behavioral category of the infant within a latency of 1 second was coded as a response. This latency window was set in correspondence with distributional analyses (Keller, Lohaus, et al., 1999). This analysis was restricted to nonverbal contingencies. Verbal contingencies were assessed separately (see next section). We first assessed the mother's behavioral events and then those of the infant during a second viewing. After each infant event had been identified, the observer decided whether it was followed by one of the previously coded maternal behaviors within an interval of 1 second (see Figure 4.8).

Maternal and infant behaviors were initially identified separately to assess the respective sets of categories as independent as possible. After extensive training, reliability was tested with a standard set of five mother–infant interactions with durations varying between 420 and 1,030 seconds. Because Cohen's kappa is not usually calculated for distinct temporal events, a proportion index of interrater agreement was calculated by dividing the number of observed agreements by the number of observed agreements plus the number of incongruent codes. Agreements were considered to be situations in which both coders identified the same behavioral event with an onset difference of no more than 1 second. All other events identified by only one coder or with a temporal difference exceeding 1 second were defined as disagreements. The mean agreement index was .83 (ranging from .70–.90) for the assessment of the behavioral categories and .76 for the assessment of contingent events.

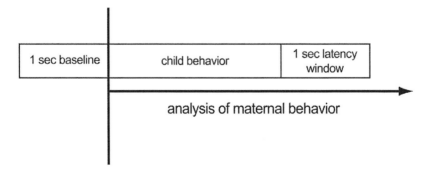

FIGURE 4.8.   Analysis scheme of contingent responsiveness toward infant signals.

Because we did not expect the face-to-face exchange to occur in every dyad of this study, we defined two different indexes to compare contingency experiences of the infants in the different cultural communities. The first was the relative frequency of latencies (Contingency 1). It indicates the number of contingency experiences a child made on average in an alert, positive state interval. This score reflects infant and maternal behavior as well, and it made it possible for us to calculate a contingency measure for every participating mother. As a second measure we calculated Watson's Responsiveness Index. This index requires the occurrence of infant signals and is therefore not to be used in cases with a low incidence of face-to-face exchanges as it was expected for subsamples in our study. It takes the above-chance association of the exchange between the two interactants into consideration. According to J. S. Watson (1979, 1985), the contingent relation between maternal and infant behavior is comprised of two independent dimensions: responsiveness and dependency. In this study we calculated Watson's Responsiveness Index (Contingency 2; see Figure 4.9), because this index seems to reflect the most relevant contingency aspects of maternal behavior during early interactions (Symons & Moran, 1994). It describes the conditional probability that a nonverbal communicative action of the child (onset of looking into the face of the mother or smiling into her face) is answered by a nonverbal communicative reaction of the mother within a reaction time of 1 second. This index is named Contingency+ in some analyses (see Figure 4.9).

Watson introduced a chance correction to reduce the conditional probability of a contingent reaction by the probability that a behavioral event of the mother occurs by chance within a latency of 1 second after an infant signal.

The indicator of contingency toward negative signals was the regulatory effort with respect to infants' crying. Because few clusters of distress signals were expected, a contingency index calculated from event-sampling data similar to the responsiveness index used for positive signals was not meaningful. The regulation of infant distress can be characterized as a persistent effort by the mother to reduce the cause of her infant's distress, with the infant continuing to cry until the mother finds an adequate response (Taubman, 1990). Therefore, the persistence of a mother to regulate the infant's state of distress, her regulatory activity, was assessed as an index of contingency toward negative signals (Contingency–).

Regulatory behaviors could include feeding to pacify hunger, change of body position to release an uncomfortable position, stimulation to alleviate boredom,

$$\text{Responsiveness index} = \frac{\text{events M within latency window}}{\text{events I}} - \left(1 - e^{-\frac{\text{events M}}{\text{total time}} \times \text{latency window}}\right)$$

where M = *Mother and* I = *Infant*

FIGURE 4.9. Responsiveness index.

providing a pacifier to promote sucking, or other goal-directed problem-solving activities that refer to possible needs of the infant assumed and tested by the mother. Because the infant often regulates weak and transient distress signals itself, only clusters of crying bouts that met a specific criterion of intensity and duration were recorded to assess regulatory behavior. At first, the intensity and duration of crying was registered by a combined index, which differentiates four degrees. The first degree refers to whimpering or very weak crying of any duration. The second degree describes distinct crying of medium or strong intensity that does not continue through the complete interval. The third degree refers to continuous distinct crying of medium or strong intensity, and the last degree to constant crying of a very strong intensity. A negative cluster was defined as a minimum of three consecutive 10-second intervals of negative signals in which at least one interval was associated with crying of the second degree. The end of a negative cluster was defined as three consecutive intervals in which none of the intervals were associated with crying of the first degree. Because we consider the demand for a regulatory activity as increasing with the intensity of crying we weighed a missing or low regulatory activity by multiplying the code of maternal behavior by the intensity of crying per interval. A coding value of zero indicates that the mother continuously attempted to regulate the infant's state for the whole 10-second interval. A value of 1 was used if a mother attempted to regulate the infant's state for only half of a 10-second interval. A value of 2 was used if the mother did not try to regulate the infant's state during an entire 10-second interval. After multiplication by crying intensity, a high value indicates low regulative effort in relation to the infant's demand. The measure of regulatory activity is therefore inversely coded. A low value indicates a high contingency to negative infant signals. The mean of the assessments of all 10-second distress intervals was used as the contingency index. The interrater reliability for negative infant signals and mother's regulatory behavior to negative infant signals was calculated on the basis of 10 video sequences. Cohen's Kappa was .87 and .85, respectively.

The Analysis of Verbal and Vocal Behavior.   In a different set of analyses we assessed contingent as well as cooccurring vocal and verbal events. Specifically we analyzed acoustic contingent and noncontingent maternal reactions toward their infants' vocalizations as well as overlapping vocal and verbal patterns in their communication. In the first step, onset and offset of every infant vocalization in the videotape was localized using Adobe Audition software. When the time span between different vocalizations was less than 1 second, one vocalization was coded; separate vocalizations are coded when the time span exceeds 1 second. An event was defined as the duration of the infant's vocalization plus 1 second after the vocalization. The events were coded using Interact software. Events constitute the time frames for contingent and noncontingent mother signals (see Figure 4.10).

Each infant vocalization was classified as positive, negative, or neutral with the help of the video picture. Moreover, vegetative (e.g., hiccup, coughing) and effort sounds (e.g., side effect of a movement) were assessed, but not further analyzed. In

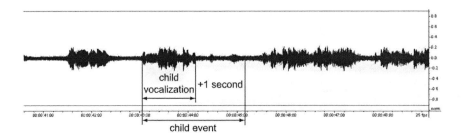

FIGURE 4.10.   Vocal and verbal analysis: Child vocalization and child event.

a different run and by a different set of coders the maternal vocalizations relating to the infant signals were assessed. If the mother sent an acoustic signal within the second after the child's vocalization, it was coded as contingent. A maternal contingent reaction may last longer than the child event as long as it started within the second after the child vocalization. In case the mother did not produce any audible sound during the specified time frame, the event was coded as noncontingent (see Figure 4.11).

Maternal sounds were assessed as verbalizations, nonverbal sounds (e.g., whistling, tongue clicking), and instrumentally generated sounds (e.g., rattles). The maternal signals were also processed by the Interact software and the vocalizations were also rated as positive, neutral, or negative.

The last step consisted of analyzing the overlap of the mother–infant exchange, again with the help of the Adobe Audition program. The accurate length of both mothers' and infants' verbal and vocal signals was assessed, allowing for precise determination of overlapping maternal talk time in infant vocalizations (see Figure 4.12).

Reliability was tested with a random sample of 10 mother–infant interactions that were coded by two independent coders. Cohen's kappa was between .84 and .90.

Maternal warmth during nondistress episodes was defined as the expression of positive affection toward the infant. Two variables were defined as indicators of maternal warmth: the amount of baby talk a mother uses while interacting with her child in a face-to-face context and the amount of maternal smiling during face-to-face context. Both values were combined to make up the warmth index according to the following scheme: A value of 4 was used to represent intervals with baby talk and smiling of 5 seconds or longer duration each. A value of 3 was coded for intervals where either baby talk or smiling lasted more than 5 seconds. A value of 2 represented intervals in which baby talk and smiling both lasted less than 5 seconds, and a value of 1 indicated baby talk without smiling. Intervals without baby talk were coded with 0. The mean value of the scores from all the intervals defined the measure of maternal warmth during the interaction of mother and infant in a face-to-face context. Reliabilities for maternal warmth were calculated based on 10 mother–infant interactions that were independently coded by two different coders. Cohen's kappa was .79 for baby talk and .85 for maternal smiling.

Maternal warmth toward negative infant signals was assessed as empathy (Warmth–) expressed by vocalizations in a rhythmic, calming manner that did not necessarily relate to the regulation of the infant's needs. For each interval of infant distress, empathic vocalizations by the mother were coded as 1. A code of 0 indicates that there were no empathic vocalizations during the interval. The mean value of all relevant intervals was calculated as an index for maternal warmth toward a negative infant. Cohen's kappa was calculated to estimate the interrater reliability. Based on 10 randomly selected video episodes, Cohen's kappa for empathic vocalizations was .84.

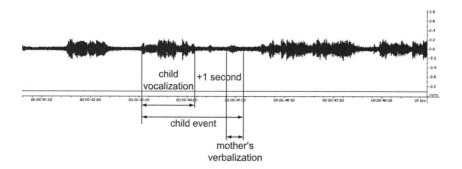

FIGURE 4.11.   Contingent maternal vocalization.

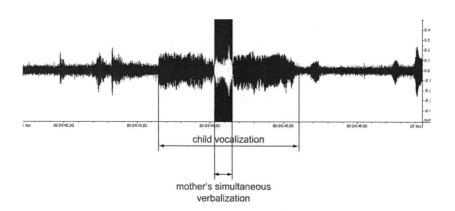

FIGURE 4.12.   Overlapping, synchronous verbal and vocal communication.

The Analysis of the Conversational Style During the Interactional Situations

The conversational style of the mother interacting with her baby during the free-play situations was analyzed with a system that was based on conversational analyses by Wang (2004; Wang et al., 2000) and comparable to the system described for the discourse style during the parenting ethnotheory interviews. Codes were defined for amount and composite scores for autonomy and relatedness.

- *Amount.* The number of words that the mother addressed to the baby during the interaction time, including vocalizations, were counted and relativized for the length of the interaction. Scores indicate mean number of words per 10-second interval.
- *Autonomy.*
  1. *Agency.* The mother refers exclusively to the child as having, developing, or initiating (not receiving).
     a. Abilities (e.g., You can already do it alone!).
     b. Volitions or intentions (e.g., Do you want to tell me a story?).
     c. Cognitions (e.g., It seems like you are not interested in our conversation. Do you remember … ?).
     d. Actions (e.g., You are looking at the trees.).
     e. Potential (e.g., You can sit here.).
     f. Preferences (e.g., You prefer to sleep, right?).
     g. Emotions (e.g., You are happy/angry/sad).
     h. Decisions (e.g., Shall I/Can I/May I give you your milk now?).

The preceding subcategories are mutually exclusive.

  2. *Evaluation.* The mother explicitly evaluates the good behavior of the child or something else:
     a. In general (not related to the child. Example: It's a nice picture, isn't it?).
     b. Praise (e.g., This morning you behaved so well).
  3. *I-statement.* The mother explicitly refers to herself as the speaking person thereby emphasizing the subjectivity of her description, evaluation, generalization, and so forth. Example: I think this is the right way of doing it.
  4. *Self-referral.* The mother refers to herself or her own experiences. Example: When I was a child like you, I used to do the same thing.
- *Relatedness.*
  1. *Concerns with authority.* The mother refers to moral correctness, social regulations, and concerns with authority. These statements are often introduced by *should,* which implicitly refers to an authority.

Example: You should listen to what I'm telling you. Daddy told you not to do things like that.

2. *Social context.* The mother talks about the social context and other persons in relation to the child (except the mother herself). Example: Yesterday we went to see Grandma.

3. *Criticism.* The mother explicitly criticizes the behavior of the child. Example: It's not nice of you to beat your friend.

4. *Coagency.* The mother refers to the child (always) together with somebody else (including the mother herself) as having, developing, or initiating one of the agency-related categories. Example: We like to go shopping, right?!

5. *Address.* The mother is addressing or speaking to the child corresponding to the family role (e.g., Son!) or in a respectful manner (e.g., *Fai!*, Queen!, Grandmother!).

The coding was conducted using the Atlas.ti software. Two trained coders independently coded the transcriptions of five randomly selected mother–infant interactions from each cultural sample. The coders' ratings were scored as the number of agreements divided by the number of agreements plus the number of disagreements. Overall interrater agreement for all categories described earlier was 91%, ranging from 80% (Los Angeles) to 94% (Berlin, Athens, and rural Nso).

The Analysis of the Parenting Quality

Interactional quality is often assessed using the conception of maternal sensitivity as introduced by Ainsworth et al. (1978) across different cultural environments.

Sensitivity in the conception of Ainsworth et al. (1978) is based on the mother's accessibility to her infant and her awareness and empathy with her communications. Sensitive mothers have insight into their babies' wishes and moods, and thus can more realistically judge their babies' behavior. Furthermore, they are aware of how their own behavior and moods affect their infants' behaviors. An inattentive, "ignoring" mother is often unable to correctly interpret the baby's signals when they break through, for she has been unaware of the prodromal signs and of the temporal context of the behavior. However, even a mother who is highly aware and accessible may misinterpret signals because her perception is distorted by projection, denial, or other marked defensive operations. Mothers who have distorted perceptions tend to bias their reading of their babies according to their own wishes, moods, and fantasies. For example, a mother not wishing to attend to her baby might interpret his fussy bids for attention as fatigue and therefore put him to bed, or a mother who is rejecting her infant somewhat might perceive him as rejecting and aggressive toward herself.

The sensitivity scale is a 9-point rating ranging from highly sensitive to highly insensitive, with every other scale point being defined as follows:

- *9-Highly sensitive.* The mother is able to see things from the infant's point of view. She knows what the infant wants and responds even to subtle, minimal, and understated cues of the infant.
- *7-Sensitive.* The mother responds promptly and appropriately to the infant's cues but there are occasions when her responses are not as consistently prompt or as finely appropriate. There might be occasional mismatches.
- *5-Inconsistently sensitive.* Although the mother can be quite sensitive on occasions, there are periods in which she is insensitive to her infant's signals. On the whole, however, she is more frequently sensitive than insensitive.
- *3-Insensitive.* The mother frequently fails to respond to the infant's communication appropriately and promptly. She is unable to see things from the infant's point of view. She may be too frequently preoccupied with other things and therefore inaccessible to the child's signals. She only responds when infant is distressed or very forceful and compelling in his or her communications and this can modify her behaviors and she shows some sensibility.
- *1-Highly insensitive.* The mother seems to be geared almost exclusively to her wishes, moods, and activity. This is not to say that she never responds to infant signals—sometimes she does if the signal is very intense, prolonged enough, or is frequently repeated. Even when she responds to the baby's signal, her response is inappropriate, fragmented, and incomplete.

Because parenting ideas and practices differ across cultural environments as we have already outlined, a Nso interactional quality scale was developed. The Yovsi scale (Yovsi, 2004) was constructed analogously to the Ainsworth scale as a 9-point scale ranging from extremely good down to good, standard, predominantly poor, and extremely bad. The scale was developed Yovsi, who is a native Nso, following Ainsworth's methodology, including comprehensive case studies, ethnotheoretical accounts, and behavioral observations, using ethnographic reports, quantitative, and qualitative methodology (Keller, Lohaus, et al., 2004; Keller, Voelker, & Yovsi 2005; Keller, Yovsi, & Voelker, 2002; Voelker, Yovsi, & Keller, 1998; Yovsi, 2003, 2004; Yovsi & Keller, 2003). Central to Nso parenting quality is keeping the baby healthy and supporting growth. Close body contact and carrying, shaking laps and bodies in a rhythmic movement, and slowly and softly lifting the baby up and down is considered central to making the baby smile and feel happy and supporting growth and development. Exercising the body is believed to make the child relaxed and smart. Babies are stimulated through massage and the straightening of legs, arms, hands, and palms. Body stimulation also helps parents to easily detect motor problems in their babies and detect when they are in pain. Another form of body stimulation is making the infant grasp an object.

Good parenting in Nso consists of closeness, monitoring, instructing, training, directing, and controlling the infant's activities. This conception of caretaking gives the parent the lead. The Yovsi scale captures this conception of caretaking with the following ratings:

- *9-Extremely good.* The mother almost always controls and directs the ongoing activities of the infant with close body contact, vestibular, and kinesthetic stimulation. The mother takes the lead showing and initiating the play for the infant. The mother is emotionally involved throughout.
- *7-Good.* The mother is predominantly in control of the child's activities, although at times she might not be emotionally involved.
- *5-Standard.* The mother provides the infant with tactile object stimulation and at the same time is preoccupied with other things, but still aware and in control of the infant. The mother is at times emotionally involved with the child by smiling.
- *3-Predominantly poor.* There is predominantly distant body contact with the infant. The mother positions the infant in a more comfortable position on her lap while providing tactile, object, and vocal stimulation. The mother overstimulates the infant with no positive emotional involvement with the infant. The mother leaves the infant almost on his or her own without controlling his or her activities.
- *1-Extremely poor.* The mother has a consistent lack of body contact with the child, with no body training or stimulation, leaving the infant completely on his or her own without controlling the baby's activities. The mother's emotion is flat and even if she reacts, she does so just with object or vocal stimulation. The mother constantly distorts the interactional process and devalues the baby.

Two groups of independent coders were trained with one scale each. Maternal interactional quality was evaluated for units of 30 seconds with a computer-based video analysis system for the interaction time of about 15 minutes. Only units where the infant was in a positive state were coded. Positive episodes were defined as the child not crying or fussing. Negative states occurred too infrequently during the free-play situations to treat them statistically. To test reliability, we computed Kendall's t, which is the adequate reliability coefficient for ordinal data. The reliability ranged from .84 to .91 for the Ainsworth scale and .86 to .94 for the Yovsi scale. Mean scores were computed for the two scales from the individual ratings.

Methodological Challenges in Cross-Cultural Research

Our research methodology has been developed with great care and respect for cultural idiosyncrasies. Nevertheless, the inclusion of samples that differ so widely with respect to lifestyle and affluence, from well-off, urban middle-class families in Western urban centers to subsistence-based farming villagers; education from illiteracy to university degree; definition of family from nuclear to extended households and clans; and norms and values of conduct from egalitarian interactions to hierarchical roles poses extreme challenges. Comparisons of behaviors and ideas across those diverse settings are only possible when there is a common point of reference. In our approach this common point of reference is defined by universal developmental tasks. We have argued that humans are predisposed to have a universal behavioral repertoire to solve these tasks. The comparisons of the behavioral expressions therefore can be assumed to reflect cultural emphases. However, the assessments are embedded in the respective cultural context. Research methodology nevertheless usually does not reflect cultural peculiarities. The ethics of research are rooted in the worldview of an independent, self-determined individual with an independent agency. In cultural environments with an interdependent worldview, a different set of ethical principles prevails, and applies to everything starting with the recruitment of families and the establishment of informed consent.

The decision about participation in a study for Western middle-class families is a temporary contract between two independent agencies that can be quit anytime. The assessment situation implies interaction between nonfamiliar individuals, which is a familiar condition; researchers are furthermore ascribed scientific authority so that their visit is potentially beneficial to mother, child, or even the family as a whole. Lastly, there is also an entertainment factor implied, as the most common scenario is that mother and baby spend the day alone, so that young mothers are often quite happy to have a conversational partner in the researcher.

In small-scale societies, the individual mother is the least likely to decide on participation in such an unfamiliar enterprise as a scientific study. First the permission of the local authority of the village is needed (e.g., a *shufay* in the Cameroonian Nso kingdom). Only when he agrees can families be contacted, where the head of the family (usually the oldest male) then decides on participation. In the Gujarati Nandesari villages the area can only be accessed with the help of an NGO cooperating with local midwives. In both cases, the contact with the mother operates through a hierarchical system.

In India things are made even more complicated by the powerful caste system that regulates every detail of social encounters. For example, it is not possible to visit a higher caste family and a lower caste family in the same village.

Inherent in the system is that the wish to quit participating cannot be openly expressed either. We sometimes faced the fact that mother and child were not at home repeatedly for appointments or that the address where they were supposed to be did not exist. This may be an expression of the wish not to participate.

In this social setting, there is not much need for and therefore not much familiarity with formal, written agreements. Besides illiteracy, written agreements may provoke distrust and suspicion, even in educated middle-class homes in Africa or India; especially when it is proposed by unfamiliar people in a social context, where people are used to interacting with familiar others only. Unfamiliar persons create anxiety (see also Abels, in press).

Once in a while it happens that families think that bad spirits and sorcery are involved in the assessments, which again causes anxiety and even disturbances.

There is a two-volume edition *The Scientist and the Irrational*, edited by alternative Nobel Prize Laureate Hans Peter Dürr (1981), in which these kinds of supernatural experiences are compiled, plus the transformations that rational scientists make themselves when confronted with the seemingly irrational that was obvious in daily encounters with their research participants and their cultural informants.

The social entrée to the family is not only based on culturally scripted roles, but also on culturally defined communication styles. The Western academic stance demands—at least in the quantitative research paradigm—the invisibility of the researcher. However, visiting a family is always a social event and follows the social and therefore cultural rules, which may be quite different in different cultural environments.

P. J. Miller (1996) described how researchers native to the study population—a Euro-American and a Chinese researcher—designed their participation:

> As it turned out, the two ethnographers negotiated roles that contrasted in some important ways. The American researcher came to be treated as a family friend who was addressed by her first name by parents and children. The Chinese researcher was granted fictive kin status. She was introduced to the family's relatives and frequently invited to family events such as dinners and picnics. Children were encouraged to address her as "Aunty." In addition, the Chinese ethnographer was much more likely than the American researcher to be invoked as an audience to the child's past transgressions. This almost never happened in the American families. (p. 189)

Abels (in press) described the challenges of negotiating social conduct that she encountered during her work in the Nandesari villages. Villagers are used to interacting with familiar people, so that it is normal to them to also collect information about the researcher that is most relevant to them (see Figure 4.13). In India, one of the key topics is naturally the family: Do you have siblings? Are your parents still alive? Most important of all, are you married and do you have children? The Western researcher, who is on the independent pathway of family formation, has problems explaining why she is not married in her mid-20s and does not have children, and to keep their respect for her work at the same time.

However, it is not always a cooperative attitude that describes the communication between researcher and participants. Marjorie Shostak (1981) has contributed to the understanding of the communication difficulties due to different motivations that she encountered with her Kenyan informant Nisa. She also reported about unrealistic expectations that Nisa claimed from Marjorie, experiences that all field researchers, natives included, can confirm. The Nandesari villagers also wanted to know exactly what the researcher, the assistant, and they themselves would get out of the research, especially in terms of money. The villagers suspect that the researchers are rich, which is obviously true compared to them, so 10 rupees for bangles that one mother requested for her child would really be very little money for the researcher. However, the Deepak Foundation maintained that monetary rewards were not to be given to the families in the villages where they work.

a.

b.

FIGURE 4.13.   Crowds of observers gathered once we entered a compound or
house. Photo from Culture and Development Lab, University of Osnabrück.

They fear that the families might not cooperate in their nonpaid projects. Moreover this could create social problems because families who do not have a child in the requisite age group would be excluded (Abels, in press).

The presents that the researchers give to participating families (e.g., clothes for the child) are more worth than the 10 rupees for the bangles, equaling what the husband earned in 1 day. Nevertheless, Abels (in press) concluded that this situation was quite unpleasant and all three—the mother, the researcher, and the assistant—lost dignity in this encounter.

We have argued that free-play situations are a common scenario across diverse cultural environments to assess infants' interactional experiences. Nevertheless, those situations are differently familiar and differently accepted during normal daily routines. Rogoff and collaborators (1993) described how the mothers-in-law of the Indian tribal participants of their study disliked the situation that the experimenter had provoked, namely letting the young mother sit with her 1-year-old child and play with a toy. The young mothers are expected to work hard and not just sit around. Again, Abels (in press) reported that one mother's answer was, "Wait until my older children come back and play with her." Playing is a luxury that the mother usually cannot afford and is not considered necessary. The child is mostly seen as self-sufficient when he or she is not showing any signs of tiredness or distress (Abels, in press).

Interview studies also pose problems. Greenfield (1997) described the different views on knowledge in independent and interdependent cultural environments. In one case, knowledge is an individual possession where the owner freely decides how to use it and with whom to share it. In the other case, knowledge is a common possession where the decision about the dissemination of that knowledge is based on the same hierarchical social model on which any other decision concerning the family is based. One consequence is that the young mothers who are lowest in the family hierarchy are not expected to answer the questions of the researcher. Therefore, it is not unusual, for example, in our Indian rural studies that whenever we sit with a young mother, besides the usual observers, husbands or grandmothers step in and answer the questions for the mothers.

Despite all these difficulties, cultural and cross-cultural research has contributed tremendously to our understanding of development and has thus created a culturally informed psychology. Every researcher involved in cross-cultural research finds idiosyncratic solutions for methodological challenges. Nevertheless, topics of comparability of procedure and assessment need to be systematically reconsidered. Our claim is that triangulation of methods—combining qualitative and quantitative approaches—will help to further advance our knowledge.

5 Cultural Models of Parenting

Parenting is a principal reason why individuals in different cultures differ from each other (Greenfield & Suzuki, 1998; Keller, 2003a, 2003b, 2003c; LeVine, 1977; Shweder et al., 1998; J. W. M. Whiting & Child, 1953). Accordingly, parenting has been regarded as a significant feature of culture (Harkness & Super, 1995), representing a major mechanism for the transmission of cultural values and practices between generations. At the same time parenting constitutes an investment that shapes individuals' life histories with respect to their reproductive strategies, and thus, their own parenting style (Chasiotis, 1990; Geary & Flinn, 2001; Keller, 2000a, 2000b, 2001; Keller & Chasiotis, 2005). It is a continuing task of parents and other caretakers to enculturate children by preparing them for socially acceptable physical, economic, and social activities that are characteristic of the culture in which they are to survive and thrive (LeVine, 1977). Enculturation is constructed and co-constructed through participation in cultural practices during everyday activities (Rogoff, 2003). Everyday activities express the values, goals, emotions, and feelings of the participating people and follow a script defining the appropriate, normative way to do that activity (Weisner, 2002). Children are introduced to culturally constituted conventions from birth on, as their postnatal environment is already saturated with cultural meaning (LeVine, 1999). The two prototypical cultural environments differ substantially with respect to their emphasis on the development of autonomy and relatedness as constitutive elements of self-construals during the developmental phase of infancy (Harwood, Miller, & Lucca Irizarry, 1995; Keller, 2003c; Keller, Lohaus, et al., 2004). I first describe the social world of infants in the two prototypical environments, and then analyze parenting strategies.

90

THE SOCIAL WORLD OF INFANTS

I have argued that infants' first experiences are social and take place within a network of genetically related people, in other words, the family. The biological definition of family comprises a mother and her child. However, the "nursing couple" (Middlemore, 1941) or the mother–child pair is embedded in a larger social system (see Figure 5.1).

In this Gujarati family, the mother–child pair is surrounded by other dyadically interacting persons and persons who are differently involved in the mother–child dyad. The older brother of the baby looks at the baby's face and the mother-in-law observes the young mother.

These social systems vary tremendously across and within cultural environments. Nevertheless the mother is the primary caregiver and, thus, the attachment figure during the first half-year in the diverse environments that we address. Breastfeeding and nursing are certainly one reason for this exclusive bond, but there may be other biological roots as well. Rhesus monkeys that were not raised by their mothers during their first months all developed behavioral problems (Suomi, 1999). In the following paragraphs, I characterize the social environments for babies in the two prototypical cultural models of independence and interdependence.

The baby who is born into a middle-class Western family spends most of the time during the first months of life exclusively with the mother. These babies also

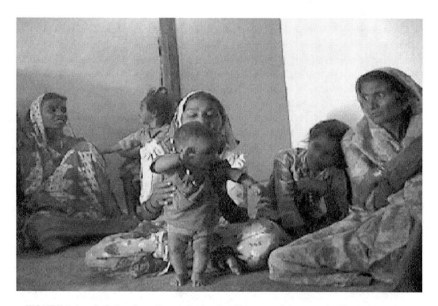

FIGURE 5.1.   A Gujarati mother–infant pair within a social network. Photo from Culture and Development Lab, University of Osnabrück.

spend a remarkable amount of time without being within bodily reach of a caregiver. Three-month-old German babies, for example, spent about 40% of an 8-hour home observation without being in physical reach of their mothers (Keller, Abels, et al., 2005). Middle-class Euro-American babies also spent time alone, although the figures vary among the existing studies. Hewlett and Lamb (2002) reported about 20%, J. W. M. Whiting (1981) reported about one third of the time being alone, and Fracasso, Lamb, Schölmerich, and Leyendecker (1997) recorded only 9% of the time being alone during a normal day (see Figure 5.2).

Infants in prototypical interdependent farming communities are never alone. They experience multiple care arrangements being surrounded by siblings and other kin. Nevertheless, the mother is the single most important caregiver in traditional farming, villager, pastoralist, and hunter–gatherer communities during the first months of life. Gujarati Rajput babies and Cameroonian Nso babies do experience multiple other caretakers on a daily basis, but together they do not match the time the mother is spending with the babies (see Figure 5.3).

Using the method of spot observations (see chap. 4, this volume), we tried to capture the social experiences of infants in the Gujarati and Nso villages as compared to middle-class German babies (Keller, Abels, et al., 2005). The results of this study confirm that the mother is the most significant caregiver in all three communities, although the participation of others differs across the communities. Due to the nuclear family situation in Germany with about three to four persons in the household and 1.3 children on average, there really are not any others who could

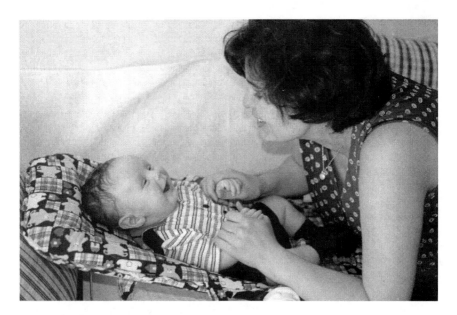

FIGURE 5.2.   A Greek mother–infant pair plays alone. Photo by Zaira Papaligoura.

a.

b.

FIGURE 5.3.   (a) Babies participate in daily activities; (b) Older siblings are reliable caretakers. Photos from Culture and Development Lab, University of Osnabrück.

take care of a baby. There is a significant proportion of others involved in baby care in the Nso villages, as well as in the Gujarati villages, although the actual amount of body contact that the infants experience differs substantially. The lesser amount of body contact that the Gujarati Rajput babies experience is based on the poor health situation of their mothers, which is due to underweight and anemia. Maternal nutritional problems also affect the infants' nutritional status. Poorly nourished infants are less active and, thus, less able to elicit maternal stimulation (Chávez,

Martinez, & Yashine, 1975; Super, 1981). This may be reflected by the fact that the Rajput infants in our study spend considerably more time sleeping than the Nso and the German infants do. Figure 5.4 demonstrates the occurrences of parenting systems of mothers and other caregivers in the three cultural communities during infants' waking hours.

The experiences within the parenting systems reveal that more others are part of infants' social worlds in the two interdependent communities than in middle-class German families. Gujarati Rajput babies experience a large amount of body stimulation from other caregivers. Although little in total, they experience even more object stimulation and face-to-face contact from others than from their mothers. Siblings are important individual other caretakers in traditional village families, although they regularly care for babies only once they are in the second part of their first year. They act as "culture-brokers" (Zukow-Goldring, 1995, p. 202), in that they introduce their younger siblings to the cultural codes of everyday life. They create intuitive and intentional learning contexts, where they teach their younger siblings routine activities (Maynard, 2002). However, in our spot observations, no single other could come close to the time mothers spent with their babies when they were a few months old.

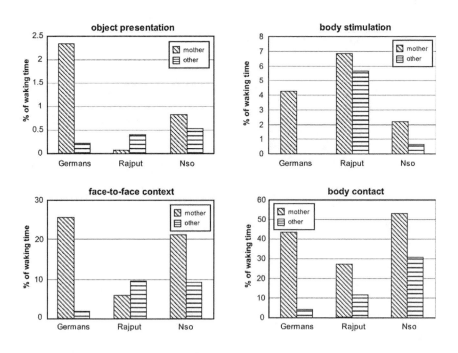

FIGURE 5.4.   Parenting activities of mother and other caregivers.

Sleeping Arrangements

The social world during waking hours differs across the two cultural models, as do nightly sleeping arrangements (cf. Morelli, Rogoff, Oppenheim, & Goldsmith, 1992; Shweder, Jensen, & Goldstein, 1995). Babies in middle-class European and Euro-American families are familiarized with their own beds and even their own rooms soon after birth. Pediatricians suggest strongly to young families that they not spoil the baby with cosleeping and warn of the risk of injuries in the parental bed. Spock and Rothenberg (1992) recommended to U.S. parents in their best-selling parenting guide that "it's a sensible rule not to take a child into a parent's bed for any reason" (p. 213). Accordingly, most middle-class Western children have their own beds from birth on, often equipped with toys (see Figure 5.5).

Nevertheless something like a cosleeping movement has emerged in the United States, emphasizing the psychological and physiological benefits of cosleeping for at least mother and baby (McKenna, 1995, 2000).

In traditional villages, on the other hand, it is unthinkable that mother and baby could sleep separately (see Figure 5.6).

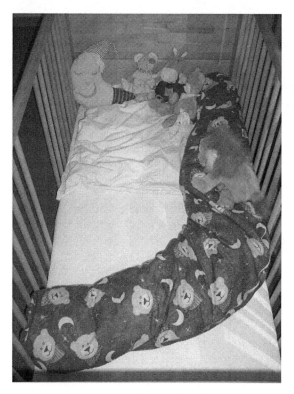

FIGURE 5.5.   A German middle-class baby's bed. Photo by Markus Lamm.

FIGURE 5.6.   A Nso baby sleeps on her mother's lap while she is preparing food.
Photo from Culture and Development Lab, University of Osnabrück.

During the focus group discussions presented later in this chapter (see also
Keller, Voelker, & Yovsi, 2005; Keller, Yovsi, & Voelker, 2002), sleeping arrangements were also discussed. Nso women just did not believe that German babies are
expected to sleep alone and in fact often do. They found this a form of child mal-
treatment that would need immediate action, such as sending a Nso woman to Germany to teach German mothers how to care for babies.

In the kitchen of the mother's house in a Nso compound there is usually a
bed used for sitting and for resting. This kitchen bed also serves as a sleeping or
siesta place for children especially when supper is delayed. Besides, children
use the kitchen bed as their play area during the day. The sleeping room is
where the mother sleeps with the baby during the first 2 to 3 years of life. When
the mother sleeps with all her children in one bed, they often position themselves according to their birth order, with the youngest one nearest to her. Children are not allowed to sleep at the side of the bed, instead they sleep behind an
older person because it is believed that they should be protected predominantly
from evil spirits and from falling out of the bed. If weaned children cannot
sleep with the mother in the same bed because there is another child and insufficient space, they may sleep with other siblings or with a grandmother.
First-time mothers do not usually sleep alone with the child in the room, as
there is someone to assist with child care. It is believed that the mother has to

master the child-care curriculum, including nocturnal care. Often fathers sleep in their own room of the house (the parlor). This is also the place where possessions are kept; it is also used as a sitting room for mostly elderly male visitors and family members.

In an interview study with 78 Nso mothers with infants from birth to 12 months old, we assessed the sleeping arrangements among the Nso farmers (Yovsi & Keller, 2006). The results confirmed that all infants (100%) slept with an adult, 97% of the infants slept with their mothers, and 3% of the infants coslept with a babysitter. The widespread reason given by mothers for cosleeping with their infants was the ease and convenience of nighttime breastfeeding and care. Mothers do not necessarily have to wake up to make the breast accessible to the infant. Other motives for cosleeping were that the infant can sleep well and safely.

The weaning period is a transitional period that has an impact on family sleeping arrangements. When the child is weaned, he or she might sleep with other siblings, a grandmother, or relatives in another bed in the same room or in another room or building.

There are other care patterns that occur during the mother–child cosleeping phase. Most children fall asleep in the midst of a social activity in the company of others like the mother, other family members, and siblings (64%); 36% of the children fall asleep in the kitchen environment in the presence of other family members. The Nso farmers usually go to bed after dinner and storytelling, which is from 7 p.m. to 8 p.m. Cosleeping decreases with increasing age of the infant. Children sleep separately from their mothers from the age of 18 months to the age of 8 years, with the average around 4 years of age. The main reasons for a child to sleep away from the mother were because the child was no longer breastfed (28.2%), the child is able to communicate his or her needs (26.9%), the child cannot fall out of bed (25.6%), parental confidentiality (19.2%), and the birth of another child (6.4%).

The pattern described for the Nso families reflects the interdependent cultural model that has also been described for rural Indian families (Saraswathi, 1994) and other interdependent cultural communities (see Figure 5.7).

It has been demonstrated that African American babies are likely to fall asleep in the presence of a caregiver and Hispanic infants are likely to be soothed to sleep by their mothers (Wolf, Lozoff, Latz, & Paludetto, 1996). Mayan children also fall asleep in their mothers' arms without preparation or bedtime rituals and objects were rarely used to help make the child fall asleep. Generally, it has been demonstrated that in families where cosleeping occurs, there is less use of transitional objects and a lack of schedules in family activities (Morelli et al., 1992). Cosleeping is associated with nocturnal breastfeeding on demand (McKenna, 1995; Mosko, Richard, McKenna, Drummond, & Mukai, 1997).

The different attitudes toward sleeping arrangements across cultures are expressed in the ideas that parents hold about the age when children should sleep alone and sleep through the night. Questionnaire data from the two prototypical cultural environments are presented in Table 5.1.

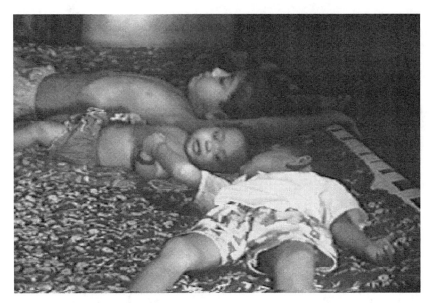

FIGURE 5.7.   Gujarati children sharing a bed. Photo from Culture and Development
Lab, University of Osnabrück.

The Berlin mothers have the earliest expectations of about 4 months of age for
sleeping alone and sleeping through the night, followed by the Los Angeles and the
Athens mothers, who have the latest expectations for sleeping alone and the earliest
for sleeping through the night within the group of independent mothers. The Gujarati and the Nso mothers, on the other hand, expect children to sleep alone and sleep
through the night only at 4 or 5 years of age, respectively. These data express substantial differences in the social life and the daily activities of children.

Fathers and Infants

The availability of fathers as caregivers during infants' early months of life is restricted in most of the world's communities. Although fathers on a universal scale
are very interested in infants, they spend little time with them (e.g.,
Eibl-Eibesfeldt, 1984). This is especially true for fathers from middle-class Western families. In a study on fathering, 26 middle-class German fathers were interviewed about the time that they spent with their 3-month-old babies. Six fathers
spent on average more than 5 hours daily with their babies, four fathers reported
between 3 and 5 hours, 14 fathers between 1 and 3 hours, and two fathers reported
less than 1 hour of daily contact with their babies (Eickhorst, 2005).

These data usually do not include weekends so that the fact that most fathers
from middle-class Western families work outside the home needs to be taken into
consideration. However, only 1.5% of German fathers take the paternity leave allowed by law in Germany.

TABLE 5.1

Ideas About Developmental Timetables: Sleeping Arrangements

	Cultural Community										
	Berlin[a]		Los Angeles[b]		Athens[c]		Rural Gujarati[d]		Rural Nso[e]		
	M	SD	M	SD	M	SD	M	SD	M	SD	$F(4, 154)$	η^2
At what age (in months) are children able to												
Sleep alone	4.03_a	8.22	5.61_a	13.63	7.56_a	7.15	46.40_b	34.35	59.62_b	31.65	56.35*	.59
Sleep through the night	4.43_a	3.11	4.36_a	2.97	3.63_a	3.60	57.33_b	43.45	40.48_b	31.57	41.16*	.52

Note. Five-level (culture) MANOVA with significant multivariate main effect for culture, Wilks's $\lambda = .32$, $F(8, 306) = 29.80$, $p < .001$, $\eta^2 = .44$, followed by univariate analyses. Indexed letters indicate results of simple main effects testing (with Bonferroni adjustment). η^2 = partial eta-square.

[a]$N = 41$. [b]$N = 50$. [c]$N = 24$. [d]$N = 15$. [e]$N = 29$.

*p < .001.

Yet even in cultural environments where fathers contribute substantially to the caregiving of their babies, as among the Aka Pygmies (Hewlett, 1991a, 1991b), who carry and hold their 1- to 4-month-old babies around 22% of the waking hours when they are in camp, mothers are involved about 51% of the time. The cultural practice in the Gujarati villages as in many Hindu families irrespective of sociodemographic background is on the other extreme. The young women leave their husbands' homesteads and return at least for the birth of the first child, but often also for births of following children, to their families of origin. They are away for months so that, especially in remote areas, there is no contact between father and baby. However, babies are surrounded by male family members of the mother's family of origin. The father's absence, in the sense that mother and infant are on their own, is, in fact, a substantial risk factor for the survival of babies, as studies with the Aché Indians have revealed (Hill & Hurtado, 1996). The consequences of a father's absence are stressed in particular by evolutionary approaches (cf. Ellis, 2004). Hrdy (1986) even suggested that the father–child bond may have been the basis for the father–mother–child bonds in human families.

Despite the different caregiving responsibilities, fathers have the same competencies in interacting with a baby as mothers do; there are no differences in their sensitivity and responsiveness to infant's signals (Lamb, 1997) and they possess the same inborn intuitive behavioral programs for interacting with babies (H. Papoušek & Papoušek, 1987). In a videotaped observational study with German fathers interacting with their 3-month-old firstborn babies, we were able to demonstrate that fathers use exactly the same parenting systems—body contact, body stimulation, face-to-face contact, and object stimulation—as mothers do (Lamm, Borke, Eickhorst, & Keller, 2006). Similar to mothers, fathers also express their parenting ideas through these parenting systems. In a study of German fathers of 3-month-old babies, fathers' parenting ideas were assessed. Ten video clips were presented individually to the participants, showing 10 different fathers interacting with their 3-month-old infants. Each clip was about 2 minutes long and covered diverse parenting behaviors. The participants were asked to comment on each clip using the same method that was used for the picture card interviews (see chap. 4, this volume). Comments that did not deal with paternal behavior at all (irrelevant comments) were excluded from further analysis (22.3% of all comments). Cohen's kappa, registered in a pretest with other trained coders, was .76. The remaining comments were coded with respect to mentions of the parenting systems body contact (9.4% of all relevant comments), body stimulation (5.6% of all relevant comments), object stimulation (9.4% of all relevant comments), and face-to-face contact (7.0% of all relevant comments; Eickhorst, 2005; Lamm et al., 2006). There were no differences concerning paternal ideas between the fathers with proximal and distal styles, which may seem surprising given the assumption that parenting behavior is an expression of parental ideas. However a one-to-one correspondence between beliefs and behaviors is too simplistic in that it does not consider the "mental steps leading to the expression of intended action" (Sigel, 1985, p. 346), especially the effect of implicit motives. I return to this belief–behavior gap in chapter 9.

However, there are also differences between mothers and fathers. Observational studies over the last 20 years revealed that paternal play is more active and exciting, less predictable, and includes more tactile and motor stimulation than maternal play (Lamb, 1997; Yogman, 1982; cf. a critical view on fathers as "playmates" by Roggman, Boyce, Cook, Christiansen, & Jones, 2004). Nevertheless, Lamb (1997) concluded that differences between fathers and mothers are far less meaningful than similarities. Figure 5.8 demonstrates fathers interacting with their babies.

a.

b.

Figure 5.8.   (a) A Gujarati father showing flowers to his baby; (b) A German father spending time with his baby. Photos by (a) Monika Abels, and (b) Bettina Lamm.

Thus, it is also important to analyze paternal influence on normal child development. I return to that in chapter 6.

Summary

The social worlds of village babies from subsistence families and middle-class infants from Western societies represent different developmental contexts, offering different opportunities. Although in both contexts mothers are the primary caretakers for the babies during the early months of life, the mother–child dyad is embedded in different social worlds. The middle-class Western mother spends most of the day alone with the baby in an apartment or a house. Fathers spend little time with the babies during the week due to their work outside the home. On the weekends there is more family time with fathers spending more leisure time with their babies. Mothers in patrilocal rural households give birth to their first child and often also to subsequent children in the household of their family of origin. In this context, the fathers are even less available than in the middle-class homes. However, there are plenty of male role models like grandfathers, brothers, cousins, and uncles. After birth, mothers are surrounded by female relatives and neighbors, so that they are never alone with their babies. Contrary to middle-class urban babies, who are expected to spend time alone from early on, village babies are in physical proximity to their mothers and other caregivers day and night. In the following chapters, I analyze the parenting strategies in the two prototypical environments. Because the mother is the main caregiver, the following analysis concentrates on the mother–infant pair.

PARENTING STRATEGIES

The analysis of parenting strategies as presented here is based on the following model, which builds on the ideas of LeVine (1977), who was the first person to link parenting strategies to broader socialization goals derived from particular ecocultural contexts. This model specifies the "socialization strategies" box in Figure 3.1 (see Figure 5.9).

Cultural models represent a "cluster of ideas that characterize cultures at a broad level and that should logically have wide-ranging functions for the organization of human development and social relationships" (Harkness, Super, & van Tijen, 2000, p. 23). They can be regarded as constituting filters through which the cluster of ideas is implemented into parenting contexts and practices (Fiske et al., 1998; Super & Harkness, 1996). Cultural models define socialization goals, which are specified in parenting ethnotheories. Parenting ethnotheories provide the ideational framework for behavioral strategies. Next I present empirical evidence for the different levels of the parenting model before I address the relations between the different levels.

In the first step, we tested whether the broader cultural models in fact differ between the rural farmers and the middle-class families. For this we used the family allocentrism scale (Lay et al., 1998; see chap. 4, this volume). Table 5.2 reports the results.

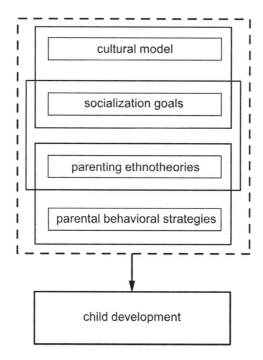

FIGURE 5.9.   The conceptual model of parenting.

The results reveal significant differences between the two groups of samples, with the farming women scoring significantly higher on family allocentrism than the urban women. There are, however, also within-group differences, with the Berlin mothers scoring significantly lower than the Los Angeles and the Athens mothers and the Nso women scoring significantly higher than the Gujarati Rajputs. Overall, these data confirm the theoretically selected research sites, for which particular sociodemographic profiles are associated with specific sociocultural orientations.

Socialization Goals

Socialization goals are supposed to serve as vehicles through which emotions, motives, and values are translated into action (Bugenthal & Johnston, 2000; L. Martin & Tesser, 1996). They capture the ideals that cultural groups have developed with respect to their priorities defining desirable endpoints (Bruner, 1986) or optimal ways of being (Csikszentmihalyi & Rathunde, 1998) within their particular ecocultural environment. Here I report data about socialization goals from our study program, comparing samples associated with the two cultural models. In a first step I present comparative questionnaire analyses, before completing these analyses with excerpts from interviews.

TABLE 5.2
Family Allocentrism

	Cultural Community										
	Berlin[a]		Los Angeles[b]		Athens[c]		Rural Gujarati[d]		Rural Nso[e]		
	M	SD	M	SD	M	SD	M	SD	M	SD	$F(4, 139)$	η^2
Allocentrism	62.92_a	11.38	70.87_b	9.46	71.42_b	9.23	92.79_c	8.33	103.89_d	1.84	75.82*	.68

Note. Five-level (culture) MANOVA with significant multivariate main effect for culture, Wilks's $\lambda = .07$, $F(20, 452.0) = 27.95$, $p < .001$, $\eta^2 = .49$, followed by univariate analyses. Indexed letters indicate results of simple main effects testing (with Bonferroni adjustment). $\eta^2 =$ partial eta-square. [a]$N = 39$. [b]$N = 23$. [c]$N = 50$. [d]$N = 14$. [e]$N = 18$.
*$p < .001$.

In the first study (Keller, Lamm, et al., 2006), we assessed socialization goals with a list of 10 statements concerning qualities that a child should learn or develop during the first 3 years of life. Participants with an independent cultural model from middle-class Berlin, Los Angeles, and Athens families scored the lowest on relational socialization goals, whereas participants with an interdependent cultural model from Nso and Gujarati Rajput villages scored highest on this scale. Concerning the autonomous socialization goals, participants with an independent cultural model scored significantly higher than the Nso (see Table 5.3).

The three samples with an independent model do not differ from each other with respect to autonomy, but they do not differ significantly from the Gujarati Rajput sample either. The Berlin mothers score significantly lower on the scale of relational socialization goals than the Los Angeles and the Athens mothers, but all three samples differ significantly from the two rural samples. Thus, the questionnaire data confirm that the two prototypical sociocultural environments are associated with different socialization goals. The model of independence focuses more on autonomy than on relatedness, whereas the model of interdependence focuses more on relatedness than on autonomy.

In a second study of mothers of 19-month-old toddlers, we assessed a different list of autonomous and relational socialization goals with samples from the middle-class Nso and Osnabrück families (Kärtner et al., 2006). Again, the German mothers valued autonomy significantly more than relatedness and the opposite was true for the rural Nso mothers (see Figure 5.10).

The same pattern emerges with respect to the individual items, the first four expressing autonomy and the last four expressing relatedness (see Figure 5.10). Some items are scored antithetically, like "developing own talents" or "doing what the parents say," whereas others differ in the degree of agreement, like "sharing with others" or "being different from others." Furthermore, the interindividual variability also differs between these two samples.

In line with an independent stance, middle-class German mothers show more variability in their opinions than the rural Nso mothers, who moreover select more extreme rating points on the questionnaire scales. For them, a statement is true or false, and there is nothing in between.

These data confirm that the Nso villagers understand themselves as a collective with a strong opinion about what is right or wrong with respect to childrearing goals. This commonality is important because children are regarded as communal obligations. There is a saying: "A child belongs to a single person when in the womb, and after birth he or she belongs to everybody." Interdependence is the thread of the communal social fabric. The survival of one person is seen as linked with that of the others: I am, because we are; and because we are, therefore I am (Mbiti, 1990; Zimba, 2001). In an interview study (Keller, Demuth, & Yovsi, 2006), rural Nso farmers confirmed that they want their children to learn to convey roles and duties, maintain social harmony, express proper demeanor, and learn by observation. Thus, Nso parents strive to have their children meet the moral standards of the community.

TABLE 5.3

Socialization Goals

	Cultural Community											
	Berlin[a]		Los Angeles[b]		Athens[c]		Rural Gujarati[d]		Rural Nso[e]		$F(4, 140)$	η^2
	M	SD	M	SD	M	SD	M	SD	M	SD		
Socialization goals												
Autonomy	3.96_a	.79	4.15_a	.57	4.09_a	.70	4.04_a	1.00	1.52_b	.68	46.55*	.57
Relatedness	3.06_a	.71	$3.60_{a/b}$	.84	3.76_b	.85	4.54_c	.68	5.0_c	.00	26.04*	.43

Note. Five-level (culture) MANOVA with significant multivariate main effect for culture, Wilks's $\lambda = .07$, $F(20, 452.0) = 27.95$, $p < .001$, $\eta^2 = .49$, followed by univariate analyses. Indexed letters indicate results of simple main effects testing (with Bonferroni adjustment). $\eta^2 =$ partial eta-square. [a]$N = 40$. [b]$N = 23$. [c]$N = 50$. [d]$N = 14$. [e]$N = 18$.
*p < .001.

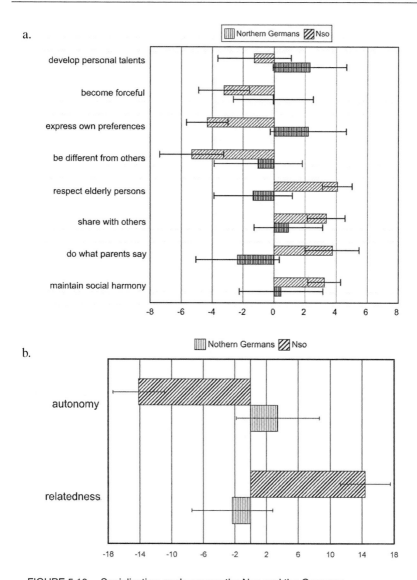

FIGURE 5.10.   Socialization goals among the Nso and the Germans.

Although the Gujarati Rajput families scored unexpectedly high on autonomous socialization goals in the questionnaire study, the interviews reveal that the relational socialization goals are of greater importance (Abels, 2006). Obedience, acceptance of norms and values, and respect for the elderly are cultural priorities, which are rooted in the Hindu religion, and, thus, in good personal qualities or *sanskaras* (Chaudhary, 2004; Saraswathi & Ganapathy, 2002). Identity in the

Hindu religion is mainly ascribed at birth; babies are born into one of the four hereditary castes in which one is destined to stay until death. Attitudes, beliefs, values, and behavior are all related to caste (Laungani, 2005).

Therefore, the two groups of subsistence farming families have very similar socialization goals, based on obedience, respect, harmony, and the moral standards of small-scale group life. These values are rooted in the spiritual systems of the social communities.

Families with an independent socialization script pursue quite different socialization goals as the questionnaire studies have demonstrated (Keller, Lamm, et al., 2006). The following excerpt of an interview about socialization goals with a 36-year-old Euro-American Los Angeles mother, who works as a self-employed office manager with a 3-month-old daughter as her only child, expresses her view, which she shares with her peers from Berlin and Athens. For her it is of utmost importance that a baby develops independence from early on:

(M = mother; I = interviewer)

M: And sometimes they do need time away, um, 'cause they get overstimulated if there are just too many people around. Or they, you know, sometimes they need just a little quiet time.

I: Mhm

M: Helps them develop a sense of, um, independence.

I: Oh, mhm, so what's important about independence?

M: Uhm, that they are able to make decisions for themselves.

I: Mhm
It is also very important to that mother that babies can be separate, and spend time on their own, alone.

M: And they don't require having someone there constantly. 'Cause sometimes they get so clingy and whiny, and that's just 'cause they don't know how to be alone. And it's important for kids, for humans to having a relationship with themselves that they can be alone.

I: Mhm. When they are older?

M: Uhm—even when they are babies, they need to be able to just not have constant—constantly somebody there.

I: Mhm

M: Helps them develop some self-identity.

This mother nicely reiterates the topics of separateness and autonomy in this excerpt. This view is similarly expressed in professional ideologies, as another 37-year-old mother of a 3-month-old baby from Los Angeles, who works as a teacher, explained:

As a teacher, I think children are happier when they are also independent, not always needing somebody there, you know, they just get fussy and they don't feel, you know,—a bab—a kid should be confident and happy to be—to play by themselves some time. I think that's OK. [laughter] But you know when they are little, you don't wanna [be] leaving them, but yeah, little by little, I think it's healthy to let them play alone.

The normative aspect of these assumptions is expressed with the reference to healthy development. These excerpts also demonstrate how socialization goals and ethnotheories are intertwined, as the women develop their socialization goals in the discourses from their ideas about valued parenting practices. Learning not to require somebody around all the time is the instruction for the socialization pathway toward independence.

In conclusion, socialization goals differ substantially between the two prototypical cultural environments. They can be regarded as cultural scripts for the development of the psychology of independence or the psychology of interdependence. The results from different studies using different methodologies confirm that the cultural model of interdependence stresses relatedness, communion, and cooperation, whereas the cultural model of independence stresses separateness and autonomy.

Parenting Ethnotheories

Socialization goals are embodied in parenting ethnotheories or parents' ideas about proper infant care (Goodnow, 1988; McGillicuddy-deLisi, 1982; Sigel, 1985; Super & Harkness, 1982), which are supposed to mediate parents' behavior toward their children. Parental beliefs and attitudes are regarded as filters through which their behavior is culturally tuned; they are interpreted as playing an important role in the mutual regulation between parent and infant (Pomerleau, Malcuit, & Sabatier, 1991).

Parenting ethnotheories represent an organized set of ideas that are shared by members of a cultural group (D'Andrade & Strauss, 1992; Quinn & Holland, 1987). These ideas and beliefs can be regarded as representational frameworks for the development of competence in particular environments (Keller, 1997, 2003b, 2003c). Ethnotheories are publicly patterned and historically reproduced symbolic practices that are available to members of a cultural community, which they use to make sense of their environment (Geertz, 1973; Gone, Miller, & Rappaport, 1999). They are explicit, but they are also often implicit ideas about what is right or wrong and how to act (H. Papoušek & Papoušek, 1991; Super & Harkness, 1981). Harkness and Super (1983) proposed a model, specifying a hierarchy of relations between cultural models and parenting behavior that starts with implicit cultural models about parenting, children, and family and narrows down to more specific and consciously held ideas about particular aspects of child development and parenting. Ethnotheories are part of the developmental niche that these authors conceptualized as a theoretical framework for understanding the interface between child and culture (Harkness & Super, 1995) in terms of a nexus through which elements of the larger culture are filtered and serve as the source of parenting practices and the organization of daily family life (Harkness & Super, 1996; Palacios & Moreno, 1996). Ethnotheories have different socialization functions. The fact that they represent shared cultural realities implies that they themselves constitute culture. Because they are acquired during socialization processes, they link generations together and allow the economical acquisition of contextually relevant knowledge.

In the next sections, I first present ethnographic portraits of the parenting ethnotheories of our study communities, and then report the results of our studies on content and style.

Ethnographic Portraits of Parenting Ethnotheories

The Interdependent Ethnopsychology: Wan Period in Nso Folk Psychology.   Among the Nso, the child is considered to be a sacred being who is a gift from the gods (*woon-ah nyuy*). Some children are believed to be reincarnated ancestors, so that the immortality of the soul comes with the birth of children. Generally the child is seen as a blessing for the family, symbolizing the "walking stick" or the "firewood of their parents" and a shield against mortality. The birth of a child is an aversion of blame. The child is initiated into his or her ancestral home by customary rituals and symbolically assigned gender identity and sex role. After the birth and naming of the child, everybody in the community has an obligation to be involved in his or her care and social development, because child care is a communal responsibility (Nsamenang, 1992). Breast milk is a baby's most cherished food. It is believed that if a child is not breastfed it can never possess the necessary potentialities to function well in a social milieu. The infant sleeps at the mother's back, and the mother faces the door to prevent the infant from being harmed by *arim* (malignant spirits). This is the most precarious period for infants, when they need the most care. Protective and magical measures are taken, like wearing amulets and the rites of *vidzee ver wan* (not raising the child away from the lineage). There are institutions in place to monitor conformity with the norms, which regulate an individual's behavior and link members together in a spirit of oneness.

The Interdependent Ethnopsychology: Indian Hindu Folk Psychology.
Indian Hindu children are also considered gifts from God and thus are valuable, welcome, and afforded the fullest protection, affection, and indulgence by the parents (Anjali, 1993; Kakar, 1978). The fusion between mother and infant is central and starts, according to the Vedas, during the prenatal period where the fetus is considered to be *chetan*—conscious and having a soul. The Hindu expression for this is *palanposhan,* meaning protection and nurturance. The actual process of caring and nurturing is *Lalan-Palan,* the affect and protection component of parenting (Anjali, 1993; Sinha, 1988). The mutual relationship is strengthened by *matri-rina,* or indebtedness toward the mother. This implies a lifelong relationship with the mother that includes the duties to protect and nurture the mother as an adult and performing

the *sanskaras* on her death for her peaceful abode to heaven. Participating in these rituals is believed to influence the peace and well-being of both ancestors and future generations, and is therefore regarded as an essential family function (Menon, 2003). *Samskara* therefore provides individuals with social affordance through which the self and self-in-relation (to significant others and to gods) are constructed and shaped (Chaudhary, 2004). Hindus conceive of motherhood as a psychospiritual experience that is infused in the spirit as *dharma* (Saraswathi & Ganapathy, 2002).

The spiritual aspect of the mother–infant relationship is manifested by protective items around the baby's neck to save the child from the "evil eye." Breastfeeding is the moral duty or *dharma* and performing the *dharma* is a sense of devotion. The father–child relationship is very restrained and circumscribed by cultural and social norms, especially for the infancy period.

Infancy (*bala*) comprises three stages according to Hindu ethnotheory: (a) *Ksirada,* when the child depends exclusively on milk for nourishment; (b) *Ksirannada,* when the child depends on both milk and cereals for nourishment; and (c) *Annada,* when the child depends solely on cereals for nourishment (Dash & Kashyap, 1992).

Summary.   There are striking similarities in these two ethnopsychological portraits of rural traditional communities. The cultural ideal is the mother–child symbiosis embedded in the close-knit social network of the group for the early phase of life, rooted in spiritual and religious prescriptions. Infants are gifts from the gods and guarantee the immortality of their parents.

The Independent Ethnopsychology.   Educated middle-class parents in Western societies are of course also very fond of their babies and want the best for them. They feel that the best way to achieve this goal is to prepare themselves to be good parents. Because their first contact with a baby is usually with their own first child, mothers and fathers do not have everyday experiences with babies that have prepared them for their future roles. Instead they visit birth preparation classes and read books and magazines. New parents' own mothers are only fourth in line when advice with respect to child care is needed in middle-class German families (Bröring-Wichmann, 2003). The healthy model of parent–infant relationships consists of separated individuals interacting with each other. Parents assign the infant an equal role for the flow of interactional exchanges as expressed in turn-taking, following a (quasi) dialogical structure (Keller, 2003c). Infants are seen as having their own will (Ainsworth, 1977) and are attributed an agency that expresses preferences, needs, and desires from early on (Keller, Hentschel, et al., 2004). Parents refer to infants' cognitions and emotions emphasizing individual abilities and cognitive skills, self-confidence, self-expression, exploration, discovery, and personal achievement (Greenfield, Keller, Maynard, & Suzuki, 2004; Keller, Harwood, & Carlson, 2006). The caregiver should be able to see things from the baby's point of view (Ainsworth et al., 1978). This model is reflected in the child-centeredness of the Western developmental sciences. German, Greek, and Euro-American mothers prize individual effort, self-actualization, expressiveness, and autonomy in children, and see optimal growth as an achievement of their children (Bellah, Madsen, Sullivan, Swidler, & Tipton, 1985; Harwood & Miller, 1991; Triandis, 1995).

Western ethnopsychology is inherent in mainstream developmental psychology. Therefore I only present one portrait for the three communities, although they contain cultural idiosyncrasies as well. Conceptions of parenting that do not fit the mainstream agenda are often regarded as dysfunctional or even pathological. The mother–child symbiosis as the cultural norm in the interdependent model is evaluated as a pathological condition. The clinical syndrome of enmeshment indicates that a symbiotic or enmeshed relationship does not have clear ego boundaries between parent and child, which are considered crucial for normal development (Bateson, 1979). These ideas are expressed in Ainsworth's (2004) conception of sensitive parenting. In the cooperation versus interference scale, she argued that the highly interfering mother has no respect for her baby as a separate, active, and autonomous person, whose wishes and activities have a validity of their own. The underlying dynamics of such an attitude are clearly located in the field of pathology as, for example, the concept of a woman whose baby continues to be a narcissistic extension of herself, who tends to treat the baby as her possession, her creature, hers. When she is in a mood to play, she may find the baby charming, provided that he or she cooperates and plays; when she tires of the baby she puts him or her aside; in either case it does not seem to occur to her to attribute any validity to how the baby feels. LeVine (2004) characterized these ideas as "prescriptive developmental psychiatry," which is deeply rooted in a Western individualistic model of what constitutes optimal development. The conceptions are not just behavioral categories; they are also a moral ideal (Harwood et al., 1995; LeVine & Norman, 2001), a judgment on maternal adequacy, and a way of distinguishing good from bad mothers (LeVine & Norman, 2001).

The Content of Parenting Ethnotheories

The Interdependent Model.   Participants with an interdependent cultural model (i.e., the Cameroonian Nso farmers and the Indian Gujarati Rajput mothers) score higher on the relationship-supporting parenting practices scale as compared to the autonomy-supporting practices scale. They agreed more often with statements concerning the importance of body contact and body stimulation as well as the importance of breastfeeding a crying baby immediately than with statements concerning object stimulation or sleeping alone, with which they actually disagreed (see Table 5.4; Keller, Lamm, et al., 2006).

Mothers from Los Angeles, Berlin, and Athens with an independent cultural model of parenting scored higher on the autonomy-supporting parenting practices scale than on the relational one; for example, they agreed with statements concerning the importance of face-to-face contact, object and toy stimulation, and early

TABLE 5.4
Content of Parenting Ethnotheories

	Berlin[a]		Los Angeles[b]		Athens[c]		Rural Gujarati[d]		Rural Nso[e]		F(4, 140)	η^2
	M	SD	M	SD	M	SD	M	SD	M	SD		
Parenting ethnotheories												
Autonomy	2.51_a	.76	$2.97_{a/b}$	.64	3.29_b	.71	2.61_a	.99	1.39_c	.44	25.02*	.42
Relatedness	3.01_a	.63	3.35_a	.64	3.29_a	.71	4.80_b	.37	4.91_b	.26	39.96*	.53

Note. Five-level (culture) MANOVA with significant multivariate main effect for culture, Wilks's $\lambda = .07$, $F(20, 452.0) = 27.95$, $p < .001$, $\eta^2 = .49$, followed by univariate analyses. Indexed letters indicate results of simple main effects testing (with Bonferroni adjustment). η^2 = partial eta-square. [a]$N = 40$. [b]$N = 23$. [c]$N = 50$. [d]$N = 14$. [e]$N = 18$.
*p < .001.

113

self-regulation like sleeping through the night and sleeping alone significantly more often than with statements concerning the importance of body contact and immediate response to infant crying (Keller, Lamm, et al., 2006).

With respect to relationship-supporting parenting ethnotheories, although the three urban samples do not differ from each other, they differ significantly from the rural ones.

The picture-based interviews revealed the following pattern concerning the mentioning of parenting systems, which is demonstrated in Figure 5.11.

Primary care is relatively high in all samples, with the Gujarati women scoring highest. Nevertheless, the developmental contexts to which women refer when they talk about primary care differ. A 29-year-old Berlin woman, who was trained as a primary school teacher and is the mother of a 3-month-old son, said:

> Because breast milk is very important and because an intensive relationship is being built. Because one needs a lot of time for breastfeeding, I need 40 minutes, then he sucks, then he falls asleep, then he opens the eyes and one has this eye contact and I like that very much. I think this is very important for the baby.

Here, the baby decides the tempo and the duration of breastfeeding, which is the context for eye contact and relationship building. A 29-year-old housewife from Los Angeles who is the mother of a 3-month-old daughter made a very similar point:

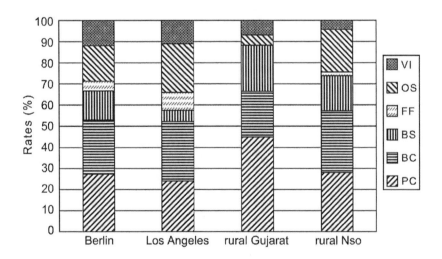

FIGURE 5.11.   The mentioning of the parenting systems in the picture-based interviews.

Um…I think breastfeeding is a good way to connect with the baby, get eye-contact, good way to smile at the baby, the baby smiles back. And touching, the feeling. It gets to feel the warmth of the body.

These mothers have multiple reasons why breastfeeding is important. On the other hand, Gujaratis and Nso mothers only have one good reason to breastfeed a baby, as a 25-year-old Gujarati mother with no formal education and two children explained:

M: Yes, if he feels hungry. Then what does that poor will do?
I: So one reason is feeling hungry that's why breastfeeding, any other reason?
M: There is only one reason for breastfeeding. He stops crying, becomes healthy and it is good for him.

Because of the emphasis on health, the technical aspects of the feeding situation become important, as a 33-year-old Nso mother of six who works as a farmer told the interviewer:

M: As this woman has nicely carried, like this, nicely the hand has supported her breast. She has cuddled him nicely, has held the nipple of the breast into the child's mouth so that if it is flowing to well, he can be reducing.
I: Mmh.
M: And he will be sucking sufficiently.

The number of mentioning of body contact is not very different across the samples either. However, the meaning systems in which body contact is embedded differ. A 32-year-old German woman who is a physician and mother of a 3-month-old daughter thought that the baby needs both body contact and time alone. However, it is important that the baby can decide when and what:

I think at 3 months a baby needs still a lot of mother warmth (*Mutterwärme*), and in case she (the baby) wants it, you see it. And only if she solves herself or shows "I do not want anymore," then we put her down and [let her] play. I think I notice with her that she [my daughter] wants to be put down. She wants to have time on her own. The same with playing, when she has a toy where she also wants to play alone with the toy, I am then a minor matter, the toy counts more.

The 33-year-old Nso farmer with six children has a more conditional view on body contact:

M: You have to hold him like this before he can sleep.
I: Mmh.
M: When you nicely cuddle him, his body will be warm, and he will then fall asleep.

As expected, body stimulation is mentioned significantly more often from the Nso and Gujarati women than from the Los Angeles and Berlin women. The contrary is true for face-to-face stimulation and vocal and verbal interaction. With respect to object stimulation, the Nso women mentioned it surprisingly often. Again, the way they mentioned it differs from the meaning system of the mothers with an independent model. The following excerpt is from a 39-year-old Nso farmer with five children:

M: When she carries [the child] like that the child will sit on the laps rattling the rattle, and when playing he will know that this is how they do [it].
I: Why is it good to give a rattle to the child?
M: It makes the child to play and not cry again.
I: What happens when a child cries?
M: When he is crying too much he can be ill.
    [And she continues later:]
M: The mother is rattling a rattle and the child is taking [it].
I: Mmh. Why is it good to be rattling a rattle to a child?
M: When you give [it] and the child rattles [it] then he will no more be giving you trouble.
I: Mmh
M: Mmm, he will not be quarrelsome, then he will be playing with it and grow.
I: Mmh
M: When the child is playing with it like that he becomes active.

This mother clearly sees object stimulation as a means of preventing crying and promoting the health of the baby, which is quite different from the value of object play as elaborated by this 35-year-old Los Angeles teacher, the mother of one son:

They need to learn to play on their own. So when they get older you don't always have to play with them. They learn how to play by themselves. You wanna make the baby choose, independent. And I think that's possible with a baby and even when they are older. And—umm—oh I do like the way she's playing with the rattle, but … !

With respect to the mentioning of the interactional mechanisms, the picture in Figure 5.12 emerges.

The data confirm our expectations in that the rural mothers talk substantially more about negative signals than the urban women, who in turn talk expectedly more about exclusive attention. Surprisingly, the rural women also talk more about positive emotions than do the urban women. Again, this result makes it necessary to refer to the narrative context in which the statements are placed. As the following examples demonstrate, Nso and Gujarati mothers both see positive emotions as one sign of monitoring health, which is central to their perception of a baby. A

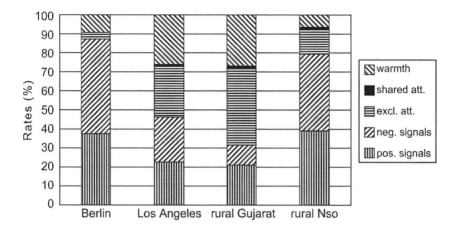

FIGURE 5.12.   The mentioning of the interactional mechanisms in the picture-based interviews.

39-year-old Cameroonian Nso farmer with five children explained, "Because she is lifting the child and making him to smile, so that the child will no more be fearful."

The same argument was put forward by a 32-year-old uneducated Gujarati mother of six children:

I: Why do you carry your child like this?
M: This way the child feels happy and won't cry. For some time, he feels happy.

The Los Angeles and Berlin mothers referred to the instantiation of positive emotionality when they talked about positive emotions. A 36-year-old Berlin woman, who holds a PhD in chemistry and has a 3-month-old son expressed, "If the child really laughs, these are the highlights of my day. Many of our friends have also said that for a smile from your baby you do the greatest Punchinello stuff."

A 30-year-old Los Angeles marketing research manager and mother of a 3-month-old daughter brought up yet another aspect:

The mother is holding her and cuddling her, but the baby is looking out so she can explore the world. I know that is something that she really enjoys to be able to see what's going on and not always be facing me. The exploration of the outside world is important and is fun!

Here the facing-out position of the baby, one that has been described, for example, for Senegalese Wolof infants as introducing the social world to the infant

(Rabain-Jamin & Sabeau-Jouannet, 1997), is explicitly directed to the exploration of the physical surrounding.

Surprisingly, the urban women also talk more about warmth than the rural women do. However, they talk more generally, abstractly, about warmth and love, as this excerpt from the same Los Angeles mother shows:

> Again the mother is looking at the baby very lovingly and they're sharing a close moment, you know, the child is maybe about to fall asleep or maybe just finished eating. Um, I think there's a lot of, a lot of love between those two.

Similarly, a 36-year-old businesswoman from Berlin with a 3-month-old daughter said, "It is like hunger, and, without, without food she cannot live. But without love she cannot live either."

The uneducated 25-year-old Gujarati mother of five had a conception of positive emotions that is more oriented toward concrete behaviors:

M: It's OK if he cries a little [its OK]. But if he cries a lot he will fall sick. In this the child laughs, the mother also laughs.
I: Is this necessary?
M: One feels good, the child laughs and the mother also laughs.
I: The child looks at the mother and laughs or the mother looks at the child and laughs?
M: The child calls the mother, the child is laughing, the child also laughs, the mother also laughs, the mother likes the child's [laughter] and the child likes the mother's.

Similarly, a 21-year-old Nso woman, who is a hairdresser and whose first child, a daughter, is 3 months old, said, "She has held the child at a distance. And she is not even smiling. She is carrying the child as if she does not love him."

The ethnotheory of the interdependent cultural model is also expressed in Nso women's evaluations of German mothers' interactional behaviors with their 3-month-old infants as discussed in the focus groups (Keller, Voelker, & Yovsi, 2005; Keller, Yovsi, & Voelker, 2002). They were concerned about the German mothers' attitudes toward primary care: "What surprises me is whether the traditionalists are now more sensitive to hygiene than Westerners, since the German mother is wiping the child's mouth with the hand instead of using a cloth." They missed German mothers' breastfeeding their infants: "When the child is crying, the Germans just try to soothe it in a very funny way—without breastfeeding." They were concerned about the lacking physical and emotional closeness. The positioning of the baby on his or her back with the mother sitting next to the baby or leaning over him or her was especially hard to understand for the Nso women: "Taking into consideration the age of the child, his back must be aching from this extended lying on the back," "Even when they take them on their laps, they lay them in a curled up position which is uncomfortable for the child." The Nso women even suspected that it may be forbidden in Germany for mothers to hold babies close to their bodies: "They handle them as if they are not their babies, as if they belong to somebody else or as if they are babysitters." Moreover, they thought body stimulation was lacking: "Lifting the child up and down is not done there, and can lead to a retardation in the child's motor skills." Nso women appreciated the focus the German mothers showed: "The Germans are good in that they talk to their infants and that can enable their infants to learn language faster and to a better degree than Nso children," because "for them, they believe every child is supposed to be intelligent" (Keller, Voelker, & Yovsi, 2005).

For the Nso women, clearly the developmental domain that is to be accelerated is motor development and the major tool used to achieve this goal is a special Nso practice of body stimulation: lifting the child up and down in a vertical position (see Figure 5.13).

a.   b.

c.

FIGURE 5.13.   (a) Without being breastfed, one cannot become a Nso; (b) Babies are in close body contact most of the time; (c) Lifting the baby up and down is the Nso practice of body stimulation. Photos from Culture and Development Lab, University of Osnabrück.

They evaluated interindividual differences in this practice carefully with respect to the baby's age ("She is lifting the baby up and straightening his legs which is really good, the only thing is that she is doing it too much. The form of hard handling should only be allowed at about 6 months of age, since the hearts are not strong enough until then") and current state ("When you feed the child, you should not lift him up and down so much, because he might throw up the food"). They also held evaluative views on the process of motor handling, as expressed when a Nso woman commented that "the bad thing is the way she suddenly lifts the child up." However general concerns were also admonished when Nso women considered the way a mother is stimulating a child "too hard, because the child can fall from her hand." These examples indicate that motor stimulation is an exclusive dyadic activity (Keller, 2003c), which expresses a mother's ability to adapt to the child's situation. The interindividual quality differences in how these behaviors are performed constitute differences in parenting quality, as defined by the Nso culture. The mechanisms of fostering growth are phrased in medical terms. Motor stimulation primarily affects the "places" (*viree,* which is their term for joints). The stimulation causes the places to become lighter and they relax and when this happens the child becomes stronger and develops well and in a healthy manner. The Nso also practice for motor milestones when they place infants in vessels or let them practice walking (see Figure 5.14).

a.

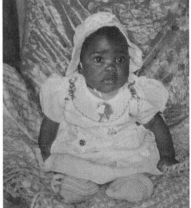
b.

c.

FIGURE 5.14.   (a, b) Sitting is practiced in bowls and chairs; (c) Walking is also practiced. Photos by Relindis Yovsi (a, c) and Bettina Lamm (b).

The German practice of keeping the infants lying on their backs was considered a retarding and even damaging practice: "She is still an infant and these places need to be trained [*nyingnin*], otherwise weakness and bad functioning of the legs and backbone will result"; "Children feel uncomfortable from the long lying position which hurts the back. It is not good for the spinal cord, growth or the development of the child." The way German women hold their babies was also thought to press the places what would result in a muscle cramp, even in an adult ("then this would happen even more in a baby"). Moreover, infants need space to "kick the legs and feet freely." The Nso women agreed that "the Germans can show a very bad example of child care."

Within an interactional context, they hold a general training theory for motor development. The effect of upright handling is explicated in a medical framework. The Nso thus combine two ethnotheoretical orientations that LeVine (1977; LeVine et al., 1994) proposed for differentiating the pedagogical orientation of agriculturalists and the more medical attitude of hunters and gatherers (Keller, Yovsi, & Voelker, 2002).

Picture-based interviews were used to discern the Gujarati Rajputs' ethnotheory of good parental care for a small baby because focus group discussions with the young women were not possible in the villages (Abels, 2002, in press). The Gujarati Rajput villagers have a similar ethnotheoretical model to the one discerned for the Nso. Health and growth are their primary concerns. Breastfeeding is the sine qua non of mothering, as expressed in the following excerpt from an interview with an 80-year-old illiterate woman who has five daughters and many grandchildren.

(GM = grandmother; I = interviewer)

I: Look at this [reference to picture].
GM: She is carrying and breastfeeding him.
I: Yes, so do you feel breastfeeding is essential?
GM: Yes, breastfeeding has to be done.
I: Why do you feel so?
GM: If [a baby] cries, breastfeeding have to be done and have to be carried.
I: So breastfeeding is essential?
GM: Yes.
I: So, what is the benefit of breastfeeding?
GM: Breastfeeding has to be done.
I: Yes, so
GM: He cries, so breastfeeding.
I: He doesn't cry, then not breastfed?
GM: He cries, so make happy by carrying.
I: No, but what I am asking, is don't cry, then not breastfed?
GM: If don't cry, don't cry, so sleeps, then why breastfed?
I: So breastfeeding is to calm the crying child?
GM: Yes.

Aside from its value for providing nutrition, breastfeeding is the main way mothers try to stop their babies from crying. Breastfeeding is not a choice but a must, a moral obligation as the formulation "breastfeeding has to be done" clearly indicates.

Body stimulation is another highly valued parenting system in the Gujarati villages. One domain of body stimulation is baby massage. In a study on baby massage in the Nandesari area, Abels (2002) reported that the interviewed women referred to the health of the baby and to the effect of baby massage making babies strong; it is good for the bones, the blood can move freely and the veins are separated. Moreover, 24% of the statements in the massage study referred to strong legs so that the infant learns to walk quickly (Abels, 2002; see Figure 5.15).

Another domain of body stimulation is infant standing, a practice that is exclusively found in this rural area and applied by the young Rajput mothers. They stand the babies in front of them on the ground during bathing and also as part of what they understand as playing (see Figure 5.16).

In the picture card interview, the same grandmother explains her view:

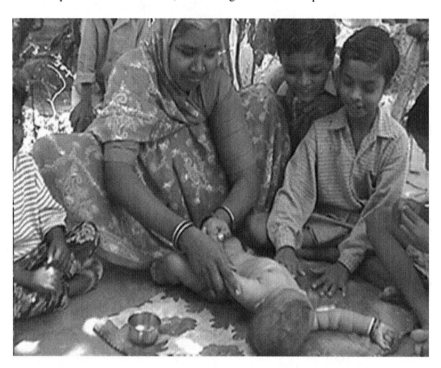

FIGURE 5.15.   Baby massage in Gujarat. Photo by Monika Abels.

I: What do you see in this photo? What is [being] done? What mother is doing? What mother is doing?

GM: Mother is sitting here. Child is standing here.

I: So child should make stand like this to child?

GM: Yes, he is kept standing.

I: So, should [be] kept standing?

GM: Yes, should [be] kept standing.

I: When should be kept, it's important or if not kept, it is OK?

GM: [pause]

I: I am asking why child have to be kept standing, why have to keep standing?

GM: Learns to walk early.

I: So child should be kept standing.

GM: Yes, OK. He learns to walk early.

I: He learns to walk early, that's why he should be kept standing?

GM: Yes.

I: And is it essential to walk early?

GM: Is it essential? It is good for him to walk early than crawl.

b.

a.

FIGURE 5.16. Babies are standing during massage or washing. Photos from Culture and Development Lab, University of Osnabrück.

Except early walking, there are other beneficial developmental consequences of the standing practice as a 32-year-old illiterate mother of six pointed out: "If we make a child stand like this, his legs will be stronger. He passes urine and he digests milk easily. It is good for the child to make him stand. First he should be fed and after that we have to keep him standing so that his digestion should be proper."

A standing baby also makes less work for the mother, as is specifically addressed in this interview with a 20-year-old mother who attended school for 7 years and has a 3-month-old second-born son.

I: What do you like in this (picture)?
M: The child is kept standing.
I: So the child should not be kept standing or should be kept standing?
M: Mean[ing], when the child defecates.
I: So while defecating is it essential to make the child stand? Do you feel so? Why?
M: This is because the clothes do not become dirty.

A similar health reason ascribed to body massage was mentioned by an illiterate 16-year-old mother of a 3-month-old daughter:

M: If we stand him, makes the child's legs free.
I: If the legs don't get free then?
M: It clots the blood while in that [standing position], the body will be healthy.
I: The child's body will be healthy, speak like that.
M: She is holding and standing.
I: Should we stand taking the child?

Rural women, even with diverse schooling experiences, ages, and numbers of children, all agree about the importance of this particular mode of body stimulation as a valuable socialization strategy.

It was apparent that it is strange for the young mothers to be interviewed and to answer questions that nobody has ever asked them before. There is a commonly shared understanding of beneficial aspects of early child care that need be neither questioned nor discussed. It was also obvious that the young Rajput women are not practiced in verbal discourse and have trouble expressing opinions. These stylistic differences are addressed later.

Body contact is also considered important for early child care. However, the Rajput mothers do not carry the babies on their back or hips when they are working. This is mainly due to their poor nutritional and health status, as mentioned earlier. In a survey about reproductive health and child health status in the villages of the Nandesari area, Lakhani and colleagues (1997) reported that during the assessment year (1996) 54% of 680 nonpregnant village women weighed less than 40 kg. Of these 18% weighed less than 35 kg, and only 23% more than 45 kg. Height was between 150 and 160 cm. Anemia was a major health problem of the women. Thirty-three percent had a hemoglobin level below 8.5 gm and only 22% of the women were above 10.5 gm. Although it can be assumed that this situation is gradually improving, there is still a major difference when compared to the well-fed and relatively healthy Nso women. Therefore, these mothers cannot constantly afford the energy investment of carrying a baby, so carrying is more of a leisurely activity, as expressed in the following interview excerpt with a 32-year-old illiterate mother of a 3-month-old son, her sixth child:

M: When I don't have work, I carry him. Whenever he is not crying, I take him and roam around. I also feed him like this and carry him like this.

I: Why do you carry your child like this?

M: This way the child feels happy and won't cry. For some time, he feels happy.

As an everyday routine small infants are kept in old saris that are hung from the ceiling or, in better-off families, cloth swings, which are supposed to wrap the baby as the arms of the mother would (see Figure 5.17).

Also similar to the Nso, the Rajput mothers consider talking to be important but they often do not have the time to engage in that kind of activity. Nevertheless they are very well aware of the developmental consequences, as another interview excerpt with the same mother indicates.

I: Should we talk to the child?

M: If we talk with him, then he can learn speaking. If we don't talk with him, he cannot learn anything. If the mother doesn't talk with him or doesn't play with him, he cannot learn anything.

Older siblings and other relatives are expected to take over that role for children's socialization. As one young illiterate Gujarati mother told us with respect to her 19-month-old son, "How can he learn to talk, he does not have siblings."

Toys do not play a special role, especially not during the first months of life, as a 32-year-old mother (six children, no formal education) said:

I: In these three photographs what can you see? Which photo do you like more?

M: Mother carry her child and play with him. I also play with him like this.

I: Which way do you like to play with him?

M: Now in this Shravan month[1], we buy toys for him and play with him. Now he can play with toys.

Toys may prevent crying as the following excerpt from a 25-year-old illiterate mother of two children explained:

---

[1]The month of Shravan is the fifth month of the Hindu calendar, which begins with Chaitra, and is the most auspicious month of the Chaturmas. On Purnima or full moon day, or during the course of the month, the star Shravan rules the sky; hence the month is called Shravan. This month is filled with innumerable religious festivals and ceremonies and almost all the days of this month are auspicious.

M: She is playing because it has [*godhood*] rattle toy. That's why she is playing. Is this [*ghughro*] rattle think it is *tamburo* [Indian guitar-type instrument].

I: Is it good play with it?

M: If the child is crying the child will be quiet, he likes it.

a.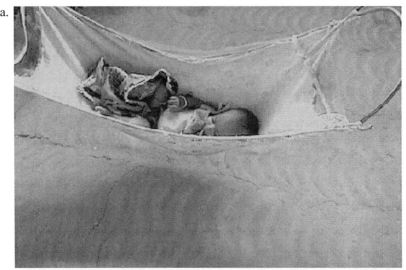

b.

FIGURE 5.17.   The cloth swing replaces body contact. Photos from Culture and Development Lab, University of Osnabrück.

We find the same ideas about adequate parenting for the two village communities who live in different parts of the world and follow different religious traditions in their everyday lives. Their parenting ideas are based on sociodemographic characteristics and living conditions. The overarching aim of both groups of village families is to support survival, health, and growth of their infants. Therefore they focus on expressions of negative emotionality and crying, which they try to prevent because crying is an expression of not feeling well and may thus be an indicator of a threat to the health and survival of the baby. All other parenting systems work toward that same goal. Body contact maintains closeness and allows monitoring of the infant's condition. Body stimulation is practiced with the goal of accelerating motor development. Early walking is important for helping with chores because every hand is needed for the subsistence of the family.

The Independent Model.   Qualitative analysis of the picture card interviews and the focus group discussions substantiates the quantitative data for the parenting model of independence as well. The face-to-face system implies a distinct focus on exclusive dyadic attention, which German mothers find the natural context of interaction, as they expressed in the focus group discussions: "The mother is completely involved with the baby—that is nice." Eye contact and the exchange of facial interactional cues are rewarding for the mother: "The mother tries to get the infant smiling," and "The mother is frustrated since the baby is not opening its eyes big and bright" (German focus group; Keller, Yovsi, & Voelker, 2002). Accordingly, the German women were somehow reluctant to accept the obviously missing focus on face-to-face exchange in the Nso videotapes ("She plays nicely, but does not have eye contact with the baby") and the exclusivity of attention ("The mother holds the baby nicely on her body, but directs her attention too often to other targets").

Object play is another asset of early care, because stimulating the senses and the cognitive system in general are considered crucial by this 29-year-old married Berlin mother of a 3-month-old firstborn daughter who wanted to continue to work as an occupational therapist after her maternity leave:

> I take this picture. Here it is not only the mother, who ehm, is in the focus of the baby, but a little toy that the baby is looking at, and, ehm, I think, other stimuli are, are also crucial, that the child, here it touches the wooden toy a little bit and also looks at it. Ehm … [belongs] to children's development, to offer toys. And this is, new material is added, that the baby can touch and possibly also a little, OK, may produce a little sound.

Beside the stimulating nature of toys, they also help the baby to be able to spend time without the mother, which is considered very important, as this 36-year-old Berlin mother (businesswoman who lives with her partner) who has a 3-month-old daughter explained:

M: In the end, it is important that the child also plays alone sometimes.
I: Yea.

M: I put her sometimes consciously alone somewhere, so that she is not always distracted or is played with all day long.

I: Ahm.

M: Has moments for herself. I find this ideal.

I: Yes. Why is it important, that she is also sometimes alone?

M: Yes, the child concentrates simply on her toys. Sometimes I deliberately put something to play with in, so that she can occupy herself with toys.

The child-centeredness as the central ingredient of the independent model of parenting is also expressed by the emphasis on the mothers paying undivided attention to their babies: "Just mother and child who are talking; listening to the baby, looking at the baby" (37-year-old single Los Angeles teacher and mother of a 3-month-old daughter). The infant-directed speech in pictures and videotapes was commended: "She adapts her style of talking nicely to the child" (German focus group; Keller, Yovsi, & Voelker, 2002).

The conversational nature of the interactions implies that both partners synchronize their activities as this Los Angeles mother (34 years old, married, two children, event manager) explained:

M: Well, it's like, "Look!" I mean as long as there's like a narrative and, and … uh. Something he was doing when you're filming was that he gives raspberries [mimics care noise with the lips] and I'll do it back, I'll do too this raspberry and you'll have a whole conversation!

I: Mhm.

M: And he'll stop all—he'll raspberry and he'll stop. And I'll raspberry and I'll stop.

I: Mhm.

M: And then he'll raspberry, like it's definitely an interaction as opposed to uh, raspberry together, you know—let's all raspberry together!

I: [Laughs] Right.

M: He definitely wants to do sort of a conversation and so I kind of look at that as OK, we're interacting with, uhm, you're playing and I'm playing near you or interacting with you.

These interactional modes leave a lot of room for the baby in terms of active involvement in his or her own development. A 35-year-old, married Los Angeles mother who is trained as a human resources manager and whose second-born son is 3 months old, reasoned about the importance of letting the baby develop his own interests in regard to this active involvement: "I was trying to play with him but he was more interested in looking in the mirror, let him look in the mirror. Here, let him explore … yeah … versus just trying to distract the baby 'cause it's more important the baby is exploring on its own."

Breastfeeding was also considered important by many of the women, but it is embedded in a different meaning system, as this 32-year-old wife and sales manager from Los Angeles, who has a 3-month-old daughter, explained with respect to the breastfeeding picture card: "It reminds me of my son, 'cause she's, he's holding her breast and she's staring into his eyes and everyone says, you know, it's a great time to do the bonding thing with your child, cause they stare in your eyes and you stare in their eyes. So that's why I like that."

However, there are other opinions, too, as a 35-year-old married resource manager who is the mother of two children explained: "And their babies are just close to them. I think it's a societal statement that you have to breastfeed. Uhm, I don't think it's the most important, I think they need more interaction. Cause some people could just nurse and then take it off and that's it."

The mothers with an independent cultural model of parenting also talk about body contact. Yet it is not body contact per se that is considered to be important by the Nso mothers. Similar to the functionality of breastfeeding, body contact is also functionally embedded into the conversational flow.

The same 35-year-old Los Angeles mother was talking generally to the interviewer about playing with the baby:

I: Mhm. And what's important about playing with the baby?
M: What's important? Just the contact, just, she's touching the baby, I don't know, I think she's touching the baby.
I: OK.
M: Well, I want the mommy touching the baby.
I: OK.
M: Just for me, it's that touching, you know, the baby can look into the mother's face. Kind of variety that it shows in the pictures, like ... .
I: Oh, we're going through them as well [the pictures].
M: Oh, OK. I just think it's the interaction, I like cooing, making the baby laugh and it looks like a good time.
I: OK. And what would be important about touching? Like if she touched him or her?
M: Oh I think the baby just loves the mother's touch.
I: OK.
M: I think the babies should be touched.

Here, the body contact, the touching again is an enabling condition for face-to-face contact, for exchanging positive interactional signals, and for conversation and dialogue. However, with the emphasis on early individuality and separateness, many mothers do not think that body contact is that important. One Los Angeles mother (34 years old, two children, married, event manager) was comparing two picture cards:

M: ... being ... uh—the difference between this and that one is that she's watching whereas this one is sort of a game, you know.
I: Mhm.

M: The parent or the adult there is doing a physical thing interacting with him. Even though they're not touching, I feel like the adult is playing with [him]. So you don't necessarily [need to] be touching, but just being present, interacting, engaging ...

The attitude of letting the baby take the lead is perhaps most expressed in the belief system about body stimulation. Both Berlin and Los Angeles mothers think that body stimulation is superimposing the babies' developmental tempo. They strictly disagree with that kind of motor training. One mother (31 years old, married, two children, event manager) from the Los Angeles sample put this perspective in plain language:

Yeah, well, I wouldn't put my baby on the feet like that. I think that's why ... uhm ... I don't know why. She doesn't like it—the baby doesn't like it and I'm always afraid that I'm gonna hurt their legs if I have them on their feet too long! So, it just doesn't feel that sturdy to me! I think of my baby as pretty sturdy but I tried ... just yesterday to hold her up on her feet and she did not like it at all ... so, that's why I chose it last.

She selected the picture demonstrating body stimulation last because she observed that her baby did not like it. The focus on independence is expressed by the following statement, also with respect to the parenting system of body stimulation, as this 37-year-old married Los Angeles mother (housewife) of a 3-month-old son explained:

M: And the baby is being held up ... uhm ... held up and building muscular development, because the baby is standing, although the baby is not looking at the mother. I don't like that, but my feeling with this is, that the baby probably spends most of the time looking at the mother and the mother is holding it up and helping the baby develop independence. Yet, there is human touch, so the baby doesn't feel observed in the process.

I: And what's important about developing, developing independence?

M: Well, I guess my feeling on that is, that babies are starting to realize that they are, they're a different person than the mother. So they're starting to develop, uhm, the knowledge that they're a separate person and that they're different.

The Berlin mothers had an identical point of view (Berlin mother, 40 years old, three children, married, has an MBA):

M: It is only ... the child does not have eye contact with the mom and [she] does not know, it's hard to say, whether the baby likes it that moment.

I: Yeah

M: Therefore I would select this last.

I: Mhm.

M: But I do not think it is wrong to hoist the baby sometimes

I: Yeah.

M: Although one should not do it, but somehow one plays with the baby, so …

I: Mhm.

M: It also is …

I: Why shouldn't one do it?

M: Because of the back. One should also not sit babies.

This perspective becomes even more pronounced when the German focus group women commented on the Nso videotapes. To put it simply, the Nso practice of body stimulation was strange for the German women: "They should not shake a small baby like this." They were equivocally concerned about what they considered to be very rough motor handling by Nso women.

Like the women with an interdependent cultural model, the women with an independent cultural model express very similar views on early child care, although they live in different countries with different histories. For them, exclusive dyadic attention, face-to-face contact, and object stimulation are the columns of good parenting. These domains are clearly pivotal even if they talk about other systems like breastfeeding or body contact. Acceleration of motor development is clearly not a part of their socialization agenda, as they expect the baby to take the lead with respect to the tempo of growth and development. The major difference between the two cultural prototypical models is that the women with an orientation toward interdependence focus on negative emotions, which they want to reduce immediately or, even better, prevent, as they may be signs of problems or sickness. Women with an orientation toward independence focus on positive emotions, which they want to maintain and maximize to keep the conversational flow going.

With respect to the methodology, we can conclude that the methods we used all draw a similar picture. Only the analysis of the content of parenting ethnotheories on the basis of the number of mentions of the different parenting systems revealed in some cases a somewhat distorted picture. It is also necessary in this case to respect the functional embeddedness of the content domains to have a complete picture. In that respect, the qualitative analysis is important to complement the quantitative data.

The Discourse Style in Parenting Ethnotheory Interviews

The excerpt examples that were presented with respect to the content analysis have already demonstrated that amount of speech differs tremendously across cultural environments. Table 5.5 presents the data for the samples of the two groups of cultural orientations. The quantitative analysis confirms the earlier impression that the amount of speech differs significantly. Middle-class Berlin and Los An-

TABLE 5.5

Amount of Maternal Speech in the Ethnotheory Interviews

	Cultural Community								
	Berlin[a]		Los Angeles[b]		Rural Nso[c]		Rural Gujarati[d]			
	M	SD	M	SD	M	SD	M	SD	F(3, 102)	η^2
Amount	63.52$_a$	32.48	49.67$_a$	23.48	25.15$_b$	11.54	10.09$_b$	8.88	23.96***	.41

Note. Four-level (culture) ANOVA. Indexed letters indicate results of simple main effects testing (with Bonferroni adjustment). η^2 = partial eta-square. [a]N = 41. [b]N = 23. [c]N = 29. [d]N = 13.
*p < .001.

geles mothers have a significantly higher amount in terms of the average number of words in one interactional turn than do the rural Nso and Gujarati mothers.

Figure 5.18 shows again that the turns of the rural Nso mothers are brief and skeletal, whereas the middle-class Los Angeles mothers' turns are embellished and elaborate.

The Los Angeles mother's answers can be seen as lectures about child care. She only needed brief prompts by the interviewer to continue talking. Her discourse expressed self-consciousness. The Nso mother needed long prompts from the interviewer to make brief statements.

The quantitative analysis of the picture-based interviews revealed that the discourse style of the German and the Euro-American mothers is characterized by more autonomy codings than that of the rural Cameroonian Nso mothers (Kärtner et al., 2006; see Table 5.6).

This pattern is consistent for the autonomy composite score with respect to mother and the subcomponents of I-statements and self-referral. German and Euro-American mothers used these discourse elements significantly more often than rural Cameroonian mothers. Euro-American mothers also referred significantly more often to a child's needs, preferences, and volitions than the rural Nso mothers. The picture is less clear for the baby's mental state composite score. Contrary to our assumption, Nso mothers talked more often about babies having cognitions and emotions than mothers from the urban middle-class samples.

For the composite score of relatedness and its subcategories reference to authority and social context the data were explicit (see Table 5.7).

Rural Cameroonian mothers referred significantly more often to the aspects of relatedness than the urban German and Euro-American mothers.

In the following section, the respective models of independence and interdependence are further elaborated based on a qualitative analysis of the interview transcripts, which reveal more details about these stylistic dimensions.

The Stylistic Embodiment of the Interdependent Cultural Model. In the picture card interview with a rural Nso mother, 21, who was raising her

Nso mother
(39 years, farmer, 8 children)

I: why is that one good?

M: Because she is lifting the child up as their are playing and he is feeling fine.

I: why is it good to be lifting the baby up like that?

M: So that the baby should become lighter.

I: Okay and what again? Have you seen how she is lifting,

M: Yes

I: why is it good to be lifting the child and laughing with him like that? What happens to the baby when the mother is playing and laughing with him?

M: The baby will be feeling fine.

LA mother (37 years, teacher, 3-month-old daughter)

I: so what it is important about um their- their health, yeah, well

M: for the health of the baby, the intelligence, you know, bonding also is important to, you know- like some people, you know train the baby to take a bottle, which I am in the process of doing, but- a lot of people do it so they can give it to somebody else the baby to feed the baby. But I think it's- it's really important in the beginning, in the first months of the baby's life for you to feed the baby, the mother to establish that bond. Especially in the first year of the baby's life.

I: hm

M: so it's for physical needs, intellectual needs, emotional needs, social- you know, everything.

I: ok, good. Here- I'll show you the next four ones.

M: ok

I: Which one would you choose next?

M: next, uh- I guess I would have to choose- I would choose this one.

I: ok- why did you choose this one?

M: uh- it looks like she is probably burping the baby <laughs> just- comes right after feeding the baby. It's very important because the baby becomes rid of gas, because if they don't they can feel falsely full and not get enough nutrition. Um- she could also be just holding the baby and soothing the baby, rubbing the baby's back which is important - something that you do all day, makes the baby feel good

I: why is it important to-

M: Well, just as a matter, in other words, there is like five- five things you're supposed to do. You're supposed to- um- soothe your baby, um- so that you can create the environment that the baby had inside you for nine months. So: the baby being close to you, um, having physical contact, um, shooshing the baby, like that it sounds like when the baby was inside you. So that why I think especially in the beginning, they really need that contact, you know, to feel, you know, loved and and safe, and again if she is burping for comfort and also not to- so that the baby can eat more, that's why you have to burp the baby in between the feedings, so

FIGURE 5.18. Comparison of turn length of a Los Angeles middle-class and a rural Nso mother.

TABLE 5.6
Composite and Component Categories of Autonomy

| | Cultural Community | | | | | | | |
| | Berlin[a] | | Los Angeles[b] | | Rural Nso[c] | | | |
	M	SD	M	SD	M	SD	F(2, 83)	η^2
Autonomy total	44.52[a]	20.11	54.35[a]	18.91	19.49[b]	12.32	22.82**	.36
Autonomy mother	38.51[a]	18.87	42.02[a]	17.68	7.44[b]	8.47	31.91**	.44
I-Statements	24.58[a]	8.86	27.78[a]	11.43	3.05[b]	3.96	55.89**	.57
Self-referral	13.93[a]	14.95	14.24[a]	13.17	4.39[b]	7.79	4.54*	.10
Mental state baby	6.01[a]	4.64	12.32[b]	7.53	12.06[b]	7.39	10.35**	.20
Preference	3.42[a]	4.25	6.46[b]	6.47	.72[a]	1.22	9.30**	.18
Emotion	.42[a]	1.01	1.64[a]	2.76	5.60[b]	3.85	30.58**	.42
Cognition	2.16[a]	2.61	4.21	4.78	5.74[b]	4.43	6.62*	.14

Note. Three-level (culture) MANOVA with significant multivariate main effect for culture on narrative style (component variables only: I-statements, self-referral, emotion, cognition, preference), Wilks's $\lambda = .23$, F(10, 158) = 17.11, $p < .001$, $\eta^2 = .52$, followed by univariate analyses. Indexed letters indicate results of simple main effects testing (with Bonferroni adjustment). η^2 = partial eta-square. All mean scores indicate relative frequency per 1,000 words. [a]$N = 40$. [b]$N = 24$. [c]$N = 22$.
*p < .01. **p < .001.

TABLE 5.7
Composite and Component Categories of Relatedness

| | Cultural Community | | | | | | | |
| | Berlin[a] | | Los Angeles[b] | | Rural Nso[c] | | | |
	M	SD	M	SD	M	SD	F(2, 83)	η^2
Relatedness	1.87[a]	3.48	4.42[a]	4.33	11.69[b]	6.19	33.58*	.45
Reference to authority	.68[a]	1.65	1.44[a]	2.68	4.86[b]	4.37	15.86*	.28
Social context	1.19[a]	2.33	2.98[a]	2.71	6.82[b]	4.21	24.84*	.37

Note. Three-level (culture) MANOVA with significant multivariate main effect for culture on narrative style (component variables only: reference to authority and social context), Wilks's $\lambda = .55$, F(4, 164) = 14.48, $p < .001$, $\eta^2 = .16$, followed by univariate analyses. Indexed letters indicate results of simple main effects testing (with Bonferroni adjustment). η^2 = partial eta-square. All mean scores indicate relative frequency per 1000 words. [a]$N = 40$. [b]$N = 24$. [c]$N = 22$.
*p < .001.

3-month-old daughter in her parents' house and working as a farmer, the following discourse emerged (Keller, Hentschel, et al., 2004):

I: These are pictures of mothers with their 3-month-old babies. Look at these five pictures and tell me which one is the best for you.

M: This one where she is breastfeeding the baby.

I: Why that one first? I would like you to always tell me the reason you choose any picture.

M: I took this because if she giving breast to child then she wants that child should be strong enough and also have strength in his body and also being fine.

Because Lamnso has no gender differences in the third-person pronoun, the original text does not offer any clues as to whether the speaker might be identifying the baby in the picture with her own son (as the English translation of the text suggests). The semantic concepts that are rather explicitly foregrounded in this turn are strength and well-being (strong enough, strength, fine).

I: Have you seen the way she is breastfeeding?
M: Mmh yes
I: Why is it good to do like that?
M: So that the mouth of the child should not be big. When you cuddle the child while breastfeeding him like this, then he will be able to suck well.

The use of the personal pronoun *you* ("When you cuddle the child") is commonly used as a generalizing indefinite pronoun, and it helps to include the interviewer within the statement. The statement reflects the shared meaning system: Everybody should cuddle their baby this way. The particular way of Nso caregiving is a normative obligation.

I: Why is it good for the child to be sucking well?
M: Then he will have much strength.

Here she reintroduced the concept of strength as a desirable developmental goal for a baby. This mother restricted her remarks to the process of optimizing breastfeeding, which is conceived of as important to ensure the success of the underlying aim; that is, to make the child strong. Growth and health are the main objectives. This rural mother focused on the relationship, and placed the mother and child in hierarchical positions of expert and novice. The mother is responsible for the child's development. The use of the collective *you* to express her parenting ideas also draws the interviewer into the social communicative process and allows communal accounts.

The following interview with a 16-year-old illiterate Rajput mother, who has a 3-month-old baby, lives with her husband's family, and works as a day laborer, reveals yet another aspect of the discourse style, which can be characterized as following an interdependent cultural model:

I: What can you see in these photographs?
M: The child is playing with the ball.

Selecting a picture that represents best parental care is a difficult task for many of the rural, poorly educated mothers, as the concept of choice is completely alien to them. She started to describe what she saw in one of the pictures.

The choices offered by the interviewer with the next question were also hard to manage for this mother:

I: What is nice, playing close to the child or away from him?
M: Everything is nice.
I: When should we make the child play with the ball?
M: When he is crying.
I: If he is crying?
M: Then only should make him play with the ball.

The statements are normative, as expressed by the verb *should.* With the next statement she also made clear that she was not referring to a personal opinion, but that there is a normative understanding of what to do. The interviewer also referred to the normative framework:

I: Why should we carry the children? What happens by that?
M: We do that always. If the child is crying we have to do it.

This excerpt also reveals that interviewers have to play different roles across cultural environments to elicit ethnotheoretical statements (see also chap. 4, this volume). As compared to the "Hmm" that is often sufficient to keep the flow of thoughts going in an urban educated mother, the rural mothers need to be interviewed with more explicit verbal instigation and questions are repeated often.

The stylistic analyses of the interview transcripts confirm, using both quantitative and qualitative methodology, the basic elements of the discourse styles that have been described for interactions with preschool children. The interdependent model is associated with a hardly elaborated, skeletal, descriptive, and repetitive style that is socially situated and carries moral meanings and communal obligations. Although in the quantitative analyses there is a lot of reference to emotions, they are not mentioned for their own sake, but as indicators of health and well-being.

The Stylistic Embodiment of the Independent Cultural Model.   In a picture card interview with a 30-year-old middle-class Euro-American mother, who lives with her 3-month-old daughter and her husband in Los Angeles and works as a self-employed personal trainer, the milestones of the independence model were elaborated on (see Keller, Hentschel, et al., 2004). The mother selected the breastfeeding photo as her highest priority.

I: Why did you choose that?
M: Uhm … because of all the research saying how good it is for the baby to [have] an hour to […] their defenses and then also for bonding. In the first 3 months breastfeeding is the only thing that distinguishes the mother from anyone else. You know what I mean?

It is obvious that this mother has an elaborative way of talking. She justified her judgment with reference to scientific authority ("research"). Justifications are typical components of narratives and discourses focusing on independence. She continued elaborating the uniqueness of the mother, which is established for the baby through breastfeeding ("distinguishing the mother from anyone else").

The same behavioral choice (breastfeeding) is embedded in a different stylistic fabric with personal evaluations that are marked quite clearly as such ("I feel," "I guess," "I think," "I mean"). She is also referring to the baby as an independent person with his or her own needs and desires for whom it is important to develop self-esteem. Attachment and bonding occur between two separate and independent persons.

A similar concept was developed by a 39-year-old middle-class German mother from Berlin who lives in an unmarried partnership, has three children, and works as a self-employed travel agent (Keller, Hentschel, et al., 2004).

I: Which of the pictures shows what you consider to be most important in caring for a 3-month-old baby?

M: Yes, OK, I mean, [the] breastfeeding is a survival measure, but, yes, sure but now purely for the child itself I mean, simply like the body contact. Well I find every mother here does in her way something now with the child.
The mother started with a statement containing three evaluations ("I mean" twice, and "I find"), referring to mentalistic states.

I: If you have to decide, which is most important?

M: The most important for the baby? Yes, breastfeeding the baby. I would say so.
The mother acts as an independent agent with a personal evaluation ("I would say so").

I: Why is breastfeeding important?

M: Yes, well I am convinced of this that this is good for the child, well, instead of the bottle and yes body contact simply all [tag question]. Yes because this is simply good. Well, I, yes, have had the experience that the children seldom fall ill. I hope that this stays like that. It is easy, it is tasty, convenient. There are only factors that speak for it. Yes, and he finds it totally great, so great no child has found it so far. He could only reach for it, yes, well, therefore. Yes, and because it's nice, too.

She continued to present herself as an independent agent ("I am convinced," "I had the experience," "I hope"). She referred to her own child (and her own experiences), presenting the baby as an individual with his or her own references and likes ("he loves it so much"; "he could breastfeed all the time"). Furthermore, she differentiated the baby from other children ("no other child loved it that much"). She justified ("children do not become ill so easily") and elaborated ("It is simple, tasty and convenient"; "it is nice") her point of view. Discourse markers appear mainly at the beginning and the end of the utterance, which shows that she followed a coherent flow of connotations that are linked to the concept of breastfeeding.

The Los Angeles and Berlin mothers clearly expressed an independent understanding of the person in their ethnotheoretical accounts. They usually referred to their own experience by using mentalistic terms. They referred to their own babies and to babies in general with an understanding of an individual with its own needs, desires and preferences, an individual agent. The relationship between mother and baby develops between two separate and independent persons. Their language was evaluative and judgmental. They justified and elaborated their opinions. Moreover, when they talked about emotions, they also referred to separate agencies. Experiencing and expressing positive emotions, having fun, and entertainment are primary objectives in their own right and they are having a good time (Umm, it just seems like she's sort of enjoying the interaction with the baby). Having positive emotions and fun justifies practices that they would normally reject as good parental care, thus even dissociating maternal and infants' emotional states. Talking about emotions can be regarded as an affirmation of the importance of the individual.

Conclusion: Independent and Interdependent Models of Parenting Ethnotheories

Like socialization goals, parenting ethnotheories also reflect the different models of parenting related to the two prototypical cultural environments. Content and style consistently express different emphases on independence and interdependence. The model of independence incorporates a roughly equal interactional exchange between parent and infant, assigning the infant wishes, desires, and wants that need to be taken seriously. The concept is child centered and nurtures the infant's individuality. The model of interdependence incorporates a hierarchical, role-defined social model with the parental responsibility being to monitor health, teach life skills, and stimulate growth and development. As such, the model is adult centered and assigns the infant the proper place in the community. The model of interdependence is closed and community controlled with the consequence that intracultural variability is low. The independent model, on the other hand, embodies more personal variability with individual nuances to the general picture. This attitude reflects the importance of individual choices. However, mothers with an independent cultural model also share the universe of meaning and feel that their worldview is part of an established knowledge system. With the linguistic analysis of particles in the Berlin interviews, Hentschel and Keller (2006) demonstrated that the Berlin corpus shows a significantly higher frequency of *halt* (just) and *eben* (even) than the texts of two comparative corpuses of language samples of German adults. These differences indicate that the mothers not only felt sure that the concepts they were speaking about were unalterable, but that they also had positive feelings about them.

To systematically analyze intracultural variations and response styles we reanalyzed the data from the questionnaire study (Lamm & Keller, 2006). Levene tests revealed that the variances within the groups differ significantly for the socialization goals and parenting ethnotheories. The samples with an independent cultural model from Los Angeles, Berlin, and Athens showed significantly more intracultural variation on the relational scales of socialization goals and parenting ethnotheories than the samples with an interdependent cultural model from rural Cameroon and India. Surprisingly, however, there was more intracultural variation on the autonomous scales of socialization goals and parenting ethnotheories in the group with an interdependent cultural model than in the group with an independent model. To better understand this result, we looked in more detail at the Nso and Gujarati samples as compared to the independent samples (see Figure 5.19).

Clearly the assumption of the low intracultural variance has been confirmed for the rural Nso women, but not for the women from rural Gujarat. Whereas the Nso participants show the lowest intracultural variation in all measures, the Gujarati women have the highest intracultural variation for autonomous socialization goals as well as autonomous parenting ethnotheories. Nevertheless, the pattern of results is the same for both samples with an interdependent sociocultural orientation. There is more intracultural variation on the autonomous subscales compared to the relational subscales in the Nso sample as well. In contrast, the intracultural variation in the groups with an independent cultural model is independent of the scale content and remains the same for all measures. Thus, this content specificity seems to be unique to the samples with an interdependent cultural model. This result confirms our assumption that the interdependent cultural model of parenting is strictly defined by a network of moral rules focusing on harmonic functioning of the group, which is the main socialization goal. That is the reason why there is very

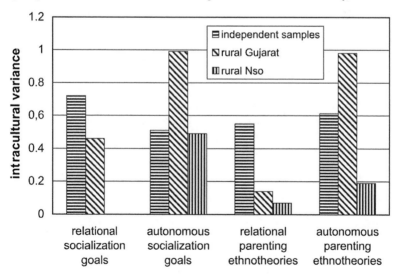

FIGURE 5.19.   Intracultural variation in the reference to autonomy and relatedness in Cameroonian Nso and Gujarati Rajput mothers as compared with the independent samples.

little intracultural variation allowed on the subscales concerning relatedness. On the other hand, the subscales about autonomy deal with an aspect that is not an explicit part of the cultural model of interdependence. Therefore there could be uncertainty concerning the required ratings on these subscales, which caused more intracultural variation.

With respect to extreme response behavior, a MANOVA revealed that the groups differ statistically significantly in the frequency of extreme scores on all scales. As expected, mothers with an interdependent cultural model showed more extreme responses than the mothers with an independent model. This result strengthens the line of arguments that opinions that are communally shared can be regarded as moral rules that are axiomatic and have to be followed (Lamm & Keller, 2006).

Thus intracultural variation and response behavior are also meaningful aspects of cultural models of parenting.

Interactional Contexts

Nonverbal Parenting Behaviors

This section deals with the occurrence of the body contact, body stimulation, face-to-face context, and object stimulation parenting systems, and the interactional mechanisms of contingency and warmth toward positive and negative stimuli as specified in the component model of parenting (see chap. 2, this volume) for the two prototypical cultural environments. I do not report data on the primary care parenting system here because the analyses are based on videotaped free-play interactions, where primary care usually does not occur. It is obvious that primary care occurs in all cultural environments, nevertheless there are also culturally informed practices (Yovsi, 2003; Yovsi & Keller, 2003) that I do not address here. I demonstrated in Figure 2.7 that the four parenting systems—body contact, body stimulation, face-to-face context, and body stimulation—occur in free-play interactions between mother and infant in sociodemographically diverse cultural communities. To find out whether there are consistent patterns that can be associated with the cultural models of independence and interdependence, respectively, we computed hierarchical cluster analyses based on these data (Keller, Kuensemueller, et al., 2005). We used the "linkage between groups" cluster method on the basis of squared Euclidian distances. A sudden increase in the distance between merged clusters revealed an optimal solution of two clusters (cf. Table 5.8).

Cluster 1 describes a caregiving pattern consisting of extensive body contact, substantial body stimulation, less face-to-face orientation, and very low object stimulation. Cluster 2 describes a pattern consisting of high amounts of face-to-face contexts, less body stimulation, less object stimulation, and very low body contact. If we identify the cultural background of the participants contributing to the clusters, we can verify that Cluster 1 consists of 83% of participants from rural Cameroonian Nso, Indian

TABLE 5.8
Cluster Analysis of the Parenting Systems

	Variable	Cluster 1[a]		Cluster 2[b]		
		M	SD	M	SD	F
Cluster variables	Object stimulation %	8.09	17.40	36.47	27.40	74.26**
	Body stimulation %	59.78	32.63	47.45	18.60	10.31*
	Body contact %	84.49	22.24	23.12	19.98	405.86**
	Face-to-face exchange %	31.31	26.19	74.25	20.95	157.58**
	Mutual eye contact %	29.06	29.78	46.85	24.80	20.29**
Additional variables	Latencies (Contingency 1)	0.049	0.087	0.150	0.147	34.30**
	Responsiveness (Contingency 2)	0.347	0.254	0.354	0.222	0.03
	Warmth combined index	0.96	0.92	1.40	0.76	3.84
	Baby talk in %	42.91	34.24	59.22	27.02	13.44**
	Smiling in %	39.65	33.66	44.67	27.52	1.28
	Regulatory activity (C-)	1.95	2.48	1.08	1.41	3.47
	Empathy (W-)	0.15	0.25	0.11	0.15	0.66
Sociodemographic profile	Years of schooling, mother	7.87	3.73	13.71	3.25	115.54**
	Age of mother	26.09	5.70	29.68	3.89	18.13**
	Locality	86 rural (87.8%); 12 urban (12.2%)		30 rural (31.6%); 65 urban (68.4%)		73.05**
	Birth order	33 firstborns (33.7%); 65 later-borns (66.3%)		83 firstborns (87.4%); 12 later-borns (12.6%)		69.34**
	Sex of infant	46 boys (46.9%); 52 girls (53.1%)		49 boys (51.6%); 46 girls (48.4%)		2.12

[a]N = 98: Cameroonian Nso = 26 (100%); Costa Ricans = 9 (90.5%); Indian Gujarati = 36 (92.3%); Greeks = 12 (23.5%); Germans = 5 (8.9%). Cameroonian Nso = 0 (0%); Costa Ricans = 2 (9.5%); Indian Gujarati = 3 (7.7%); Greeks = 39 (76.5%); Germans = 51 (91.1%).
*p < .01. **p < .001.

Gujarati, and low-income Costa Rican[2] mothers, whereas Cluster 2 is comprised of 95% participants from German and Greek middle-class households. To test the occurrence of interactional mechanisms as part of these parenting styles, we computed the respective values for the two clusters (see Table 5.8). We find significantly more contingent responsiveness toward infants' positive signals in Cluster 2 than in Cluster 1. The indexes of warmth as expressed in vocal and facial expressions do not differ between the clusters. With respect to contingency and warmth toward negative infant cues, we find more regulatory activity (Contingency–) and slightly more empathy (Warmth–) in Cluster 1, which, however, both fail to reach the 5% significance level. These data confirm the existence of two patterns of parenting in the nonverbal domain that can be clearly associated with the two prototypical sociocultural environments. Distal parenting with a focus on face-to-face contact with contingent responsiveness and object stimulation occurs in middle-class Western families, whereas proximal parenting with a focus on body contact and, thus, body warmth and body stimulation occurs in rural villagers and families belonging to lower socioeconomic levels with similar sociodemographic characteristics like low levels of education and early reproduction (Keller, Lohaus, et al., 2004).

To substantiate these styles we conducted more studies with the same empirical setup; that is, videotaping free-play situations between mothers and their 3-month-old infants with different samples from the same cultural communities (Keller, Borke, et al., 2005). The results of these studies are presented in Table 5.9.

The data clearly confirm the existence of the two styles associated with the two sociocultural environments. There are significant differences among the four parenting systems. Based on the results of the ethnotheory interviews, we formed two styles from the four parenting systems: Body contact and body stimulation form a proximal style of parenting and face-to-face context and object stimulation form a distal style of parenting. These two styles also differ significantly in the expected direction. In regard to the similarity among the samples selected to represent the respective cultural model, the body contact and the object stimulation systems reveal the clearest picture. The three independent samples do not differ from each other, nor do the two interdependent samples. Concerning the face-to-face system, the Los Angeles mothers use the face-to-face context surprisingly little, whereas the rural Nso mothers use this system to a surprising degree. The Los Angeles data may be explained by the prevalence of the object stimulation system, which has the highest occurrence among all samples and may overrun to some extent the face-to-face system. Amazingly, the Los Angeles mothers were already using the interactional format of joint attention—reading books together with the baby and other situations—where both directed their attention jointly to an object. These kinds of interactional situations are usually performed with children in the second part of the first year in middle-class Western families. Nevertheless, the early emphasis of joint attention supports the view of a mental agent

---

[2]We included a low-income, low-education sample from Costa Rica here because the sociodemographic characteristics are similar to those of the villagers.

TABLE 5.9

The Occurrence of the Parenting Systems and Parenting Styles in the Independent and Interdependent Communities

	Cultural Community										
	Germans[a]		Los Angeles[b]		Athens, Greece[c]		Rural Nso, Cameroon[d]		Rural Gujarati, India[e]		
Parenting system	M	SD	M	SD	M	SD	M	SD	M	SD	$F_{(4, 307)}$	η^2
Body contact	32.96_a	31.1	$43.20_{a/b}$	31.0	20.28_a	27.7	80.77	21.3	59.73_b	29.9	50.05*	.39
Face-to-face context	77.82_a	19.7	56.80_b	22.4	77.07_a	18.4	58.50_b	28.8	26.04	23.9	45.06*	.37
Body stimulation	59.28_a	21.3	55.00_a	21.8	51.34_a	25.4	77.72	20.0	29.79	23.5	40.62*	.35
Object stimulation	39.54_a	28.0	44.95_a	35.3	38.72_a	34.8	10.30_b	23.6	2.15_b	5.8	31.64*	.29
Distal parenting	58.68_a	18.5	50.88_a	22.6	57.90_a	19.9	34.40	19.3	14.09	12.3	62.14*	.45
Proximal parenting	46.12_a	19.2	49.10_a	20.8	35.81_a	22.8	79.24	15.7	44.76_a	18.0	59.97*	.44

Note. Five-level (culture) MANOVA with significant multivariate main effect for culture on parenting system, Wilks's $\lambda = 27$, $F_{(16, 929.4)} = 31.28$, $p < .001$, $\eta^2 = .28$, followed by univariate analyses. Indexed letters indicate results of simple main effects testing (with Bonferroni adjustment). η^2 = partial eta-square. All mean scores indicate the appearance of the respective parenting system (in per cent).
[a]N = 119 (Berlin, 2002, n = 39; Marburg, 2000, n = 59; Muenster, 1993, n = 21). [b]N = 20. [c]N = 29. [d]N = 96. [e]N = 48.
*p < .001.

model of the baby. The Nso data might be related to the prevalence of the body stimulation system; they have the highest occurrence among all samples. Body stimulation as demonstrated by the Nso mothers represents an activity that is performed in an en face position. It is a rhythmic lifting up and down of the baby a couple of times, which is interrupted with bouts of face-to-face contact. As such, the face-to-face context scores may be regarded as a consequence of the focus on body stimulation. As the analysis of the parenting ethnotheories has revealed, particular systems may be regarded as pivotal with other systems supporting them, like breastfeeding creating a situation that is optimal for face-to-face contact, as one of the Los Angeles mothers explained. Body stimulation is lowest in the Indian Gujarati sample, which can be explained by the poor physical condition of the Rajput mothers, who cannot afford high-energetic parenting behaviors. These data from different samples clearly reveal that the two cultural environments emphasize different parenting styles in the nonverbal domain, which can be summarized as distal and proximal parenting styles.

To better understand the cooccurrences of the parenting systems we analyzed the percentage distribution of the 10-second intervals for all possible combinations of the four systems separately for the two cultural models. The exclusive combination of body contact and body stimulation is more frequent in the interdependent sample (23.8% of the intervals) and the exclusive combination of face-to-face context and object stimulation appears more often in the independent samples (17.5% of the intervals). Other patterns of parenting occurring during the 10-second intervals are exclusive face-to-face context (12.1%); face-to-face context and body stimulation (21.0%); face-to-face context, body stimulation, and object stimulation (10.1%) in the independent samples; and body contact and face-to-face context (16.8%) in the interdependent sample.

Generally, all combinations in which body contact occurs occur more frequently in the interdependent samples, and all combinations in which face-to-face context occurs occur more frequently in the independent samples. These results demonstrate the dominance of these two parenting systems for the two cultural models for the early phase of infancy. The special case of the combination of face-to-face context and body contact occurs more frequently in the interdependent sample. It might be easier to simultaneously organize a body contact priority with a face-to-face context than the other way around. The results demonstrate that all combinations are physically possible but empirically they are realized differently.

The relations among the four parenting systems were further analyzed with Pearson product–moment correlations (Keller, Borke, et al., 2005). Table 5.10 shows the correlations for the combined independent and interdependent samples. There are negative correlations between body contact and face-to-face exchange, and object stimulation. There are also negative correlations between object stimulation and body stimulation. There is a positive correlation between body contact and body stimulation.

To test the relation between the two combined parenting styles we included proximal parenting and distal parenting as additional variables. Again we com-

TABLE 5.10

Correlations Between Parenting Systems and With Parenting Styles

	Body Stimulation	Object Stimulation	Face-to-Face Context	Distal Parenting	Proximal Parenting
Body contact	.22**	−.51**	−.39**	−.55**	.85**
Body stimulation	—	−.12*	.20**	.04	.71**
Object stimulation		—	.34**	.83**	−.44**
Face-to-face context			—	.81**	−.18**

Note. N = 312.
*p < .05. **p < .01.

puted Pearson product–moment correlations to test the relations. We found a significant negative correlation between the two parenting styles ($r = -.52, p < .01$).

The behavioral analyses of the free-play situations convincingly reveal that the four systems—body contact, body stimulation, face-to-face context, and object stimulation—are appropriate for analyzing interactional behavior. The two prototypical cultural environments emphasize the four systems differently. With different statistical methods we were able to demonstrate that the face-to-face context is central for the independent cultural model, whereas the body contact system is central to the interdependent model. The Euro-American mothers moreover show an unexpected early focus on joint attentional processes with toys during the free-play situations. The nonverbal interactional experiences of the 3-month-old babies can be described as proximal (body contact and body stimulation) in the interdependent cultural model, and distal (face-to-face context and object stimulation) in the independent cultural model.

The Timing of the Interactional Flow

Contingency Analyses.   As we saw in Figure 2.9, contingency toward positive infant signals differs across the two prototypical sociocultural environments. In line with the independent model of parenting, infants in middle-class Western families experience more contingent responsiveness in the face-to-face context than do infants of rural farmers, irrespective of the amount of the face-to-face context. To substantiate these results, we conducted several cross-cultural analyses. In the first study we tested the contingent responsiveness during free-play situations with the mother and the 3-month-old infant in the three middle-class Western samples (Keller, Chasiotis, & Runde, 1992): German mothers from Osnabrück and Munich, Euro-American mothers from Salt Lake City, and Greek mothers from an urban area in northern Greece. The onsets and offsets of infants' behaviors (smiling, looking into the mother's face, looking at the surroundings, vocalizing) and mothers' behaviors (smiling, looking into the infant's face, looking at the surroundings, vocal and verbal behavior, eye greeting) were assessed. The results revealed similarly structured behavioral regulations in the three samples. The nonverbal contingent responses of the mothers from the three samples did not differ, although the German mothers used the verbal and vocal mode significantly more often than the Greek and the Euro-American mothers.

In another study we compared the contingency experiences of 21 3-month-old Cameroonian Nso babies and 31 German middle-class babies with our empirical setup of interactional free-play situations in the families' homes (Keller, Kärtner, et al., 2005).

Using a time-sampling method based on 10-second intervals, the infant's state (awake or sleepy) and mood (negative, neutral, or positive) was coded from the videotapes. The analysis was restricted to nonverbal contingent responses (see chap. 4, this volume).

To analyze differences between the two samples concerning mothers' contingent responses, we conducted analyses of covariance (ANCOVAs) controlling for a set of variables that may be potential confounds. The variables for the babies were gender and birth order (firstborn or later-born). The variable for the mothers was education operationalized as years of schooling z standardized within cultures. There was a highly significant main effect of culture on contingent responsiveness, $F(1, 44) = 13.49$, $p < .01$, with German mothers ($M = .23$, $SD = .16$) showing higher degrees of contingent responsiveness toward their 3-month-old babies than Nso mothers ($M = .07$, $SD = .16$). The same held true for the latency score, indicating the number of latencies per minute with the baby being in an alert positive state. German babies ($M = .97$, $SD = .99$) experienced significantly more latencies than Nso babies ($M = .39$, $SD = .42$), $F(1, 46) = 5.44$, $p < .05$ (Keller, Kärtner, et al., 2005).

In a study comparing 30 Nso mother–infant vocal and verbal patterns with those of 20 middle-class German mother–infant pairs (the babies were 3 months old for both groups; Keller, Otto, Yovsi, & Lohaus, 2006), the results revealed that contingent responses showed statistically significant differences between Nso and German mothers with respect to neutral child vocalizations. German mothers reacted contingently more often to neutral and positive child vocalizations than the Cameroonian Nso mothers, $\chi^2(1, N = 4,495) = 10,08$, $p < .001$. There was no statistical effect between the two groups concerning negative child vocalizations.

The results for the noncontingent maternal reactions, that is, no verbal and vocal response within the 1-second interval following the child vocalization, showed significant effects relating to negative infant signals: German mothers showed no verbal and vocal reaction to crying or whining signals more often than the Cameroonian Nso mothers, $\chi^2(1, N = 2,210) = 4.08$, $p < .05$. There were no differences in noncontingent reactions with respect to neutral signals.

This set of different studies confirms that contingent responsiveness in the face-to-face context is part of a distal parenting style that characterizes middle-class urban families more than rural subsistence-based families.

Synchronous Verbal and Vocal Interactions.   Gratier (2003) found there were interesting cultural differences in vocal mother–infant interactions. She compared Indian mother–infant pairs living in India, French mother–infant pairs living in France, and Indian mother–infant pairs living in the United States. All families lived in urban areas. As compared to the French and Indian immigrant mothers, the Indian mothers expressed more togetherness with their babies, as indexed by less space between vocal turns and more overlap of mother and baby vocalizations. This pattern can be interpreted as supporting symbiosis and interpersonal fusion as the expression of the cultural model of interdependence.

To test the validity of this pattern with respect to the two prototypical pathways, we analyzed the vocal and verbal interactions of the 30 Cameroonian Nso farmer mothers and 20 middle-class German mothers with respect to overlapping, synchronous vocal and verbal patterns during the first 3 months of life (Keller, Otto, et al., 2006). The data revealed that Cameroonian Nso mothers talk and vocalize significantly more often during infants' vocalizations than German mothers for the three assessments at 4, 8, and 12 weeks (see Figure 5.20).

This holds true for all types of vocalizations: positive, negative, and neutral (see Figure 5.21). To increase the database, we compiled the three assessments.

However, Cameroonian Nso mothers vocalize most synchronously during infants' negative vocalizations. German mothers verbalize equally during positive and negative infant vocalizations. Both groups of mothers vocalize and verbalize least during neutral vocalizations.

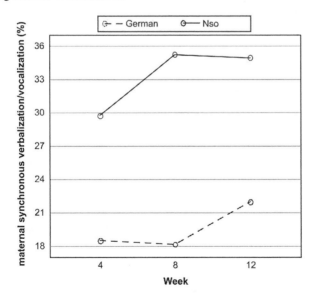

FIGURE 5.20.   The amount of synchronous vocalizations in Nso and German mother–infant interactions during Weeks 4, 8, and 12.

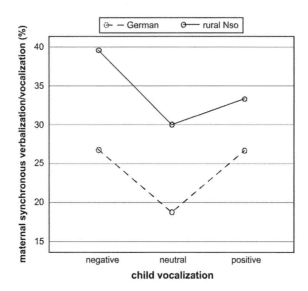

FIGURE 5.21.   Synchronous vocalizations during positive, negative, and neutral infant vocalizations.

Our data imply that mothers with an interdependent cultural model pattern the interactional flow more synchronously with overlapping vocalizations and verbalizations. The middle-class German mothers, on the other hand, emphasize the ego boundaries of the baby with their prevalent turn-taking pattern of interactional exchange. The Indian mothers in Gratier's (2003) study can also be assumed to be more oriented toward the cultural model of interdependence than the French mothers. Both sets of data, Gratier's (2003) and ours (Keller, Otto, et al., 2006), can therefore be regarded as revealing similar results.

The Narrative Envelope: Conversational Styles

Cultural environments also differ as to the emphasis they put on the verbal enactment of behavior, intentions, moods, and states. Accordingly, the tendency to react verbally to infant cues also differs as we have demonstrated with the contingency analyses. In an earlier cross-cultural study comparing middle-class German and Greek mothers with Trobriand islanders and Yanomami Indians interacting with their babies who are a few months old (Keller, Schölmerich, & Eibl-Eibesfeldt, 1988; Schölmerich, Keller, & Leyendecker, 1991) we found that German and Greek infants vocalized more than Trobriand and Yanomami infants and in turn received more vocal and verbal responses from their caregivers. These data also highlight that caregivers' and infants' behaviors are not independent from each other but linked in a meaningful way.

To compare the amount of the mothers' vocal and verbal behavior during the free-play interactional situations with their 3-month-old infants, we analyzed the amounts of language spoken in terms of vocal and verbal utterances during 10 minutes of interaction time for our different samples (see Table 5.11). Due to translation problems, data are not available for the rural Gujarati sample.

TABLE 5.11
Amount of Maternal Speech in Mother–Infant Interaction

	Cultural Community									
	German[a]		Los Angeles[b]		Athens[c]		Rural Nso[d]			
	M	SD	M	SD	M	SD	M	SD	F(3, 194)	η^2
Amount	568.77$_a$	29.88	585.00$_a$	56.41	247.06$_b$	159.18	259.70$_b$	179.25	22.93*	.26

Note. Four-level (culture) ANOVA. Indexed letters indicate results of simple main effects testing (with Bonferroni adjustment). η^2 = partial eta-square.
[a]German mothers were sampled in Berlin, Muenster, and Marburg; N = 82. [b]N = 23. [c]N = 49. [d]N = 44.
*$p < .001$.

The data reveal that the Berlin and Los Angeles mothers use a similarly high amount of language when interacting with their 3-month-old babies, whereas the rural Nso mothers use the expected low amount of language during the same situations. However, the Athens mothers also have a surprisingly low amount, which also differs from earlier data sets in which the Greek mothers scored as high as the Euro-American mothers (Keller, Chasiotis, & Runde, 1992).

What mothers say to their small babies during interactional situations and how they phrase it is another window into their cultural model of parenting. For these analyses, the verbal and vocal exchanges of mothers with their 3-month-old babies in free-play interaction situations were analyzed with the coding schemes autonomy and relatedness (see chap. 4, this volume).

Table 5.12 reports the composite score of autonomy and relatedness for three samples with an independent cultural model as compared to a sample of rural Cameroonian Nso mothers representing the interdependent cultural model.

TABLE 5.12
Composite Measures of Maternal Conversational Style in Mother–Infant Interaction

	Cultural Community									
	German[a]		Los Angeles[b]		Athens[c]		Rural Nso[d]			
	M	SD	M	SD	M	SD	M	SD	F(3, 194)	η^2
Autonomy	47.49$_{a/b}$	2.05	56.63$_a$	3.87	42.58$_b$	2.65	11.44$_c$	2.80	45.63*	.41
Relatedness	12.80$_a$	3.90	18.98$_{a/b}$	7.35	40.29$_b$	5.04	80.98$_c$	5.32	37.70*	.37

Note. Four-level (culture) MANOVA with significant multivariate main effect for culture on conversational style, Wilks's λ = .44, F(6, 386) = 32.22, $p < .001$, η^2 = .33, followed by univariate analyses. Indexed letters indicate results of simple main effects testing (with Bonferroni adjustment). η^2 = partial eta-square. All mean scores indicate relative frequency per 1000 words.
[a]German mothers were sampled in Berlin, Muenster, and Marburg; N = 82. [b]N = 23. [c]N = 49. [d]N = 44.
*$p < .001$.

The results demonstrate that the three samples of middle-class urban mothers refer significantly more to autonomy than the rural Cameroonian mothers when they converse with their babies during interaction situations. In contrast, the Nso mothers talk significantly more about relatedness than the Western urban mothers. There are, however, also differences among the three samples having an independent model, with the Athens mothers talking in about equal amounts about autonomy and relatedness.

In a second study we compared again the conversational styles during free-play interactions of middle-class German mothers and Cameroonian Nso farmer mothers with two different samples (Keller, Yovsi, et al., 2004).

The results again show a significant main effect for the cultural group, $F(2, 47)$ $= 64.09, p < .001, \eta^2 = .73$. The univariate analyses show that the proportion of verbal interactions related to supporting autonomy is significantly higher in the German sample, $F(1, 48) = 92.40, p < .001, \eta^2 = .66$, whereas relatedness supporting verbal interactions is more prominent in the Nso sample, $F(1, 48) = 52.50, p < .001, \eta^2 = .529$. Figure 5.22 shows the distributions.

The two conversational styles were also able to be confirmed with qualitative analyses of the interaction transcripts (Demuth, Abels, & Keller, in press; Keller, 2004b; Keller & Demuth, in press).

The following excerpts from transcripts of free-play situations between middle-class Los Angeles mothers and their 3-month-old babies demonstrate the focus on autonomy and separateness: The mothers generally ask for the baby's opinion: "Want to look at mommy for a second or are you busy? Busy huh? Yes … "

The mother lets the child make the decision about what to do while they are interacting. "OK, should I read another little book to you, in Greek?" She assigns the baby autonomous agency in the interaction. Giving choices is especially important to Euro-Americans (Fiske et al., 1998). "What are you looking at? What are you looking at, darling? Do you need this instead? Will this get your attention?"

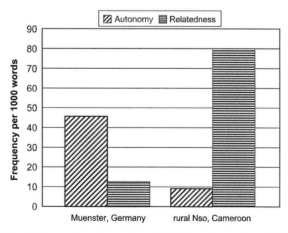

FIGURE 5.22. Reference to autonomy and relatedness in mother–infant conversations: Nso and German middle-class mothers.

Autonomy in the independent model is associated with separateness, as this Los Angeles mother expressed: "I am going to leave you alone so you can play all by yourself." In general, the baby is praised for being somebody special: "OK, you're the tallest boy in the world, huh? Look how tall you are. Look at those strong legs. [...] Look how big that big boy is? [...] Super baby, super baby. Look at that, look at that big boy, look at that big boy ... ."

The Nso, women on the other hand, instantiate relatedness and interdependence: "Mm."

The Los Angeles mothers addressed their children as "mama," or "little baby." Nso babies are addressed as mother, grandmother, and queen to express respect for the baby as being linked to the ancestors.

"Do you know that they are filming you?" References to the social environment are made often. It is evident that the conversational style is less voluminous than that of the Los Angeles mothers and that it utilizes more vocalizations than verbal statements. In line with low variability in a closed cultural model, individual mothers have very similar conversational styles.

Figure 5.23 contrasts excerpts of 2 minutes of completely transcribed free-play interaction.

Time:	LA Mother	Rural Nso Mother
00:00:00	How about the finger Cab? How about the finger Cab? Ready? Oops, No not that one, not that one. Ready? one, two, you like that? three, kisses. Little neck, little neck. Little neck huh?	Look, look, look at mama. Mama, look. Voc
00:30:00	Huh? huh? little neck? Okay, let's go to your bouncy k? You want to play in the bouncy? Okay, let's see, let's the big baby. Let's see the big baby, let's see the big baby. The cutesy baby, the cutesy baby. K? Play without mommy. Huh?	Look, belch. Have you not sucked to satisfaction? Voc Voc Voc Voc Voc Where are you?
01:00:00	You want to play without mommy? Okay, okay, you want to laugh for me huh? You want to laugh for me? Okay, how do I get you to talk for me? huh? Jahard you can talk, give me a kiss and then you we'll talk k? okay, okay. Want to play with Ziggy? huh?	Mum. Look, who is that?
01:30:00	Here he comes, here he comes. Did you kiss him? Did you kiss him? Yea cute baby, you kissed him huh? O, that little baby likes to kiss the giraffe huh? He's over here you can't see him. Here he comes, here he comes. yea, okay?	Voc

FIGURE 5.23.   The amount of language of a Los Angeles and a rural Nso mother during a free-play interaction.

The transcripts clearly demonstrate that the two conversational styles differ substantially in the amount of language spoken, reflecting different emphases on the verbal enactment of the interactional situation.

Summary. The verbal and vocal environment of small infants also clearly reflects the existence of the two prototypical styles of independence and interdependence. There are three structural differences. First, the prevalence of verbal reactions differs in that Western middle-class mothers are more prone to react verbally to infant cues than traditional village women. Second, the amount of the verbal and vocal enactment of interactions differs, in that the farmer women talk skeletally and highly repetitively, whereas the middle-class mothers talk voluminously and elaborately. Third, the content of the conversations differs. Middle-class Western mothers refer to autonomy, give the infant choices, and praise the uniqueness of the baby. The village mothers refer to the social context and moral rules and link the baby to the continuity of kin and the ancestors.

Analysis of the Quality of Parenting

The occurrence of parenting systems and interactional mechanisms and their distributions does not inform us directly about qualitative parameters of these behavioral regulations. Interactional quality is often assessed with the concept of maternal sensitivity as introduced by Ainsworth et al. (1978) across different cultural environments. Maternal sensitivity is regarded as a key indicator of the quality of mother–child interaction during the first year of life and predictive of children's later developmental outcomes across cultures. It is defined as the mother's ability to recognize her infant's signals as well as to interpret them accurately and respond to them appropriately and promptly (Ainsworth, Bell, & Stayton, 1971; Ainsworth et al., 1978; van IJzendoorn & Sagi, 1999). The four essential components of sensitivity are awareness of the infant's signals, accurate interpretation, appropriate response, and prompt response. The caregiver should be able to see things from the baby's point of view and know the meaning of even subtle, minimal, understated infant cues. A sensitive mother almost always gives the baby what he or she indicates that he or she wants, although perhaps not invariably so (Ainsworth et al., 1974, 1978).

However, cross-cultural psychologists have argued that this notion of sensitivity is founded in a conception of the self that is oriented toward the cultural model of independence and therefore not really applicable to parenting associated with the cultural model of interdependence (Goldsmith & Alansky, 1987; Greenfield, 1997; Harwood et al., 1995; Keller, 2004a; Keller, Harwood, & Carlson, 2006; LeVine & Miller, 1988; Main, 1990; Nakagawa, Lamb, & Miyake, 1992; Schneider-Rosen & Rothbaum, 1993).

Yovsi, Keller, Kärtner, and Lohaus (2006) therefore argued that conceptions of parenting quality need to be developed from a culture-specific point of view and informed by the respective socialization goals and ethnotheories. As outlined previously, central to the Nso conception of parenting quality are the goals of keeping the baby healthy and supporting growth. Parenting is aimed at preventing and suppressing distress and crying as indicators of poor health. Good parenting consists of parents taking the lead with monitoring, instructing, training, directing, and controlling the infant's activities.

For the German sample, the Ainsworth scores for Week 4 correlated highly with the scores of Week 8 and Week 12 (see Table 5.13). However, there was no correlation between the latter two. For the Yovsi scale, only Week 8 and Week 12 correlated significantly for the German sample. Stabilities were generally higher in the Nso sample. For the Ainsworth and the Yovsi scale Week 4 correlated highly with Week 8, which in turn correlated highly with Week 12. In both cases, there was no direct relation between Week 4 and Week 12. Accordingly, both scales turned out to be reasonably stable across time for each of the two samples. The Ainsworth and the Yovsi scales do not seem to be related as there were no significant correlations between the Ainsworth and the Yovsi scores for the different weeks.

TABLE 5.13
Intercorrelations Across Time for the Cultural Samples Separately

	Ainsworth Scale			Yovsi Scale		
	Week 4	Week 8	Week 12	Week 4	Week 8	Week 12
Ainsworth Week 4	—	.62*	.31+	.24	.19	.12
Ainsworth Week 8	.67**	—	.55*	.27	.22	.10
Ainsworth Week 12	.55*	.26	—	.28	.23	.23
Yovsi Week 4	.21	.15	.24	—	.64**	.21
Yovsi Week 8	.37	.10	.36	.31	—	.51**
Yovsi Week 12	.10	.01	−.14	.32	.49*	—

Note. Correlations for the German sample ($N = 20$) are below and correlations for the Nso sample ($N = 30$) are above the diagonal.
$^+p < .10$. $^*p < .05$. $^{**}p < .01$. $^{***}p < .001$.

To test whether there were differences between the two cultural samples as hypothesized, we calculated a repeated measures MANOVA with the within-subjects factor of time (Weeks 4, 8, and 12) and the between-subject factor of cultural sample, and both sensitivity measures (Ainsworth and Yovsi) as the dependent variables. For the multivariate analysis we found a significant main effect for cultural sample, $F(2, 47) = 79.46$, $p < .001$, $\eta^2 = .77$.[3]

---

[3]Eta-square (η^2) was used as an index of the strength of association between an independent variable and a dependent variable; η^2 values of .01, .06, and .14 can be interpreted as small, medium, and large effect sizes, respectively (see Cohen, 1988).

To qualify these findings, we computed univariate repeated measures ANOVAs with the within-subjects factor of time (Weeks 4, 8, and 12) and the between-subject factor of cultural sample for each sensitivity scale separately. For the Ainsworth scale, the repeated measures ANOVA yielded a significant main effect for sample, $F(1, 48) = 4.70$, $p < .05$, with a medium effect size of $\eta^2 = .09$. As hypothesized, mothers in the German sample scored higher on the Ainsworth scale than mothers in the Nso sample (see Table 5.14).

The differences between the two samples are even more pronounced for sensitivity as measured by the Yovsi scale. Here, the repeated measures ANOVA resulted in a significant main effect for sample, $F(1, 48) = 127.17$, $p < .001$, with a very large effect size of $\eta^2 = .73$. As can be seen in Table 5.12, the Nso mothers were much more sensitive than were the mothers of the German sample.

The data from this study reveal that culturally sensitive definitions of parenting quality have to be utilized when different cultural samples are compared. Parents not only focus on different parenting systems, they also have a different understanding of what constitutes parenting quality. This analysis reconfirms the different conceptions that have been elaborated in the analyses of socialization goals and ethnotheories.

TABLE 5.14
Ainsworth and Yovsi Sensitivity Scores Across Time for the Two Cultural Samples

| | Cultural Community | | | | Sample | | Time | |
| | German[a] | | Nso[b] | | | | | |
	M	SD	M	SD	F(1,48)	η^2	F(2,47)	η^2
Ainsworth Week 4	7.22	1.07	7.06	.68	4.70*	.09	1.07	.04
Ainsworth Week 8	7.46	1.02	7.06			.68		
Ainsworth Week 12	7.66	.92	6.94			.71		
Yovsi Week 4	4.76	1.32	7.05	.80	127.17**	.73	3.21[+]	.12
Yovsi Week 8	4.74	1.38	7.02			.93		
Yovsi Week 12	4.15	.78	6.99			.73		

Note. Repeated measures ANOVAs with the between-subject factor sample and the within-subject factor time for the Ainsworth and the Yovsi scale separately. η^2 = partial eta-square. All mean scores indicate relative frequency per 1,000 words.
[a]N = 20. [b]N = 30. [+]p < .10. *p < .05. **p < .001.

Consistency of the Parenting Patterns

The empirical evidence for cultural differences in parenting styles is mainly based on comparisons of cross-sectional samples; in other words, assessing one sample in one cultural environment at one point in time and comparing it with samples that have been likewise assessed at one point in time in other cultural environments. Although the samples in our research program are carefully selected with respect to sociodemographic characteristics that can be linked to cultural models, it is nevertheless important to confirm the findings by using multiple sampling.

First we replicated the hierarchical cluster analysis of the two parenting styles, distal and proximal, in 119 free-play interactional situations between mothers and their 3-month-old infants in five cultural communities (Keller, Borke, et al., 2006). Linkage between groups on the basis of squared Euclidian distances was used as the cluster method.

Cluster 1 (80 families) represents a behavioral style with a less proximal parenting and more distal parenting. Cluster 2 (39 families) represents a behavioral style with more proximal parenting and less distal parenting (see Table 5.15). The two clusters differed in a statistically significant manner concerning the extent of proximal, $F(1, 212) = 255.90, p < .001, \eta^2 = .55$, and distal parenting, $F(1, 212) = 136.79, p < .001, \eta^2 = .39$.

As Table 5.15 shows, almost all of the German and Greek mothers, and most of the Euro-American mothers, are in Cluster 1, whereas most of the rural Indian and rural Nso families are in Cluster 2. Thus the analysis confirms our previous results, which showed that the middle-class urban samples form one cluster of distal parenting that differs significantly from the rural samples, which demonstrate a more proximal style of parenting.

TABLE 5.15
Two-Cluster Solution

	Cluster 1[a]	Cluster 2[b]
Proximal parenting style		
M	35.85	73.42
SD	17.85	14.28
Distal parenting style		
M	58.20	26.54
SD	19.09	11.63
Los Angeles	15	5
Berlin	29	2
Athens	25	4
Rural Gujarati	4	12
Rural Nso	7	16

[a]N = 80. [b]N = 39.

In a different study (Keller, Borke, et al., 2005), we analyzed a sample of middle-class German families and compared it to a sample of rural Nso farming families. The Nso sample includes 96 families; the German sample includes 119 families. As the simple main effects in Table 5.16 show, there are significant differences concerning face-to-face context, object stimulation, body contact, and body stimulation as well as proximal and distal parenting style (see Table 5.16).

These observational studies are based on interactional situations with 3-month-old infants. To further test the consistency of these patterns and their validity as socialization environments, research needed to be done to see if the patterns are stable over the first months of life and, thus, the first developmental period. We therefore conducted longitudinal studies with middle-class German families and Cameroonian Nso farming families during the first 3 months of life. We videotaped free-play situations at home weekly during the first 12 weeks. We analyzed body contact and face-to-face contact as the two dominant parenting systems of the distal and proximal style (Keller, Yovsi, et al., 2004; Keller, Yovsi, Borke, Lohaus, & Lamm, 2006).

First, we calculated the interrelatedness between the parenting systems for all 12 points of time. The face-to-face contact and the body contact assessments correlate positively with each other. The mean correlation of the face-to-face assessments is $r = .51$ ($SD = .24$), and the mean correlation of the body contact assessments is $r = .56$ ($SD = .25$). The face-to-face contacts and body contact are negatively correlated with the mean $r = -.33$ ($SD = .17$). The calculation of the means and standard deviations was based on Fisher's z transformation.

To analyze the development of both the face-to-face and body contact systems over the 12 assessments and the differences between the two samples repeated measures MANOVAs with time as within-subjects factor and sample as between-subject factor were calculated. The dependent variables were face-to-face contact and body contact.

TABLE 5.16
German and Rural Nso Mother–Infant Interaction

Parenting System	Rural Nso Cameroon[a]		German[b]		F(1, 77)
	M	SD	M	SD	
Body contact	80.77	21.28	32.96	31.15	164.19*
Face-to-face context	58.50	28.81	77.82	19.67	33.93*
Body stimulation	77.72	19.97	59.28	21.29	42.10*
Object stimulation	10.30	23.61	39.54	28.02	66.43*
Distal parenting	34.40	19.30	58.68	18.51	88.00*
Proximal parenting	79.24	15.75	46.12	19.23	184.81*

[a]N = 96. [b]N = 119.
*$p < .001$.

The results show a significant main effect for the difference between the samples, $F(2, 46) = 28.68$, $p < .001$, $\eta^2 = .55$. As predicted, the univariate analyses show that the two samples differ significantly in the amounts of both parenting systems, $F(1, 47) = 33.45$, $p < .001$, $\eta^2 = .42$, concerning the face-to-face system, and $F(1, 47) = 42.03$, $p < .001$, $\eta^2 = .47$, concerning the body contact system. Face-to-face situations occur significantly more frequently in the German sample than in the Cameroonian Nso sample (see Figure 5.24) over the 12 points of time.

As expected, body contact is significantly higher in the Cameroonian Nso sample than in the middle-class German sample over all 12 assessments (see Figure 5.25).

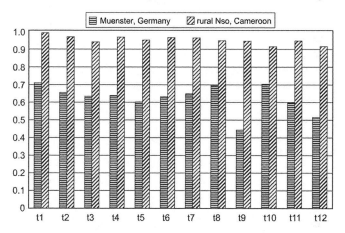

FIGURE 5.24.   The distribution of face-to-face context over the first 3 months in a Nso and a German middle-class sample.

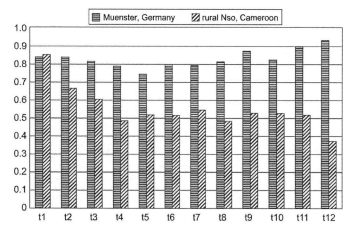

FIGURE 5.25.   The distribution of body contact over the first 3 months in a Nso and a German middle-class sample.

The relevant effect for the longitudinal differences is the interaction between the within-subjects factor (time) and the between-subject factor (sample). The results of the MANOVA indicate a significant interaction, $F(22, 1,034) = 3.40, p < .001, \eta^2 = .07$. The univariate analyses show that the interaction is significant for the face-to-face system, $F(11, 517) = 5.71, p < .001, \eta^2 = .11$. This effect is due to the increasing percentage of face-to-face situations in the German sample and to the decrease in the Nso sample (see Figure 5.24). The interaction is not significant for the body contact system, $F(11, 517) = 1.42, p > .05, \eta^2 = .03$.

It is interesting to mention that the variances are also different between the middle-class German sample and the Cameroonian Nso sample. The Levene test shows significant differences for each of the 12 body contact assessments and for 4 of the 12 face-to-face contact assessments (at Times 7, 9, 11, and 12, each with $p < .05$). The main reason for these differences is, however, that the body contact measures for the Nso sample and the eye contact measures in the German samples are close to the maximum reachable values, which reduces the variability in these cases.

The increase in face-to-face context in the middle-class German sample confirms distributions that we analyzed with an earlier longitudinal study (Keller et al., 1985). In that study we analyzed the occurrence of eye contact in mother–infant and father–infant dyadic free-play interactional situations in a middle-class German sample during the first year of life. The percentage of eye contact at the interaction time of about 5 minutes was the highest at 2 to 3 months and steadily declined to basically zero at about 12 months. During the same time period, the infant eye contact behavior was the most prominent topic in the parents' conversations with about 36% of all topics mentioned (Keller & Keller, 1981).

To analyze differences with regard to autonomy and relatedness in the verbal interactions of the mothers with their infants in the first longitudinal study (Keller, Yovsi, et al., 2004), a second MANOVA was calculated with time as the within-subjects factor and sample as the between-subject factor. Dependent variables were the proportions of verbal interactions relating to supporting autonomy and relatedness. In this case, assessments were made only at the ages of 4, 8, and 12 weeks. The results again show a significant main effect for the differences between the samples, $F(2, 47) = 64.09, p < .001, \eta^2 = .73$. The univariate analyses show that there are significant differences for both dependent variables: The proportion of verbal interactions related to supporting autonomy is significantly higher in the German sample, $F(1, 48) = 92.40, p < .001, \eta^2 = .66$, and relatedness supporting verbal interactions is more prominent in the Nso sample, $F(1, 48) = 52.50, p < .001, \eta^2 = .529$. Figure 5.26 shows the distributions. The interaction between the within-subjects factor (time) and the between-subject factor (sample) is not significant in this case.

Therefore, the conversational styles also show consistency across the developmental period of the first 3 months of infants' lives.

Our studies demonstrate that the parenting styles that we analyzed in the free-play interactional situations between mothers and their 3-month-old babies

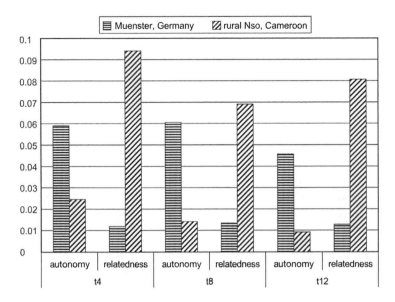

FIGURE 5.26.   The distribution of the conversational styles for weeks 4, 8, and 12.

can be reliably replicated. Middle-class urban mothers prefer the distal behavioral style consisting of face-to-fact context and object stimulation; rural farming women prefer the proximal style consisting of body contact and body stimulation. These results are consistent across different samples representing the two prototypical cultural models. The central systems of body contact and face-to-face context also demonstrate temporal stability as we have demonstrated with a short-term longitudinal study over the first 12 weeks. The conversational styles show also consistency over time, in that middle-class German mothers refer predominantly to autonomy and rural Nso mothers to relatedness in their verbal conversations during the first months.

Outlook: The Behavioral Parenting Model

In line with the different social contexts in which babies grow and develop, their interactional experiences also differ. The middle-class urban babies experience face-to-face contact and object stimulation as the primary nonverbal parenting systems. They experience an embellished and elaborated verbal environment. Prompt contingent reactions toward their facial and vocal cues support the perception of independent, separate agency. Their parents explore their wishes and needs during early verbal conversations and surround them with the voice of autonomy. There are differences among samples sharing an independent worldview and there are also interindividual differences that express individuality. Nevertheless, they all differ substantially from the farming families in rural villages. Those babies experience body contact and body stimulation as the primary nonverbal parenting systems. Their verbal environment is more vocal than verbal, skeletal, and repetitive, focusing on the social surroundings and moral lessons. Moreover, it is more cooccurring and overlapping and therefore less dialogical in nature. Differences among the Gujarati Rajput and the Nso women are mainly due to different physical and health conditions, with the Gujarati women being weaker and more vulnerable, a situation that precludes highly energetic forms of child care. Their parenting concept is parent centered and emphasizes stimulation and training. Parenting represents a closed system, where interindividual variability is less pronounced.

In general, the social contexts and the interactional experiences match the socialization goals and parenting ethnotheories, so that the different dimensions of infant developmental contexts all transmit the same message to the infant with different communicational means.

This chapter has convincingly documented that there are systematic differences in cultural models of parenting that are defined by broader cultural models of the self and relationships. Parenting is understood to be an evolved behavioral program that supports the infant's mastery of the first integrative developmental task: the formation of a relational matrix that is developed in its basic structure at about 3 months of age. We have contrasted two prototypes that are adaptive to extremely different environmental contexts. The model of interdependence is adaptive for life in subsistence-based families with a low educational profile and a reproductive strategy that is characterized by reproduction beginning at a young age and many children. The model of independence is adaptive for life in the anonymity of Western urban centers. The high educational profile of mothers and fathers is associated with late reproduction and few children.

The cultural models are rooted in the cultural conception of the self and can be described as encompassing particular combinations of autonomy and relatedness. The resulting conception informs cultural models of parenting, which have the goal of raising offspring who are competent in these particular environments.

6 Variations of Independence and Interdependence

In the previous chapter, I discussed the two prototypical cultural models of independence and interdependence. I argued that the two models constitute independent dimensions with the possibility of multiple combinations resulting in multiple psychologies. In this chapter, I analyze different sets of those combinations.

The first set of studies relates to Kağitçibaşi (1996a, 2005) proposal of autonomous relatedness. Kağitçibaşi proposed this concept as a third prototypical model resulting from the combination of autonomy as one endpoint of the agency dimension and relatedness as one endpoint of the interpersonal distance dimension (see Figure 6.1).

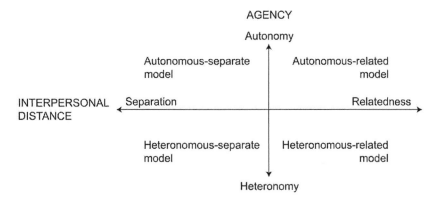

FIGURE 6.1.   Kağitçibaşi's model of autonomy and relatedness.

The combination of heteronomy and separateness is not further elaborated. It may express parental neglect or indifference in hierarchical families (Kağitçibaşi, 2005). The underlying assumption of Kağitçibaşi's proposal is that agency and interpersonal distance form two independent dimensions, so that "one's standing on the interpersonal distance dimension may or may not affect one's standing on the agency dimension" (Kağitçibaşi, 2005, p. 404).

Kağitçibaşi (1996a, 2005) described this cultural model of autonomous relatedness as emotional interdependence without economic interdependence. It has emerged within a model of family change reflecting a global pattern of urbanization and socioeconomic development in the "majority world" with collectivistic cultures of relatedness (Kağitçibaşi, 1990, 1996b, 2005). It is therefore considered to be adaptive for educated middle-class families in traditionally interdependent societies, where the economic value of children is no longer needed for the family. In particular, formal education for a competitive labor market has increased autonomy, whereas family cohesion and an intrafamilial relatedness have remained important values. Previous studies have demonstrated that women in rural environments who take part in formal educational programs changed their parenting ideas and practices, for example, in Turkey (Kağitçibaşi, 1996b), Cameroon (Tchombe, 1997), Mexico (LeVine, 1994), and the Zinacantecan Mayas, also in Mexico (Greenfield, 2000; Greenfield, Maynard, & Childs, 2000). However, urban environments also host pockets with different educational attainments (Kusserow, 1999; Palacios & Moreno, 1996).

However, with the assumption of a dimensional character of cultural models, other combinations besides the coexistence of endpoints should also be possible. Our research agenda analyzes possible combinations in cultural models of parenting in middle-class, urban, educated samples of traditionally interdependent societies in San José (Costa Rica), Beijing (China), and Delhi (India).

Our second set of studies is aimed at directly analyzing the influence of education within the same cultural environment. Therefore, we compare families from the same geographical area, sharing a common language and historical background, yet differing with respect to the level of formal education and, thus, having different *Lebenswelten* (life worlds; Schütz & Luckmann, 1984) in rural and urban life contexts. We compare rural Cameroonian Nso with an interdependent model of parenting with urban educated middle-class families, also belonging to the ethnic tribe of the Nso in Cameroon. Likewise, we compare Indian Hindu Gujarati villagers with urban middle-class Hindu families from the city of Vadodara in Gujarat and Hindu families from Delhi. Finally, we compare German fathers with different educational attainments.

Our third set of studies is aimed at comparing similarly defined sociodemographic samples within cultural communities belonging to different historical time epochs. Although cultural models of parenting can be assumed to be stable and consistent, as demonstrated in chapter 5, they are integrated into cultural dynamics that develop and change over historical time in conjunction with sociodemographic changes (Greenfield, 1997, 2004; Rogoff, 2003). So, cultural models reflect the zeitgeist of an epoch. Consistent with this view, Abramovitz (1976) demonstrated that since the early colonial period each phase of historical development in the United States has produced different ideas about children's inherent nature at birth, proper care, and the estimated socialization goals. Thus historical epochs also constitute cultural environments, to which parenting strategies need to be adapted (Kessen, 1979). We analyzed parenting patterns over historical time in middle-class German families and Nso farming families, representing the prototypes of independence and interdependence, and Costa Rican families, representing one model of variation.

Finally, the fourth set of studies addresses generational differences by assessing parenting ethnotheories of mothers and grandmothers in different sociocultural environments. Variation across generations within the same sociocultural milieu is a quite neglected area in the literature. Historical analyses revealed dramatic changes in the Western world with respect to childrearing ideas and practices as reported earlier (see also Grant, 1998; Hulbert, 2003). The different pace of change across cultures that we have discussed with respect to cross-sectional comparisons may result in larger changes in some cultural environments as compared to others. Cho, Sandel, Miller, and Wang (2005) reported that there is a greater overlap in parenting folk theories between Taiwanese mothers and grandmothers as compared to Euro-Americans. We assessed mothers' and grandmothers' parenting ethnotheories with the picture card interview (see chap. 4, this volume) with Berlin, Delhi, and Nso middle-class mothers and grandmothers, and rural Nso mothers and grandmothers, thus covering the two prototypes (Berlin and rural Nso) and two examples for variations.

The organization of the following sections follows the structure of chapter 5 in that I present data for the different dimensions of the cultural model of parenting.

URBAN MIDDLE-CLASS FAMILIES IN TRADITIONALLY INTERDEPENDENT SOCIETIES

For this set of analyses, we selected research sites of middle-class families in large cities in different geographical parts of the world with different cultural histories and religions: the Central American capital of San José, Costa Rica; the Indian capital of Delhi; and the Chinese capital of Beijing. In the following sections I briefly describe the ecocultural environments and the ethnopsychology of the self for our study sites.

The Case of Costa Rican Ticos

For historical and geographical reasons, the Costa Rican population lacks a significant indigenous substrate. Although many authors emphasize the "European" origin of Costa Ricans, the Costa Rican population is composed mainly of ethnically mixed groups, which make up 90% of the population, resulting in the *mestizo* type (Rosabal-Coto, 2004). Due to a highly developed health care system, which covers approximately 90% of the Costa Rican population, life expectancy at birth is 76.8 years. The age structure is 0 to 14 years, 28.9%; 15 to 64 years, 65.5%; 65 years and older, 5.6%. The global fertility rate is 2.28 for 2005, declining gradually from 7.11 in 1960. The infant mortality rate has also been steadily diminishing in recent decades; it was 9.95 per 1,000 live births in 2005—a decrease of more than 7% from 1985.

Costa Rica has one of the highest literacy rates in Latin America, with 96% of the population age 15 and older being able to read and write. Over the last 15 years, there has been an average annual rate of increase of 1.9% in children who register for the first time for first grade in public elementary schools. Primary and secondary education (comprising 11 years of elementary and high school studies) is funded by the state. Higher education was founded in 1843 with the University of Costa Rica—still the largest university in the country—and now includes four state universities; there are more than 40 small private universities.

The Costa Rican economy is a basically stable economy based on (commercial) agricultural (bananas, coffee, sugar cane, cocoa, cotton, pineapple, etc.) and livestock activities. In recent decades tourism has become a very important source of foreign currency, as have electronic exports.

The two-generation nuclear family is the prevalent urban household pattern, making up 56.4% (Vega-Robles, 2001). At the same time, there is a decreasing tendency in the predominance of the conjugal family, and a substantial trend toward single-parent families and one-person households. Separation and divorce rate increases are a compelling reason for these changes (Vega-Robles, 2001). Nevertheless the sense of family and its unity still plays an important role in Costa Ricans' everyday life. That is why it is common to encounter relatives living in the same neighborhood or nearby areas (Miranda & Rosabal-Coto, 1997). The home is considered a private refuge to which nonrelatives rarely gain access. Family life is rooted in Catholicism, to which 76.3% of the population belongs; 13.7% of the population is Protestant.

Children are cherished and most welcome in Costa Rican society. Small children are indulged by mothers and the members of the extended family. Gender differentiation is supported from early on with different dress codes and differential reinforcement of activities. Costa Rican parents want a good education for their children and favor socialization goals related to values such as being well mannered, obedient, and respectful (Alvarez, Brenes, & Cabezas, 1990; Miranda & Rosabal-Coto, 1997). Social desirability and the ability to interact appropriately in a social context are the values that parents cherish the most (Rosabal-Coto, 2000). In line with a relational value orientation, Costa Rican mothers expect their infants to develop social skills earlier and cognitive skills later than German mothers (Keller, Miranda, & Gauda, 1984).

Positive affect expressions by the child, such as kissing, hugging, and caressing, are highly estimated by parents, particularly mothers, although this is not the case with negative affect expressions, which are undesired and immediately rejected and sanctioned (see Figure 6.2 for a Costa Rican family party).

FIGURE 6.2.   Costa Rican middle-class family. Photo by Elsa van Putten.

The Case of Middle-Class Chinese Families

China is still a developing country with a relatively low per-capita income. It has nevertheless experienced tremendous economic growth since the late 1970s, which goes hand in hand with urbanization and migration from other Chinese provinces into the urban centers. The capital, Beijing, with more than 7 million citizens, is located in the northeastern part of the country and represents a major commercial, industrial, political, educational, and cultural center of the country. The standard of living has improved significantly since economic reforms were started in 1978. Life expectancy at birth is 72.3 years. The age structure is 0 to 14 years, 22.3%; 15 to 64 years, 70.3%; and 65 years and older, 7.5%. Although "one child" has been promoted as an ideal since 1979, and the limit was strongly enforced in urban areas, the actual implementation varied from location to location. In most rural areas, families were allowed to have two children if the first child was female. Additional children would result in fines, or more commonly, the families would be required to pay fees for public services such as education for the children that otherwise would be free.

Moreover, in accordance with China's affirmative action policies toward ethnic minorities, all non-Han ethnic groups are completely exempted from child birth constraints, including financial penalties. Thus the overall fertility rate of 1.7 is closer to two children per family than to one child per family, which results in a population growth rate of 0.57%. The infant mortality rate is 24.2 per 1,000 live births with a substantial sex difference favoring males (21.2 per 1,000 boys vs.

27.5 per 1,000 girls). China has emerging public health problems, particularly in relation to air and water pollution.

Ninety percent of the total population (males, 95.1%; females, 86.5%) over 15 years of age can read and write. China is working toward 9-year compulsory education. The enrollment rate for schoolchildren at the elementary school level was 99.1% in 1999. Illiteracy has declined rapidly in recent years, from 23.5% in 1978 to 12.0% in 1997 (X. Chen & He, 2005). China has a differentiated system of higher education, including many renowned universities.

China recognizes 56 distinct ethnic groups, of which the largest is Han Chinese, comprising 92% of the total population. Mandarin is the dominant Chinese language, spoken by 70% of the population. On January 1, 1979, the government officially adopted the *pinyin* system for spelling Chinese names and places in Roman letters. Religion plays an important part in the lives of Chinese people. Buddhism and Taoism are the most practiced religions.

Due to socioeconomic factors, joint families have decreased and nuclear families have increased in numbers in the large cities. About one third of families consist of three generations: parents of husband or wife, parents, and children (X. Chen, 1998). The average family size decreased from 4.8 in 1985 to 3.6 in 1999 (X. Chen & He, 2005). Most families have close emotional and financial connections with their families of origin. The divorce rate is rising, especially among members of the young generation with a high educational level, as is the number of single-parent families.

The main task of parents is considered training their children to control individualistic behaviors and to display cooperative, compliant, and interdependent behavior (X. Chen & He, 2005). The understanding of the Chinese self is expressed in Hsu's (1971) concept of *yen*. Interpersonal transactions are the core of the meaning of *yen*, representing an alternative to the Western conception of personality. With this concept the nature of the individual's behavior is not seen as an expression of individual traits and mental states but rather as a reflection of how the behavior fits the interpersonal standard. Personal transactions are embedded in social hierarchies to contribute to the harmonic functioning of the social unit, in particular the family (Bond, 1991; Chao, 1995; Hsu, 1971).

Chinese parenting strategies have been described as emphasizing obedience, respect, and filial piety (Chao, 1995; Hu & Meng, 1996) in an adult-centered hierarchical environment. The Chinese approach to childrearing is assumed to be rooted in Confucian ethics, which places a high value on social hierarchy and moral rectitude and is still regarded as valid today (Bond, 1991, 1998; Tobin, Wu, & Davidson, 1989; Wu, 1985). Chinese parents therefore rely on training, which expresses the parental responsibility to carry out moral education for the child (Wu, 1985).

Chinese parents intend to foster a very close relationship with the child throughout his or her life (Chao, 1994). Nevertheless, increasing education and a changing economy have had an impact on childrearing, although less so than in Western cultures (Xiao, 2000; see Figure 6.3).

FIGURE 6.3.   Chinese middle-class family from Beijing. Photo by Yanjie Su.

The Case of Indian Hindu Middle-Class Families

India is also still a developing country with a relatively low per-capita income, but it has had an increasing economic growth rate since the 1980s. It recorded one of the highest annual growth rates (6.9%) for 2004–2005. Services are the major force of economic growth, with the information technology industry being especially prominent, although two thirds of the workforce is still in agriculture. The greatest disappointment of economic development is the failure to reduce India's widespread poverty to a greater degree. Studies have suggested that income distribution changed little between independence in 1947 and the early 1990s, although it is possible that the poorer half of the population improved its position slightly. Nevertheless, 25% of the population lives below the poverty line.

By the early 1990s, economic changes led to an increase in the number of Indians with significant economic resources. About 10 million Indians are considered upper class, and roughly 300 million are part of the rapidly increasing middle class. Typical middle-class occupations include owning a small business or being a corporate executive, lawyer, physician, white-collar worker, or land-owning farmer.

After China, India is the most populous country in the world. The overall fertility rate is 2.78 children born to a woman, which results in a population growth rate of 1.4%. The infant mortality rate is 56.2 deaths per 1,000 live births. Life expectancy at birth is 64.35 years. The age structure is 0 to 14 years, 31.2%; 15 to 64 years, 63.9%; and 65 years and older, 4.9%.

The capital, Delhi, which has more than 15 million citizens, is one of the most affluent urban centers in India and it is at the heart of India's largest consumer belt. It is located in the northern part of the country and has always been an important economic, cultural, and intellectual center. Delhi has a high standard of education. It is home to many major educational institutions in India. Delhi also hosts a great number of quality schools. As compared to 59.5% of the total national population (males, 70.2%; females, 48.3%) over 15 years of age who can read and write, Delhi has a literacy rate of 78.5%. It has one of the highest per-capita incomes in India and is one of the fastest growing metropolitan areas in Asia. Migrants account for 60% of the increase in population.

Delhi has a number of governmental and private colleges offering quality education in the fields of science, engineering, medicine, arts, law, and management. There are more than nine universities situated in the Delhi metropolitan area. In 2001, Delhi University had 220,000 students, making it one of the largest universities in Asia. In 2003–2004, more than 310,000 students were enrolled in Delhi's 4,800 primary and secondary schools.

The Indian population consists of 72% Indo-Aryans, 25% Dravidians, and 3% Mongoloid and others. English enjoys associate status but is the most important language for national, political, and commercial communication. Hindi is the national language and primary tongue of 30% of the people. There are 14 other official languages. Religion is important in everyday life and is a visible part of all life contexts. The population is 80.5% Hindu, 13.4% Muslim, 2.3% Christian, 1.9% Sikh, and 1.8% others.

Typically, Indian families are large structures characterized by coresidence of several generations. The traditional joint family system finds expression in everyday ideology where affiliation and affection with extended kin can be found even when couples may live separately. In urban life, many new forms of "jointness" have emerged, such as extended units, where some members may live with a couple and their children, and parallel joint families, where nuclear units may live nearby or on different floors of the same house and cooperate to care for children, the elderly, and ailing, but maintain different kitchens and sometimes even different accounts. It has been found that the ideology of togetherness has persisted, despite the pressures of modern living and increased urbanization (Uberoi, 2005).

The Hindu sense of self is believed to be context-dependent and changeable. Bodies are considered to be relatively "porous," "permeable," and predicated on different life circumstances and relationships (Menon, 2003). The possible transformations are determined by one's social and biological states, of being woman or man, pregnant or young, and so on. Furthermore, a fundamental connectedness is assumed among all living beings (collective selves or *advaita*). The existence of human beings is seen as essentially linked to society, and social processes are believed to have the same organicity as bodies (Menon, 2003).

The Hindu life cycle prescribes ardent interdependence in childhood, uncritical "follower-ship" in youth, complete devotion to family and pursuit of wealth in early adulthood, gradual detachment with aging, and complete seclusion and distance from others in old age (Chaudhary, 2004).

Perhaps the only avenue for which the importance of the family has been somewhat reduced is the recognition of school as a powerful social institution. Despite faltering rates of school attendance for its children, the accomplishments in the field of education and literacy in India have been nothing short of remarkable. People from every strata of society, even the very poor, believe deeply in schooling and its positive effect on individuals (see Figure 6.4).

Summary

The brief descriptions of the three urban environments from traditionally interdependent societies reveal that they can indeed be characterized by emotional interdependence, as Kağitçibaşi (1996b) proposed. Children are raised in multigenerational networks that are smaller than the joint and extended families in rural environments, but definitely larger than nuclear two-generation families prevalent in the Western middle class. Parents try to instill conformity and respect, obedience and self-control, and maintenance of parental authority in their children. The developmental goals are rooted in different religions and historical traditions: Catholicism in Costa Rica, Confucianism in China, and Hinduism in India. Education, which is highly available in urban metropolises, plays a major role in children's life trajectories. Education reduces economic interdependence. Sometimes the family

FIGURE 6.4.   Indian middle-class family from Delhi. Photo by Nandita Chaudhary.

of origin supports their grandchildren's education economically, a model that is also popular in middle-class Western families. As a corollary of increasing education, changes in lifestyle become manifest, such as increasing divorce rates, numbers of single-parent families, ages for marriage, and ages for reproduction. Our study samples reflect the sociodemographic characteristics of late reproductive life in these environments. Table 6.1 also contains the data for the urban Nso sample and the Vadodara sample from Gujarat, India, which are portrayed later.

As can be seen in Table 6.1, the sociodemographic characteristics of the mothers in our study families are different from the women with an interdependent model. Their educational profile is similar to that of the women with an independent model. With respect to the other sociodemographic variables, they are situated between the independent and interdependent model samples, for example for their age at the birth of their first child, the number of children, and the household size. Nevertheless, there are also differences among the samples with respect to these characteristics.

THE CULTURAL MODEL OF PARENTING IN FAMILIES WITH AN ASSUMED AUTONOMOUS-RELATED ORIENTATION

Family Cohesion and Socialization Goals

In a first step we tested the concept of family cohesion, as assessed with the family allocentrism scale (Lay et al., 1998). Table 6.2 presents the scores in comparison with the mean values of the samples with an independent and interdependent orientation, respectively.

In accordance with the concept of the autonomous-related model, these samples should score as high on the family allocentrism scale as the samples with an interdependent model did. The results reveal however, that they score in between the samples with an independent cultural model and the samples with an interdependent cultural model, with the San José sample scoring lowest and thus being most similar to the independent samples in this respect.

In a next step we analyzed these mothers' socialization goals, assessing them with the socialization goals questionnaire described in chapter 4 (Keller, Lamm, et al., 2006). The results for the relational and autonomous socialization goals are also presented in Table 6.2. The samples from San José, Beijing, and Delhi score lower in relational socialization goals and higher in autonomous socialization goals than the samples with an interdependent cultural model. They score similarly to the independent samples with respect to autonomous and relational socialization goals, except the Costa Rican mothers, who score high on relational socialization goals. With the exception of the Beijing families, relational and autonomous socialization goals are expressed equally. The Beijing families value autonomy much more than relatedness. Here again, the different samples do not reveal a consistent pattern. Moreover they differ in both orientations from the samples with an independent model and from the samples with an interdependent model.

TABLE 6.1
Sociodemographic Profiles of the Autonomous-Related Samples

				Cultural Community			
	Independent Samples[a]	Beijing, China[b]	San José, Costa Rica[c]	Delhi, India[d]	Vadodara, India[e]	Urban Nso, Cameroon[f]	Interdependent Samples[g]
Mean age of mothers	30.6	27.5	26.4	29.0	27.6	29.9	25.9
Mean age at birth of the first child	30.0	27.5	24.2	26.3	25.2	24.1	19.5[k]
Mean years of school attendance	14.4	15.0	9.6	15.6	13.2	12.9	5.9[l]
Mean number of children	1.2	1.0	1.6	1.6	—[h]	2.4	2.6
Percentage of first-born infants	88.2	100	60	41.7	30	38.9	31.4
Percentage of female infants	48.6	61.9	40.7	45.7	50	65	52.2
Percentage of married mothers (living together in an unmarried partnership)	72.4[i] (13.5)	100	60 (25)	100	100	65	81.8
Mean number of persons per household	3.3[j]	4.4	—[h]	5.8	—[h]	6.3	6.9

[a]N = 228. [b]N = 21. [c]N = 27. [d]N = 37. [e]N = 30. [f]N = 29. [g]N = 134. [h]No information available. [i]N = 178. [j]N = 158. [k]N = 93. [l]N = 111.

TABLE 6.2

Results for Family Allocentrism and Socialization Goals

	Cultural Community										
	Independent Samples[a]		Beijing, China[b]		San José, Costa Rica[c]		Delhi, India[d]		Interdependent Samples[e]		$F(4, 208)$	η^2
	M	SD	M	SD	M	SD	M	SD	M	SD		
Allocentrism	68.35_a	10.77	80.50_b	5.32	68.85_a	9.93	84.74_b	5.16	99.03_c	7.89	76.18*	.59
Socialization goals												
Autonomy	$4.05_{a/b}$	.71	4.57_a	.44	$4.26_{a/b}$	.57	3.61_b	.81	2.63_c	1.51	23.10*	.31
Relatedness	3.48_a	.85	3.31_a	.79	$4.27_{b/c}$	.57	$3.87_{a/b}$	.67	4.80_c	.50	23.89*	.32

Note. Five-level (culture) MANOVA with significant multivariate main effect for culture, Wilks's $\lambda = .16$, $F(20, 677.5) = 25.70$, $p < .001$, $\eta^2 = .37$, followed by univariate analyses. Indexed letters indicate results of simple main effects testing (with Bonferroni adjustment). $\eta^2 =$ partial eta-square.
[a]$N = 113$. [b]$N = 18$. [c]$N = 27$. [d]$N = 23$. [e]$N = 32$.
*$p < .001$.

In a second study (Kärtner et al., 2006), we tested the degree of autonomous and relational socialization goals of the Delhi sample as compared to the Berlin and Los Angeles samples with an independent model on the one hand, and rural Nso with an interdependent model on the other hand. A ratio score (autonomous socialization goals score divided by relational socialization goals score) revealed that the Delhi mothers' score of around .90 indicates a slight prevalence of relational socialization goals. This falls between the Berlin and the Los Angeles mothers, who score higher than 1.0, and the rural Nso mothers, who have score of about .40, which indicates a clear preference for relational socialization goals. These results again support an intermediate position for the Delhi sample.

The results of these studies reveal that the samples with an assumed autonomous-related model differ from both the independent and the interdependent samples with respect to autonomy and relatedness. They also differ from each other, yet not in systematic ways.

Parenting Ethnotheories

The questionnaire study (Keller, Lamm, et al., 2006; for a description of the questionnaire, see chap. 4, this volume) reveals that the samples with an assumed autonomous-related model score between the independent and interdependent samples. The relational parenting ethnotheory score is lower than that of the Nso and the Gujarati women and higher than that of the Berlin, Los Angeles, and Athens mothers. The Delhi mothers, who score similarly to the independent samples, are an exception. With respect to the autonomous parenting ethnotheory score, the Beijing and Delhi mothers score similarly to the mothers with an independent model, whereas the Costa Rican mothers score similarly to the mothers with an interdependent model (see Table 6.3).

The mothers in these samples score between the independent and interdependent samples with respect to their ideas concerning the night sleep patterns of small babies (see Table 6.4). The Delhi mothers expect a child to sleep alone at about 2 years of age, the Beijing mothers at about 15 months. The Costa Rican mothers express the most extreme opinion of about 6 months. With respect to sleeping through the night, the Beijing mothers express the earliest expectation among this group of mothers with younger than 1, the Delhi mothers expect sleeping though the night to occur at about 2 and the Costa Rican mothers at more than 3.

The Content of the Parenting Ethnotheories.   The parenting ethnotheories of the Beijing and Delhi mothers are elaborated by the picture card interviews. Figure 6.5 reports the data on parenting systems and interactional mechanisms as compared to the mean profiles for the independent and interdependent samples.

The Delhi and Beijing mothers do not differ with respect to the amount of object stimulation or verbal interaction from each other, nor do they differ with respect to the interactional mechanisms of warmth, shared and exclusive attention,

174

TABLE 6.3
Results for Parenting Ethnotheories

	Independent Samples[a]		Beijing, China[b]		San José, Costa Rica[c]		Delhi, India[d]		Interdependent Samples[e]		F(4, 208)	η^2
	M	SD	M	SD	M	SD	M	SD	M	SD		
Parenting ethnotheories												
Autonomy	$2.95_{a/b}$	.79	$3.12_{a/b}$	.59	$2.49_{a/c}$	.56	3.11_b	.73	1.93_c	.95	14.13*	.21
Relatedness	3.21_a	.74	4.16_b	.48	$3.79_{b/c}$	.68	$3.43_{a/c}$	.54	4.86_d	.31	44.76*	.46

Note. Five-level (culture) MANOVA with significant multivariate main effect for culture, Wilks's $\lambda = .16$, $F(20, 667.5) = 25.70$, $p < .001$, $\eta^2 = .37$, followed by univariate analyses. Indexed letters indicate results of simple main effects testing (with Bonferroni adjustment). η^2 = partial eta-square. [a]N = 113. [b]N = 18. [c]N = 27. [d]N = 23. [e]N = 32.
*p < .001.

TABLE 6.4
Results for Sleeping Arrangements

	Independent Samples[a]		Beijing, China[b]		San José, Costa Rica[c]		Delhi, India[d]		Interdependent Samples[e]		F(4, 227)	η^2
	M	SD	M	SD	M	SD	M	SD	M	SD		
At what age (in months) are children able to												
Sleep alone	5.89_a	9.25	17.83_a	16.77	5.72_a	5.84	39.70_b	20.67	55.11_c	32.81	72.51*	.56
Sleep through the night	4.07_a	3.30	8.83_a	6.88	7.25_a	5.55	13.24_a	9.39	46.23_b	36.45	53.83*	.49

Note. Five-level (culture) MANOVA with significant multivariate main effect for culture, Wilks<2146>s $\lambda = .34$, $F(8, 452) = 40.27$, $p < .001$, $\eta^2 = .42$, followed by univariate analyses. Indexed letters indicate results of simple main effects testing (with Bonferroni adjustment). η^2 = partial eta-square. [a]N = 115. [b]N = 21. [c]N = 30. [d]N = 23. [e]N = 44.
*p < .001.

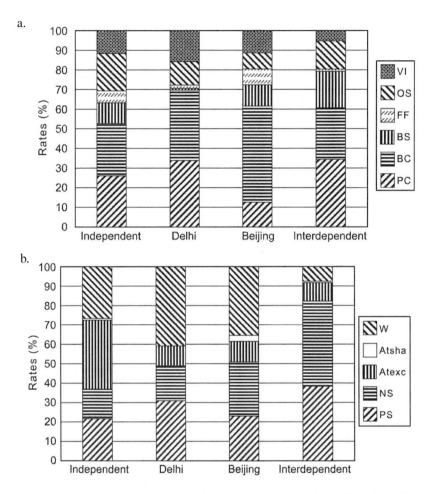

Figure 6.5.   (a) The address of parenting systems in the picture card interviews of the Delhi and Beijing mothers as compared to the interdependent and independent mothers (VI = verbal interaction; OS = object stimulation; FF = face-to-face context; BS = body stimulation; BC = body contact; PC = primary care); (b) The address of interactional mechanisms in the picture card interviews of the Delhi and Beijing mothers as compared to the interdependent and independent mothers (W = warmth; Atsha = attention shared; Atex = attention exclusive; NS = negative signals; PS = positive signals).

and how positive and negative stimuli are addressed. Yet they differ significantly with respect to the amount of primary care—the Beijing mothers also address it significantly less than the independent and interdependent samples. The Beijing mothers address body contact significantly more than the Delhi mothers; they also address body stimulation significantly more than the Delhi mothers, being similar to the independent mothers in this respect. They address face-to-face context significantly more often than the Delhi mothers, to a degree similar to that of the independent mothers. Taken together, the orientation toward autonomy and relatedness is expressed in parenting ethnotheories as follows (see Figure 6.6).

The Delhi and Beijing mothers differ significantly from each other in their emphasis on autonomy and relatedness as expressed in the reference to the parenting systems. Although both refer to relatedness more than to autonomy, the Delhi mothers clearly refer more often to autonomy than the Beijing mothers do. Com-

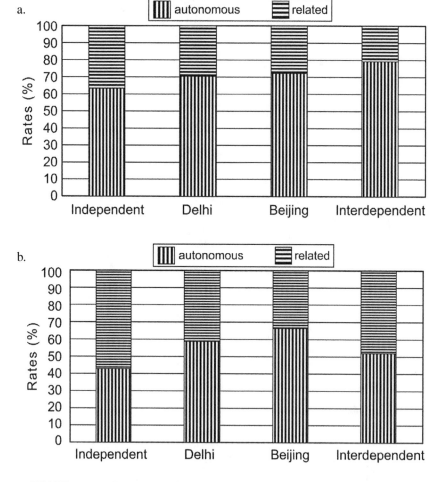

FIGURE 6.6.   (a) The content of the parenting ethnotheories related to autonomy and relatedness of the Delhi and Beijing mothers as compared with the interdependent and independent mothers; (b) The interaction mechanisms related to autonomy and relatedness of the Delhi and Beijing mothers as compared to the interdependent and independent mothers.

pared to the independent and interdependent groups, they fall somewhere in the middle. With respect to the reference to interactional mechanisms, both samples refer significantly more to mechanisms expressing relatedness than to those expressing autonomy. Both groups refer more to interactional mechanisms representing relatedness than the interdependent and independent women do. Both samples refer to autonomy-related interactional mechanisms less than the interdependent and independent women.

The qualitative analysis exemplifies the special interrelation between parenting ideas promoting autonomy and relatedness, independence and interdependence of the mothers with an assumed autonomous-related cultural model.

Body contact as part of an interdependent orientation was described as follows by a mother from Delhi (32 years old, two children, university degree):

> Yes, it does. I am not saying that one should always be cuddling, there are lines to be drawn. Not always you should be cuddling the child, but there are times when the cuddling has to be there. Especially in the night when you are sleeping, saying to the child that I love you. That kind of thing makes a lot of difference to the child. Whenever you are lying down in the bed, cuddling with the child. For both me and my husband, make it a point that at least in a day two or three times, we have a nice hug with the children, a nice kiss and I love you types so that the child is feeling happy and she also feels good and she has also started doing it as a regular this thing so …

It is obvious that body contact is important, but it is not a permanent state of being. As this mother says, "lines need to be drawn," and contexts need to be defined in which body contact is permitted. Body contact even has to be restricted in some cases as the following excerpt from the same Delhi mother explains:

> He is playing on his own which is good as long as he is not asking for attention and in this one [picture card] if the child is happy then why keep the child in your lap? Put the child down, like even if you don't have a place like for him, when he is in a good mood, after waking up, I just get his this thing and I make him lie down and whoever plays with him he is not in lap, which I think is a lot of trouble if they get into the habit of getting into the lap and staying there.

This view is clearly different from the evaluation of body contact as a moral obligation as expressed by the rural Nso and Indian Gujarati mothers. It is even closer to the attitude of the Berlin and Los Angeles mothers, who also look for opportunities in the daily routine to have the babies spend time on their own.

The Beijing mothers have a similarly moderate view of body contact. On the one hand, body contact is important as this Beijing mother (25 years old, one daughter, social scientist) explained: "When you hold the baby like this often in your arms, then it is good for the health and the growth. If a baby is held in the arms from early on, then this has effects on the development."

There is also the focus on growth and development as likewise stressed by the mothers with an interdependent model. Nevertheless, there should not be too much body contact, as the same mother further explained: "In this picture the baby has fallen asleep. Should it have been fallen asleep already some time ago, one should not hold him all the time in the arms. I think, on this picture it looks as if he is just fallen asleep. One should put him on the bed."

The views on the second parenting system, body stimulation, reveal an unconfined proximal view; body stimulation is viewed unanimously positively among the Delhi and the Beijing mothers.

This excerpt from an interview with a Delhi mother (28 years old, two children, teacher) illustrates:

M: This one (chooses picture card) because the mother is doing a sort of exercise and the baby is also in good relationship with the mother, he is also concentrating and this will help in the development of the child.
I: So you feel that exercising is good?
M: Exercise and massage is good for the child
I: Why is it good?
M: One thing is that even while lying down the child gets tired and that goes away and the child feels fresh so it is a must. You can do alternate day, but massage is good for the development of the baby and also for body ache also it is good.

It is not the rough handling and the strong massage that is valued in the village families, however, but a softer form of exercising.

The view of the Beijing mothers is more straightforward. They relate body stimulation to growth and physical development, where acceleration is obviously seen positively. A 29-year-old mother from Beijing (one son, technical assistant) narrated:

I: Why do you think that more movement is important?
M: It is important for the child now to have exercise movement of all four limbs. Now it is passive. This will promote the child's developmental growth. Especially with coordination. This will help with coordination movement. This hand can grasp, left hand can grasp, right hand can grasp, give her a toy, this will promote her development.

Both the Delhi and Beijing mothers also value distal modes of interaction, such as talking and object stimulation, which may even replace body contact. It is also obvious that the child has needs and wants that need to be taken seriously. A Delhi mother (32 years old, two children, BA) told the interviewer:

M: In this the mother and the child both are paying attention to each other. They are playing, laughing, talking with each other.
I: Is that important?

M: Yes it is important and the child also demands this at this age that someone should talk to me play with me. It is important also you also feel happy yourself and he also stays happy.

I: And for the child?

M: It is good for him.

However, the stimulation value of objects clearly dominates, as it also does in the view of this Chinese mother (26 years old, one daughter, BA):

Because you look above at the pinwheel windy toy. I also have [one] in my house, half of the children have them. To say that they have pretty good leisure time. ... This is a good situation. She sees the pinwheel windy toy. The pinwheel windy toy exercises her vision. The toy rotates. It has music. She loves to hear it. Listening is also an exercise. Also sometimes the hands would dance with the music. Her muscles can grow and develop. This way she can learn to play by herself. Learning how to play is good for intellectual progress. She can become smart and [she] views the pinwheel windy toy with interest. ... In the future during her studies, she will progress far in her studies.

In line with the emphasis on stimulation, mere face-to-face contact is not seen as especially meaningful. A Delhi mother (22 years old, one daughter, BA) expressed her view:

Both mother and child are complacent seeing each other happy so I think that this is okay, there is no need for the mother—I mean at this particular point the mother is just smiling at the baby and the baby is responding back smiling but the mother is not creating any activity [so] that the child can talk, she is just holding the baby so they are both complacent enough so I think this is third.

A Beijing mother (28 years old, one daughter, university teacher) also focused on training when reflecting on face-to-face contact:

M: It should be like this, I think when taking care of an infant, there should be eye contact. I think that she should be able to see my eyes directly. This will help a lot with the child's intellectual development.

I: Why do you think it's important to have this eye contact?

M: I feel that from the mother, the child should be able to feel the love given. This viewpoint relationship [agrees with] what my child's doctor says. They also say the same, to look at the child's eyes.

The interview excerpts with the Delhi and Beijing mothers clearly substantiate the quantitative analysis, which supports a view on parenting ethnotheories of an assumed autonomous-related model as representing an intermediate position between the independent and the interdependent model of parenting. These mothers clearly have an autonomous picture of the baby, stressing his or her needs, wishes, and wants. They follow the baby's lead, as the Delhi mother elaborated—when the baby is protesting being left alone, she sits down and communicates with him. They share a focus on stimulation with the mothers following an interdependent model. They highly estimate body stimulation, they see object stimulation as training for concentration and they even add face-to-face contact to that conception. Merely looking at each other, which is the *via regio* of the mothers with an independent model, does not make much sense to them. With respect to body contact, they hold an intermediate position between the independent and interdependent model. They value body contact, but it has to be restricted to particular situations.

The excerpts also make clear that the discourse style of these mothers is highly elaborated and embellished. To document this impression quantitatively as well, we compared the Delhi mothers with respect to their discourse style assessed in the ethnotheory interviews with the Berlin and Los Angeles mothers on the one hand and the rural Nso mothers on the other hand. The same codes that were described in chapter 4 were applied. The results are presented in Tables 6.5a and 6.5b.

Again, the data demonstrate that the Delhi women fall between the independent and the interdependent women with respect to the orientation toward autonomy, as well as with respect to the orientation toward relatedness.

The analysis of the parenting ideas of mothers with an assumed autonomous-related model reveals that it is not just a combination of the relational aspects of the interdependent model and the autonomous aspects of the independent model. It is clearly a different model with unique features. It combines domains of both models that are more or less mutually exclusive in the two prototypes, as, for example, the autonomous view of the child and the focus on stimulation. However, the orientation toward both autonomy and stimulation is not as pronounced as in their models of origin. The focus on health and growth is also there, yet not as dominant as in the interdependent model. Communication does not serve the main purpose of following the baby's communicational cues and responding sensitively to them, but to train proper demeanor, as a Beijing mother (25 years old, one daughter, social scientist) explained:

> Then I have an exchange with her, I communicate with her, talk with her, teach her some gestures. I think she just kisses him or communicates with him or just tells him, "Little treasure, be a good boy." Often when I kiss her, I tell her, "Little treasure, be a good girl. You have to be a good girl."

Parenting Practices

In this section I report findings concerning the behavioral interactions of the Beijing, Delhi, and San José mothers with their 3-month-old infants. I report the results concerning nonverbal behavioral systems and conversational styles separately.

TABLE 6.5a

Composite and Component Categories of Autonomy

	Cultural Community							
	Berlin + Los Angeles[a]		Delhi[b]		Rural Nso[c]			
	M	SD	M	SD	M	SD	$F(2, 119)$	η^2
Autonomy total	48.20$_a$	20.09	34.39$_b$	15.53	19.49$_c$	12.32	23.37***	.28
Autonomy mother	39.83$_a$	18.37	26.04$_b$	16.92	7.44$_c$	8.47	32.57***	.35
I-Statements	25.78$_a$	9.94	19.54$_b$	13.87	3.05$_c$	3.96	37.91***	.39
Self-referral	14.05$_a$	14.20	6.50$_b$	8.76	4.39$_b$	7.79	7.79**	.12
Mental state baby	8.37	6.60	8.35	6.96	12.06	7.39	2.62[+]	.04
Preference	4.56$_a$	5.36	3.54	4.31	.72$_b$	1.22	5.78**	.09
Emotion	.88$_a$	1.94	2.23$_a$	4.06	5.60$_b$	3.85	19.30***	.25
Cognition	2.93$_a$	3.69	2.58$_a$	3.86	5.74$_b$	4.43	5.25*	.08

Note. Five-level (culture) MANOVA with significant multivariate main effect for culture on narrative style (component variables only: I-statements, self-referral, emotion, cognition, preference), Wilks's $\lambda = .40$, F(10, 230) = 13.28, $p < .001$, $\eta^2 = .37$, followed by univariate analyses. Indexed letters indicate results of simple main effects testing (with Bonferroni adjustment). η^2 = partial eta-square. All mean scores indicate relative frequency per 1000 words.
[a]N = 64. [b]N = 36. [c]N = 22. [+]p < .10. *p < .05. **p < .01. ***p < .001.

TABLE 6.5b

Composite and Component Categories of Relatedness

	Berlin + Los Angeles[a]		Cultural Community Delhi[b]		Rural Nso[c]			
	M	SD	M	SD	M	SD	$F(2, 119)$	η^2
Relatedness	2.83$_a$	3.99	7.33$_b$	6.94	11.69$_c$	6.19	24.04*	.29
Reference to authority	.97$_a$	2.11	4.55$_b$	5.22	4.86$_b$	4.37	15.21*	.20
Social context	1.86$_a$	2.61	2.78$_a$	3.83	6.82$_b$	4.21	18.40*	.24

Note. Five-level (culture) MANOVA with significant multivariate main effect for culture on narrative style (component variables only: Reference to authority and Social context), Wilk's $\lambda = .65$, F(4, 236) = 14.43, $p < .001$, $\eta^2 = .20$, followed by univariate analyses. Indexed letters indicate results of simple main effects testing (with Bonferroni adjustment). η^2 = partial eta-square. All mean scores indicate relative frequency per 1,000 words.
[a]N = 64. [b]N = 36. [c]N = 22. *$p < .001$.

The Nonverbal Parenting Systems.   We compared the expression of the body contact, body stimulation, face-to-face contact, and object stimulation parenting systems for a sample of 24 middle-class Costa Rican mothers from San José interacting with their 3-month-old babies with a sample of 46 Greek mothers from Athens with an independent model of parenting and with a rural Nso sample of 32 women with an interdependent model of parenting (Keller, Yovsi, et al., 2004). According to the model of autonomous-relatedness, the San José mothers should score as high on body contact and body stimulation as the rural Nso mothers and as high on face-to-face contact and object stimulation as the Athens mothers.

For the dimension of autonomy the object stimulation and face-to-face contact parenting systems were entered as dependent variables in a three-level, between-subject MANOVA design controlling simultaneously for age, gender, birth order, and education of the mother. Because only birth order turned out to be a significantly confounding variable, analyses were rerun controlling for birth order only. According to Wilks's criterion, there is a significant multivariate main effect of culture on the latent construct of independence, $F(4, 170) = 8.49$, $p < .001$, with the control of birth rank as a significantly confounding variable, $F(2, 85) = 4.64$, $p < .05$. Univariate analyses to test specific effects reveal that cultural differences hold for both variables: object stimulation, $F(2, 86) = 14.77$, $p < .001$, and face-to-face contact, $F(2, 86) = 3.38$, $p < .05$. Both dimensions were observed least frequently in rural Nso mothers ($M = 2.67$, $SD = 7.71$; $M = 54.68$, $SD = 24.80$), more often in mothers from San José ($M = 11.83$, $SD = 16.19$; $M = 59.91$, $SD = 23.15$), and most often in mothers from Athens ($M = 40.31$, $SD = 33.94$; $M = 74.23$, $SD = 24.77$). The linear contrast testing of the hypotheses turned out to be significant for both object stimulation (contrast estimate = 22.73, $SD = 4.42$, $p < .001$) and face-to-face contact (contrast estimate = 10.48, $SD = 4.28$, $p < .05$).

For the dimension of relatedness the body contact and body stimulation parenting systems were defined as dependent variables in a three-level between-subject MANOVA design. According to Wilks's criterion, there is a highly significant multivariate main effect of culture on the latent construct of interpersonal distance, $F(4, 172) = 23.66$, $p < .001$. The univariate analyses indicate that there are significant main effects for both the body contact, $F(2, 87) = 59.87$, $p < .001$, and body stimulation, $F(2, 87) = 4.60$, $p < .05$, parenting systems. The linear contrast is highly significant for body contact (contrast estimate = –48.58, $SD = 4.45$, $p < .001$) and body stimulation (contrast estimate = –10.27, $SD = 3.48$, $p < .01$), indicating a linear decrease of observed body contact and object stimulation from rural Nso mothers ($M = 100$, $SD = 0.00$; $M = 70.72$, $SD = 20.89$) over San José mothers ($M = 65.00$, $SD = 32.99$; $M = 56.96$, $SD = 22.95$) to Athens mothers ($M = 31.30$, $SD = 34.31$; $M = 55.75$, $SD = 21.34$).

The results reveal that the mothers from San José hold a position midway between the mothers with an independent and those with an interdependent model. Thus, these data reconfirm the autonomous-related model as occupying an intermediate position between the prototypical models of independence and interdependence.

In a second set of analyses we compared a combined sample of two subsamples from San José with 41 mothers and the samples from Delhi and Beijing with the combined samples with an independent model and those with an interdependent model with respect to the same nonverbal parenting systems (see Table 6.6).

The results reveal that the Delhi and Beijing samples are similar to the independent samples and different from the interdependent samples with respect to body contact and object stimulation. With respect to face-to-face contact the three samples with an assumed autonomous-related model are more similar to the interdependent samples than to the independent ones. With respect to body stimulation there are no differences among the samples. Moreover, the San José sample is more similar to the interdependent samples with respect to body contact and body stimulation.

In general, the San José sample resembles the interdependent model more than the autonomous-related model. The Beijing and the Delhi mothers are similar with the exception of object play, which Delhi mothers use less. However, they also do not represent the autonomous-related model, because they demonstrate less body contact than the interdependent samples. The data indicate that there is less of an autonomous-related prototype than is the case for the independent and the interdependent model. The differences among the samples that are assumed to be oriented toward autonomy and relatedness may reflect different amounts of schooling. Whereas the Delhi and Beijing mothers hold educational degrees comparable to the mothers with an independent model, the San José mothers have, with 9.5 years of schooling on average, a notably lower educational level.

THE RURAL–URBAN DIFFERENCE WITHIN SOCIETIES

Formal education has been related to changes in cultural models of parenting in diverse environments. The results indicate equivocally that higher educational levels increase the orientation toward autonomy in socialization goals, parenting ethnotheories, and parenting behaviors. We have already dealt with the role of education, because educational achievements are constituent for the definition of our cultural prototypes of independence and interdependence. Education can also be regarded as the engine of change with respect to the urban families in traditionally interdependent societies whose parenting models were presented in the previous section. In this section I address the role of education directly by comparing low-educated rural women with high-educated urban ones belonging to the same culture of origin. I contrast two sets of samples: low-educated rural Nso women and high-educated urban Nso women, and low-educated rural Gujarati Hindu women with high-educated urban Hindu families from the cities of Vadodara, Gujarat, and Delhi, respectively.

The Case of Rural and Urban Nso Women's Cultural Models and Practices of Parenting

Differences in Socialization Goals and Parenting Ethnotheories of Rural and Urban Nso. In a questionnaire study we compared the family orientation, socialization goals, and parenting ethnotheories of 28 rural and 28 urban Nso

TABLE 6.6

The Parenting Systems of the Autonomous-Related Samples as Compared to the Interdependent and Independent Samples

	Cultural Community										
	Independent Samples[a]		San José, Costa Rica[b]		Beijing, China[c]		Delhi, India[d]		Interdependent Samples[e]			
Parenting system	M	SD	M	SD	M	SD	M	SD	M	SD	$F(3, 113)$	η^2
Body Contact	31.99	31.0	61.02	31.0	32.30_a	33.4	37.89_a	33.2	73.76	26.3	7.33*	.14
Face-to-face Context	75.19	20.8	59.22_a	24.8	60.40_a	25.5	53.91_a	24.5	47.68	13.2	.60	.01
Body Stimulation	57.40	22.2	67.66_a	20.4	59.30_a	17.2	60.49_a	22.7	61.74	31.0	1.61	.03
Object Stimulation	40.04	30.0	10.37	19.3	44.30_a	29.3	29.14_a	30.5	7.58	19.9	12.41**	.21
Distal Parenting	57.61	19.3	34.79_a	15.9	$52.35_{a/b}$	15.2	$41.53_{a/b}$	19.1	27.63	19.7	7.20*	.13
Proximal Parenting	44.70	20.4	64.34	18.6	45.80_a	19.1	49.19_a	21.6	67.75	23.2	8.19**	.15

Note. Three-level (culture) MANOVA with significant multivariate main effect for culture on parenting system, Wilks's $\lambda = .72$, $F(8, 180.0) = 3.93$, $p < .001$, $\eta^2 = .15$, followed by univariate analyses. Indexed letters indicate results of simple main effects testing (with Bonferroni adjustment). $\eta^2 =$ partial eta-square. All mean scores indicate the appearance of the respective parenting system (in per cent). [a]N = 168. [b]N = 41. [c]N = 35. [d]N = 20. [e]N = 144.*$p < .01$. **$p < .001$.

185

women. The rural women lived in villages in the western grassfields and had an average education of about 7 years. The urban women also belong to the same ethnic tribe of the Nso and live in different cities throughout Cameroon, such as Douala, Yaounde, Bamenda, Kumbo, and Buea. They had about 13 years of formal education (Keller, 2005). As predicted by the autonomous-related model of parenting, both groups of women had equally high scores on family allocentrism, 103.9 for the rural women ($N = 19$) and 90.0 for the urban women ($N = 10$). The relational socialization goals were equally high with a maximum score of 5 for the rural women and a comparable score of 4.9 for the urban women. The scores for the autonomous socialization goals were low, as expected, in the rural sample ($M = 1.3$) and high for the urban women with 4.1 equaling the score of the Los Angeles women. The scores for the parenting ethnotheories were also as expected. Both rural and urban Nso women value relational parenting ethnotheory highly ($M = 4.9$ and $M = 4.0$), but urban women also value autonomous parenting ethnotheory highly ($M = 2.6$), thus equaling middle-class German mothers from Berlin ($M = 2.5$), whereas rural Nso mothers score low on the autonomous ethnotheory scale ($M = 1.3$). Rural and urban women differ from each other significantly in all these domains. However, this may also be partly related to the very low variability of the answers of the rural women, which were discussed in chapter 5. The questionnaire data confirm that the educated urban Nso women follow the autonomous-related model of parenting as predicted by Kağitçibaşi. In this way they differ from the urban educated samples from Delhi, Beijing, and San José.

The picture-card interviews helped to develop a more differentiated picture about the ideas of rural and urban Nso mothers concerning their parenting ethnotheories. As Figure 6.7 demonstrates, there are no differences in how the different parenting systems are addressed.

With respect to mentioning the interactional mechanisms, there is a significant difference concerning warmth. The urban Nso emphasize warmth more than the rural Nso, but this difference may be due to their more abstract—and more frequent—reference to love and general positive feelings (see Figure 6.7).

The composite score of autonomy-oriented and relatedness-oriented verbal ethnotheoretical accounts does not reveal differences between the two samples. With respect to the parenting systems, relatedness is addressed more often; with respect to interactional mechanisms, relatedness and autonomy are addressed about equally (see Figure 6.8).

However, talking about the same subject may mean different things. This rural mother (19 years old, one son, 7 years of formal education) values motor stimulation of the child and likes training for sitting: "This one fits me because if you [are] carrying the child as I am now carrying like this and wanted to do something or whether you wanted him to sit, then you can lay him inside the bowl as he is now like this."

An urban mother (31 years old, four children, 12 years of formal education) also expressed that she likes to train babies to sit, but she has a more conversational

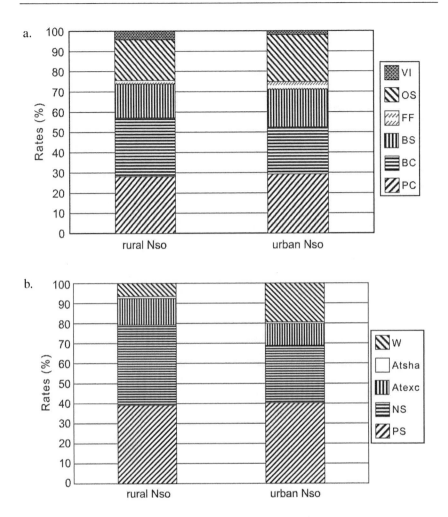

FIGURE 6.7.   (a) The content of the parenting ethnotheories of the rural and urban Nso mothers (VI = verbal interaction, OS = object stimulation, FF = face-to-face context, BS = body stimulation, BC = body contact, PC = primary care); (b) The address of interactional mechanisms in the picture-card interviews of the rural and urban Nso mothers (W = warmth, Atsha = attention shared, Atex = attention exclusive, NS = negative signals, PS = positive signals).

attitude toward it: "Like this one, as I was saying that he is also recognizing me because when I am sitting him I also turn him to be looking at me from the eyes."

Also with respect to the address of object stimulation, there are striking differences. The rural woman (19 years old, two children, 7 years of formal education) related object play to health as previously discussed in chapter 5:

a.

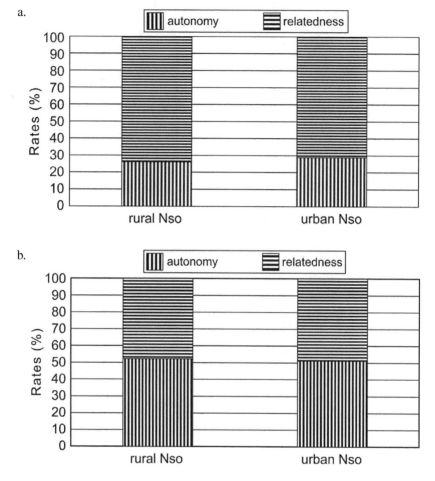

b.

FIGURE 6.8.   (a) The content of the parenting ethnotheories related to autonomy and relatedness of the rural and urban Nso women; (b) The interactional mechanisms related to autonomy and relatedness of the rural and urban Nso women.

M: Because you are supposed to carry the child and have a plaything and make him to smile.

I: Why? Why is it important to have a plaything that can make the child to smile?

M: If you carry the child you should be making him to laugh because at times when he is not playing that means he is ill.

For one urban mother (27 years old, two children, 12 years of formal education), object stimulation is embedded in a much more well-elaborated framework:

M: Yes this one is the various ways the child can take to play. Either you present flowers or present toys to him to play with. So that he should be used to nature and, artificial and natural things. [I: Mmh.] Yes you can present him with any of the things whether it's flowers or toys for him to play with.

I: Why is it good for the child to be used to things like nature and toys?

M: He too is admiring nature, but [it] is just that he too cannot express it to you that he is admiring nature. He has his own way he takes to admire the nature. [I: Mmh.] When he is at the age where he recognizes things, he will know the difference between flowers. Because in a case where you present a child with a toy and a flower, he will prefer to leave that toy and come to the flower and it is because he is really admiring the thing, but it's just that he does not know how he can ask what that is.

The amount of words per turn in the interviews does not differ between rural and urban Nso. The 28 urban women had a mean score of 28.26 (SD = 12.12) and the rural women had a mean score of 25.15 (SD = 11.54), $F(1, 55)$ = .98, $p > .05$.

With respect to the discourse styles in the ethnotheory interviews, there are significant differences with regard to the orientation toward autonomy. Urban mothers address the autonomy-related categories significantly more often than the rural mothers. With respect to the orientation toward relatedness, there is only a marginal significance, indicating more similarities than differences between the two groups of women (see Tables 6.7a and 6.7b).

The following two excerpts highlight the differences in the discourse styles of rural and urban Nso women again. Both excerpts are from the beginning of the picture-card interview. The answers of the rural woman (31 years old, four children, 6 years of formal education) are short and affirmative: Breastfeeding is necessary for the health of the baby.

I: Look at these five pictures and choose the best one. Choose which one is the best for you and the reason you have chosen the picture. They are all mothers with their babies.

M: [Laughs] All I can start giving the breast to the child.

I: Why have you taken that one? Why does that one fit you?

M: Because it is the food you are giving him to eat. When he is sucking he will then be healthy, and you are not giving him any other food.

TABLE 6.7a
Composite and Component Categories of Autonomy

| | Cultural Community | | | | | |
| | Urban Nso[a] | | Rural Nso[b] | | | |
	M	SD	M	SD	F(1, 48)	η^2
Autonomy total	27.87	9.83	19.49	12.32	7.15*	.13
Autonomy mother	11.42	11.45	7.44	8.47	1.86	.04
I-statements	5.18	5.19	3.05	3.96	2.54	.05
Self-referral	6.24	9.30	4.39	7.79	.56	.01
Mental state baby	16.45	6.56	12.06	7.39	4.94*	.09
Preference	1.92	2.40	.72	1.22	4.60*	.09
Emotion	6.45	6.45	5.60	3.85	.30	.01
Cognition	8.07	5.53	5.74	4.43	2.60*	.05

Note. Two-level (culture) MANOVA with significant multivariate main effect for culture on narrative style (component variables only: I-statements, Self-referral, emotion, cognition, preference), Wilks's $\lambda = .77$, $F(5, 44) = 2.63$, $p < .05$, $\eta^2 = .23$, followed by univariate analyses. η^2 = partial eta-square. All mean scores indicate relative frequency per 1,000 words. [a]N = 28. [b]N = 22. *$p < .05$.

TABLE 6.7b
Composite and Component Categories of Relatedness

| | Cultural Community | | | | | |
| | Urban Nso[a] | | Rural Nso[b] | | | |
	M	SD	M	SD	F(1, 48)	η^2
Relatedness	8.26	7.32	11.69	6.19	3.09[+]	.06
Reference to authority	3.15	4.10	4.86	4.37	2.03	.04
Social context	5.11	5.47	6.82	4.21	1.47	.03

Note. Two-level (culture) MANOVA with significant multivariate main effect for culture on narrative style (component variables only: Reference to authority and Social context), Wilks's $\lambda = .94$, $F(2, 47) = 1.55$, *n.s.*, $\eta^2 = .06$, followed by univariate analyses. Indexed letters indicate results of simple main effects testing (with Bonferroni adjustment). η^2 = partial eta-square. All mean scores indicate relative frequency per 1,000 words.

The urban women also stress the importance of breastfeeding and its relation to the baby's health. Yet their answers are more elaborate; in the example the urban woman (27 years old, two children, 12 years of formal education) developed her viewpoint during the discourse:

M: Okay. This is the best one.
I: Why do you like that one?

M: I like this one because when you give birth to a child, when he is still really young, at least like 1 month, you hear [I: Yes.] when he is still fearful, when anything makes noise he will be afraid. So when he is like 1 month you can be flinging him up so that his heart should be stronger. [I: Mmh.] So that if there is noise he cannot shake so that when you are flinging him up like that at least you are giving him the opportunity to play.

I: Why it is necessary for the child to be playing?

M: At least it is important because if the child is not playing you cannot know whether he is healthy or not. You see, because if a child just stays quiet, when he is playing you know that he is healthy and when he is quiet you should know that there is something wrong with him. So it is really important that when you are with the child he should be playing with you so that at times you can always notice changes in him whether he is sick or not, or anything that can be worrying him.

The mother needed only brief prompts to continue talking. However, the content is very similar.

In a different study analyzing the effects of education on parenting strategies, we interviewed Nso mothers with different educational profiles concerning their socialization goals and parenting ethnotheories (Keller, Demuth, & Yovsi, 2006). Ten Nso women with children participated in this study. Four participants were born and raised in a rural area and 6 participants lived in towns at the time of the study. The families of the rural mothers lived off subsistence farming, whereas the families of the urban mothers lived on a cash economy. The rural sample included participants with primary education ranging from 0 to 7 years of formal education (primary school). The mean age of the rural sample was 49 years, ranging from 37 to 70 years, with 1 participant for whom age was not known. Two women were Muslims (1 married, 1 a single mother) and 2 were Catholic (both married). The number of children varied from 3 to 9. The urban sample included participants with education levels higher than 7 years, ranging from form five (12 years of formal education) to BA at the university level. The mean age of the urban sample was 31; the range was 24 to 45 years. Five women were Catholic (1 divorced, 1 single, 3 married) and 1 woman was a married Presbyterian. The number of children varied from one to four.

The higher educated women lived in the town of Kumbo in northwest Cameroon, whereas the lower educated women lived in villages in the same province. Semistructured interviews were conducted in the local Lamnso language by a multilingual native speaker of the same cultural background and then transcribed and translated word for word into English. The data were analyzed using qualitative grounded theory methodology (Glaser & Strauss, 1967; Strauss & Corbin, 1990). Overall, all participants value the Nso concept of relatedness with the purpose of ensuring social functioning. Especially important are the exchange of resources (material help as well as knowledge):

Because there are so many people who don't have. If you have you can share with them because if you don't have too they would share theirs with you, so it is very important to share or live in harmony with other people. (Rural Nso mother, 45 years old, two children, 5 years of formal education)

On receiving support during critical life events, one mother remarked:

Because something can be happening like illness, dea[th] or suffering, or even a good one, and you will not have anybody to send; or a person who can stand to relieve you of such problems or do help do that with you. If something comes like a good one, and many people do it that would be nice. Or even if it is a bad one, people would come and support you then it will be good, and you will not shoulder the burden alone. (Rural Nso mother, 42 years old, nine children, 5 years of formal education)

On maintaining social harmony, one mother said:

And then when you cooperate like that, you see life goes, it moves. You see days are just running out like that. But when you tend to have a bad impression and don't share with people, you are just in chaos with people, in short you don't see days moving. You don't even live longer. That is one important thing. You don't live longer when you are angry with people. But when you share with people, they encourage you and you see days moving faster. (28 years old, two children, undergraduate)

Although interdependence is a general Nso value, there is a tendency among higher educated mothers to refer to interdependence mainly in the closer family context. Lower educated mothers refer to interdependence in all social contexts, which, however, are more narrowly composed of familiar people than those of the urban women.

Autonomy is also valued among all Nso, especially for survival, as one urban mother (28 years old, two children, undergraduate) explained:

M: At times she even tries to wash her dresses even though she cannot do it well. She forces herself that mummy I want to wash my dresses but she cannot do it well.
I: Why are all those things important?
M: They are important because at times you like a mother does not really predict that you die, but at times it helps that child when anything happens and you are no more the child can still try and help herself in one way or the other.

For the rural women, independence is restricted to adulthood:

… and when he is big enough then he can choose his own work to do that is within his reach and strength. … Then in future when he is grown up and his senses are matured enough before he can start doing what is good for him while doing what he is doing. (Rural Nso mother, nine children, 4 years of formal education)

Agency is not valued in the context of limited resources that need to be shared, which is the everyday context of the rural women:

> If there are many siblings that he has, you cannot allow him do such a thing. … Because there are many of them. He cannot just be doing his things alone and only thinking about himself, what will the others then do? They have to share from there equally. If you see a child doing that way and being selfish, you only have to be teaching him slowly so that it should not be part of him. (Rural Nso mother, nine children, 4 years of formal education)

Urban women also value independence as a way to enhance self-development:

> It is very important because it is not good to always interfere in somebody's affairs, even a child. Sometimes you allow the child's interests to grow. … It is good because if you allow her to open up she might grow in a talent that would have covered. … Yes, a talent that would have been covered. So you allow her to do what ever she likes to do. To explore her interest and what she would like to do. … So, that can open up a talent that maybe was hidden in her and which you were not seeing. But if you close him up, it will just be buried in her and it will never come out. (Urban Nso mother, 36 years old, four children, BA)

Figure 6.9 demonstrates an interaction between an urban Nso mother and her baby.

In summary, mothers with less education value autonomy in the context of survival and in particular contexts for adults. Otherwise, autonomy is seen as selfishness, which seems inappropriate in light of the limited resources and the cultural value of sharing. Mothers with higher education value autonomy in a more general sense in the context of self-actualization (see Figure 6.10).

FIGURE 6.9.   Urban Nso mother–infant interaction. Photo by Relindis Yovsi.

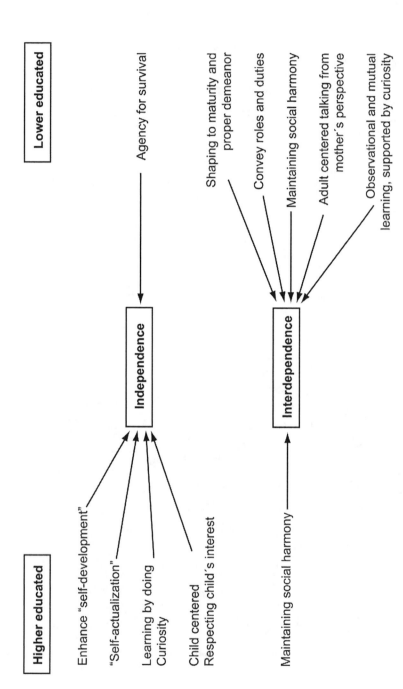

FIGURE 6.10. Socialization goals of higher and lower education Nso women.

The analysis of these interviews reveals that there are commonalities between the lower educated and the higher educated women with respect to autonomy as well as with respect to relatedness. Nevertheless, there are also substantial differences with respect to the emphasis put on these two domains. It is obvious that low-educated rural women and high-educated urban women do not share the same conception of relatedness. This adds important information to our analyses, as the differences between lower educated and higher educated Nso women are not quantitative, but reflect qualitative nuances.

The rural and the urban women differ significantly from each other with respect to autonomy-oriented and relatedness-oriented discourse categories. The urban Nso mothers' discourse style is similar to that of the Delhi mothers. The following excerpt of an interview with an urban Nso mother (30 years old, one son, BA) depicts the similarities of the urban Nso mothers to the Delhi and Beijing women: They also value face-to-face contact, but not as a behavior per se:

M: The mother has to observe, she is observing her baby. She is having a face-to-face contact with the baby.
I: Why is it good for the mother to have a face-to-face contact with the baby?
M: With the face-to-face contact the mother knows whether the baby has a problem or not. Because looking at the baby everyday, you realize whether there are changes or not.

Face-to-face contact needs to serve a purpose, in this case to check whether the baby is healthy or has a problem. On the other hand, face-to-face contact can be combined with primary care, as is done by the interdependent mothers, as demonstrated by this urban Nso mother (27 years old, three children, 12 years of formal education):

I: Why is that one good?
M: When you are breastfeeding the child you should look at the face of the child well. [I: Mmh.] Yes.
I: Why is it good to be breastfeeding the child and looking at his face?
M: So that you and the child should be conversing. [I: Mmh.] Yes.
I: Why is it good to be conversing with the child?
M: The child will be happy.

Here again, happy means basically to be in good health and have no problems.

The training orientation that is part of the interdependent model and also expressed by the Delhi and Beijing mothers is also part of the urban Nso mothers' thinking:

Because even from birth when you wake up in the morning you are supposed to greet the child. [I: Mmh.] You are supposed to say good morning. Yes, you have to greet him. You should not just think that they only greet adults, in the morning even to babies. When you do that way, he grows knowing things.

You are training him from birth to know that when he wakes up in the morning he must greet, greet his mother, father, and other neighbors, too. (Urban Nso mother, 27 years old, two children, 12 years of formal education)

This is a another nice example of the importance of not only social contact from birth on, but of extended contact and the proper way of doing it.

Our studies reveal that education makes an obvious difference in the cultural models of parenting, especially with respect to the orientations to autonomy and relatedness, even within the same ethnic group. Whereas quantitative analyses reveal that the urban Nso are oriented toward relatedness just as strongly as the rural Nso are, the qualitative analyses unmask obvious differences. Relatedness in the rural families is a pervasive characteristic pertaining to all domains of life. Relatedness in the urban families is bound to the traditional and respectful relations between children and their parents and grandparents. In every other respect, relatedness is calibrated with self-actualization and self-enhancement. With respect to the ideas supporting autonomy, urban Nso mothers feel that face-to-face contact is at least supporting the emotional development of the child. Even more important is having the opportunity to check whether everything is right with the baby, an endeavor that they share with their rural peers.

Rural and Urban Nso Parenting Behaviors. With respect to the parenting behaviors, we compared a rural Nso sample with an urban Nso sample; we also computed the composite scores of distal and proximal parenting. The results are presented in Table 6.8.

TABLE 6.8
The Occurrence of Parenting Systems in the Rural and Urban Nso Samples

Parenting System	Rural Nso[a]		Urban Nso[b]		
	M	*SD*	*M*	*SD*	*F(1, 56)*
Body contact	91.60	10.52	60.80	36.29	19.85***
Face-to-face context	37.35	24.93	58.63	28.58	9.16**
Body stimulation	87.50	14.91	56.98	27.89	27.52***
Object stimulation	7.40	21.04	24.52	33.69	5.46*
Distal parenting	22.38	17.13	41.57	15.09	20.39***
Proximal parenting	89.55	8.14	58.89	26.57	36.33***

[a]N = 30. [b]N = 28.
*p < .05. **p < .01. ***p < .001.

The data reveal significant differences with respect to all parenting systems and to the composite scores. The urban Nso mothers perform less body contact behavior and less body stimulation and more face-to-face context behavior and object stimulation than the rural mothers. Consequently, the scores for the proximal and distal styles also differ significantly. In summary, the urban Nso mothers show a different parenting pattern when interacting with their 3-month-old babies from the rural mothers. In line with the expected changes brought about by higher formal education, they emphasize distal parenting more than proximal modes.

Sleeping Arrangements. In another study we assessed the sleeping arrangements in 78 Nso households with children from birth to 12 months of age. The households differed with respect to education and household economy (Yovsi & Keller, 2006). The results revealed that children from subsistence-based families slept exclusively with their mothers in one bed with possibly another person in the same room, whereas higher educated, income-earning mothers slept with the child and another person, predominantly the father, in the same bed. In a next step, the socioeconomic status dichotomy (income vs. subsistence families) indexing the educational background and the standard of living of the family was entered as an independent variable into an ANOVA. The analysis controlled for the number of rooms used for sleeping, household composition, birth rank of the child, and sex of the child. The ANOVA confirmed the existence of different sleeping arrangements between the two groups, $F(1, 67) = 4.46$, $p < .05$.

The traditional practice is that the mother sleeps exclusively with the child in one bed. The father is absent, because the mother needs to concentrate on the baby and breastfeed him or her well to grow before the birth of another child. The sleeping pattern thus constitutes the main source of family planning for the farming communities. The results indicate that although mother–infant cosleeping is the cultural norm among the Nso, there are substantial intracultural variations with respect to the specification of the social context of sleeping. With whom the child falls asleep also differed significantly between the two groups. The groups of families did not differ in their ideas about the age at which the child should be sleeping alone, which was about 4 years old for both groups.

The time the child goes to bed (bedtime schedule) also differed significantly among the two groups. Children in subsistence-based families do not have a bedtime schedule and go to bed later than children in income-earning families, who usually have a bedtime schedule. Differences were also found with respect to bedtime routines. Subsistence-based families do not have bedtime routines, whereas income-earning families do.

The two groups of families also differed significantly in their planned weaning age. The subsistence-based families expected to wean the children at the mean age of 23 months, ranging from 12 to 36 months, whereas the income-earning families planned to wean their children at a mean age of 18 months, ranging from 12 to 24 months. This indicates that the subsistence-based families breastfeed their children 5 months longer on average than the income-earning families.

Schooling and income earning exert significant, enduring effects on the way parents organize the sleeping environment of their children. Parents with a higher educational level and occupational position often engage in Western independent parenting practices as is demonstrated by their age of childbearing, planned weaning age, and timing of sleeping arrangements. They also focus on the mother–father–child bond, whereas the traditional family focuses more on the mother–child unit within the family system. Formal education creates an environment void of traditional practices and forms a measure of Westernization (Richman, Miller, & LeVine, 1992; Yovsi, 2003) that is inculcated into the way parents care for their children. Schooling and income for the family, no matter how low it is, make a difference for the family's lifestyle and constitute socialization for a particular type of parenting, which also involves autonomy and independence.

The differences between the rural and urban Nso can be summarized as representing two different models of parenting. The rural families follow an interdependent model, as described previously, whereas the educated urban Nso women follow a combination that can be described as one variation on an autonomous-related model. With respect to family allocentrism, relational socialization goals, and relational parenting ethnotheories, the urban women do not differ from their rural peers. With respect to autonomous socialization goals and parenting ethnotheories, however, there is a clear difference. Urban Nso women value autonomous socialization goals to the same extent that independent women do. The qualitative analysis of the ethnotheories reveals that in fact autonomy-related socialization goals supersede relational ones in urban Nso women. It also became apparent that their conception of relatedness differs from that of the rural women in that it is more domain specific; relatedness is constrained to family relationships and not a general attitude like for the rural Nso. On the other hand, the rural Nso's conception of autonomy also differs from that of the urban women. For them, autonomy is more domain specific, centering on survival. With respect to parenting behaviors, urban women express more autonomy-related practices than do the rural women with higher amounts of distal parenting and lower amounts of proximal parenting. This pattern is also expressed by the sleeping arrangements, which originally were another avenue to closeness and family cohesion. This pattern is not maintained in its original form either, but undergoes changes and modifications with increasing education and cash economy. Urban infants leave the parental bed earlier and are weaned earlier than their rural peers. Moreover sleeping becomes an activity that is clearly separated from daily life with bedtime schedules and routines.

The Indian Case: Socialization Goals and Parenting Ethnotheories of Rural and Urban Women

In our questionnaire study we compared 14 rural Gujarati Rajput women with 23 urban middle-class Hindu families from Delhi (Keller, Lamm, et al., 2006). With an average of 3.4 years of formal schooling, the Rajput mothers have the lowest formal educational attainment among all our cultural samples. The Delhi mothers, on the other hand, have, with 15.3 years on average, one of the highest educational levels among our samples (Berlin women had 15.0 years, Los Angeles women had 17.2 years). As expected, both groups of women score high on family allocentrism, although the rural mothers ($M = 92.8$) score even higher than the urban mothers ($M = 84.7$). Both the autonomous and relational socialization goals and the respective scores for the parenting ethnotheories of the rural and urban Indian participants are indicated in Table 6.9.

The data reveal somewhat surprising results. Whereas the rural women hold higher relational socialization goals than the urban women, there are no differences with respect to autonomous socialization goals. With respect to parenting ethnotheories, the same holds true: The rural women score higher on the relational dimension and there is no significant difference on the autonomous dimension, although descriptively the rural women score lower than the urban women. Thus, the data indicate that there are differences, but they are not always in the expected direction: Rural women express more relatedness and less autonomy in all dimensions than urban women.

This study has documented that rural and urban women from the same ecocultural context who have differing degrees of formal education not only differ with respect to their emphases, but also with respect to their evaluations and the normative underpinning of what constitutes normal and healthy development.

In a different study we analyzed the conceptions of educated, urban middle-class women from the Gujarati city of Vadodara with respect to the parenting practices of the rural Rajput mothers interacting with their 3-month-old babies (Keller, Voelker, Yovsi, & Shastri, 2005).

Vadodara is a city with approximately 1.15 million inhabitants in the state of Gujarat, India. Vadodara is surrounded by an industrial belt where the main industries are oil, petrochemicals, and pharmaceuticals. Education is available at a great variety of private and public schools and from the Maharaja Sayajirao University of Baroda, an internationally renowned university. The total literacy rate for the city is 71.1%, with females lagging behind males. This does not, however, typify the literacy of young members of the middle class, who achieve higher education

TABLE 6.9
Results for Socialization Goals and Parenting Ethnotheories

| | *Delhi*[a] | | *Rural Gujarati*[b] | | | |
	M	*SD*	*M*	*SD*	*F(1, 35)*	η^2
			Cultural Community			
Socialization goals						
Autonomy	3.61	.81	4.04	1.00	2.11	.06
Relatedness	3.87	.67	4.54	.68	8.67*	.20
Parenting ethnotheories						
Autonomy	3.11	.73	2.61	.99	3.10[+]	.08
Relatedness	3.43	.54	3.43	.26	70.95**	.67

Note. Two-level (culture) ANOVA. η^2 = partial eta-square.
[a]N = 23. [b]N = 14. [+]p < .10. *p < .01. **p < .001.

levels to a large extent. Health care is available from the numerous clinics and private practices that are scattered all over Vadodara. Apart from allopathic treatments, many middle-class Indian families also value traditional, especially Ayurvedic remedies (e.g., Kakar, 1978).

Infant mortality was estimated to be 45 per 1,000 live births in urban Gujarat in 1999 (Registrar General of India, 2003). This rate can be expected to be lower in middle-class families. The fertility rate was 3.8 in urban Gujarat in 1991.

The majority of the families in Vadodara follow the Hindu religion, but there is a fair representation of religions like Islam, Christianity, and Jainism. Families from different regions of the country reside in Vadodara, giving it a cosmopolitan culture. All the families in our study belong to the Hindu religion.

We held focus group discussions with the 19 urban women in our sample using the video prompt method described in chapter 4. The women differed in age (ranging from 22–44) and parity ($M = 1.6$ children); all had high levels of formal education with college degrees. They watched video sequences of rural Indian women from the Nandesari area, which is located about 20 km from Vadodara. The Indian women spoke English and Gujarati, using the local code-switching style.

The comments of the women to the video clips were analyzed according to the code system presented in chapter 4. Frequencies of comments were accumulated per category, resulting in total scores per respondent for each category that were divided by the total amount of each respondent's comments.

The categories were grouped with respect to their association toward autonomy and toward relatedness (see chap. 4, this volume). The data are contrasted with results from a focus group discussion of 19 middle-class northern German mothers (M age = 27.8 years, range = 21–42) with a high level of education (at least 15 years of formal education) and 1.2 children on average. Unfortunately, it was not possible to do the same study with rural Indian women because the social attention that the video setup was disturbing village life.

The analysis of the categories that can be associated with relatedness for the middle-class Gujarati and German mothers are presented in Figures 6.11.

It is surprising that the German women talk more about distress regulation and body contact than the Indian women. The major difference, however, is the enormous gap in the reference to primary care. This difference can be entirely explained by the Gujarati urban women's rejection of the rural women's practice of standing their 3-month-old babies when they wash them or just for the sake of having them stand (see Figure 6.12). They feel that the three-month-old baby is not yet mature enough for this kind of treatment and they get quite upset with the rural women's behavior, which they credit to lacking information about proper child care (Keller, Voelker, Yovsi, & Shastri, 2005).

Accordingly, most of the comments made by the urban Indian women had a negative tone. In line with a general orientation toward positive emotions with respect to early child care, the German women's comments are mainly positive.

The data reveal that the German women talk a lot more about all aspects of autonomy than the urban Gujarati women do.

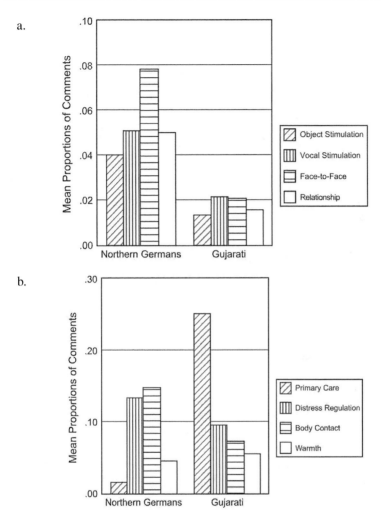

FIGURE 6.11.   Mentioning of parenting dimensions related to (a) autonomy, and
(b) relatedness of urban Indian and German women.

Parenting Practices.   We assessed the parenting practices of rural and urban
Gujarati mothers interacting with their 3-month-old babies using the method of
spot observations, explained in chapter 4 (Abels et al., 2005). In line with the autonomous-related orientation of the urban women, we expected them to have amounts
of body contact, caressing, and body stimulation (as the parenting practices that can
be assumed to support relational socialization goals) similar to those of the rural
women. Our data confirm this assumption with respect to caressing and body stimulation, but not, however, with respect to body contact.

FIGURE 6.12.   Mother and father with standing baby in rural Gujarat. Photo by
Monika Abels.

The difference in body contact may be mainly due to the fact that urban infants
receive more passive touch than their rural peers. It can be assumed that this is
rooted in the differences in rural and urban women's chores. Rural mothers' chores
include fetching water, washing clothes, and sometimes even working in the
fields, during which time they have to leave their infants behind. The middle-class
urban women have employees or technical devices to help them with their work
that gives them more freedom with respect to their involvement with their babies.
This interpretation also goes well with the correlation of the covariate family income with body contact as better off families can spend more money on devices,
employees, or both. The covariate family income also was significant for body
stimulation. This may be due to the fact that, in urban areas in particular, well-off
families employ somebody to massage their infants or find time to do it
themselves.

Although the amount of caressing was equal for the two samples as expected, it
was unexpectedly low. This finding may express a characteristic of Hindu Indian
parenting that has been described as *diffuse mothering*. Children are encouraged to
form affective bonds with adult female relatives but discouraged from forming
close mother–child bonds (Kurtz, 1992; Seymour, 1999). Another aspect of this
parenting strategy is that an open display of a mother's emotions in the presence of

other people is regarded as inappropriate (Chaudhary, 2004). However, in our study there was not much caressing from persons other than the mother either, which may be a characteristic of the early age range of the infants in our study.

We also expected urban infants to experience more exclusive attention, eye-to-eye contact, and object stimulation. Our data confirm that urban infants experience more eye-to-eye contact and more exclusive attention; there were no differences, however, with respect to object stimulation (Abels et al., 2005). Object stimulation was rare in both settings. It does not seem to play the role it does in Western cultural communities that stress an independent agency, such as German and U.S. middle-class societies (Keller, Lohaus, et al., 2004; Keller, Voelker, & Yovsi, 2005).

In fact, rural Gujarati women believe that a 3-month-old baby cannot understand toys and see their advantage mainly in distracting a fussy or crying baby, as analyzed in the interviews. Urban mothers expressed that toys are not that important for 3-month-olds. They also expressed their fear of the baby getting hurt by or catching an infection from the toy.

The father's age was correlated with the exclusive attention the infant experienced. It could be that older fathers interacted more, and maybe more exclusively, with their infants. It may be that the older fathers' positions in their families were different and their occupational status might have been more secure than that of the younger fathers and might have allowed them a closer relationship with their infants.

The role of the other people who supposedly play an especially important role in children's socialization in India (Keller, Abels, et al., 2005) seems to differ somehow in rural and urban families. In rural homes other people are both within reach and within view of the child to a larger extent than in urban families. In urban homes, others are more involved in care activities than in rural families. On the one hand, this may reflect the greater affluence of the urban families, which have servants to massage the baby; others may have fewer chores and therefore can spend more time caring for the baby. On the other hand, this could be the expression of a general rural mentality that suggests that as long as a baby does not cry he or she does not need any special attention.

The comparison of rural Gujarati women with educated urban women from Delhi and Vadodara, all belonging to the Hindu religion, also reveals that parental education has major implications for infants' experiences. However, these differences are not expressed equally in all dimensions of parenting. The urban women clearly represent a variety of the autonomous-related model, whereas the rural women follow the interdependent model. Rural women's attitudes and behaviors are influenced greatly by their physical weakness and their workload. Our data reveal both intracultural differences and different reference systems. This is obvious, particularly for the rural technique of standing babies, which is vigorously rejected by the urban women. In line with the Nso data, the Indian data also reveal that education and its consequences for daily life substantially influence parenting.

German Fathers With Different Educational Backgrounds

The third set of studies refers to urban German fathers with different levels of formal education. In a longitudinal study, 24 German fathers and their firstborn children (12 girls, 12 boys) participated (Lamm et al., 2006). All 24 families lived in urban areas in northern Germany and belonged to the middle class. The majority of the participants had a high level of education: 41.7% had a university degree, another 29.2% had passed the *Abitur* (general qualification for university entrance), and the remaining 29.2% had completed secondary school. The fathers' mean age was 32.2 years ($SD = 4.28$ years); 18 fathers (75%) were married at the time, and 6 fathers lived together with the mother of the child without being married. The fathers and their 3-month-old infants were videotaped during free-play situations, which were later analyzed with respect to the occurrence of the four parenting systems of body contact, body stimulation, face-to-face contact, and object stimulation. To test the assumption that there is intracultural variation concerning the father–infant interaction related to educational level, a hierarchical cluster analysis with the four parenting systems as variables was computed. Linkage between groups on the basis of squared Euclidian distances was used as the cluster method. A sudden increase in the distance between merged clusters revealed an optimal solution of two clusters.

Cluster 1 (11 fathers; 6 male, 5 female children) describes a more proximal parenting style with extensive body contact. Cluster 2 (13 fathers; 6 male, 7 female children) represents a more distal parenting style with a low amount of body contact, extensive object stimulation, and a high frequency of face-to-face contact (see Table 6.10). The two clusters differed statistically significantly concerning the extent of body contact and object stimulation. Although fathers in Cluster 2 showed more face-to-face contact with their infants, this difference was not statistically significant. Neither was there a statistically significant difference between the clusters with respect to the body stimulation system.

Although the two groups of fathers did not differ statistically significantly in the amount of face-to-face contact, there was a descriptive difference as expected. The missing statistical significance may be due to the fact that a German mid-

TABLE 6.10
Two Cluster Solution (ANOVA)

Cluster variables	Cluster 1 (11 fathers)		Cluster 2 (13 fathers)		
	M	SD	M	SD	F(1, 22)
Body contact	87.16	12.10	36.17	14.67	84.20**
Body stimulation	59.44	19.19	60.67	10.19	.04
Object stimulation	16.48	18.75	52.33	26.41	14.18*
Face-to-face context	56.91	25.40	65.92	22.60	.85

*p < .01. **p < .001.

dle-class sample was studied; this sample can generally be expected to emphasize face-to-face contact more than participants from other cultural environments (Keller, Lohaus, et al., 2004; Keller, Yovsi, et al., 2004), hence making it difficult to find statistically significant differences at a relatively high level of occurrence. With respect to body stimulation, there was not the expected difference between the fathers emphasizing the proximal and the distal style of parenting, respectively. This finding may express fathers' general inclination for bodily stimulations in interaction with their infants (Lamb, 1997; Yogman, 1982).

To analyze the differences between the two clusters concerning the educational achievement of the fathers, a one-way ANOVA with the cluster solution as the independent variable and the sociodemographic context variables as dependent variables was calculated. There were no differences between the two clusters with respect to gender and age of the infant, age and birth rank of the father, and the duration (in hours) the father was interacting with his child on a daily basis. However, there were statistically significant differences with respect to education (years of schooling) of the fathers. The fathers in Cluster 2 with the more distal parenting style had a higher educational level ($M = 15.46$ vs. $M = 12.64$ in Cluster 1), $F(1, 22) = 4.36$, $p < .05$.

Conclusion

The intracultural comparisons of mothers and fathers with the same cultural background but different educational attainments revealed that education is indeed the major force behind changing parenting attitudes and behaviors. Our data help us understand parameters that influence patterns of caregiving in the same cultural environment. Generally, changes occur in the direction of increasing autonomy and independence. However, it is not a simple quantitative increase but a qualitative transformation; for example, face-to-face contact is increasingly emphasized with increasing education, not as the sole communication channel that the independent families appreciate, but as a scenario for training and health checks. It is evident that the economic situation of a family has important consequences for caregiving. Affluence allows the families to hire helpers in the household who give the mother more time for exclusive care of the infant. It may also influence the amount of body contact, as our Indian data suggest. Our data do not reveal gender differences, although the Nso culture and the Hindu way of life emphasize hierarchical gender segregation (Anandalakshmy, 1991). It is possible that gender differences only become manifest in attitudes and behavior later in life. Generally the data support the results of the analyses of middle-class samples from previous interdependent societies presented earlier.

HISTORICAL CHANGES

Modernization, globalization, and individualization processes constitute a widespread phenomenon, something that is also being discussed by sociologists and psychologists with respect to the impact on family life. In this paragraph we address the situation in Germany first. Since the mid-1980s, sociologists have discussed a new phase of individualization as being a particular German phenomenon (Beck, 1986/1994; McClosky & Zaller, 1984; Neubauer & Hurrelmann, 1995). A large increase in the material standard of living, increased social and geographical mobility, and the expansion of education have been related to the breakdown of traditional forms of lifestyles and emancipation from normative ties and social dependencies (Beck, 1986/1994). Reunification of the two German states in 1989 further reinforced the demand for individualization. As a corollary, major demographic changes occurred. The number of marriages has declined (6.3 per 1,000 inhabitants in 1980 vs. 5.1 in 2002) and divorce rates have increased from 1.8 per 1,000 inhabitants in 1980 to 2.4 in 2002. The average age of marriage is delayed for women, from 23.4 in 1980 to 28.5 in 2000 and for men from 26.1 in 1980 to 31.3 in 2000. The average age of mothers when their first child is born has increased from 25.2 in 1980 to 28.9 in 1999. Children live in one of only three types of households in Germany. Paralleling these changes, education has improved significantly. The number of university students in West Germany has increased from about 1.04 million in 1980 to 1.63 million in 2001. The percentage of women studying at a university has increased from 36.7 in 1980 to 46.1 in 2000. Women's participation in the labor force has also increased from 36.4% (women with children under 6 years of age) in 1980 to 52.9% in 2001. (All figures are from the Statistisches Bundesamt, Wiesbaden, Germany.) All figures represent the national level of the western part of Germany, so it can be expected that the figures are even more pronounced for middle-class families.

All these changes amount to the definition of individuality as a social demand on each member of a society (Heitmeyer & Olk, 1995; Sünker, 1995). These changes can also be assumed to affect the nature of parent–child relationships, as parents want to give their children skills for the future. We therefore expected that the sociocultural orientation toward increased independence would also be recognizable in changing parenting practices with infants (Keller & Lamm, 2005).

To test these assumptions we compared parenting in 1977–1978 with parenting in 2000 in free-play situations involving mothers and their 3-month-old babies (Keller & Lamm, 2005). The two samples were comparable with respect to sociodemographic characteristics. We assumed that an increased focus on independence would be reflected in increased amounts of contingency to positive infant signals in the face-to-face context and increased frequency of object play. The focus on the cultural model of independence might also be expressed in decreased expressions of warmth in terms of the amount of bodily proximity or facial and vocal expression of warmth in the face-to-face context. The participants in the study were 67 ethnically German mothers of 3-month-old firstborn infants. The 25 mothers in the 1977–1978 cohort lived in Mainz and the surrounding area; the 42 mothers in the 2000 cohort lived in Marburg and the surrounding area. The two cities are comparable in size, economic bases, and demographic profile. Both are traditional German university cities. The two samples consist of highly educated middle-class participants who had just started a family. The age of the mothers of the two cohorts differed in accordance with the demographical changes. The average age was 26.5 (range = 21–32) for the mothers of Cohort 1 and 29.7 for the mothers of Cohort 2 (range = 24–39).

Free-play interactional situations were videotaped and analyzed according to parenting systems and interactional mechanisms as conceptualized in the component model of parenting (see chap. 3, this volume). Group differences were analyzed using a MANOVA with the cohort of the mother as the independent variable and gender of the child and age of the mother as covariates. The dependent variables were the measures of contingency, object play, body contact, smiling, and baby talk. The results revealed significant differences in most of the parenting behaviors of the mothers depending on the cohort of the mother, $F(5, 59) = 9.37, p <$ .001 (see Table 6.11). There were no effects from the covariates. Neither the gender of the infant nor the age of the mother affected maternal contingency to infant signals, the use of toys, or the expressed warmth. The analysis of contingency experiences revealed significant differences between the cohorts. Mothers of the 2000 cohort reacted more frequently (within a latency window of 1 second) to infants' positive signals than did mothers in the 1977–1978 Cohort 1. The use of toys and objects also differed significantly between the two cohorts of mother–infant dyads. Mothers belonging to the 2000 cohort used objects while interacting with their infants in 39.8% of the analyzed observational intervals, whereas mothers of the 1977–1978 cohort used toys only in 15.3% of the observational time.

Looking at the role of warmth in early mother–child interactions, we found significant differences with respect to both modes of warmth. The expression of bodily warmth by means of body contact and the facial or vocal expression of warmth assessed by smiling and baby talk decreased significantly from the 1977–1978 cohort to the 2000 cohort. Mothers of the 1977–1978 cohort had significantly more close body contact with their infants during play interaction than mothers of the 2000 cohort. At the same time the frequency of smiling decreased significantly from the 1977–1978 cohort to the 2000 cohort.

Only the frequency of baby talk did not change. The data thus confirm that these two generations of mothers differ in their interactional patterns with their

TABLE 6.11
Group Differences Between Mothers of the Two Cohorts

Dependent Variables	1977/78 Cohort	2000 Cohort	F (1, 63)	p	η^2
Contingency toward positive infant signals	0.09	0.34	18.94	.000	.231
Object play	0.15	0.40	8.57	.005	.120
Body contact	1.29	0.70	15.38	.000	.196
Smiling	0.70	0.50	4.03	.049	.060
Baby talk	1.06	1.04	0.04	.843	—

3-month-old babies. The younger generation of mothers demonstrates significantly more parenting practices that can be assumed to support independent socialization goals (i.e., contingency experience and object play), and at the same time a decrease in parenting practices that can be assumed to support interdependent socialization goals (i.e., bodily warmth as well as facial and vocal expressions of warmth). Infants from these two generations of middle-class German families thus have different social experiences during the early phase of life.

These differences are also reflected in mothers' conversational styles, in other words, how they address their babies in interactional situations and how they try to convey autonomy and relatedness in these dialogues. We analyzed the conversational styles of middle-class German mothers of different samples belonging to different epochs interacting with their 3-month-old babies in free-play situations. Sociodemographically comparable samples were assessed in Mainz, Muenster, Marburg, and Berlin. The transcripts of the mothers' verbal and vocal behaviors were analyzed with the coding system presented in chapter 4. The data were compiled for categories supporting autonomy and those supporting relatedness. The results are presented in Figure 6.13.

The conversations expressing relatedness did not change over historical time. Yet, the conversations supporting autonomy increase over time, although not statistically significantly.

The results of our studies suggest that historical epochs form distinct cultural environments that undergo substantial change in Western postindustrialized information societies.

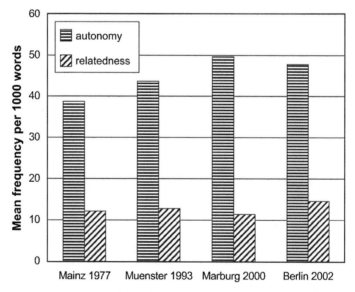

FIGURE 6.13. Verbal production relating to autonomy and relatedness in German mother–infant interactions over historical time.

Because the pace of change may be different in different societies, we analyzed changes in parenting patterns in three cultural communities that represent the three cultural models of parenting. We selected a shorter time span of 5 years (Keller, Borke, et al., 2005). The study included 129 families with 3-month-old children from three cultural communities (33 rural Nso families from Cameroon, 50 urban middle-class families from Costa Rica, and 46 urban middle-class families from Germany).

The sociodemographic profiles (see Table 6.12) support the macrolevel changes over the period of 4 to 5 years, but to different degrees in the three cultural communities. Literacy and economy increased, as did life expectancy; infant mortality decreased.

Mother–infant interactional situations were videotaped and analyzed with respect to the occurrence of the four parenting systems: body contact, body stimulation, face-to-face contact, and object stimulation. First, for all the subsamples Mann–Whitney –U tests were calculated to test whether there were in-group differences concerning the parenting systems between male and female and between firstborn and later-born children. There were no significant differences among the subsamples.

We expected that in all of the cultural samples that we analyzed in this study changes in parenting could likewise be attributed to an increase in independence. We therefore compared the combined early samples with the combined later samples from all cultural contexts. Table 6.13 presents the results of the Mann–Whitney U test separately with the parenting systems for the early and later assessments. The results of the Mann–Whitney U tests showed significant differences with respect to body stimulation. In the later samples there was less body stimulation than in the earlier ones.

Table 6.14 presents the results of Mann–Whitney U tests with separate comparisons of the parenting systems between the two rural Nso, urban middle-class Costa Rican, and urban middle-class German samples. The results for the rural Nso samples show that the differences between the two samples were not significant. For the urban Costa Rican samples, the results of the Mann–Whitney U test show a significant difference in the variable body stimulation. In the 1997 sample there was more body stimulation than in the 2001 sample. In the case of the urban German samples, the results of the Mann–Whitney U test show significant differences with respect to object stimulation and body stimulation. In the 1999 sample there was more object stimulation and less body stimulation than in the 1993 sample.

Although we only analyzed a brief time span of 4 to 5 years in this study, we were able to demonstrate changes in line with an increase in an orientation toward a more independent model of parenting. However, the pattern of changes does not apply to all cultural communities and all parenting systems. There were no changes between the two rural Nso samples. There was a significant decrease in body stimulation between the two urban Costa Rican samples. There was also a significant decrease in body stimulation, but also a significant increase in object

TABLE 6.12
Sociodemographic Changes

	Cameroon		Costa Rica		Germany	
	1998	2002	1997	2001	1993	1999
Literacy	63.4[a]	79.0[b]	94.8[a]	96.0[b]	99.0	99.0
Gross domestic product (per capita, U.S.$)	2,000.0	1,700.0	6,700.0[c]	8,500.0	16,700.0	22,700.0
Life expectancy total (years)	51.4	54.4	75.8	76.0	76.0	77.2
Life expectancy, men (years)	49.9	53.5	73.4	73.5	73.0	74.0
Life expectancy, woman (years)	53.0	55.2	78.4	78.7	79.0	80.5
Total fertility rate	5.0	4.6	2.7	2.1	1.4	1.4
Divorce rate (per 100 marriages)	—[d]	—[d]	18.0	31.0	15.6	18.8[c]
Infant mortality rate (per 1,000 live births)	77.0	70.1	14.3	10.8	7.0	5.1
General mortality rate (per 1,000 inhabitants)	14.0	12.1	3.9	3.9	11.0	10.8

[a]1995. [b]2003. [c]1998. [d]No information available.

TABLE 6.13
General Differences Between the First and the Second Cohort (Over All Samples)

	N	T1[a] Mean Rank	T2[b] Mean Rank	Z
Face-to-face context (%)	129	68.24	62.44	−.88
Object stimulation (%)	129	62.57	66.92	−.69
Body contact (%)	129	69.75	61.24	−1.33
Body stimulation (%)	129	78.66	54.19	−3.69*

[a]$n = 57$. [b]$n = 72$.
*$p < .001$.

TABLE 6.14
Differences in the Parenting Systems for the Different Samples Separately

Variable	n	T1[a] Mean Rank	T2[b] Mean Rank	Z
Cameroonian Nso				
Face-to-face context (%)	33	18.86	15.63	−.95
Object stimulation (%)	33	19.29	15.32	−1.43
Body contact (%)	33	17.50	16.63	−.86
Body stimulation (%)	33	19.00	15.53	−1.02
Costa Ricans				
Face-to-face context (%)	50	27.00	24.32	−.64
ObjectsStimulation (%)	50	24.50	26.29	−.47
Body contact (%)	50	27.91	23.61	−1.05
Body stimulation (%)	50	30.77	21.36	−2.27*
Germans				
Face-to-face context (%)	46	23.24	23.30	−.11
Object stimulation (%)	46	18.14	28.00	−2.49*
Body contact (%)	46	26.26	21.18	−1.28
Body stimulation (%)	46	31.00	17.20	−3.47**

[a]$n = 57$. [b]$n = 72$.
*$p < .05$; **$p < .001$.

play in the urban German samples. These data suggest that sociodemographic changes reveal different dynamics in different sociocultural environments. The lifestyle of the Nso farmers is still traditional, although education and other sociodemographic parameters have changed. The Nso still live in their extended family system and make their living communally with respect to farming and other subsistence activities, described in the Nso portrait earlier.

The reported sociodemographic changes for Germans are biggest among the cultural communities that we addressed with this study. Therefore, it is not surprising that the changes in parenting are also most pronounced among the three cultural communities. Discontinuity in parenting in German middle-class families can be expected, as horizontal transmission of information concerning childrearing is prevalent. The urban Costa Rican mothers demonstrated significantly less body stimulation across the two samples, which may also express an inclination toward greater independence among the younger generation.

Our studies clearly reveal that historical epochs represent distinct cultural environments. Demographic changes support an increasing orientation toward the cultural model of independence, which finds its expressions in parenting practices that are more and more oriented toward autonomy and less oriented toward relatedness. This is especially visible in quickly changing societies like Germany. Babies experience more face-to-face context and contingent responses and more object stimulation with toys. On the other hand, they also experience more separateness in that they experience less body contact and warmth in interactional situations.

GENERATIONAL CHANGES

The grandmothers in this study are the mothers or the mothers-in-law of the participating mothers. The grandmother who had most contact with the 3-month-old baby was interviewed in our studies. In the case of the rural Nso sample, this was, in the majority of families, the mother-in-law due to the patrilocal homesteads. Some single mothers live with their families of origin, so that their mothers were interviewed. Likewise, in the urban Nso sample mainly the paternal grandmothers were interviewed. The sociodemographic data of the samples are included in Table 6.15.

The mentioning of the parenting systems primary care, body contact, body stimulation, face-to-face context, object stimulation, and vocal interaction were coded and relativized by the amount of all mentioning of the six parenting systems for each participant individually. The data reveal that the mothers from the different cultural communities differ significantly from each other concerning all parenting systems except primary care. The grandmothers differ from each other significantly with respect to the mentioning of primary care, body stimulation, object stimulation, and vocal interaction (see Figure 6.14). There are no significant differences with respect to body contact and face-to-face context. This is interesting, because on the one hand, one would have expected cultural differences to be more pronounced in the younger generation because global changes toward individualization that have a similar effect could be expected to increase. On the other hand, however, it could also be that the older generations are more similar, as they all adhered to a more interdependent mode. Our cross-sectional comparisons of parenting behaviors confirm this latter view.

The mother–grandmother comparisons reveal different results with respect to the different samples. The rural Nso mothers and grandmothers do not differ from each other. This likewise confirms the cross-sectional comparisons, in which we did not

TABLE 6.15

Sociodemographic Profiles of the Grandmothers

	Mothers				Grandmothers		
	Berlin, Germany[a]	Delhi, India[b]	Urban Nso, Cameroon[c]	Rural Nso, Cameroon[d]	Berlin, Germany[e]	Delhi, India[f]	Urban Nso, Cameroon[f]	Rural Nso, Cameroon[g]
Mean age of mothers/grandmother	34.0	28.9	29.8	29.2	63.0	57.2	58.3	57.8
Mean years of school attendance	15.3	15.5	12.9	6.7	11.6	12.0	3.2	1.0
Mean number of children	1.4	1.6	2.6	3.4	2.5	2.9	5.8	5.9[h]
Mean number of persons per household	3.5	6.1	6.7	7.5	2.1	6.3	7.3	6.3

[a]N = 41. [b]N = 36. [c]N = 28. [d]N = 29. [e]N = 22. [f]N = 12. [g]N = 20. [h]N = 7.

213

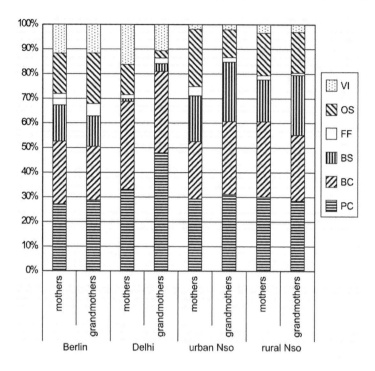

FIGURE 6.14. Mothers and grandmothers reference to the parenting systems in the picture-card interviews.

find differences in parenting behaviors over a time span of 4 years. The time span of the generational comparisons, however, is much larger, indicating stability across generations. The urban Nso mothers differ from the grandmothers with respect to the number of times object stimulation was mentioned. Mothers talk significantly more about this parenting system than grandmothers do. The object stimulation system is strongly associated with the independent model of parenting. In the Delhi samples there is a trend toward significant differences with respect to primary care (grandmothers more than mothers) and object stimulation (mothers more than grandmothers). There is no difference between the Berlin mothers and grandmothers. This result is surprising when we consider the shift toward the independent model in parenting that we found in behavior in the historical comparison between the 1977 and 2000 cohorts. However, our interview data reveal that grandmothers try to adapt to the mothers' attitudes toward parenting as this excerpt from an interview with a Berlin grandmother (69 years old, two children, three grandchildren, 10 years of formal education, retired bookkeeper) illustrates:

GM: Oh well, how should I say, one needs to take care, one needs to talk to him and I don't know. And they get excited and do. It's okay for me.

I: Yes.

GM: Not only feeding and then putting them back to bed. I mean, we did not do as much when we were you[ng], I honestly confess.

I: Uhm.

GM: But we didn't know [any] better, one shouldn't go out with them either, they should be lying [down] and what do I know. Everything was different, okay?

I: Uhm.

GM: But his ... today, I really like it a lot.

Later she explicitly admired her daughter for how she parents:

GM: Yeah, breastfeeding is certainly very important.

I: Uhm.

GM: And most importantly to stay calm. My daughter, well she is so calm, and only the child, and caressing and "Sweetheart, do you like this?" Honestly, she is unique.

I: Uhm.

GM: I really like that.

If we compile the parenting systems with the two composite scores of autonomy (face-to-face context, object stimulation, verbal interaction) and relatedness (primary care, body contact, body stimulation), the analysis confirms the results of the component categories. A 4×2 ANOVA reveals significant main effects for cultural community, $F(3, 192) = 7.42$, $p < .001$, as well as generation, $F(1, 192) = 5.72$, $p < .05$, and significant interaction, $F(3, 192) = 3.23$, $p < .05$. In specific, we find no significant cultural differences concerning the composite scores of autonomy and relatedness among the mother samples, but we do with respect to the grandmother samples. The grandmothers from Berlin score significantly higher in autonomy and lower in relatedness than all the other grandmothers. Differences among mothers and grandmothers are also found in the Delhi and urban Nso samples, where the mothers score significantly higher in autonomy than the grandmothers. The Berlin and rural Nso samples revealed no generational differences (see Figure 6.15).

With respect to the discourse styles, we also found significant main effects for cultural community, $F(6, 182) = 12.04$, $p < .001$, as well as for generation, $F(2, 191) = 9.33$, $p < .001$, and a significant interaction, $F(6, 382) = 2.97$, $p < .01$. There are significant cultural differences between the mother samples and significant differences between the grandmother samples in the expected direction. Concerning the comparison between mothers and grandmothers, the Delhi samples reveal the most clear-cut pattern: The mothers use significantly more discourse elements that refer to autonomy, and the grandmothers refer more often to relatedness. The Berlin grandmothers' style refers significantly more to relatedness, but there are no differences between mothers and grandmothers from Berlin with respect to au-

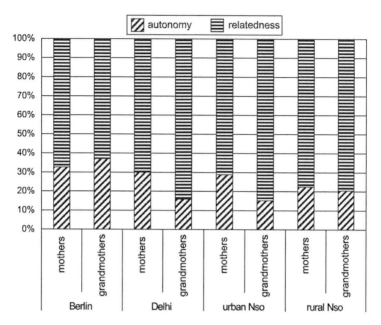

FIGURE 6.15.   Mothers and grandmothers reference to autonomy and relatedness as expressed in the parenting systems.

tonomy. The results with respect to the Nso samples are less clear. The Nso farmer mothers use more discourse elements referring to relatedness than the grandmothers do, but the mothers also tended to use more elements of autonomy. The urban Nso mothers and grandmothers do not differ from each other with respect to discourse style.

Generational comparisons also shed some light on the processes of cultural change. The discourse styles reveal more and systematic differences between the two generations. The comparisons of mothers and grandmothers reveal different pictures in the different samples. The similarities between the German mothers and grandmothers were unexpected, as there are substantial behavioral differences across generations, as reported earlier. The interviews reveal that these similarities are based on adjustments that the grandmothers did with respect to the opinions of their daughters or daughters-in-law. For example, grandmothers told the interviewer that they did not breastfeed their children, because nobody did it at that time. However, now that they see how much it means to their daughters, they also find it the most important thing for early care. This may be a method for family cohesion, because mothers in Western middle-class society are the authority for child care. Also Cho et al. (2005) identified a group of Euro-American grandmothers (9 of 16) who echoed their daughters' views. Mothers may have the impression that the views of the elder generation are outdated and wrong, when these views may in fact express differences in adaptational pressures. If grandmothers insisted in their opinions, this would definitely lead to decreasing contact between grandmother and grandchild.

CONCLUSION

In the preceding sections I presented the first sets of studies that systematically address variations of independence and interdependence in cultural models of parenting. In general our studies confirm Kağitçibaşi's suggestion that there are more cultural models than the model of independence and the model of interdependence. We can also confirm that autonomy and relatedness are two independent dimensions that can vary independent of each other. The interview studies in particular reveal that these aspects can coexist. Moreover, autonomy and relatedness change their meaning in different contexts. These considerations have implications for the definition of the cultural model of autonomous-relatedness. Our data suggest that there is not a prototypical model of autonomous-relatedness as the combination of autonomy as defined in the independent model and relatedness as defined in the model of interdependence. Our studies reveal different patterns across the different dimensions of parenting for the different samples. The most common pattern falls midway between the model of independence and interdependence.

The different sets of studies have revealed that changes to models of parenting occur in all cultural environments in line with demographic changes. The most powerful variable of change is formal education. It is not clear whether it is the experience of formal schooling per se or the changes in lifestyle and living environment that become possible with better education. However, there are some indicators that suggest it is education per se. One way to test this assumption would be to analyze the parenting model of low-educated and high-educated urban citizens within the same environment. Palacios and Moreno (1996) reported, for example, differing parenting models in the same Spanish environment depending on education and socioeconomic status. Our data of low-educated Costa Rican mothers clustering in the interdependent cluster of parenting practices (see chap. 5, this volume) also points in the same direction. Finally, the results of fathers' parenting patterns reported in this chapter also support this assumption, as the only sociodemographic variable in which they differed was the level of formal education. Nevertheless, more studies are needed that systematically compare the different dimensions of the cultural model of parenting of higher educated and lower educated parents from the same environment.

7

Relations Among the Dimensions of the Parenting Model

In chapter 3, I presented the conceptual model of parenting that defines the structural dimensions of our research program. So far, I have presented evidence for the two cultural prototypes and for the different forms of variations with respect to the different dimensions of this model by analyzing the mothers' orientation toward the family, their socialization goals, ethnotheories, and parenting strategies. However, we looked at all these different dimensions separately. Theoretically, we assume that all these different dimensions are related to each other and complement each other in defining the cultural model of the specific cultural environments. To further prove this assumption, I analyze the interrelations among these different dimensions in this chapter. In terms of theory, these considerations are based on LeVine's earlier ideas that parenting constitutes patterned activities with parenting goals as an organizing principle (LeVine, 1974; LeVine, Miller, & West, 1988).

In this chapter I present evidence that parenting dimensions relate in a meaningful way as depicted by our model. Because we do not have all the data from all the samples I present different analyses that are based either on a few dimensions from many samples or on more dimensions from fewer samples. The basic idea of our research plan is to contrast homogeneous groups from different sociocultural environments. As a result, within-group variance of sociodemographic marker variables that are the driving force for different developmental pathways is rather small. Therefore, I do not address the question of whether these different dimensions are related to each other by computing relational analyses, but instead I look at the potency of these analyses for differentiating among the samples and their specific relative contribution. Thus, these analyses are aimed at identifying patterns across different domains of data, reaching from the more abstract dimensions (e.g., socialization goals or family orientation) to more specific data (e.g., interview or behavioral data).

Basically, we combined those data to identify the underlying latent construct, which we called the *cultural model*. Theoretically, this cultural model is composed of all the different dimensions, which, therefore, were incorporated in the analyses simultaneously. For each dimension, we condensed the data to one single score and entered these scores as dependent variables in a MANOVA with the cultural sample as the independent variable. After doing these analyses we performed discriminatory function analyses to assess the relative contribution of the single dimensions to the latent construct of the cultural model and to evaluate which groups differ from each other by assessing how precisely the participant's sample affiliation can be predicted by the discriminatory function.

The condensed scores used for the analyses are relative scores relating the composite score for autonomy to the composite score for relatedness. A score greater than 1.0 means that autonomy is emphasized more strongly than relatedness, whereas a score smaller than 1.0 indicates that relatedness is emphasized more strongly than autonomy. With this procedure, response sets were mostly precluded as far as questionnaire data were concerned. For the discourse style and content of the interviews and for the conversational style in the videotaped sequences the ratio scores are proportional scores indicating the percentage of codes that were related to autonomy. For instance, a score of .90 would indicate that 90% of all codes were related to autonomy.

In what follows, I present three sets of analyses. First, I present data on the relation among the mothers' family orientation, socialization goals, and parenting ethnotheories based on questionnaire data from eight different samples. Second, I report findings for the relation among mothers' socialization goals, discourse style and content during interviews, and observed parenting behavior based on five samples. Third, I present data about the relation among mothers' socialization goals, their discourse style and content during interviews, and their conversational style and observed parenting behavior during interactions based on four samples.

RELATIONS AMONG SOCIALIZATION GOALS, FAMILY ORIENTATION, AND PARENTING ETHNOTHEORIES

The relations among the nonbehavioral dimensions of the parenting model were addressed in a questionnaire study described in chapter 4 (Keller, Lamm, et al., 2006). We presented data for 214 mothers of 3-month-old babies from eight samples. Mothers lived in Berlin, Los Angeles, Athens, Beijing, Delhi, San José, rural Nso, and rural Gujarat.

We computed a MANOVA with the ratio score for the socialization goals, the parenting ethnotheories, and the total score for family orientation as the dependent variables and we used cultural sample as the independent variable. As can be seen in Table 7.1, the cultural model differs significantly among the samples. On a descrip-

TABLE 7.1

Results for the Latent Construct Cultural Model Based on Socialization Goals, Family Allocentrism, and Parenting Ethnotheories

	Socialization Goals		Family Allocentrism		Parenting Ethnotheories	
	M	SD	M	SD	M	SD
Berlin (N = 39)	1.34	.33	62.90	11.52	.89	.41
Los Angeles (N = 23)	1.19	.22	70.87	9.46	.93	.30
Athens (N = 50)	1.17	.46	71.42	9.23	1.07	.44
Delhi (N = 23)	.94	.18	84.74	5.16	.93	.25
San José (N = 29)	1.01	.13	69.34	9.74	.68	.17
Beijing (N = 18)	1.46	.40	80.50	5.32	.76	.19
Rural Gujarati (N = 14)	.90	.20	92.79	8.33	.54	.19
Rural Nso (N = 18)	.30	.14	103.89	1.84	.28	.08

tive level, the scores for socialization goals and parenting ethnotheories are higher for the independent samples, medium for the variation samples, and lowest for the interdependent samples, whereas it is the other way around for family orientation.

In the post hoc analysis the prior dependent variables were entered as discriminatory variables and the prior independent variable was entered as the criterion variable in the discriminatory function analysis. There were three significant discriminatory functions that define a latent variable that is essentially the same as the cultural model latent construct defined by the dependent variables entered in the MANOVA already described. To evaluate the relative contribution of the three dimensions to this latent construct, we used the standardized discriminatory coefficients for the first function, which accounted for 85.5% of the explained variance. Accordingly, family orientation was of major importance for the cultural model ($\beta = -.76$), followed by socialization goals ($\beta = .47$) and parenting ethnotheories ($\beta = .38$).

MANOVA results do not carry any information on between-group differences or their direction. Again, the discriminatory function analysis results help to clarify these questions (see Table 7.2).

The classification function predicts the sample affiliation of each mother based on the data of the three dimensions (socialization goals, family orientation, parenting ethnotheories). The more precise this prediction is, the better these dimensions are qualified to discriminate between the cultural samples. Furthermore, the mean discriminatory scores for each of the cultural samples (group centroids) contain information on how similar these groups are to each other.

As hypothesized, three groups of samples can be distinguished according to the group centroids. The Berlin, Los Angeles, and Athens samples have rather high scores; the rural Gujarati and rural Nso samples have very low scores; and, finally, the

TABLE 7.2

Observed and Predicted Group Affiliation Based on Socialization Goals, Family Orientation, and Parenting Ethnotheories

Observed Group Affiliation	Predicted Group Affiliation							
	Berlin	Los Angeles	Athens	Delhi	San José	Beijing	Rural Gujarati	Rural Nso
Berlin (N = 39)	**56.4** **(18.2)**	0.0	30.8	0.0	10.3	2.6	0.0	0.0
Los Angeles (N = 23)	17.4	**0.0** **(10.7)**	60.9	0.0	17.4	4.3	0.0	0.0
Athens (N = 50)	20.0	0.0	**58.0** **(23.4)**	8.0	10.0	4.0	0.0	0.0
Delhi (N = 23)	0.0	0.0	30.4	**56.5** **(10.7)**	4.3	0.0	8.7	0.0
San José (N = 29)	10.3	0.0	27.6	6.9	**55.2** **(13.6)**	0.0	0.0	0.0
Beijing (N = 18)	5.6	0.0	33.3	11.1	5.6	**44.4** **(8.4)**	0.0	0.0
Rural Gujarati (N = 14)	0.0	0.0	0.0	28.6	7.1	0.0	**57.1** **(6.5)**	7.1
Rural Nso (N = 18)	0.0	0.0	0.0	0.0	0.0	0.0	0.0	**100.0** **(8.4)**
Group centroids	1.59	.72	.80	-.89	.27	.07	-2.12	-4.31

Note. Classification table and group centroids (for the first function) of the discriminant function analysis. The expected hit ratios are given in parentheses. Hit ratio = 61.9%. Boldface represents percentage of correctly predicted group affiliations.

Delhi, San José, and Beijing samples lie somewhere in between. This is mirrored in the predicted group affiliation of the classification function. Overall, 62% of the mothers were assigned correctly to their samples. That is far above the level one would expect by chance alone. In the diagonal of Table 7.2 one can see the percentage of correct classifications that would have been expected by chance and the percentage of mothers who were assigned correctly. For each cultural sample, except the Euro-American sample from Los Angeles,[4] the percentage of mothers that was assigned correctly was far above chance. The pattern of false predictions is particularly interesting here. As one can see, most mothers in the independent samples that were not classified correctly were assigned to the two other independent samples. Taken together, about 80% of mothers were classified correctly if one takes the broader sociocultural orientation as the point of reference. What is interesting about the variation samples is that about 60% fall into this category, whereas another 30% of each sample was classified as Greek. The similarity to the Greek sample may be rooted in the fact that our Greek sample has some features of interdependence, especially in the verbal mode. The move from interdependence to independence in Greek mainstream society is more recent than in Euro-American and German society (Georgas, 1989). The Greek sample may therefore be the least independent among the independent ones. However, it clearly belongs empirically to the group of independent samples. Moreover, most rural Indian mothers who were not classified correctly were assigned to the urban Indian sample. Here, in fact, common attitudes may be rooted in Hinduism.

In sum, the classification of mothers based on their family orientation, socialization goals, and parenting ethnotheories is quite precise. Furthermore, the false classifications revealed an interesting pattern. Mothers from independent samples were falsely assigned to the other independent samples and mothers from rural India were falsely assigned to the urban Indian sample. Thus, there seems to be some logic in these attributions, which needs to be analyzed further.

RELATIONS AMONG SOCIALIZATION GOALS, DISCOURSE STYLE AND CONTENT IN ETHNOTHEORY INTERVIEWS, AND OBSERVED PARENTING BEHAVIOR

For this analysis we combined the data concerning the socialization goals, the discourse style and content of the ethnotheory interviews, and the nonverbal interactional data. We included five samples for which we had complete data sets. The samples from Berlin and Los Angeles represent the independent cultural model, the rural Nso sample represents the interdependent cultural model, and the samples from Delhi and the urban Nso represent the variation samples. This analysis is aimed at identifying patterns across different domains of data reaching from the more abstract levels (i.e., socialization goals) to more specific data (i.e., verbal and nonverbal behavioral data). Theoretically, the cultural model is composed of all these

---

[4]The fact that a greater percentage of Euro-Americans was assigned to the other independent samples than to the Euro-American sample was due to the unequal sample sizes influencing the a priori probabilities.

different facets and therefore we incorporated all of these domains simultaneously. As in the previous analysis, we condensed the data to one single score for each domain and then entered these scores as dependent variables in a MANOVA with cultural sample as the independent variable. This analysis was followed by a discriminatory function analysis to assess the relative contribution of the single dimensions to the cultural model latent construct and to evaluate how precisely the participants can be attributed to the different cultural samples by the discriminatory function. As can be seen in Table 7.3, these condensed scores closely resemble the results of the more close-grained analyses presented in the previous chapters.

The cultural model differed significantly among the cultural samples. For most domains, the Berlin and Los Angeles mothers were similar to each other but distinct from the mothers of the other samples, and most distinct from mothers of the rural Nso sample. The mothers from the variation samples formed a distinct group concerning the socialization goals but were similar to the independent or interdependent groups in most other domains. The pattern of results summarizes and supports the conclusions drawn in earlier chapters.

In the post hoc discriminatory function analysis there was one significant discriminatory function, Wilks's $\lambda = .20$, $\chi^2(16, N = 134) = 207.1$, $p < .001$, which accounted for 98.1% of the explained variance. According to the standardized discriminatory coefficients the socialization goals were of major importance for the cultural model ($\beta = .83$), followed by the discourse style ($\beta = .53$) and the content ($\beta = .20$) of the interviews and, lastly, the nonverbal behavioral data ($\beta = .15$). From the MANOVA results alone, we do not know the nature of these differences. Again, the discriminatory function analysis results help to clarify (see Table 7.4).

The classification function predicts the sample affiliation of each individual based on the data of the four dimensions (socialization goals, discourse style and content, nonverbal behavior). As hypothesized, the group centroids are similar for the Berlin and the Los Angeles samples, as well as for the urban Indian and the urban Nso samples, and all of them differ substantially from the group centroid of the rural Nso sample. Looking at the percentage of mothers whose sample affiliation was predicted correctly, it is evident that for all groups the hit ratio is well above the ratio that would have been expected by chance alone (see Table 7.4). The overall hit ratio is 61.9%. This is a very good result compared to an overall expected hit ratio of 20%. The smallest percentages of correct predictions were found in the urban Indian and the Euro-American sample. Even if the hit ratio is above chance for both samples, a greater proportion of the samples were assigned to an "incorrect" sample. However, this "incorrectness" again sheds light on a pattern that underlies these wrong assignments. In three out of four cases the largest incorrect sample affiliation was with the sample with the same cultural model. For example, in addition to the 33% of the Los Angeles sample that was predicted correctly, 43% of the Los Angeles mothers were assigned to the Berlin sample.[5] Simi-

---

[5]The fact that a greater percentage of Euro-Americans was assigned to the German sample than to the Euro-American sample was due to the unequal sample sizes influencing the a priori probabilities.

TABLE 7.3

Results for the Domain-specific Ratio Scores of the Latent Construct Cultural Model

| | Cultural Community | | | | | | | | | |
| | Berlin[a] | | Los Angeles[b] | | Delhi[c] | | Urban Nso[d] | | Rural Nso[e] | |
	M	SD	M	SD	M	SD	M	SD	M	SD
Socialization goals	1.31_a	.31	1.17_a	.25	$.95_b$	.19	$.84_b$	.24	$.29_c$	.16
Content (Int.)	$.35_{a/b/c}$	.18	$.42_b$	.19	$.27_{c/d}$	.20	$.29$	.10	$.22_d$	.14
Style (Int.)	$.96_a$	.07	$.93_a$	.07	$.87_{a/b}$	.15	$.78_b$	.16	$.60_c$	.22
Behavior systems	1.32_a	.71	1.59_a	2.40	1.24	.95	1.17	1.76	$.26_b$	.21

Note. Five-level (culture) MANOVA with significant multivariate main effect for cultural sample on cultural model, Wilks's $\lambda = .20$, $F(16, 385.6) = 16.57$, $p < .001$, $\eta^2 = .33$. Indexed letters indicate results of simple main effects testing (with Bonferroni adjustment). η^2 = partial eta-square. Int. = Interview. [a]N = 39. [b]N = 21. [c]N = 20. [d]N = 26. [e]N = 28.

TABLE 7.4

Observed and Predicted Group Affiliation Based on Socialization Goals, Discourse Style and Content, and Parenting Behavior

Observed Group Affiliation	Predicted Group Affiliation				
	Berlin[a]	Los Angeles[b]	Delhi[c]	Urban Nso[d]	Rural Nso[e]
Berlin	**71.8** **(29.1)**	12.8	12.8	2.6	0.0
Los Angeles	42.9	**33.3** **(15.7)**	19.0	4.8	0.0
Delhi	30.0	5.0	**20.0** **(14.9)**	40.0	5.0
Urban Nso	11.5	3.8	7.7	**69.2** **(19.4)**	7.7
Rural Nso	0.0	0.0	0.0	7.1	**92.9** **(20.9)**
Group centroids	1.83	1.39	0.16	−0.50	−3.25

Note. Classification table and group centroids of the discriminant function analysis. The expected hit ratios are given in parentheses. Hit ratio = 61.9%. Boldface represents percentage of correctly predicted group affiliations. [a]N = 39. [b]N = 21. [c]N = 20. [d]N = 26. [e]N = 28.

larly, besides the 20% of the Delhi mothers that were assigned correctly, 40% were assigned to the urban Nso sample. This result, however, contributes to the understanding of cultural models and confirms the hypothesis that they are not specific to particular countries or societies but to the sociodemographic parameters of the samples.

The implications of these post hoc analyses for the initial MANOVA results are as follows. First, the cultural model latent construct as measured by socialization goals, discourse style and content, and observed parenting behavior is primarily influenced by the socialization goals and the mothers' discourse style. The content of the interviews and the nonverbal behavioral data also exert an influence, although less powerfully. Second, the group differences are, as hypothesized, most distinct for the independent and variation samples as compared to the interdependent sample. Again, these analyses confirm the validity of the cultural models.

They also confirm the fact that socialization goals are powerful descriptors of differences between cultural models. The substantial association between the discourse style and the cultural model may be rooted in the nonconscious and intuitive nature of verbal behaviors. They may be subject to conscious control to a lesser degree than other behaviors. In the following section I address these relations explicitly.

RELATIONS AMONG SOCIALIZATION GOALS, DISCOURSE STYLE AND CONTENT, CONVERSATIONAL STYLE, AND NONVERBAL PARENTING BEHAVIOR

In the final step we added another dimension of the theoretical model. This dimension is the way in which mothers talk to their 3-month-old babies while interacting with them. Adding this dimension meant reducing the number of samples because the analyses of the conversational styles of the urban Nso are not finished yet. Furthermore, the sample sizes decreased marginally because some of the videos could not be transcribed due to the insufficient quality of the soundtrack. We condensed the conversational style to one score indicating the percentage of total codes that were related to autonomy. The data analysis was parallel to the analyses described earlier. The cultural samples differed significantly on the cultural model latent construct, defined by the socialization goals, discourse style and content, conversational style during the mother–child interactions, and observed parenting behavior, Wilks's $\lambda = .20$, $F(15, 204.7) = 17.79$, $\lambda < .001$, $\eta^2 = .54$. The score for conversational style was highest for Euro-American mothers ($M = 1.59$, $SD = 2.39$), followed by German ($M = 1.25$, $SD = .65$), Indian ($M = 1.17$, $SD = 1.02$), and, lastly, the rural Nso mothers ($M = .27$, $SD = .23$). The means and standard deviations for all other scores changed only slightly as compared to the results reported in Table 7.3.

The post hoc discriminatory function analysis revealed one significant discriminatory function, Wilks's $\lambda = .10$, $\chi^2(15, N = 82) = 176.3$, $p < .001$, which accounted for 98.2% of the explained variance. Again, socialization goals contributed most ($\beta = .74$) to the explanation of the cultural model latent concept, followed by conversational style ($\beta = .68$), discourse style ($\beta = .41$), and, less influential, content of the interview data ($\beta = .11$) and nonverbal behavioral data ($\beta = .07$; see Table 7.5).

Table 7.5 shows that for each sample the percentage of correct classifications is far above what was expected by chance. The overall percentage of mothers who were classified correctly is 72%. The group centroids show that the discriminatory function differentiates best between rural Nso and Berlin or Los Angeles mothers. The Indian mothers are located in between. A consequence of the similar group centroids of the Berlin and Los Angeles sample is that most "false" classifications concern the German and Euro-American sample. However, nearly all "misclassifications" are accounted for by the sample with the same sociocultural orientation. That is, most Los Angeles mothers who were not classified as Los Angeles mothers were assigned to the Berlin sample and vice versa. Less than 5% of both samples were falsely assigned to the Delhi or the rural Nso sample.

CONCLUSIONS

Across the different analyses presented in this chapter several basic findings and conclusions can be drawn. First, the different dimensions of the theoretical model, ranging from abstract goals to specific behaviors, are central aspects of the cultural

TABLE 7.5

Observed and Predicted Group Affiliation Based on Socialization Goals,
Discourse Style and Content, Conversational Style, and Parenting Behavior

Observed Group Affiliation	Predicted Categories			
	Berlin[a]	Los Angeles[b]	Delhi[c]	Rural Nso[d]
Berlin	**56.5** **(28.0)**	39.1	4.3	0.0
Los Angeles	42.9	**52.4** **(25.6)**	4.8	0.0
Delhi	6.3	12.5	**81.3** **(19.5)**	0.0
Rural Nso	0.0	0.0	0.0	**100.0** **(26.8)**
Group centroids	2.42	2.03	−.42	−4.16

Note. Classification table and group centroids of the discriminant function analysis.
The expected hit ratios are given in parentheses. Hit ratio = 62.0%. Boldface represents
percentage of correctly predicted group affiliations.
[a]N = 23. [b]N = 21. [c]N = 16. [d]N = 22.

model. Socialization goals, family orientation, parental ethnotheories, discourse
style in interviews and mother–child interactions and, to a lesser degree, the content of interviews and the nonverbal behavioral data, all describe characteristic
facets that are relevant to the proper description of the cultural model. Second,
these different dimensions form meaningful patterns. If one looks at the differences at the sample level, for most samples all dimensions differed as expected.
Additionally, there is a relative emphasis on autonomy within the independent
samples that decreases for the variation samples and is lowest for the interdependent samples. This supports our theoretical argument that these different dimensions relate to each other and complement each other. However, this does not mean
that the more abstract dimensions fully determine the more behavior-based aspects of the cultural model, which brings us to the next point.

Each of these dimensions contributes specifically to the cultural model. If the
more concrete dimensions were determined mainly by more abstract concepts, the
specific contribution of these factors should be negligibly small. However, instead
it seems as if each of these components has a specific influence on the cultural
model. This underlines the importance of taking into consideration all the different
dimensions of the cultural model. Although all these dimensions relate to each
other in a meaningful way, each of them carries cultural knowledge that is specific
to this domain, regardless of whether it is manifested in abstract values or concrete
behaviors.

8

Developmental Consequences of the Early Parenting Experiences

The concept of life-span development to which we subscribe is based on the assumption that there are universal developmental tasks that have evolved and that have to be solved in culture-specific ways to represent adaptations to particular ecocultural contexts. Each task becomes developmentally possible at a particular stage of the life cycle and there is a focal time period for each task when mastery is newly acquired and performance is characterized by *Funktionslust* (Bühler, 1918), or the inherent desire to engage in a particular behavior with seemingly endless but joyful repetitions (Keller, 1992, 2002a). So far we have dealt with the first integrative developmental task: the formation of a matrix of primary relationships. Mastery of this developmental task begins at birth or even before. At around 3 months of age the first relationships are formed based on the preceding interaction experiences.

The concept of developmental pathways implies a coherent and meaningful organization of developmental tasks over a life span. The mastery of earlier tasks lays the foundation for later tasks without functioning in a deterministic way. The coherent organization of developmental results along the pathway thus implies structural continuity (Keller, 1991). The selection of early and later developmental achievements for assessing structural continuity should therefore not be random, but should be integrated in a theoretical model. Because our pathway model is based on the developmental goal of self-construals, the subsequent developmental tasks have to reflect further achievements of self-development. We assume that early social experiences lay the foundations for the self-concept differently (Keller & Greenfield, 2000; LeVine, 2002; B. B. Whiting, 1963). We further assume that

228

the different foundations have developmental consequences for the solution and the timing of children's subsequent developmental tasks. Accordingly, children are expected to manifest specific behaviors at a precociously early age depending on the standards of different cultures (LeVine & Norman, 2001). So far, pathways have been reconstructed mainly by building on existing studies on different cultural communities and on different life stages. Shweder and colleagues (1998) stated accordingly that relatively little research has been done on the behavioral consequences of cultural variations in early childhood experiences. Research that is pertinent to these questions is often referential. For example, different cultural models are supposed to be responsible for cross-cultural differences, but they have not been assessed (e.g., equating national samples with an independent or interdependent orientation); other studies are correlative and demonstrate that categories of environment and individual covary (e.g., sleeping arrangement and interrelated beliefs about childrearing; Caudill & Plath, 1966; cf. Greenfield & Suzuki, 1998). To overcome these shortcomings, I examine here the developmental pathways in different cultural environments empirically with a longitudinal design. I relate the early social experiences around the focal time of 3 months to the salient aspects of the self-concept at 18 to 20 months of age, self-regulation and self-recognition. The latter age range can also be regarded as a time of developmental transition when self-regulation and self-recognition become developmental milestones (e.g., Bischof-Köhler, 1991; Kopp, 2001).

THE DEVELOPMENT OF SELF-RECOGNITION

Studies on children's self-recognition have established that toddlers begin to respond to their mirror image as if they know that it is their own face between the ages of 15 and 18 months (Bard et al., 2005; Lewis & Brooks-Gunn, 1979; Lewis, Sullivan, Stranger, & Weiss, 1989). These behaviors are taken as evidence that the child has acquired conceptual self-knowledge, which forms a categorical self-concept in terms of the awareness that the self is a separate, physical entity and a source of actions, words, ideas, and feelings (Edwards & Liu, 2002). The most prominent method of assessing this capacity is mirror self-recognition (see Figure 8.1).

The toddlers' self-referential behavior in front of the mirror after being marked with some rouge on their faces (the classic rouge test) can be taken as evidence for the acquisition of conceptual self-knowledge (Amsterdam, 1972; Bard et al., 2005; Gallup, 1977). Mirror self-recognition represents a capacity that seems to be independent of the child's familiarity with reflecting surfaces, as was shown in a field study with nomadic Bedouin participants from the Negev region (Priel & de Schonen, 1986). Applying a longitudinal design with monthly assessments between 14 and 24 months, Hart and Fegley (1994) demonstrated that exposure to the mirror and the mark test did not lead to earlier mirror self-recognition. The children in this study showed mirror self-recognition on average at the age of 18.1 months, which is comparable to cross-sectional studies of Western toddlers. There

a.

b.

FIGURE 8.1.   Mirror self-recognition in Nso and German middle-class toddlers.
Photos from Culture and Development Lab, University of Osnabrück.

is ample evidence that although children are able to produce self-referential behavior in the rouge test, they do not know many of the properties of reflecting surfaces (Butterworth, 1990). Thus, mirror self-recognition as a single measure of
self-referential behavior appears to remain the best index of the construct of "me"
(Lewis, 1994) available, even in cultural environments that differ with respect to
the familiarity of children with mirrors.

THE DEVELOPMENT OF SELF-REGULATION

Self-regulation refers to the development of a child's ability to follow everyday customs and valued norms embraced and prescribed by their parents and others (Kopp, 2001). Emde, Biringen, Clyman, and Oppenheim (1991) stressed that the development of self-regulation reflects the dos and don'ts of early moral development. Self-regulation encompasses compliance, the ability to delay actions, and the modulation of emotions to contextual demands. Parents' childrearing styles play a critical role in social development and the development of self-regulatory behaviors. Studies, however, mainly assess concurrent parenting behaviors, when pressure to perform self-regulatory behaviors begins during the second year of life in many cultural communities (Kopp, 1982; Maccoby & Martin, 1983; B. B. Whiting, 1963; B. B. Whiting & Edwards, 1988). Although the study of compliance (i.e., the ability and willingness to modulate behavior in accordance with caregivers' commands and expectations) has been one of the most actively studied areas in toddler research, most of the research has been conducted in Euro-American families (Edwards & Liu, 2002). Children's compliance in these studies is related to maternal correlates, mainly maternal warmth and (low-key) control in interactive contexts (cf. Crockenberg & Litman, 1990; Kochanska & Aksan, 1995). Mothers who display warmth, support, and guidance are more likely to get their toddlers to comply (Crockenberg & Litman, 1990; Power & Chapieski, 1986). Furthermore, these maternal behaviors lead to the acceptance of norms and values and the development of compliance and obedience (Bandura, 1977; Hetherington & Frankie, 1967; Keller, 2003c; MacDonald, 1992).

Parenting that supports compliance in these studies deemphasizes control that uses power and emphasizes shared positive affect between mother and toddler (Kochanska & Aksan, 1995). The use of control strategies and the display of positive affect in mother–child or caregiver–child interactions, however, differ substantially across cultures. As demonstrated in chapter 4, high levels of maternal control are authentic to the socialization agenda of Nso farmers (see also Chao, 1995, for the Chinese culture, and LeVine, 1994, for the Gusii; Keller, 2003c; Yovsi, Keller, et al., 2006). The display of positive affect is regarded as instantiating self-enhancement of the independent self (Shweder & Bourne, 1984). Accordingly, the display of positive affect is deemphasized in many cultural environments with an interdependent cultural model (Chaudhary, 2004; Wang, 2004, Wang et al., 2000). Moreover, it has been demonstrated that the emphasis on compliance is more consistent and absolute for toddlers in interdependent cultural communities (Chao, 1995; Z. Chen & Siegler, 2000; Ho, 1986; Nsamenang, 1992; Ogunnaike & Houser, 2002) and noncompliance is considered a moral transgression (Nsamenang, 1992). Also, based on the ethnotheoretical accounts presented earlier in chapter 4, it can be expected that compliance is developed earlier in cultural environments that have an interdependent cultural model as compared to cultural environments that have an independent cultural model (where noncompliance is tolerated as expressing children's developing skills as autonomous agents; Crockenberg & Litman, 1990; Kuczynski & Kochanska, 1990; Kuczynski, Zahn-Waxler, & Radke-Yarrow, 1987).

To test the culture-specific timing of universal developmental tasks as a consequence of early parenting experiences, we assessed self-recognition and self-regulation in three different cultural environments: 46 middle-class Greek families representing the independent model, 32 Nso farmers representing the interdependent model, and 12 middle-class Costa Rican families representing one variation of the autonomous-related model (Keller, Yovsi, et al., 2004).

The Greek families lived in the capital, Athens, and the mothers had an average educational level of 13 years of schooling. The Nso families lived in villages in the Bui division of northwestern Cameroon and the mothers had an educational level of about 7 years. The Costa Rican families lived in the capital, San José, and had an average educational level of about 9 years.

In line with our conception of different developmental pathways, we assumed that the fact that face-to-face interactions and object play are prevalent in independent cultural communities promotes the development of separateness and individuality, and, thus, the earlier formation of a categorical self as expressed in mirror self-recognition. In interdependent communities, on the other hand, the experience of body contact and body stimulation supports a self-conception that is based on relatedness and communalism.

The parenting system that can be thought of as being functionally equivalent to warmth, support, and guidance is body contact (Harlow, 1958; Montagu, 1958; Oleson, 1998). We therefore assumed that children's experiences with proximal parenting in cultural environments with an interdependent cultural model would support the development of relatedness and heteronomy. Thus, we expected children with these parenting experiences to develop self-regulation in terms of compliance earlier than children with the experience of distal parenting in cultural communities with an independent cultural model.

We assumed that children in cultural communities with an autonomous-related sociocultural model, who experience both distal and proximal parenting styles, develop autonomy and relatedness at the same time. These toddlers should develop self-regulation and self-recognition at an intermediate point in time.

ASSESSING SELF-RECOGNITION

Self-recognition was assessed using the standard method, the rouge test (Amsterdam, 1972; Bard et al., 2005; Bischof-Köhler, 1989).

Rouge Test

To test this task a mirror was used in which the child could at least see his or her upper torso and face. In the Greek and Costa Rican samples we used the family's mirror. For the Nso sample, the experimenters brought a mirror, although some families owned a mirror. First the child was shown the mirror so he or she could become familiar with the situation. After 10 minutes, the mother blew the nose of the child, coloring it at the same time. The child was shown the mirror again after the mark was put on his or her face (Bischof-Köhler, 1989). The mirror viewings were videotaped (see Figure 8.2).

Coding the Rouge Test.   According to Bischof-Köhler (1991), children re-act in one of four possible behavioral ways when they look into the mirror with the color mark on their faces, and these responses were coded.

A. The child points at or tries to clean his or her nose (act to self).
B. The child points at or rubs the mirror image of his or her nose (act to image).
C. The child looks at the mirror without any special reaction (look without acting).
D. The child does something else (e.g., avoids the mirror, does not look into the mirror, touches mirror exploratively, no special reaction; see Figure 8.3).

In a second step, a dichotomous variable was calculated: act to self was defined as self-recognition; act to image, look without acting, and no special reaction were defined as lack of self-recognition.

FIGURE 8.2.   The setup for the assessment of mirror self-recognition in a Nso vil-lage. Photo by Joscha Kärtner.

a.

b.

c.

Figure 8.3.   Different mirror interactions. Photos from Culture and Development Lab, University of Osnabrück.

ASSESSING SELF-REGULATION

In accordance with the literature, we assessed self-regulation as compliance with prohibitions and compliance with requests separately (Bandura, 1997; Kochanska & Aksan, 1995; Mischel, Shoda, & Rodriguez, 1989).

Conceptually we differentiated compliance with requests (toddlers performing desired behaviors) from compliance with prohibitions (toddlers suppressing an undesired act).

Assessing Compliance With Requests

To assess compliance with request, the mother asked the child to bring three objects to her and to bring three objects to another place or person (e.g., Crockenberg & Litman, 1990). The six tasks were distributed over the whole assessment period. The mother selected objects that were familiar to the child so that the child would know where to find them; they needed to be within the child's reach and emotionally neutral (not objects the child likes or wants very much nor objects that are emotionally negatively charged for the child). Examples include the following: "Would you please bring me a glass of water?" and "Would you please take the pot to your grandma?" When the child showed no reaction or reactions that had nothing to do with the request, the mother was instructed to repeat the request up to six times. If the child still did not react, the mother was supposed to ask for the next task without any sign of being negatively impacted by the noncompliance of the child during the previous task. The mother was instructed not to interfere with the task other than to repeat the request if necessary.

Assessing Compliance With Prohibitions

To test this task the experimenter gave the toddler attractive food items in a transparent container that was closed. The experimenter instructed the child not to open the container until she came back. Then the experimenter left the room for about 2 minutes. During this time the child was in the room with his or her mother and the second experimenter who was videotaping the child. The mother was instructed to remind the child not to take the food until the experimenter came back if the child approached the container. She was not, however, supposed to actively stop the child from taking the food (e.g., Kochanska & Aksan, 1995).

Coding Compliance With Requests

The behavioral reactions of the child during each of the six compliance-to-request tasks were coded. The following codes were adopted from the literature (e.g., Crockenberg & Littman, 1990; Kochanska & Aksan, 1995; Pipp-Siegel & Foltz, 1997).

    A. The child performs according to the request without having to be reminded or coerced (internally regulated compliance).

B. The child generally complies with the request, but stops several times and has to be reminded at least once to finish the task (externally regulated compliance).

C. The child starts acting according to the request but does have the correct end result (e.g., bringing the wrong object or going to the wrong person; partially regulated compliance).

D. The child does not obey the request (noncompliance).

For each compliance-to-request task one of the four categories was coded, so that each child received six codes.

Coding Compliance With Prohibitions

With the help of the video recording, one of three possible categories was coded for each child (Kochanska & Aksan, 1995).

A. The child is waiting without being reminded (internally regulated compliance).

B. The child is only waiting when the mother is reminding him or her one or several times not to eat the food (externally regulated compliance).

C. The child is not waiting at all (noncompliance).

The assessments of compliance with prohibitions, compliance with requests, and the rouge test were analyzed by different (in each case native-speaking) coders who had no information about any of the other data sets. The native coders were trained by the German coordinator of this study. Cohen's kappa for the Greek coder was .85, for the Spanish coder .80, and for the Nso coder .82.

In the analyses we first controlled for gender and exact age of the toddlers at 3 months or at 18 months depending on the phenomenon in question. Second, we controlled for the toddler's birth rank, which was either firstborn or later born. Third, we controlled for the education of the mother indicated by the years spent in school. This last variable was z standardized within cultures as it is not the absolute level of education, but the relative level of education within one's own culture that needed to be controlled for. In the final analyses we only controlled for those variables that had a significant effect as covariates. In the hierarchical regression analyses we entered the whole set of confounding variables in Step 1, regardless of whether they contributed significantly to the analyses or not.

Mean Differences in Self-Recognition

The dichotomous variable (self-recognition: yes vs. no) was entered into a three-level between-subject ANOVA design. Because none of the possibly confounding variables reached the level of significance, they were excluded from further analysis. Furthermore, we specified a linear contrast according to the hypothesis that there is an increase in the self-recognition rate across cultures. Both the main effect for culture, $F(2, 84) = 24.09$, $p < .001$, and linear contrast (contrast estimate = .46, $SD = .07$, $p < .001$) were highly significant. Self-recognition was lowest in Nso toddlers ($M = .03$, $SD = .18$), on an intermediate level in Costa Ricans ($M = .50$, $SD = .52$), and most prominent in Greek toddlers ($M = .68$, $SD = .57$).

Mean Differences for Compliance

To test the hypothesized mean differences across cultures for compliance with requests, we computed four variables each indicating the percentage of one of the four codes of possible behavioral outcomes (internally regulated compliance, externally regulated compliance, partially regulated compliance, and noncompliance) for the six tasks. These variables were entered in a three-level between-subject MANOVA design controlling simultaneously for the same set of variables as previously. Because the toddler's gender alone turned out to be a significant confounding variable, it was the only variable to be controlled for in the final analysis. As earlier, we specified linear contrasts, hypothesizing a linear decrease of internally regulated compliance and a linear increase of partial compliance and noncompliance across cultures. We expected externally regulated behavior to be in a middle position. As Wilks's criterion illustrates, there was a significant multivariate main effect for culture, $F(6, 164) = 6.29$, $p < .001$, and gender, $F(3, 82) = 3.40$, $p < .05$, the latter being controlled for. Univariate analyses revealed that the differences in compliance were due to three of the four dependent variables: internally regulated compliance, $F(2, 84) = 19.81$, $p < .001$, which was high in Nso toddlers, moderate in the Costa Rican sample, and low in the Greek sample; and partially regulated compliance and noncompliance, $F(2, 84) = 5.36$, $p < .01$, and $F(2, 84) = 5.58$, $p < .01$, which were low in Nso toddlers, moderate in the Costa Rican toddlers, and high in the Greek sample. The specified linear contrasts were highly significant for internally regulated compliance (contrast estimate = $-.29$, $SD = .05$, $p < .001$), partially regulated compliance (contrast estimate = .11, $SD = .04$, $p < .01$), and noncompliance (contrast estimate = .12, $SD = .04$, $p < .01$). Girls showed internally regulated behavior more often than boys, $F(1, 84) = 5.79$, $p < .05$, and boys exhibited externally regulated compliance more often than girls, $F(1, 84) = 7.19$, $p < .01$. There were no significant differences concerning the two other types of compliance.

To test the result of the compliance tasks, we entered the percentage of successfully completed requests as the dependent variable in a three-level between-subject ANOVA design. We did not control for possibly confounding variables, as they did not significantly contribute to the analysis. There was a significant main effect for culture, $F(2, 85) = 12.92$, $p < .001$, with Nso toddlers being the most successful ($M = .82$, $SD = .22$), Costa Rican toddlers being in between ($M = .57$, $SD = .41$), and Greek toddlers being the least successful ($M = .50$, $SD = .27$). The specified linear contrast reached the level of significance (contrast estimate = $-.23$, $SD = .05$, $p < .001$).

Finally we analyzed compliance with prohibitions. The three behavioral measures (internally regulated compliance, externally regulated compliance, noncompliance) were entered as dependent variables in a three-level between-subject MANOVA design. Because none of the confounding variables contributed significantly to the effects, they were excluded from the final analysis. As Wilks's criterion indicates, there was a significant multivariate main effect for culture, $F(6, 170) = 11.20$, $p < .001$, which held for all three behavioral outcomes in the univariate analyses: for internally regulated compliance, $F(2, 87) = 39.00$, $p < .001$; for the externally regulated compliance, $F(2, 87) = 7.52$, $p < .01$; and for noncompliance, $F(2, 87) = 3.14$, $p < .05$. As the significant linear contrast shows, internally regulated compliance decreased substantially across cultures (contrast estimate $= -.49$, $SD = .06$, $p < .001$), being most prominent in Nso toddlers, less frequent in Costa Ricans, and rare in Greek toddlers; whereas the significant linear contrasts for externally regulated compliance and noncompliance (contrast estimate $= .27$, $SD = .07$, $p < .001$, and contrast estimate $= .19$, $SD = .08$, $p < .05$, respectively) confirmed an increase in these types of compliance being least frequently observed in Nso toddlers, more often in Costa Ricans, and most often in Greek toddlers. Figure 8.4 shows a Cameroonian Nso toddler following the request immediately. The Costa Rican toddler needed several reminders from his mother (see Figure 8.5). The Greek toddler shown in Figure 8.6 did not obey the request at all.

FIGURE 8.4. A Nso toddler complies completely and immediately. Photo from Culture and Development Lab, University of Osnabrück.

FIGURE 8.5. A Costa Rican toddler needs reminders. Photo from Culture and Development Lab, University of Osnabrück.

FIGURE 8.6. A Greek toddler does not follow at all. Photo from Culture and Development Lab, University of Osnabrück.

239

The analysis of the toddlers' achievements in the developmental tasks of self-recognition and self-regulation confirms the expected differences between the cultural communities. To test our assumption that these differences are related to early parenting experiences, we computed a hierarchical logistic regression analysis with the dichotomous variable of self-recognition as the dependent measure. In the first step, the possibly confounding variables of age, gender, and birth rank of the toddler, and the relative education of the mother were entered, followed by the hypothesized predictors of object stimulation and face-to-face context in the second step. Predictors were z standardized before being entered in the regression. To assess the significance of the overall model fit for Step 1, we used the chi-square distributed measure of G (J. Cohen, Cohen, West, & Aiken, 2003), which showed that the model was significant at a marginal level, $G(4) = 7.89, p < .10$. As a measure of the overall goodness of fit we used Nagelkerke's R^2, which for Step 1 was $R^2 = .118$. After adding the second set of predictor variables in Step 2, the overall model fit was significant, $G(6) = 21.40, p < .01$, and the overall goodness of fit increased to Nagelkerke's $R^2 = .296$. A hierarchical likelihood ratio test can be used to assess whether the second set of predictors contributes significantly over and above the first set of variables (J. Cohen et al., 2003). The difference of the deviance measure is chi-square distributed with degrees of freedom equal to the number of predictors entered in Step 2 (deviances are labeled −2 log likelihood in SPSS). The likelihood ratio chi-square test with 2 degrees of freedom = 109.65 to 96.14 = 13.51, $p < .01$, was significant for indicating a considerable contribution by the predictors. The coefficient was significant for object stimulation, $B = 1.00$, Wald(1) = 11.05, $p < .001$, EXP(B) = 2.71. The high odds ratio of EXP(B) = 2.71 indicated that the more object stimulation the children experienced during early childhood, the more likely they recognized themselves at the age of 18 to 20 months. The coefficient for face-to-face context did not reach a level of significance. This confirmed our hypotheses only partially with respect to object stimulation.

Therefore, we conducted a second hierarchical logistic regression analysis, for which we included mutual eye contact instead of face-to-face context in the second step. Eye contact is the actually occurring and actively established mutual eye contact within sequences of face-to-face context. The drop in the number of toddlers (from $N = 86$ to $N = 74$) is due to the fact that in some cases mutual eye contact did not occur or could not be rated due to problems of visibility on the tapes. The overall model fit for Step 1 including the set of confounding variables was significant, $G(4) = 9.75, p < .05$. Adding the second set of predictors—object stimulation and mutual eye contact—the overall model fit became highly significant, $G(6) = 29.82, p < .001$. The likelihood ratio test indicated that the second set of predictors contribute significantly more than the first set of variables. The coefficient was significant for object stimulation, indicating that the more object stimulation the children experienced during early infancy, the more likely they recognized themselves at the age of 18 to 20 months. The coefficient for eye-to-eye contact was significant as well. These data confirm that the more mutual eye contact and object stimulation the toddlers experienced during infancy, the earlier they recognized themselves in the mirror (see Keller, Yovsi, et al., 2004).

With respect to the development of compliance, we analyzed mean differences in compliant behavior across cultures. In the compliance-with-request tasks, the behavioral responses were recoded into a metric compliance score with noncompliance being least compliant (getting a value of 1), partial compliance being not completely compliant (getting a value of 2), externally regulated behavior being moderately compliant (getting a value of 3), and internally regulated behavior being compliant (getting a value of 4). A mean score of the six tasks was computed ranging from 1 to 4. For the compliance with prohibition, a similar logic was applied. A metric score was computed ranging from 0 (*no delay*) to 1 (*externally regulated delay*) to 2 (*internally regulated delay*). These three scores were used as dependent measures in separate hierarchical regression analyses.

To test the contribution of the body contact and body stimulation parenting systems to explaining toddlers' compliance with requests, a hierarchical regression was computed. In the first step, the set of confounding variables was entered, and in the second step the hypothesized predictors of body contact and body stimulation were simultaneously entered into the regression equation.

The final model accounted for 20.1% of the variance (adjusted $R^2 = .201$), almost entirely attributable to the predictors entered in the second step of the analysis (change in $R^2 = .183$), $F(2, 80) = 9.83, p < .001$. The regression coefficient was significant for body contact ($\beta = .43, t = 3.88, p < .001$) but not for body stimulation ($\beta = .11, t = 1.01, p > .05$). If, in the second step, body stimulation was entered as the only predictor, its regression coefficient became marginally significant ($\beta = .22, t = 1.98, p = .051$). Thus, we can conclude that body stimulation does contribute to the explanation of compliance, but this effect was overridden by the effect of body contact.

With respect to compliance with prohibition, again we computed a regression analysis with the same confounding variables and predictors being entered in two steps. The final model explained 18.8% of the variance (adjusted $R^2 = .188$), which was almost entirely attributable to the predictors entered in the second step of the analysis (change in $R^2 = .166$), $F(2, 80) = 8.81, p < .001$. The regression coefficient of body contact was significant ($\beta = .45, t = 4.07, p < .001$); the coefficient of body stimulation did not reach the level of significance ($\beta = -.01, t = -.08, p > .05$).

The results of this study provide evidence that the early social experiences during the first months of life have a measurable impact on children's performance of subsequent developmental tasks. Our data confirm differences in toddlers' behavioral development that coincide with different cultural emphases on the development of self-recognition and self-regulation. Greek toddlers demonstrate more self-recognition than any of the other cultural groups, Cameroonian Nso toddlers demonstrate more self-regulation than any of other the cultural groups, and Costa Rican toddlers are situated in between these two groups with respect to self-recognition and self-regulation.

These differences are systematically related to early parenting experiences. Children who experience the proximal parenting style demonstrate more self-regulation on an individual level at 18 to 20 months of age. Body contact turned out to be the central predictor for this relation. The children who experience the distal parenting style demonstrate more self-recognition on an individual level at 18 to 20 months of age. It is the actual experience of eye contact that is important, as the differential impact of the face-to-face system (as provision of a possibility) and the actually occurring mutual eye contact have demonstrated (see also Blain, Thompson, & Whiffen, 1993). Children who experience the proximal or distal style of parenting are situated between the two other groups with respect to the development of self-recognition and self-regulation. These data confirm that the Costa Rican toddlers develop self-recognition and self-regulation to medium degree, in line with their parenting experiences, which are also located between the independent orientation of the Greek middle-class mothers and the interdependent orientation of the Nso farmers.

CONTINGENCY EXPERIENCE AND MIRROR SELF-RECOGNITION

As we discussed earlier, the interactional mechanism of contingent responsiveness toward infants' positive facial signals is another parenting dimension that supports the cultural model of independence. Therefore, the experience of contingent responsiveness during infancy should also be related to the timing of mirror self-recognition. To test this assumption, we conducted another study comparing 41 middle-class German families from Berlin with 31 Cameroonian Nso farmer families (Keller, Kärtner, et al., 2005). The two samples differed with respect to their sociodemographic profiles in the characteristic ways: Rural Nso parents held a low level of formal education of about 6 years, whereas the mothers and fathers from Berlin had on the average 16 years of formal education. The Berlin sample consisted of more firstborn children, the Nso sample of more later-born children, and the Nso mothers were younger than the Berlin mothers. When the babies were 3 months old, free-play interactional situations were videotaped and analyzed according to the nonverbal contingency manual described in chapter 4. Self-recognition was assessed with the mirror self-recognition task as described earlier in this chapter.

The distribution of children recognizing and not recognizing themselves was analyzed in the two cultural samples using a chi-square test for this two-by-two contingency table. Whereas the overall percentage of children recognizing themselves was 50.9%, only 15% of the Nso toddlers recognized themselves and 72% of the Berlin toddlers did. The differences in observed frequencies compared to expected frequencies were highly significant, $\chi^2 (1, N = 53) = 16.61, p < .001$.

To test whether recognizers experienced more contingent reactions from their mothers at the age of 3 months than nonrecognizers, we computed point-biserial correlations. Self-recognition correlated with the responsiveness score on a marginal level, $r_{pb} = .25$, $p < .10$, and significantly with the relative frequency of latencies, $r_{pb} = .29$, $p < .05$ (Keller, Kärtner, et al., 2005).

To further substantiate the differences in mirror self-recognition between the middle-class German toddlers and the Cameroonian Nso farmer toddlers, we conducted a short-term longitudinal study with weekly assessments over 6 weeks from the 18th month on with 40 German toddlers from Osnabrück and 30 rural Nso toddlers (Kärtner, Keller, & Yovsi, 2005). Again, the samples reflected the typical differences in mothers' education (75% of the mothers from Osnabrück and 3% of the rural Nso mothers have a high school certificate of a higher degree) and other sociodemographic characteristics (60% of the Osnabrück toddlers were firstborn versus 24% of the Nso toddlers, and Nso toddlers had 2.53 siblings on the average, whereas the toddlers from Osnabrück had only .55). The rouge test was done in the families' homes using a standard mirror in which the toddlers were able to see their whole body. Figure 8.7 shows the percentages of toddlers who recognized themselves in Week 1 and the combined Weeks 5 and 6 of the assessment.

Figure 8.7 demonstrates that there are highly significant differences for the first assessments in the expected direction. The difference remains significant the for the assessment during Weeks 5 and 6, but is now substantially smaller. Toddlers of both groups increased mirror self-recognition over the weeks, but the Nso substantially more than the toddlers from Osnabrück. Although the cultural differences represent a stable pattern, familiarization may, nevertheless, also play some role in an environment where mirrors are not part of the everyday life of the toddlers.

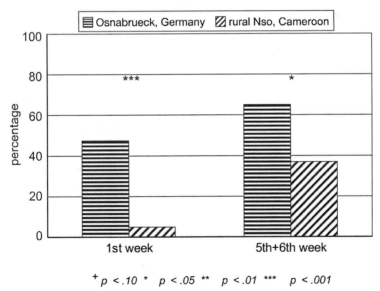

FIGURE 8.7.   German and Nso toddlers' self-recognition. Photo from Culture and Development Lab, University of Osnabrück.

CHAPTER 8

THE ROLE OF FATHERS FOR MIRROR SELF-RECOGNITION
IN GERMAN TODDLERS

In a longitudinal study of 24 German fathers and their firstborn children (12 girls, 12 boys), Lamm et al. (2006) assessed 3-month-old infants' early social experiences with their fathers during free-play situations, the fathers' parenting ethnotheories, and mirror self-recognition when the children were 18 to 20 months old. The first assessment of this study is reported in chapter 5. Ten families had a second child at the time of the second assessment. The same two experimenters who had visited the family for the first assessment also conducted the second assessment when the children were between 18 and 20 months old. Self-recognition was assessed using the rouge test (see earlier in this chapter). A coder who was not familiar with the assumptions of this study coded the mirror self-recognition. Cohen's kappa, registered in a pretest with other trained coders, was .85.

To test the relation between parenting styles (proximal and distal) of the father and children's mirror self-recognition, we calculated a two-by-two contingency table. The chi-square test was significant, $\chi^2(1, N = 24) = 5.91, p < .05$. Nearly 85% of the children who were raised with a predominantly distal paternal style—but only 36% of the children who were raised with a predominantly proximal style—were able to recognize themselves in the mirror. So, we were able to predict correctly whether a child could recognize himself or herself in the mirror in 75% of the cases by knowing the parenting style of the father.

To further analyze which elements of parenting style and parenting ethnotheories fostered the development of self-recognition, we conducted a two-level between-subject MANOVA with mirror self-recognition as an independent variable. This analysis revealed significant differences between the children who recognized themselves in the mirror and those who did not, $F(8, 15) = 3.01, p < .05$. Children who recognized themselves had experienced significantly less body contact and more object stimulation (marginal significant effect) from their fathers during early infancy. The parenting ethnotheories of fathers of self-recognizers focused more on face-to-face contact and less on body contact compared to fathers of children who did not recognize themselves in the mirror (see Table 8.1). The number of mentions of object stimulation and body stimulation in the parenting ethnotheories did not differ between the groups. Furthermore, we tested whether these two groups of children differ with respect to sociodemographic characteristics, but there were no differences concerning the gender of the child, the child's age at the second assessment, the number of children in the family, or the education level of the father (Lamm et al., 2006).

As we demonstrated in chapter 6, German fathers interacting with their 3-month-old firstborn babies predominantly use one of two parenting styles, a proximal style of parenting focusing on body contact or a distal style emphasizing object stimulation and face-to-face contact. These differences are due to different educational levels.

TABLE 8.1

Differences Between Self-Recognizers and Nonrecognizers Concerning
Parenting Experiences in Infancy and Paternal Ethnotheories

	Self-Recognizers[a]		Nonrecognizers[b]			
	M	*SD*	*M*	*SD*	*F(1, 22)*	η^2
Parenting behavior						
Body contact	.48	.27	.78	.23	7.83*	.26
Body stimulation	.60	.14	.60	.17	.00	.00
Object stimulation	.44	.27	.23	.29	3.27[+]	.13
Face-to-face context	.60	.27	.64	.18	.17	.01
Parenting ethnotheories						
Body contact	.04	.05	.09	.07	4.52*	.17
Body stimulation	.07	.06	.05	.06	.63	.03
Object stimulation	.07	.05	.05	.05	1.86	.08
Face-to-face context	.06	.06	.01	.02	5.43*	.20

Note. Two-level (self-recognition) ANOVA. η^2 = partial eta-square. [a]N = 15. [b]N = 9.
[+]p < .10. *p < .05.

The results of the second assessment done by Lamm et al. (2006) demonstrated that fathers' parenting ideas and behavioral styles influence child development. The results also indicate that parenting attitudes and practices independently influence child development within the developmental niche by transmitting the same cultural information via different channels (Harkness & Super, 1996).

This study reconfirms the impact of early socialization experiences for children's development. It further demonstrates that fathers also contribute substantially to this development. Fathers are often forgotten in developmental analyses, as mothers are the primary caregivers during infancy.

SUMMARY

Taken together, the three studies confirm that early parenting experiences that are related to an independent cultural model—that is, face-to-face contact, contingent responsiveness during face-to-face contact, and object stimulation—accelerate the timing of the developmental milestone of self-recognition, whereas experiencing body contact and body stimulation accelerates the timing of the development of self-regulation.

The different socialization strategies that parents pursue may find their expression in precociousness (LeVine & Norman, 2001) in the developmental domains emphasized in different cultural communities. In contrast to research demonstrating that parental expectations regarding the timing of developmental milestones differ depending on the cultural model—as outlined earlier for the expectation for a baby to sleep alone (see also Goodnow, Cashmore, Cotton, & Knight, 1984; Joshi & MacLean, 1997; Keller, Miranda, & Gauda, 1984; Ninio, 1979; Pomerleau et al.,

1991)—our results show differences in the actual behavior of the toddlers. Cultural environments with an interdependent cultural model emphasize a communal agenda and hierarchical social stratification. It is important to learn norms and roles as early as possible. Cultural environments with an independent cultural model emphasize individual distinctness among equal social partners, so that the early timing of self-recognition is stipulated. One implication of this view is that the developmental roots of similar behavioral achievements in different cultural communities may be different. Whereas in an interdependent socialization agenda obedience to the parents may be the precursor of compliance, it may be the development of autonomy in an independent socialization agenda. Accordingly, the development of compliance is assumed to be rooted in a child's autonomy in the Western literature (Feldman & Klein, 2003), where compliance based on obedience is often regarded as immature. On the other hand, in contexts with an interdependent cultural model, obedience is more of a duty, expressing social maturity (Keller, Yovsi, et al., 2004; Le Vine, 2004). In this sense, Weisner (1989) suggested that the Kenyan Aba-Luyia mothers "use evidence that a child has the ability to give and receive social support, and assist others, as markers of a child's more general developmental level, much as an American parent may use literacy skills such as knowing the alphabet, or verbal facility, to show how grown-up or precocious his or her child is" (p. 86). Overall, our data are the first to confirm coherent developmental pathways from infancy to toddlerhood empirically as well.

DEVELOPMENTAL MILESTONES OF SELF-DEVELOPMENT BEYOND INFANCY

The next integrative developmental tasks for the development of a conception of the self are autobiographical memory and the theory of mind. Both concepts are briefly introduced in the following sections.

The Development of Autobiographical Memory

Based on the pathway model, it can be assumed that the developmental achievements during the second year of life set the stage for the processing of subsequent developmental tasks. In the literature, the categorical self-concept is referred to as a precondition of the capacity to memorize autobiographical information.

One's autobiographical story is a central part of the individual's sense of self (M. Ross, 1989). Infants begin to develop a stable, reliable memory for routine events before the age of 3, but children's memory activities cannot be characterized as being autobiographical in nature until after this time (Fivush & Nelson, 2004; K. Nelson, 1996). Because adults generally cannot recall any episodes from before this time, this threshold marks the end of the so-called infantile amnesia (for a review see Pillemer & White, 1989). The child's ability to store experiences in a narrative structure starts developing when language mastery allows children to participate in discussions about past events with family members (Mullen, 1994). Accordingly, the average age of the earliest memory consistently found in U.S.

samples is about 3.5 years (Sheingold & Tenney, 1982). There are, however, distinct cultural differences with respect to the onset of autobiographical memory. Mullen (1994) confirmed with questionnaire studies that the earliest memories of a mixed group of Asians and Asian Americans were on the average 6 months later than those of Euro-Americans. A subsequent comparison of ethnic Koreans with ethnic Euro-Americans revealed an even larger difference of almost 17 months. The differences in the onset of autobiographical memories are associated with differences in how past events are narrated. An earlier onset is associated with more voluminous, specific (one point in time events), emotionally elaborate, and self-focused narrations of one's earliest childhood memories. A later onset is associated with more skeletal, routinely related, emotionally unexpressive, and relation-centered narrations of earliest childhood memories (Han, Leichtman, & Wang, 1998; P. J. Miller et al., 1997; Wang, 2001). The cultural differences in talking about past events are thus reflective of the early verbal interactional environments described in chapter 5. They emphasize the creation and elaboration of an early distinct sense of self, as compared to a socially bound construction of the self where personal distinctness is not cherished (cf. Markus & Kitayama, 1991).

The processing of autobiographical information can be distinguished between a differentiated and an integrated way of organizing content and structure, which determines the cognitive complexity of the narrative (Woike, Gershkovich, Piorkowski, & Polo, 1999). Differentiation refers to the number of distinct and contrasting aspects in a topic, whereas integration is characterized by expressions of causalities and similarities between aspects. Both operate together, but serve different purposes: perceiving oneself as being different and unique as opposed to feeling interdependent and connected. Thus, these structural processes capture key elements of the functions of autobiographical memory for the self (differences, uniqueness) and social purposes (relationships and interdependence).

Therefore different conceptions of autobiographical memories can be related to the cultural models of independence and interdependence (Fiske et al., 1998; Keller, 2003a, 2003b; Wang et al., 2000).

It can be assumed that autobiographical memory develops as part of the social structure of family narratives (K. Nelson, 1993). Accordingly, different styles of maternal narration with children across cultures have been documented (Reese et al., 1993; Tessler & Nelson, 1994; Wang, 2001). Independent or high-elaborative mothers speak often about the past with their children, provide extended, descriptive information about past events, and prompt children to produce similar narratives. Interdependent or low-elaborative mothers talk relatively little about past events and provide fewer details about these events. They tend to pose pointed questions with single correct or incorrect answers (Fivush & Fromhoff, 1988; Han et al., 1998; Reese et al., 1993).

Howe and Courage (1997) regarded mirror self-recognition as the point in time when autobiographical memory begins. Furthermore, Welch-Ross (2001) found that an awareness of self in time, measured by the delayed self-recognition paradigm, was directly linked to the construction of autobiographical memory. Mirror self-recognition is thus understood to be the theoretically grounded link between early socialization experiences and the development of the autobiographical memory. High levels of contingency and an emphasis on the distal style of parenting lead to an earlier development of the categorical self-concept. This is expected to lead to a more advanced autobiographical memory in 3-year-olds due to an earlier onset of autobiographical remembering. Cross-sectional data thus support the concept of developmental pathways and the developmental logic implied.

In a study comparing German and Cameroonian Nso preschoolers, Chasiotis, Bender, Kießling, and Hofer (2005) found that the Nso children dated their earliest memories significantly later than German preschoolers. Nso preschoolers showed more integrative cognitive complexity compared to German preschoolers. The German toddlers processed information analytically, with a focus on the perception of contrasting aspects of objects and persons.

The Development of a Theory of Mind

The last step in the development of a core conception of the self is the conviction that other humans are mental beings whose ways of behavior are based on certain states of mind and processes of consciousness (e.g., needs, beliefs, and emotions) and thus differ from one's own state of mind.

The concept of a theory of mind implies two generic sorts of mental states—beliefs and desires—that are purported to structure mental life and intentional action, as understood in our everyday reasoning. Wellman and Miller (2005) summarized the core assumptions "that beliefs and desires are (a) prototypical inner psychological states, not overt behaviors, (b) frame a conception of persons as intentional agents, and (c) along with related constructs such as perceptions and emotions, provide explanations of human action and life."

The understanding of "false belief" situations is regarded as a central aspect of children's theory of mind, because it indicates the presence of representational abilities (Dennett, 1983). Children's understanding of false belief situations is subject to considerable change, especially from the ages of 3 to 4.5 (Wellman, Cross, & Watson, 2001). Verbal competence is a central contributor to this development (Astington, 2001; Cutting & Dunn, 1999; Jenkins & Astington, 1996).

Thus, the acquisition of a theory of mind can also be regarded as a universal developmental task that evolved during human phylogeny (Keller & Chasiotis, 2006a, 2006b). Accordingly, there is evidence from meta-analyses that false-belief understanding is a universal human capability (Wellman et al., 2001).

However, there is also increasing evidence that suggests that sociocultural environments influence the development of a theory of mind differently. Studies with Western as well as non-Western samples have demonstrated that the development of false-belief understanding is significantly related to the socioeconomic status of the family and number of (older) siblings, even when the studies control for age and verbal skill of the child (Cole & Mitchell, 2000; Cutting & Dunn, 1999; Perner, Ruffman, & Leekham, 1994; Ruffman, Perner, Naito, Parkin, & Clements, 1998).

Socioeconomic status and the presence of siblings, however, represent developmental contexts that differ with respect to the support of cultural models of independence and interdependence. Consequently, it has been demonstrated that parenting style can affect the development of the theory of mind (e.g., Ruffman, Perner, & Parkin, 1999; Vinden, 2001). In particular, more opportunities for discussing mental states and reasoning about social issues, fantasy play, and managing social conflict influence the development of a theory of mind. Thus, the maternal narrative style, especially mind-mindedness, defined as mothers' tendency to focus on their children's independent mental states and mental-state talk, is important (Dunn, Brown, Slomkowski, Tesla, & Youngblade, 1991; Ruffman et al., 1999; Ruffman, Slade, & Crowe, 2002). The same setting also increases the speed of language development (Cummins, 1996; Ruffman et al., 1998).

In line with these results, there is empirical evidence for an age effect in the development of false-belief understanding across cultures (Naito, 2003, 2004; Wellman et al., 2001). Wellman et al. (2001) found in a meta-analysis that Japanese children's false-belief performance was significantly lower than that of Western children. Naito (2003; Naito & Koyama, 2005) reported that Japanese children understood false beliefs more than a year later than Western children. Moreover, Japanese children base their justifications for false-belief judgments primarily on the protagonist's overt behaviors and social rules rather than their internal mental states. J. G. Miller (personal communication, July, 2004) also emphasized that the anchorage of the theory of mind of children in different cultural environments may be different. Based on her interviews with Indian children, she speculated that the pathway of a morally based and duty-based theory of mind may be an alternative to the Western mentalistic model.

Aspects of mothers' narrative style and characteristics of the mother–child interaction in discussions about past events were related to a set of theory of mind tasks as Welch-Ross (1997) demonstrated. I propose that the processes involved in collaborative remembering not only affect the child's theory of mind, but also facilitate the construction of autobiographical memory. Thus, one can expect there to be meaningful associations between the development of autobiographical memory and theory of mind development.

Lastly, it could be demonstrated that a composite theory of mind score, including second-order belief understanding, also differs across cultural environments: German preschoolers performed better than Cameroonian Nso preschoolers in false-belief understanding (see also Chasiotis, Bender, et al., 2005). This finding lends further support to the notion that an independent cultural model may be closely intertwined with the development of an understanding the minds of others.

Investigating the interrelations between complexity in autobiographical memories, independent motive orientation, and theory of mind, Chasiotis, Bender, et al. (2005) were able to show that more differentiation in a child's narratives is related to more independent implicit motive realizations and to a better theory of mind understanding. Merely based on the correlational nature of this result, they speculated whether a motivation to realize one's desires and needs in an independent manner might enhance false-belief understanding.

In summary, there is compelling evidence that development after infancy also continues cultural pathways in line with the cultural models of independence and interdependence. Again, the timing of the mastery of a universal developmental task may be regarded as an indicator of the emphasis that is put on this developmental task in the respective cultural environment. As we have seen and empirically demonstrated compliance is rooted in different connotative systems across cultures, the theory of mind may also have different developmental precursors.

OUTLOOK

We were able to empirically confirm our conceptualization of developmental pathways for the first 2 years of life. We have demonstrated that early parenting experiences with respect to different cultural models of parenting have developmental consequences for the mastery of the next developmental milestones. The parenting model of independence sets the stage for the early development of a categorical self as assessed using the mirror self-recognition task. In particular, the experience of face-to-face contact, contingent responsiveness to facial cues, and object stimulation are the instigators of the independent developmental pathway. The parenting model of interdependence primes the development of early self-regulation. In particular, the experience of body contact, and thus warmth, and body stimulation are the instigators of the interdependent developmental pathway. The experience of a variation model of parenting, which has elements of both distal and proximal parenting, but not to the same degree as the prototypical models, primes the development of self-recognition and self-regulation at an intermediate point in time. Thus, this developmental pathway deviates from the independent as well as the interdependent model. Although we are not yet able to present longitudinal data on the development of autobiographical memory and the theory of mind, the existing literature confirms the continuation of the pathways described for the early years.

Our data also confirm that fathers exert a direct influence on their children's development. Although fathers spend less time with their infants than mothers do during infancy, their style of parenting is directly related to their children's achievement of developmental milestones. So far, two different cultural models are presented in the literature. More studies are needed to assess more variation samples to further explore cultural emphases on the interplay between autonomy and relatedness for the solution of developmental tasks.

9

Cultural Models of Parenting and Developmental Pathways: Synthesis and Conclusion

In the preceding chapters, I developed a concept of cultural pathways marked by universal developmental tasks. Developmental pathways are tailored to meet the demands of specific ecocultural environments. I specified two prototypical environments: rural, subsistence-based ecologies with families who closely cooperate for their joint economy and whose formal education is low; and urban, middle-class, Western families in which everybody is supposed to develop his or her own talents and formal education level is high. I have argued that these two environments are associated with two different psychologies that are embodied in different construals of the self. The interdependent self is adapted to rural environments; the independent self is adapted to urban Western environments. These self-concepts can be understood as cultural models of the person specifying the underlying dimensions of relatedness and autonomy. The independent model focuses on autonomy; the interdependent model focuses on relatedness. Kağitçibaşi (1996a, 2005) proposed a third prototype, the autonomous-related self, that applies to urban educated people from traditionally interdependent societies. Our analyses revealed, however, that autonomous relatedness does not just represent the combination of the relatedness from the interdependent model and the autonomy from the independent model. I propose that autonomy and relatedness be understood as independent dimensions and not as the extremes of the agency and the interpersonal distance dimension, respectively. Autonomy and relatedness can form multiple combinations and therefore multiple psychologies. However, their interrelation is complex. Autonomy and relatedness undergo quantitative and qualitative changes while moving along the dimensions.

I have theoretically argued and empirically demonstrated that early socialization experiences lay the groundwork for the development of different self-ways. Parenting strategies that create scenarios for particular developmental trajectories are key. Parenting strategies form organized sets of beliefs and practices that inform socialization goals. Socialization goals directly translate the cultural model of the self into developmental goals for particular developmental periods. I have analyzed the parenting strategies for the developmental phase of infancy for the two prototypical cultural models: the model of independence and the model of interdependence. I have also explored combinations of autonomy and relatedness from different perspectives across cultures, contexts, and historical epochs.

I was able to demonstrate that the two prototypes represent distinct models that are significantly different from each other with almost no overlap. Table 9.1 gives an overview of the data for the different dimensions of the cultural model of parenting for the two prototypical environments.

The two models follow different socialization goals, embody different parenting ethnotheories, and emphasize different behavioral practices. The middle-class urban families follow the script of autonomy; the rural farmer families follow the script of interdependence. Moreover, parents following one model do not appreciate—and even reject—the ideas and practices of parents following the other model. Rural Cameroonian Nso women, for example, felt that the practices of middle-class German mothers, such as laying a baby on its back, were bad for children's development, whereas middle-class German women reject many of the practices that are central to the rural Nso parenting style, such as motor stimulation. Highly esteemed practices in one model are often regarded as pathological in the other model: The mother–child symbiosis that is normality in the interdependent model is regarded as sick and threatening for self-development in the independent model.

The parenting models are multidetermined in that cultural messages are conveyed through different channels and with different means. Proximal parenting, consisting mainly of body contact and body stimulation that supports interdependent socialization goals, is associated with a conversational style that is skeletal, directive, and repetitive, and that focuses on social contexts and moral rules and also supports interdependent socialization goals. Distal parenting, consisting mainly of face-to-face contexts and object stimulation, is associated with a conversational style that is voluminous and elaborated, and that focuses on the mental agency of the individual and also supports independent socialization goals. Proximal parenting and the interdependent conversational style are negatively related to distal parenting and an independent conversational style. The coherence and consistency of these styles becomes especially apparent in qualitative analyses. These contextual analyses demonstrate that there are cultural key systems that are pivotal for the other systems. An illiterate, rural Nso mother and a highly educated, middle-class Euro-American mother may both indicate that breastfeeding is the most important parenting behavior for a 3-month-old baby. However, they may express these preferences for very different reasons. The Nso mother is primarily concerned about the

TABLE 9.1

Overview Over the Parenting Dimensions for the Independent and Interdependent Samples

	Cultural Community				
	Berlin[a]	*Los Angeles*[b]	*Athens*[c]	*Rural Gujarati*[d]	*Rural Nso*[e]
Allocentrism	*62.90*	*70.87*	*71.42*	**92.79**	**103.89**
Socialization goals					
Autonomy	*3.93*	*4.15*	*4.0*	4.04	1.52
Relatedness	3.02	3.60	3.76	**4.54**	**5.0**
Parenting ethnotheories					
Autonomy	*2.49*	*2.97*	*3.29*	2.61	1.39
Relatedness	2.15	2.39	2.37	**3.43**	**3.51**
Discourse style in the ethnotheory interview					
Amount	*63.52*	*49.67*	—[f]	**10.09**	**25.15**
Autonomy	*44.52*	*54.35*	—[f]	—[f]	19.49
Relatedness	1.87	4.42	—[f]	—[f]	11.69
Maternal speech in mother–infant interaction					
Amount	*7.80*	*9.66*	5.36	—[f]	**4.25**
Autonomy	*47.49*	*56.63*	42.58	—[f]	11.44
Relatedness	12.80	18.98	40.29	—[f]	**80.98**
Parenting behavior					
distal	*58.68*	*50.88*	*57.90*	14.09	34.40
proximal	46.12	49.10	35.81	**44.76**	**79.24**

Note. >_Italicized values indicate support for the independent model and bold values indicate the interdependent model. [a]N = 39. [b]N = 23. [c]N = 50. [d]N = 48. [e]N = 96. [f]No information available.

health and growth of her baby, whereas the Los Angeles mother thinks that breast-feeding is the perfect context for face-to-face contact. The interdependent parenting model embodies a training and stimulation model that is parent centered. Here, the mother knows what the baby needs. The independent parenting model embodies a quasi equal dialogue model that is infant centered. Here, the baby communicates his or her needs and the mother has to sensitively respond to these needs.

The interdependent model focuses on the health and physical development of the baby. Constant nonverbal monitoring, especially of negative signals, and stimulating growth and development are the measures of good parenting.

The independent model is focused on the mental agency of the baby. From early on, the baby is the center of the communication and the baby's autonomy is supported. Cognitive stimulation through toys and objects emphasizes the importance of mental development. The second asset is supporting a baby's ability to be alone, which is considered a necessary prerequisite for healthy development toward autonomy. Being able to spend time alone and get along without others does not seem to represent the antipode of relatedness. Independent mothers also value relatedness, but their conception of relatedness is different from that of interdependent mothers. Being able to get along alone may be one pole of a separateness dimension with the other pole being isolation and loneliness, which may indicate being alone but not feeling good about it and competent in handling it.

Part of the model of independence is variability among caregivers. Although the model of parenting can be clearly defined as outlined earlier, every family tries to find its own expressions within the general framework so that more intracultural variability results. Parenting is, except for cases of serious neglect and abuse where the state has to intervene, the sole responsibility of the individual family and the individual parent. Part of the interdependent model, on the other hand, is public control of the individual parent's efforts and behaviors. This is expressed by the fact that family life takes place mainly outdoors and is therefore displayed publicly (see Figure 9.1).

As a result, interindividual variability across families with respect to parenting ideas and practices is lower in the interdependent model. We demonstrated in the previous chapters that the independent women are eager to explain their individual point of view and justify it almost with scientific expertise; the rural village women do not understand why we are interested in matters that are so obvious and that everybody knows, so that it would really never occur to anybody to talk about them. These differences are associated with different response styles in interviews and questionnaires. In the recent literature extreme response styles, or the greater tendency of respondents to select the endpoints of a response scale when answering a question, are discussed as expressing an individualistic orientation. Individualists are supposed to seek and to achieve clarity in their explicit verbal statements (Triandis, 1995), because they are less concerned with the consequences of expressing strong opinions. Johnson, Kulesa, Cho, and Shavitt (2005) argued that collectivism is associated with a greater emphasis on interpersonal harmony and with less emphasis on individual opinions. Ambiguity in communication is adaptive in these cultural contexts. In this view, extreme response style is equated with

a.

b.

FIGURE 9.1.   Contexts for family life (a) outdoors and (b) inside the house. Photos from Culture and Development Lab, University of Osnabrück.

an individual opinion, reflecting an independent stance that assumes that opinions are always individually based. In our rural samples, most pronounced in the Nso sample, we find an extreme response style with respect to the socialization goals scales with zero individual variation. All the farmer women strongly agree (with interdependent socialization goals) or strongly disagree (with independent socialization goals). The answers are not based on individual reasoning but on normative cultural conceptions that are unquestioned and shared. These data reflect the dimension of tightness (Pelto, 1968) in cultural models.

Interactions and conversations between parents and their babies are permanent cultural lessons. Parents explicitly and implicitly communicate their worldview to their children. Everyday life is saturated with cultural meaning, as LeVine (1994) suggested earlier. Nevertheless, infants are not the passive recipients of these messages. They process information actively and coconstruct their psychology and their selves.

Although the cultural parenting models of independence and interdependence are distinct and consistent, there are differences among the samples that we selected to represent these two models. Nevertheless, these differences can be explained within the same conceptual framework. Mothers from Los Angeles, for example, have significantly more body contact and significantly fewer face-to-face contexts than mothers from Berlin and Athens, who do not differ from each other. Yet the Los Angeles mothers do not follow a proximal parenting style. The Los Angeles mothers hold their babies on their laps and explain the outside world to them; that is, they establish an extradyadic, object-related focus. This increases body contact and reduces the number of face-to-face contexts. One Los Angeles mother (37 years old, teacher turned housewife after the birth of the child), for example, read two books to her 3-month-old daughter during the 10 minutes of interaction time (see Figure 9.2). The German mothers, on the other hand, introduce toys into the dyadic face-to-face context, as can be seen in Figure 9.3.

FIGURE 9.2.   A Euro-American middle-class mother reads a book with her 3-month-old child. Photo from Culture and Development Lab, University of Osnabrück.

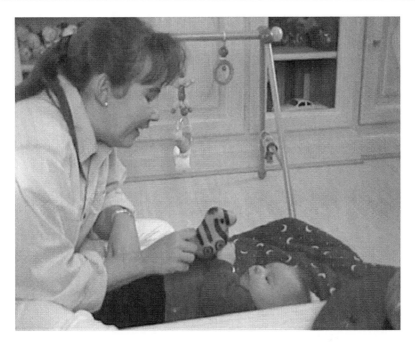

FIGURE 9.3.   A German middle-class mother with toy and face-to-face context.
Photo from Culture and Development Lab, University of Osnabrück.

The parenting style of the Los Angeles mothers can be regarded as an acceleration of the independent model, which may be due to the fact that the Los Angeles
mothers also hold the highest level of formal education among our samples. I return to the role of education later.

The Nso and the Gujarati mothers also differ from each other. The Gujarati
mothers demonstrate less body contact, less body stimulation, and less
face-to-face context than the Nso mothers. However, their socialization goals and
ethnotheories are very similar. These differences can be attributed to differences in
health and bodily strength. The Nso women are much better nourished, healthier,
and stronger than the Gujarati mothers and can therefore afford to invest more energy in their parenting style. Their higher face-to-face orientation can be attributed
to face-to-face positions that occur during performing body stimulations, as
discussed earlier.

THE NATURE OF THE TWO PARENTING STYLES

Our empirical analyses are mainly focused on maternal parenting style, reflecting
the fact that mothers are the primary caregivers during the first months of their infants' lives. We have also demonstrated that fathers' behavior has a direct impact
on children's development. Nevertheless, there are vast differences in

alloparenting and multiple caretaking among the cultural communities that we studied. Infants who grow up with an interdependent cultural model of parenting experience the network of a large family and kin from birth on, whereas infants growing up in an independent model of parenting experience mothers and fathers primarily. However, the parenting experiences do not change with the number of persons interacting with the baby. Even if we compile the socialization experiences infants had with the mother and all other persons together as assessed with the spot observation method described in chapter 4, we still find these different parenting styles: the proximal style for the interdependent families and the distal style for the independent families (see Figure 9.4).

a.

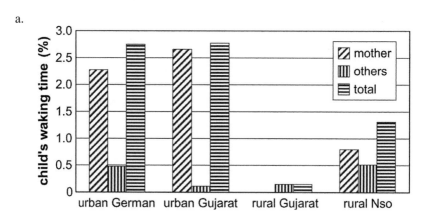

b.

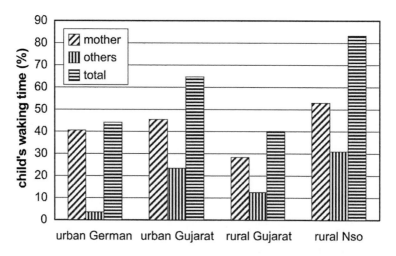

FIGURE 9.4. Mothers' and others' involvement in (a) object stimulation and (b) body contact.

As Figure 9.4 demonstrates, other people are the only ones who do object stimulation with the baby in the Gujarati sample and other people contribute a lot to the amount of object stimulation in the Nso families, but the total amount is nevertheless much lower than in the urban German and Indian samples. Although other people provide a lot of body contact for the Nso babies, mothers also provide more than the mothers in the other samples.

The two parenting strategies can be regarded as mutually exclusive, but they are not antagonistic in the sense that they represent the two endpoints of one dimension. This is mainly due to the fact that relatedness and autonomy do not have one, but several meanings that differ qualitatively, not just quantitatively. Relatedness in the interdependent model means interconnectedness with defined other people based on a system of obligations. Relatedness in the independent model means intentional relations, based on self-determined choices. This does not mean that obligations do not play a role in the independent model and choices are not part of the interdependent model. The difference is that obligations are a choice in the independent model and choices in the interdependent model are based on obligations.

The meaning of autonomy also differs between the two prototypical models. Autonomy as the expression of an independent, separate, consistent agency is the precondition for the independent definition of relationships. Autonomy in the interdependent model is context bound and only appreciated with respect to survival. As the rural Nso women explained, autonomy is valued only in particular segments of life, foremost in the context of personal hygiene so that good health and survival are ensured (Keller, Demuth, & Yovsi, 2006). Personal choice is only acceptable later in adult life, when a person is considered mature enough to know right from wrong and to make decisions, but not in childhood. Other aspects of autonomy that are crucial in the independent model, like respecting a child's interest and will, are generally seen as something negative that should be suppressed because the child's interest might lead to socially inappropriate and embarrassing behavior. Primarily thinking of one's own benefit is interpreted as selfish and as a sign of bad character (Keller, Demuth, & Yovsi, 2006).

The two dimensions of autonomy and relatedness are independent, yet they are organized in hierarchical patterns that differ across the two prototypes. Autonomy is the dominant dimension in the independent model, and relatedness is the dominant dimension in the interdependent model. Therefore, relatedness is in the service of autonomy in the independent model and autonomy is in the service of relatedness in the interdependent model.

These thoughts may leave room for speculation that the model of independence may have evolved out of the model of interdependence. In fact, images of infancy have undergone dramatic historical changes. Up through the 17th century, the belief persisted in the Western world that all people, including infants, were part of a larger cosmos of God in partnership with the family (Kessen, 1979). Children were typically given names of family members, often that of an older sibling who had died, to emphasize the historical and sacred connection of one person to another. These cultural practices are alive and well in the interdependent cultural model. During the 18th century a shift to individuality was based on earlier Judeo-Christian beliefs about the value of individual life. Changes continue as part of the dynamics of culture. As we demonstrated with the empirical historical analyses, there has been a shift from a more proximal style of parenting to a more distal style of parenting over the years in middle-class German families that is accompanied by greater orientation toward agency in verbal conversations. Changes in meaning of autonomy and relatedness accompany these shifts.

These considerations have implications for the conception of autonomous relatedness. Based on the argument developed here, relatedness in the sense of the interdependent model and autonomy in the sense of the independent model are mutually exclusive and cannot form another prototype. Our data, presented in chapter 6, confirm Kağitçibaşi's (1996a) important proposal that there are other models besides the model of independence and interdependence and that autonomy and relatedness are part of independent dimensions. However, we do not find support for the autonomous-related prototype where autonomy is as high as in the independent model and relatedness is just as important as in the interdependent model. The most frequent empirical type that we could identify is in between; that is, autonomy-related ideas and behaviors are more pronounced than in the interdependent model and less pronounced than in the independent model and relatedness-oriented ideas and behaviors are less pronounced than in the interdependent model and more pronounced than in the independent model. Table 9.2 presents an overview of the different dimensions of parenting for the samples with an autonomous-related model as compared to the models of independence and interdependence.

Based on these data, we have concluded that the autonomous-related model of parenting does not represent an empirical prototype as the independent and the interdependent model do. Yet there are multiple combinations of socialization goals, ethnotheories, and behaviors that simultaneously adhere to different cultural models.

However, the quantitative analyses do not paint a complete picture. The qualitative analyses reveal that there are multiple meaning shifts. The Beijing and Delhi mothers, for example, establish the face-to-face context less than the independent samples, but definitely more than the interdependent samples; however, they accord a meaning to it that is different from the independent practice. They use it as a context for stimulation, thus combining a parenting system that is typical for the independent model with a functional application that is typical for the interdependent model. They also have their own meaning system for the body contact system. They perform it less than it is performed in the interdependent samples, but more than in the independent samples. They express that body contact is very important, but only if the child wants it. Thus, they combine a parenting system that supports relatedness but gives the baby the lead, which is typical for the independent model. In line with the interdependent model they value body stimulation and devalue object stimulation. This may be a manifestation of the roots of this system being in the interdependent model of parenting, which experiences gradual transforma-

TABLE 9.2

Overview over the Parenting Dimensions of the Autonomous-Related Samples as Compared to the Means of the Independent and Interdependent Ones

	Independent Samples	Autonomous-Related Cultural Communities				Interdependent Samples
		Delhi	Beijing	San José	Urban Nso	
Allocentrism	68.35	**84.73**	**80.50**	68.85	**96.6**	99.03
Socialization goals						
Autonomy	4.05	3.61	4.57	4.26	4.07	2.63
Relatedness	3.48	3.87	3.31	4.27	**4.89**	4.80
Parenting ethnotheories						
Autonomy	2.95	3.11	3.12	2.49	2.57	1.93
Relatedness	3.21	3.43	4.16	3.79	4.04	4.86
Discourse style in the ethnotheory interview						
Amount of language	58.54	51.46	42.14	—[a]	**28.26**	20.49
Autonomy	48.20	34.39	—[a]	—[a]	27.87	19.49
Relatedness	2.83	7.33	—[a]	—[a]	**8.26**	11.69
Maternal speech in mother–infant interaction						
Amount of language	7.10	5.72	7.28	—[a]	—[a]	4.25
Autonomy	47.60	29.61	47.78	—[a]	—[a]	11.44
Relatedness	22.61	42.67	11.08	—[a]	—[a]	80.98
Parenting behavior						
distal	57.61	41.53	52.35	34.79	39.93	27.63
proximal	44.70	49.19	45.80	**64.34**	55.79	67.75

Note. Italicized values indicate similarity to the independent model and bold values indicate similarity to the interdependent model.
[a] No data available.

tions. It is interesting that these transformations occur in the respective key systems of both models. Thus, the different parenting systems are not performed consistently as they are in the two prototypical systems, but every cultural sample of the variation sets of studies follows its own logic.

Unfortunately, we do not have all data from all of the cultural communities. However, the existing data allow us to draw some conclusions. The first observation is that these cultural models are not consistent. The San José mothers, for example, have a low allocentrism score (comparable to the independent samples), they value autonomous and relational socialization goals and parenting ethnotheories just as much, but their behavioral interactional style is similar to the interdependent model with a clear bias toward proximal parenting.

The Beijing mothers, on the other hand, have a high allocentrism score, value autonomous socialization goals more than relational ones, their parenting ethnotheory is almost equally oriented toward autonomy and relatedness, and they have a more distal nonverbal and verbal parenting style, similar to the independent samples.

The Delhi mothers also have a high allocentrism score, express autonomous and relational socialization goals to a similar medium degree, and also perform distal and proximal parenting relatively similarly.

Finally, the urban Nso have a very high allocentrism score, equally high autonomous and relational socialization goals and parenting ethnotheories, and a proximal parenting style. Overall, the four samples have high allocentrism scores, with the exception of the San José mothers. All samples value autonomous socialization goals more than the interdependent samples, with the exception of the Delhi mothers. With respect to relational socialization goals, the Beijing and Delhi mothers are similar to the independent samples, whereas the San José mothers and the urban Nso are similar to the interdependent samples. With respect to autonomous ethnotheory, the Beijing and Delhi mothers are once again similar to the independent samples, and the San José mothers and the urban Nso score lower, yet they are still higher than the interdependent samples. The Delhi mothers score similarly to the independent samples in relational ethnotheory, whereas the Beijing, San José, and urban Nso mothers score higher, yet they are still lower than the interdependent samples. The Delhi mothers speak as many words during the ethnotheory interviews as the independent mothers, the urban Nso mothers are similar to the interdependent mothers in this respect, and the Beijing mothers are in between. During the interaction, however, the Beijing mothers speak as much as the independent mothers. The Beijing mothers are also closest to the independent mothers with respect to distal parenting, whereas the Delhi, San José, and urban Nso mothers score lower than the Beijing mothers, but higher than the interdependent mothers. Finally, proximal parenting of the Delhi and Beijing mothers is similar to the independent mothers, whereas the San José and urban Nso mothers are closer to the interdependent mothers. Thus, individual cultural profiles reflect combinations of the models of independence and interdependence. The prototype of autonomous relatedness, however, as the combination of the relatedness of the interdependent model and the autonomy of the independent model, did not occur in our samples and in the developmental domains that we analyzed.

THE RELATION BETWEEN BEHAVIORS AND IDEAS

There are some discrepancies between behavioral styles and parenting ideas: Socialization goals and parenting ethnotheory may express more of an autonomous orientation, whereas the behavioral parenting style is more proximal and thus relational. Some authors call the theoretically expected but insufficiently verifiable relation between behavior and beliefs the belief–behavior dilemma, which may be based on theoretical as well as methodological reasons (Davidson & Thompson, 1980). Even if ideas and practices are assessed within the same theoretical framework using identical dimensions, as we partly did with the framework of the component model of parenting, the link may be missing (Eickhorst, 2002). Beliefs are generally regarded as motivational forces for actions (D'Andrade, 1984; Sigel, 1985). However a one-to-one correspondence between beliefs and behaviors is a too-simplistic assumption in that it does not consider the "mental steps leading to the expression of intended action" (Sigel, 1985, p. 346). One way to conceive of this relationship is McGillicuddy-deLisi's (1985) demonstration that beliefs may have an independent influence on child outcomes, in addition to their indirect effect on parental practices. Moreover, Goodnow and Collins (1990) stressed that parental ideas or beliefs encompass more than the child; that is, the parents themselves as well as the relationship.

One aspect that is rarely mentioned in the literature is the role of implicit motivational forces. McClelland, Koestner, and Weinberger (1989; see also deCharms, Morrison, Reitman, & McClelland, 1955) distinguished between two motivational systems: On the one hand, there is a motivational system operating on the conscious level (explicit or self-attributed); on the other hand, another motivational system works on the preconscious level (implicit). The latter system represents highly generalized affective preferences for certain states or behaviors. These preferences explain long-term spontaneous behavioral trends (McClelland, 1987). It is assumed that implicit motives are built on early prelinguistic affective experiences and remain affectively aroused by them rather than by salient social experiences (McClelland et al., 1989). This seems to be the reason for their substantial predictive validity concerning long-term behavior compared to self-reports of explicit goals and values (McClelland & Pilon, 1983; see also Hofer & Chasiotis, 2003; Hofer, Chasiotis, & Campos, 2006).

Chasiotis, Hofer, and Campos (2005) combined the assessment of explicit and implicit motivation for parenthood with a cross-cultural developmental perspective. They assumed that the childhood context is important for the emergence of prosocial power motivation. By being exposed to interactive experiences with younger, genetically related children, prosocial, nurturant motivations and caretaking behaviors are elicited. These implicit motivations, in turn, lead on the conscious level to a higher amount of positive, loving feelings toward children, which ultimately affect reproductive behavior. After verifying that measurements of the constructs used were psychometrically sound across cultures, Chasiotis, Hofer, and Campos (2005) were able to show that the structural path model of these psychological mechanisms of parenting behavior is valid in male and female participants and in all cultures under examination. Their data support the view that context variables, such as birth order in the case of their study, might exert similar influences on psychological, somatic, and reproductive trajectories across different cultures. These analyses further support our view that contextual factors define cultural environments.

THE ROLE OF EDUCATION

Our analyses have confirmed that formal education is the engine of change, and this applies to parenting, too. It is important to keep in mind that we are talking about the special case of formal education here. There is no doubt that there is education in subsistence-based villages. Formal, school-based education, however, differs from indigenous educational systems in significant aspects, in content as well as mode of learning (Greenfield, Keller, Fuligni, & Maynard, 2003; Maynard & Martini, 2005; Tomasello et al., 1993). Contrasting the official Zambian system of schooling with the indigenous Chewa perspective, Serpell and Hatano (1996) concluded that the theories of pedagogy and instruction are more explicit, cognitive functions are segregated more sharply from the conative and emotional aspects of thought, and the responsibility for children's socialization is highly differentiated (see also Rogoff, Paradise, Mejfa Arauz, Correa-Chávez, & Angelillo, 2003). Figure 9.5 shows classroom posters in a Cameroonian school.

Formal education changes the availability of economic opportunities and lifestyle. Higher education is associated with a trend toward smaller, nuclear households; delayed family formation; and delayed childbearing. A higher educational level also correlates to a lower number of children (Alvarez, Brenes, & Cabezas, 1990) and a simultaneous decrease in infant mortality (Simmons & Bernstein, 1982). Education also increases attention to maternal and child health (Tapia Uribe, LeVine, & LeVine, 1994). Thus, formal education initiates a trend toward the cultural model of independence.

Our analyses with lower educated and higher educated Nso and Gujarati Hindu families have confirmed that the amount of formal education instigates qualitative and quantitative changes that deemphasize the model of interdependence and emphasize the model of independence. The different economic conditions based on educational differences allow greater exclusive dyadic attention and more playful activities with the baby. Accordingly, object and toy play increase and body contact and body stimulation decrease. Language becomes more important in daily practice. The amount of language increases (LeVine, Miller, Richman, & LeVine, 1996). LeVine (2002) interpreted the association of an emphasis on verbal communication with the cultural model of independence, so that physical separation of infant and mother makes the mother more likely to use verbal rather than tactile

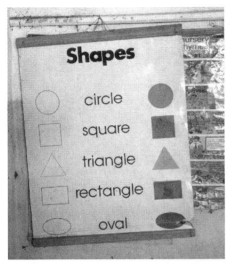

a.   b.

FIGURE 9.5.   Patterns and shapes in Cameroonian schools. Photo by Florian Kießling.

communication. Moreover, a woman who has attended school is not only inclined to learn more in the verbal mode, but also to teach more in that mode (Tapia Uribe et al., 1994). With the increase in frequency of language as a socialization context, the expression of and the reference to autonomy also becomes more pronounced.

Greenfield (1994) stated different theses about the role of formal schooling for the development of independence (see also Richman et al., 1988; Tapia Uribe et al., 1994). She argued that school-based literacy undermines interdependence. Literacy is detrimental to social intelligence (Mundy-Castle, 1974), as knowledge becomes related to unknown authorities and detached from the generational repositories (i.e., parents and grandparents). Thus, schooling also undermines the family as an educational institution. At the same time, the style of information processing and learning changes from legitimate peripheral participation (Lave & Wenger, 1991) and apprenticeship with observation and imitation to trial-and-error and instructed learning (Greenfield, 2004; Rogoff, 2003). Learning becomes separated from the social context, and holistic thinking becomes analytical and technological (Mundy-Castle, 1991). In line with these changes, the experience of formal education undermines the respect for authority. The locus of authority for formulating a logical argument is irrespective of age. However, children from interdependent sociocultural environments are expected to be respectful to elders and not to argue with them (Delgado-Gaitan, 1994). Schooling also reduces a willingness to share resources with the extended family and knowledge becomes an individual possession (Greenfield, 1994, 1997). Nevertheless children actively participate in building a new classroom, for example (see Figure 9.6).

FIGURE 9.6.   Schoolchildren help with building a new classroom.

These statements indicate that the impact and consequences of formal education on human psychology and family life are not always unanimously welcomed,
and the lack of indigenous curricula in the school setting is criticized (Nsamenang,
2003). Nsamenang elucidated the different points of view in that "international ad-
vocacy tends to condemn the participatory role of the African child as exploitative
child labor ... whereas in the subsistence economies of Africa, such labor is legiti-
mately interpreted as indigenous educational strategy that keeps children in contact with existential realities and the activities of daily life" (Nsamenang, 1992, p.
223). This view is condensed in Bruner's (1996) statement that "schooling may
even be at odds with a culture's other ways of inducting the young into the require-
ments of communal living" (p. ix). Another approach is taken by Kağitçibaşi and
collaborators (Bekman, 2003; Kağitçibaşi, Bekman, Özkök, & Kuscul, 1995;
Kağitçibaşi, Bekman, & Sunar, 1991) with the Mother–Child Education Program,
which aims at fostering cognitive and psychosocial development in the home environment and hopes to promote school readiness by supporting preliteracy and nu-
merical skills. Pursuing either way may have consequences for the development of
cultural models of the self.

Sometimes researchers regret that the influence of the parents' religious orientation is often overlooked in research on parenting. Our data reveal similarities of
parenting ideas and practices across diverse religious orientations. It seems as if
the relevant variable would be a religious orientation per se and not so much the
particular one. Likewise, in Western societies, parents with a religious orientation
differ from those who do not have one. However, religion is more visible in every-

day life in traditional communities than in Western urban centers. Places of worship are everywhere in Indian Hindu communities (see Figure 9.7). Human ontogeny is patterned with religious-based rituals, like the hair-shaving ceremony in Gujarat (see Figure 9.8). The assistance of God is crucial for all matters of life. Figure 9.9 shows part of a ceremony for the opening of a dairy farm in Gujarat. Thus religious ceremonies and worship are displayed as openly as family life is.

CULTURAL PATHWAYS OF DEVELOPMENT

Our studies have confirmed that early experiences have developmental consequences for the mastery of further developmental milestones. The models of independence and interdependence reveal consistent patterns with respect to the developmental pathways. The parenting strategy supporting the model of independence accelerates self-recognition as the first expression of a categorical self. The parenting strategy supporting the model of interdependence accelerates self-regulation as a first expression of an interdependent self. Although both developmental tasks can be regarded as universal, they nevertheless may be based on different meaning systems. Compliance in the independent model is based on an autonomous agent who intentionally and voluntarily enacts compliance, whereas in the interdependent model obedience and respect may form the basis for compli-

FIGURE 9.7.   Lord Ganesha in a worship place in a wall. Photo by Heidi Keller.

a.

b.

FIGURE 9.8. Impressions of a hair-shaving ceremony of a small boy. Photos by Monika Abels.

ance. The independent pathway to compliance may need more time, because it is based on autonomy that needs to be established developmentally first.

As Chasiotis and collaborators were able to show (Chasiotis, Kießling, Hofer, & Campos, 2006; see also Chasiotis, Kießling, Winter, & Hofer, 2006), the delay inhibitory part of self-regulatory abilities is more pronounced in interdependent cultures, as shown by their Cameroonian sample, whereas false-belief understand-

FIGURE 9.9.   Religious ceremony during the opening of a dairy farm. Photo by
Monika Abels.

ing is significantly lower than in more independent cultures, as shown by their
German sample. Cameroonian parents favor obedient and inhibited behavior in
their children (Nsamenang & Lamb, 1994, 1995; Yovsi, 2003). Accordingly, we
were able to demonstrate that 19-month-old Cameroonian children showed more
obedient reactions to parental requests compared to Costa Rican and Greek children (Keller, Yovsi, et al., 2004). From that perspective, the parenting goals of
strict obedience and mastery of impulse control might lead to less exposure to
interactional conversational contexts, which foster the development of mentalistic
abilities such as false-belief understanding. Thus, whereas independent, authori-
tative parenting might be more likely to disregard impulse control while fostering
children's false-belief understanding through mentalistic conversational contexts,
interdependent parenting goals of obedience and compliance might be related to
better delay inhibitory performances and less false-belief understanding in
children.

This does not mean, however, that the two conceptions of compliance reflect
different degrees of maturity, a view that is expressed in Western developmental
psychology. Compliance based on obedience and respect reflects the mature de-

velopmental achievement in the interdependent model, whereas compliance based on autonomy reflects the mature developmental achievement in the independent model.

Generally, it is important to note that our conceptualization of developmental pathways does not reflect any sort of value judgment, either in terms of modernity, or in quality. The pathways represent adaptations to contextual demands and the context defines which actions and beliefs are better or worse. Adaptations do not carry evaluative meanings by definition. Individuals following each pathway may represent better or inferior versions of the modal cultural type. Therefore, it is important to define culture-specific variations of parenting qualities. In a first approximation of that, we reported about an indigenous Nso parenting quality scale, which obviously assesses a different parenting conception than the popular instruments that were developed on the basis of the independent cultural model. This view has implications for developmental counseling, therapeutic interventions, and policymaking. Programs should be based on the cultural orientation of the people who are to be addressed.

BEYOND A WESTERN INDEPENDENT BIAS

Our study program has revealed that there is no one human psychology and no one pathway of development. However, textbooks of developmental psychology paint a picture of a universal human psychology (e.g., Berk, 2004; Siegler, Deloache, & Eisenberg, 2003). This is not meant to imply that cultural variation is not acknowledged (see especially Cole & Cole, 1989). However, culture is rarely attributed with the intrinsic and systematic role that it plays for developmental processes. Moreover, the model of one universal human psychology is assumed to be the healthy one—deviations are pathological. I argue however, that cultural variation follows systematic rules, and these are bound to socioeconomic conditions. This point of view is often criticized as materialistic, deterministic, and not paying enough tribute to humans' intentionality and free will. Our studies help to disentangle these issues. We observed parents' behaviors and asked them about their intentions and opinions. We find that their behaviors and their representations are closely related to socioeconomic conditions, with formal education being key. Our study program therefore also supports evolutionary assumptions of life strategies, although we mainly analyzed the culture of parenting and its developmental consequences. The acknowledgment of different cultural models and different developmental pathways is not only a must for developmental science, but also for multicultural societies. Migrants often bring an interdependent cultural model into an environment where the social mainstream is oriented toward an independent cultural model. Stereotypical judgments and misunderstandings are preprogrammed on both sides. The realization and appreciation of different models, their coexistence, and merging should offer new developmental opportunities for the future, in theory as well as in practice.

References

Abels, M. (2002). *Baby massage in rural Gujarat, India: Physical growth, motor development and caregivers' ethnotheories.* Unpublished master's thesis, University of Osnabrück, Faculty of Human Sciences, Department of Culture and Development, Osnabück, Germany.

Abels, M. (2006). *The expression of emotional warmth: Ethnotheories of rural and urban Indian mothers and grandmothers.* Unpublished doctoral dissertation, University of Osnabrück, Faculty of Human Sciences, Osnabrück, Germany.

Abels, M. (in press). Ethnotheories of parenting: Experiences from rural Gujarat. In N. Chaudhary, S. Anandalakshmy & N. Sharma (Eds.), *Constructing methods: Research and the Indian community.* Thousand Oaks, CA: Sage.

Abels, M., & Kärtner, J. (2004, May). *Validation of picture cards used for ethnotheories interviews in Cameroon, Germany, and the USA.* Poster presented at The Saskatchewan Workshop on Culture and Human Development, Saskatoon, Canada.

Abels, M., Keller, H., Mohite, P., Mankodi, H., Shastri, J., Bhargava, S., et al. (2005). Early socialization contexts and social experiences of infants in rural and urban Gujarat, India. *Journal of Cross-Cultural Psychology, 36,* 717–738.

Abramovitz, R. (1976). Parenthood in America. *Journal of Clinical Child Psychology, 5*(3), 43–46.

Ainsworth, M. D. S. (1973). The development of infant–mother attachment. In B. M. Caldwell & H. N. Ricciuti (Eds.), *Review of child development research* (Vol. 3, pp. 1–94). Chicago: University of Chicago Press.

Ainsworth, M. D. S. (1977). Attachment theory and its utility in cross-cultural research. In P. H. Leiderman, S. R. Tulkin, & A. Rosenfeld (Eds.), *Culture and infancy: Variations in the human experience* (pp. 49–67). New York: Academic.

Ainsworth, M. D. S. (1979). Attachment as related to mother–infant interaction. In J. S. Rosenblatt, R. A. Hinde, C. Beer, & M. Busnel (Eds.), *Advances in the study of behavior* (Vol. 9, pp. 1–51). New York: Academic.

Ainsworth, M. D. S. (2004). *Maternal sensitivity scales.* Retrieved October 20, 2004, from http://www.psychology.sunysb.edu/ewaters/measures/senscoop.htm

Ainsworth, M. D. S., Bell, S. M., & Stayton, D. J. (1971). Individual differences in strange situation behavior of one-year-olds. In H. R. Schaffer (Ed.), *The origins of human social relations* (pp. 17–57). New York: Academic.

Ainsworth, M. D. S., Bell, S. M., & Stayton, D. J. (1974). Infant–mother attachment and social development: Socialization as a product of reciprocal responsiveness to signals. In M. P. M. Richards (Ed.), *The integration of a child into a social world* (pp. 97–119). London: Cambridge University Press.

Ainsworth, M. D. S., Blehar, M. C., Waters, E., & Wall, S. (1978). *Patterns of attachment: A psychological study of the strange situation.* Hillsdale, NJ: Lawrence Erlbaum Associates, Inc.

Alexander, R. D. (1979). *Darwinism and human affairs.* Seattle: University of Washington Press.

Alvarez, A. T., Brenes, A., & Cabezas, M. (1990). *Patrones de crianza en la familia costarricense* [Patterns of raising in the Costa Rican family]. San José, Costa Rica: Universidad de Costa Rica, Instituto de Investigaciones Psicológicas.

Amsterdam, B. K. (1972). Mirror self-image reactions before age two. *Developmental Psychology, 5,* 297–305.

Anandalakshmy, S. (1991). The female child in a family setting. *The Indian Journal of Social Work, 52,* 29–36.

Anjali. (1993). *An analysis of the concept of Lalan-Palan as directing mother–baby interactions.* Paper presented at the Regional Conference of the International Society for the Study of Behavioural Development, Bandung, Indonesia.

Astington, J. W. (2001). The future of theory-of-mind research: Understanding motivational states, the role of language, and real-world consequences. *Child Development, 72,* 685–687.

Baillargeon, M. W., Bistline, R. G., Jr., & Sonnet, P. E. (1989). Evaluation of strains of *geotrichum candidum* for lipase production and fatty acid specificity. *Applied Microbiology and Biotechnology, 30,* 92–96.

Bakan, D. (1966). *The duality of human existence: Isolation and communication in Western man.* Chicago: Rand McNally.

Bandura, A. (1977). Self efficacy: Toward a unifying theory of behavioral change. *Psychological Review, 84,* 191–215.

Bandura, A. (1997). *Self-efficacy: The exercise of control.* New York: Freeman.

Bandura, A., & Huston, A. C. (1961). Identification as a process of incidental learning. *Journal of Abnormal and Social Psychology, 63,* 611–618.

Bandura, A., Ross, D., & Ross, S. A. (1963). A comparative test of the status envy, social power and the secondary-reinforcement theories of identification learning. *Journal of Abnormal and Social Psychology, 67,* 527–534.

Bard, K. A. (2002). Development processes in empathy. *Behavioral and Brain Sciences, 25,* 25–26.

Bard, K. A., Myowa-Yamokoshi, M., Tomonaga, M., Tanaka, M., Quinn, J., Costall, A., et al. (2005). *Cultural variation in the mutual gaze of chimpanzees (Pan troglodytes).* Manuscript submitted for publication.

Barr, R. G., Konner, M. J., Bakeman, R., & Adamson L. (1991). Crying in !Kung San infants: A test of the cultural specificity hypothesis. *Developmental Medicine and Child Neurology, 33,* 601–610.

Bateson G. (1979). *Mind and nature: A necessary unity.* Toronto: Bantam Books.

Baumrind, D. (1971). Harmonious parents and their preschool children. *Developmental Psychology, 4,* 99–102.

Beck, U. (1994). *Risk society.* London: Sage. (Original work published 1986)

Becker, W. C. (1964). Consequences of different kinds of parental discipline. In M. L. Hoffman & L. W. Hoffman (Eds.), *Review of child development research* (Vol. 1, pp. 169–208). New York: Russell Sage Foundation.

Bekman, S. (2003). From research project to nationwide programme: The mother–child education programme of Turkey. In T. S. Saraswathi (Ed.), *Cross-cultural perspectives in human development* (pp. 287–325). New Delhi, India: Sage.

Bell, R. Q. (1968). A reinterpretation of the direction of effects in studies of socialization. *Psychological Review, 75,* 81–95.

Bellah, R. N., Madsen, R., Sullivan, W. M., Swidler, A., & Tipton, S. M. (1985). *Habits of the heart: Individualism and commitment in American life.* Berkeley: University of California Press.

Belsky, J. (1999). Interactional and contextual determinants of attachment security. In J. Cassidy & P. R. Shaver (Eds.), *Handbook of attachment: Theory, research, and clinical applications* (pp. 249–264). New York: Guilford.

Belsky, J., Steinberg, L., & Draper, P. (1991). Childhood experience, interpersonal development, and reproductive strategy: An evolutionary theory of socialization. *Child Development, 62,* 647–670.

Berk, L. E. (2004). *Development through the lifespan* (3rd ed.). Boston: Pearson Education.

Berry, J. W. (1976). *Human ecology and cognitive style: Comparative studies in cultural and psychological adaptation.* New York: Sage/Halsted.

Bigelow, A. E. (1998). Infants' sensitivity to familiar imperfect contingencies in social interaction. *Infant Behavior and Development, 21,* 149–162.

Bischof, N. (1985). *Das Rätsel Ödipus* [The enigma of Oedipus]. Munich, Germany: Piper.

Bischof, N. (1996). *Das Kraftfeld der Mythen: Signale aus der Zeit, in der wir die Welt erschaffen haben* [The force field of myths: Signals from an area in which we created the world]. Munich, Germany: Piper.

Bischof-Köhler, D. (1989). *Spiegelbild und Empathie: Die Anfänge der sozialen Kognition* [Reflection and empathy: The beginnings of social cognition]. Bern, Switzerland: Huber.

Bischof-Köhler, D. (1991). The development of empathy in infants. In M. E. Lamb & H. Keller (Eds.), *Infant development: Perspectives from German speaking countries* (pp. 245–273). Hillsdale, NJ: Lawrence Erlbaum Associates, Inc.

Bjorklund, D. F. (1987). A note on neonatal imitation. *Developmental Review, 7,* 86–92.

Bjorklund, D. F. (1997). In search of a metatheory for cognitive development (or, Piaget is dead and I don't feel so good myself). *Child Development, 68,* 142–146.

Bjorklund, D. F. (2000). *Children's thinking: Developmental function and individual differences* (3rd ed.). Pacific Grove, CA: Brooks/Cole.

Bjorklund, D. F., & Pellegrini, A. D. (2002). *The origins of human nature: Evolutionary developmental psychology.* Washington, DC: American Psychological Association.

Blain, M. D., Thompson, J. M., & Whiffen, V. E. (1993). Attachment and perceived social support in late adolescence: The interaction between working models of self and others. *Journal of Adolescent Research, 8,* 226–241.

Blossfeld, H. P. (Ed.). (1995). *The new role of women.* Boulder, CO: Westview.

Bogin, B. (1990). The evolution of human childhood. *BioScience, 40,* 16–25.

Bogin, B. (1999a). Evolutionary perspective on human growth. *Annual Review of Anthropology, 28,* 109–153.

Bogin, B. (1999b). *Patterns of human growth* (2nd ed.). New York: Cambridge University Press.

Bond, M. H. (1991). *Beyond the Chinese face.* Hong Kong: Oxford University Press.

Bond, M. H. (1998). Social psychology across cultures: Two ways forward. In J. G. Adair, D. Belanger, & K. L. Dion (Eds.), *Advances in psychological science: Social, personal, and cultural aspects* (Vol. 1, pp. 137–150). Sussex, England: Psychology Press.

Bowlby, J. (1969). *Attachment and loss: Vol. 1. Attachment.* New York: Basic Books.

Boyd, R., & Richerson, P. J. (1985). *Culture and evolutionary process.* Chicago: University of Chicago Press.

Branco, A. (2003). Social development in cultural context: Cooperative and competitive interaction patterns in peer relations. In J. Valsiner & K. J. Connolly (Eds.), *Handbook of developmental psychology* (pp. 238–256). London: Sage.

Brazelton, T. B. (1977). Implications of infant development among the Mayan Indians of Mexico. In P. H. Leiderman, S. R. Tulkin, & A. Rosenfeld (Eds.), *Culture and infancy: Variations in the human experience* (pp. 151–187). New York: Academic.

Bril, B. (1989). Die kulturvergleichende Perspektive: Entwicklung und Kultur [The cross-cultural perspective: Development and culture]. In H. Keller (Ed.), *Handbuch der Kleinkindforschung* (pp. 71–88). Heidelberg, Germany: Springer.

Bronfenbrenner, U. (1979). *Ecology of human development.* Cambridge, MA: Harvard University Press.

Bröring-Wichmann, C. (2003). *Vorbereitung auf die Geburt eines Geschwisters* [Preparation for the birth of a sibling]. Unpublished master's thesis, University of Osnabrück, Department of Human Sciences, Department of Culture and Development, Osnabrück, Germany.

Bruesseler, R. (1992). Industrialisierung und Regionalplanung in einem Entwicklungsland: Das Beispiel des indischen Bundesstaates Gujarat [Industralization and regional planning in a developing country: The example of the Indian state Gujarat]. In F. Ahnert, H. Breuer, D. Havlik, J. Schultz, F. Stang, & R. Zschocke (Series Eds.), *Aachener Geographische Arbeiten, Heft 25.* Aachen, Germant: Geographisches Institut der RWTH Aachen im Selbstverlag.

Bruner, J. J. (1986). *Actual minds, possible worlds.* Cambridge, MA: Harvard University Press.

Bruner, J. J. (1996). *The culture of education.* Cambridge, MA: Harvard University Press.

Budwig, N. (1995). *A developmental-functionalist approach to child language.* Mahwah, NJ: Lawrence Erlbaum Associates, Inc.

Bugenthal, B. B., & Johnston, C. (2000). Parental and child cognitions in the context of the family. *Annual Review of Psychology, 51,* 315–344.

Bühler, K. (1918). *Die geistige Entwicklung des Kindes* [The mental development of the child]. Jena, Germany: Fischer.

Bushnell, I. W. R. (1998). The origins of face perception. In F. Simion & G. Butterworth (Eds.), *The development of sensory, motor and cognitive capacities in early infancy: From perception to cognition* (pp. 70–86). Hove, England: Psychology Press.

Buss, D. M., Haselton, M. G., Shackelford, T. K., Bleske, A. L., & Wakefield, J. C. (1998). Adaptations, exaptations, and sprandels. *American Psychologist, 53,* 533–548.

Bussab, V. S. R., & Ribeiro, F. J. R. (1998). Biologicamente cultural [biologically cultural]. In L. Souza, M. F. Q. Freitas, & M. M. P. Rodrigues (Eds.), *Psicologia: Reflexões (im)pertinentes* (pp. 195–224). São Paulo, Brazil: Casa do Psicólogo.

Butterworth, G. (1990). Self-perception in infancy. In D. Cicchetti & M Beeghly (Eds.), *The self in transition: Infancy to childhood* (pp. 119–137). Chicago: University of Chicago Press.

Caudill, W., & Plath, D. (1966). Who sleeps by whom? Parent–child involvement in urban Japanese families. *Psychiatry, 29,* 344–366.

Chao, R. K. (1994). Beyond parental control and authoritarian parenting style: Understanding Chinese parenting through the cultural notion of training. *Child Development, 65,* 1111–1119.

Chao, R. K. (1995). Chinese and European American cultural models of the self reflected in mothers' childrearing beliefs. *Ethos, 23,* 328–354.

Chasiotis, A. (1990). *Soziobiologie und Entwicklungspsychologie der frühesten Kindheit* [Sociobiology and developmental psychology of early infancy]. Unpublished master' thesis, University of Osnabrück, Faculty of Human Sciences, Department of Culture and Development, Osnabrück, Germany.

Chasiotis, A., Bender, M., Kießling, F., & Hofer, J. (2005). *The emergence of the independent self: Autobiographical memory as a mediator of false belief understanding and sociocultural motive orientation in Cameroonian and German preschoolers.* Manuscript submitted for publication.

Chasiotis, A., Hofer, J., & Campos, D. (2005). *When does liking children lead to parenthood? Younger siblings, implicit power motivation, and explicit love for children predict parenthood across cultures.* Manuscript under review.

Chasiotis, A., Kießling, F., Hofer, J., & Campos, D. (2006). Theory of mind and inhibitory control in three cultures: Conflict inhibition predicts false belief understanding in Germany, Costa Rica, and Cameroon. *International Journal of Behavioral Development, 30,* 249–260.

Chasiotis, A., Kießling, F., Winter, V., & Hofer, J. (2006). Sensory motor inhibition as a prerequisite for theory of mind: A comparison of clinical and normal preschoolers differing in sensory motor abilities. *International Journal of Behavioral Development, 30,* 178–190.

Chaudhary, N. (2004). *Listening to culture: Constructing reality from everyday day talk.* New Delhi, India: Sage.

Chauhan, N. (1991). *Demographic profile of women in Gujarat.* Unpublished paper, M. S. University of Baroda, Department of Human Development and Family Studies, Baroda, India.

Chávez, A., Martinez, C., & Yashine, T. (1975). Nutrition, behavioral development and mother–child interaction in young rural children. *Federation Proceedings, 34,* 1574–1586.

Chen, X. (1998). The changing Chinese family: Resources, parenting practices, and children's socio-emotional problems. In U. P. Gielen & A. L. Communian (Eds.), *Family and family therapy in international perspective* (pp. 150–167). Trieste, Italy: Edizioni LINT.

Chen, X., & He, Y. (2005). The family in mainland China: Structure organization, and significance for child development. In J. L. Roopnarine & U. P. Gielen (Eds.), *Families in global perspective* (pp. 51–62). Boston: Allyn & Bacon.

Chen, Z., & Siegler, R. S. (2000). Across the great divide: Bridging the gap between understanding of toddlers' and other children's thinking. *Monographs of the Society for Research in Child Development, 65*(2, Serial No. 261), 1–96.

Chirkov, V., Ryan, R. M., Kim, Y., & Kaplan, U. (2003). Differentiating autonomy from individualism and independence: A self-determination theory perspective on internalization of cultural orientations and well-being. *Journal of Personality and Social Psychology, 84,* 97–110.

Chisholm, J. S. (1992). Death, hope, and sex: Life-history theory and the development of reproductive strategies. *Current Anthropology, 34*(1), 1–24.

Chisholm, J. S. (1999). *Death, hope, and sex: Steps to an evolutionary ecology of mind and morality.* Cambridge, England: Cambridge University Press.

Chisholm, J. S. (2003). Uncertainty, contingency, and attachment: A life history theory of theory of mind. In K. Sterelny & J. Fitness (Eds.), *From mating to mentality: Evaluating evolutionary psychology* (pp. 125–153). New York: Psychology Press.

Cho, G. E., Sandel, T. L., Miller, P. M., & Wang, S.-H. (2005). What do grandmothers think about self-esteem? American and Taiwanese folk theories revisited. *Social Development, 14,* 701–721.

Cicchetti, D., & Tucker, D. (1994). Development and self-regulatory structures of the mind. *Development and Psychopathology, 6,* 533–549.

Clancy, B., Darlington, R. B., & Finlay, B. L. (2001). Translating developmental time across mammalian species. *Neuroscience, 105,* 7–17.

Cohen, J. (1988). *Statistical power analysis for the behavioral sciences.* Hillsdale, NJ: Lawrence Erlbaum Associates, Inc.

Cohen, J., Cohen, P., West, S., & Aiken, L. (2003). *Applied multiple regression/correlation analysis for the behavioral sciences* (3rd ed.). Hillsdale, NJ: Lawrence Erlbaum Associates, Inc.

Cole, K., & Mitchell, P. (2000). Siblings in the development of executive control and a "theory of mind." *British Journal of Developmental Psychology, 18,* 279–295.

Cole, M. (2005). Cultural-historical activity theory in the family of socio-cultural approaches. *ISSBD Newsletter, 1*(47), 1–4.

Cole, M., & Cole, S. (1989). *The development of children.* New York: Freeman.

Cosmides, L., & Tooby, J. (1987). From evolution to behavior: Evolutionary psychology as the missing link. In J. Dupre (Ed.), *The latest on the best: Essays on evolution and optimality* (pp. 277–306). Cambridge, MA: MIT Press.

Crockenberg, S., & Litman, C. (1990). Autonomy as competence in 2-year olds: Maternal correlates of child defiance, compliance and self-assertion. *Developmental Psychology, 26,* 961–971.

Csikszentmihalyi, M., & Rathunde, K. (1998). The development of the person: An experiential perspective on the ontogenesis of psychological complexity. In W. Damon (Series Ed.) & R. M. Lerner (Vol. Ed.), *Handbook of child psychology: Vol. 1. Theoretical models of human development* (5th ed., pp. 635–684). New York: Wiley.

Cummins, D. (1996). Evidence for the innateness of deontic reasoning. *Mind & Language, 11,* 160–190.

Cutting, A. L., & Dunn, J. (1999). "Theory of mind," emotion, language and family background: Individual differences and interrelations. *Child Development, 70,* 853–865.

D'Andrade, R. (1984). Some proposition about the relations between culture and human cognition. In J. W. Stigler, R. A. Shweder, & G. Herdt (Eds.), *Cultural psychology. Essays on comparative human development* (pp. 65–129). New York: Cambridge University Press.

D'Andrade, R., & Strauss, C. (1992). *Human motives and cultural models.* Cambridge, England: Cambridge University Press.

Dash, B., & Kashyap, L. (1992). *Five specialised therapies of Ayurveda (Panca Karma)* (Todarananda Ayurveda Saukhyam Series No. 8). New Delhi, India: Concept Publishing.

Davidson, A. R., & Thompson, E. (1980). Cross-cultural studies to attitudes and beliefs. In H. C. Triandis & R. W. Brislin (Eds.), *Handbook of cross-cultural psychology: Social psychology* (Vol. 5, pp. 25–71). Boston: Allyn & Bacon.

Dawson, G., & Fisher, K. W. (Eds.). (1994). *Human behavior and the developing brain.* New York: Guilford.

DeCasper, A. J., & Fifer, W. (1980). On human bonding: Newborns prefer their mothers' voices. *Science, 208,* 1174–1176.

DeCasper, A. J., & Spence, M. J. (1986). Prenatal maternal speech influences newborns' perception of speech sounds. *Infant Behavior and Development, 9,* 133–150.

deCharms, R., Morrison, H. W., Reitman, W. R., & McClelland, D. C. (1955). Behavioral correlates of directly and indirectly measured achievement motivation. In D. C. McClelland (Ed.), *Studies in motivation* (pp. 414–423). New York: Appleton-Century-Crofts.

Deepak Medical Foundation, Deepak Charitable Trust. (2000). *Annual report.* Baroda, India: Author.

Deka, N. (1993). India. In L. Loeb Adler (Ed.), *International handbook on gender roles* (pp. 122–143). Westport, CT: Greenwood.

Delgado-Gaitan, C. (1994). Consejos: The power of cultural narratives. *Anthropology & Education Quarterly, 25,* 298–316.

Demuth, C., Abels, M., & Keller, H. (in press). Autobiographical remembering and cultural memory in a socio-historical perspective. In G. Zheng, K. Leung, & J. Adair (Eds), *Perspectives and progress in contemporary cross-cultural psychology.* Beijing: China Light Industry Press.

Dennett, D. C. (1983). Intentional systems in cognitive ethology: The "Panglossian paradigm" defended. *Behavioral and Brain Sciences, 6,* 343–390.

De Vries, M. W. (1984). Temperament and infant mortality among the Masai of East Africa. *American Journal of Psychiatry, 141,* 1189–1194.

de Wolff, M. S., & van IJzendoorn, M. H. (1997). Sensitivity and attachment: A meta-analysis on parental antecedents of infant attachment. *Child Development, 68,* 571–591.

Doumanis, M. (1983). *Mothering in Greece: From collectivism to individualism.* London: Academic.

Draper, P. (1975). Cultural pressure on sex differences. *American Ethnologist, 4,* 602–615.

Draper, P., & Harpending, H. (1988). A sociobiological perspective on human reproductive strategies. In K. B. MacDonald (Ed.), *Sociobiological perspectives on human development* (pp. 340–372). New York: Springer.

Dunbar, R. (1995). *The trouble with science.* Cambridge, MA: Harvard University Press.

Dunbar, R. (1996). *Grooming, gossip and the evolution of language.* London: Faber & Faber.

Dunham, P. J., & Dunham, F. (1995). Developmental antecedents of taxonomic and thematic strategies at three years of age. *Developmental Psychology, 31,* 483–493.

Dunn, J., Brown, J., Slomkowski, C., Tesla, C., & Youngblade, L. (1991). Young children's understanding of other people's feelings and beliefs: Individual differences and their antecedents. *Child Development, 62,* 1352–1366.

Dürr, H. P. (1981). *Der Wissenschaftler und das Irrationale* [The scientist and the irrationale] (2 vols.). Frankfurt, Germany: Syndikat.

Edwards, C. P., & Liu, W.-L. (2002). Parenting toddlers. In M. H. Bornstein (Eds.), *Handbook of parenting: Vol. 1. Children and parenting* (2nd ed., pp. 45–71). Mahwah, NJ: Lawrence Erlbaum Associates, Inc.

Eibl-Eibesfeldt, I. (1984). *Die Biologie des menschlichen Verhaltens: Grundriß der Humanethologie* [The biology of human behavior: Outline of human ethology]. Munich, Germany: Piper.

Eickhorst, A. (2002). *Vater-Säuglings-Interaktionen und Theorien über Vaterschaft* [Father–child interactions and theories about fatherhood]. Unpublished master's thesis, University of Osnabrück, Faculty of Human Sciences, Department of Culture and Development, Osnabrück, Germany.

Eickhorst, A. (2005). *Vater-Erleben, integrative Kompetenzen und Wohlbefinden: Eine quer- und längsschnittliche Studie an 40 deutschen Vätern 19–20 Monate alter Kinder* [Father-experience, integrative competencies and well-being: A cross-sectional and longitudinal study with 40 German fathers of 19- to 20-month-old children]. Unpublished doctoral dissertation, University of Osnabrück, Faculty of Human Development, Osnabrück, Germany.

Eimas, P. D., & Quinn, P. C. (1994). Studies on the formation of perceptually based basic-level categories in young infants. *Child Development, 65,* 903–917.

Ellis, B. J. (2004). Timing of pubertal maturation in girls: An integrated life history approach. *Psychological Bulletin, 130,* 920–958.

Ellsworth, C. P., Muir, D. W., & Hains, S. M. J. (1993). Social competence and person–object differentiation: An analysis of the still-face effect. *Developmental Psychology, 29,* 63–73.

Emde, R. N. (1984). The affective self: Continuities and transformations from infancy. In J. D. Call, E. Galenson, & R. L. Tyson (Eds.), *Frontiers of infant psychiatry* (pp. 38–54). New York: Basic Books.

Emde, R. N., Biringen, Z., Clyman, R. B., & Oppenheim, D. (1991). The moral self of infancy: Affective core and procedural knowledge. *Developmental Review, 11,* 251–270.

Engel, S. (1995). *The stories children tell: Making sense of the narratives of childhood.* New York: Freeman.

Erikson, E. H. (1950). *Childhood and society.* New York: Norton.

Erikson, E. H. (1968). *Identity, youth, and crisis.* New York: Norton.

Fantz, R. L. (1961). The origins of form perception. *Scientific American, 204,* 66–72.

Fantz, R. L. (1963). Pattern vision in newborn infants. *Science, 140,* 296–297.

Feldman, R., Greenbaum, C. W., & Yirmiya, N. (1999). Mother–infant affect synchrony as an antecedent of the emergence of self-control. *Developmental Psychology, 35,* 223–231.

Feldman, R., & Klein, P. S. (2003). Toddlers' self-regulated compliance to mothers, caregivers, and fathers: Implications for theories of socialization. *Developmental Psychology, 39,* 680–692.

Fernald, A. (2004). Hearing, listening, and understanding: Auditory development in infancy. In G. Bremner & A. Fogel (Eds.), *Blackwell handbook of infant development* (2nd ed., pp. 35–70). Malden, MA: Blackwell.

Fiske, A. P., Kitayama, S., Markus, H. R., & Nisbett, R. E. (1998). The cultural matrix of social psychology. In D. T. Gilbert, S. T. Fiske, & G. Lindzey (Eds.), *The handbook of social psychology* (4th ed., Vol. 4, pp. 915–981). Boston: McGraw-Hill.

Fivaz-Depeursinge, E., & Corboz-Warnery, A. (2001). *Das primäre Dreieck: Vater, Mutter und Kind aus entwicklungstheoretisch-systemischer Sicht* [The primary triangle: A developmental systems view of fathers, mothers, and infants]. Heidelberg, Germany: Carl-Auer-Systeme, Verl. und Verl.-Buchhandlung.

Fivush, R. (1994). Constructing narrative, emotions and self in parent–child conversations about the past. In U. Neisser & R. Fivush (Eds.), *The remembering self: Construction and accuracy in the self-narrative* (pp. 136–157). New York: Cambridge University Press.

Fivush, R., & Fromhoff, F. (1988). Style and structure in mother–child conversations about the past. *Discourse Process, 11,* 337–355.

Fivush, R., & Nelson, K. (2004). Culture and language in the emergence of autobiographical memory. *Psychological Science, 15,* 586–590.

Flores, J. P., Teuchner, U. C., & Chandler, M. J. (2004, May). *Telling selves in time: Aboriginal and non-aboriginal accounts of identity.* Paper presented at the University of Saskatchewan Culture and Human Development Workshop, Saskatoon, Canada.

Fontaine, R. (1984). Imitative skill between birth and six months. *Infant Behavior and Development, 7,* 323–333.

Fox, N. A. (1991). If it's not left, it's right: Electroencephalographic asymmetry and the development of emotion. *American Psychologist, 46,* 863–872.

Fracasso, M. P., Lamb, M. E., Schölmerich, A., & Leyendecker, B. (1997). The ecology of mother–infant interaction in Euro-American and immigrant Central American families living in the United States. *International Journal of Behavioral Development, 20,* 207–217.

Fung, H. (1994). *The socialization of shame in young Chinese children.* Unpublished doctoral dissertation, University of Chicago, Chicago.

Gallup, G. G. (1977). Self-recognition in primates. *American Psychologist, 32,* 329–338.

Gauda, G., & Keller, H. (1987). Das subjektive Familienkonzept schwangerer Frauen [The subjective family concept of pregnant women]. *Zeitschrift für Entwicklungspsychologie und Pädagogische Psychologie, 19,* 32–45.

Geary, D. C., & Flinn, M. V. (2001). Evolution of human parental behavior and the human family. *Parenting: Science and Practice, 1,* 5–61.

Geber, M., & Dean, R. (1959). The state of development of newborn African children. *Lancet, 1,* 1215.

Geertz, C. (1973). *The interpretation of culture.* New York: Basic Books.

Georgas, J. (1989). Changing family values in Greece: From collectivist to individualist. *Journal of Cross-Cultural Psychology, 20,* 80–91.

Georgas, J., Christakopoulou, S., Poortinga, Y., Angleitner, A., Goodwin, R., & Charalambous, N. (1997). The relationship of family bonds to family structure and function across cultures. *Journal of Cross-Cultural Psychology, 28,* 303–320.

Gewirtz, J., & Pelàez-Nogueras, M. (1992). B. F. Skinner's legacy to human infant behavior and development. *American Psychologist, 47,* 1411–1422.

Glaser, B. G., & Strauss, A. L. (1967). *The discovery of grounded theory: Strategies for qualitative research.* Chicago: Aldine.

Goheen, M. (1996). *Men own the fields, women own the crops: Gender and power in the Cameroon grassfields.* Madison: University of Wisconsin Press.

Goldsmith, H. H., & Alansky, J. A. (1987). Maternal and infant temperamental predictors of attachment: A meta-analytic review. *Journal of Consulting and Clinical Psychology, 55,* 805–816.

Gone, J., Miller, P. J., & Rappaport, J. (1999). Conceptual self as normatively oriented: The suitability of past personal narrative for the study of cultural identity. *Culture & Psychology, 5,* 371–398.

Goodnow, J. J. (1988). Parents' ideas, actions, and feelings: Models and methods from development and social psychology. *Child Development, 59,* 286–320.

Goodnow, J. J., Cashmore, J., Cotton, S., & Knight, R. (1984). Mothers' developmental timetables in two cultural groups. *International Journal of Psychology, 19,* 193–205.

Goodnow, J. J., & Collins, W. A. (1990). *Development according to parents: The nature, sources and consequences of parents' ideas.* Hillsdale, NJ: Lawrence Erlbaum Associates, Inc.

Gottlieb, G. (1992). *Individual development and evolution: The genesis of novel behavior.* New York: Oxford University Press.

Gould, S. J. (1977). *Ontogeny and phylogeny.* Cambridge, MA: Harvard University Press.

Grant, J. (1998). *Raising baby by the book: The education of American mothers.* New Haven, CT: Yale University Press.

Gratier, M. (2003). Expressive timing and interactional synchrony between mothers and infants: Cultural similarities, cultural differences, and the immigration experience. *Cognitive Development, 18,* 511–531.

Greenfield, P. M. (1994). Independence and interdependence as developmental scripts: Implications for theory, research, and practice. In P. M. Greenfield & R. R. Cocking (Eds.), *Cross-cultural roots of minority child development* (pp. 1–40). Hillsdale, NJ: Lawrence Erlbaum Associates.

Greenfield, P. M. (1996). Culture as process: Empirical methods for cultural psychology. In J. W. Berry, Y. H. Poortinga, & J. Pandey (Eds.), *Handbook of cross-cultural psychology: Vol. 1. Theory and method* (2nd ed., pp. 301–346). Boston: Allyn & Bacon.

Greenfield, P. M. (1997). You can't take it with you: Why ability assessments don't cross cultures. *American Psychologist, 52,* 1115–1124.

Greenfield, P. M. (1999). Historical change and cognitive change: A two-decade follow-up study in Zinacantecan, a Maya community in Chiapas, Mexico. *Mind, Culture and Activity, 6,* 92–108.

Greenfield, P. M. (2000). Three approaches to the psychology of culture: Where do they come from? Where can they go? *Asian Journal of Social Psychology, 3,* 223–240.

Greenfield, P. M. (2004). *Weaving generations together: Evolving creativity in the Maya of Chiapas.* Santa Fe, NM: Sar Press.

Greenfield, P. M., & Childs, C. P. (1991). Developmental continuity in biocultural context. In R. Cohen & A. W. Siegel (Eds.), *Context and development* (pp. 135–159). Hillsdale, NJ: Lawrence Erlbaum Associates, Inc.

Greenfield, P. M., & Keller, H. (2004). Cultural psychology. In C. D. Spielberger (Ed.), *Encyclopedia for applied psychology.* Oxford, UK: Elsevier.

Greenfield, P. M., Keller, H., Fuligni, A., & Maynard, A. (2003). Cultural pathways through universal development. *Annual Review of Psychology, 54,* 461–490.

Greenfield, P. M., Keller, H., Maynard, A., & Suzuki, L. (2004). Lifespan development and culture. *Encyclopedia of Applied Psychology, 2,* 567–574.

Greenfield, P. M., Maynard, A. E., & Childs, C. P. (2000). History, culture, learning and development. *Cross-Cultural Research, 34,* 351–374.

Greenfield, P. M., & Suzuki, L. (1998). Culture and human development: Implications for parenting, education, pediatrics, and mental health. In I. E. Sigel & K. A. Renninger (Eds.), *Handbook of child psychology: Vol. 4. Child psychology in practice* (5th ed., pp. 1059–1109). New York: Wiley.

Greenough, W. T., Black, J. E., & Wallace C. S. (1987). Experience and brain development. *Child Development, 58,* 539–559.

Gross, D. R. (1984). Time allocation: A tool for the study of cultural behavior. *Annual Review of Anthropology, 12,* 519–558.

Guisinger, S., & Blatt, S. J. (1994). Individuality and relatedness: Evolution of a fundamental dialectic. *American Psychologist, 49,* 104–111.

Han, J. J., Leichtman, M. D., & Wang, Q. (1998). Autobiographical memory in Korean, Chinese and American children. *Developmental Psychology, 34,* 701–713.

Harkness, S., & Super, C. M. (1983). The cultural construction of child development: A framework for the socialization of emotion. *Ethos, 11,* 221–231.

Harkness, S., & Super, C. M. (1995). Culture and parenting. In M. Bornstein (Ed.), *Handbook of parenting* (pp. 211–234). Mahwah, NJ: Lawrence Erlbaum Associates, Inc.

Harkness, S., & Super, C. M. (Eds.). (1996). *Parents' cultural belief systems: Their origins, expressions, and consequences.* New York: Guilford.

Harkness, S., Super, C. M., & van Tijen, N. (2000). Individualism and the "Western mind" reconsidered: American and Dutch parents' ethnotheories of the child. In S. Harkness, C. Raeff, & C. M. Super (Eds.), *Variability in the social construction of the child* (pp. 23–39). San Francisco: Jossey-Bass.

Harlow, H. F. (1958). The nature of love. *American Psychologist, 13,* 673–685.

Harré, R. (1992). Introduction. *American Behavioral Scientist, 36,* 3–8.

Hart, D., & Fegley, S. (1994). Social imitation and the emergence of a mental model of self. In S. Parker, R. Mitchell, & M. Boccia (Eds.), *Self-awareness in animals and humans: Developmental perspectives* (pp. 149–165). Cambridge, England: Cambridge University Press.

Harwood, R. L., & Miller, J. G. (1991). Perceptions of attachment behavior: A comparison of Anglo and Puerto Rican mothers. *Merrill-Palmer Quarterly, 37,* 583–599.

Harwood, R. L., Miller, J. G., & Lucca Irizarry, N. (1995). *Culture and attachment: Perceptions of the child in context.* New York: Guilford.

Hauser, P., & Schnore, L. F. (1965). *The study of urbanization.* New York: Wiley.

Hayne, H., Rovee-Collier, C., & Perris, E. (1987). Categorization and memory retrieval by 3-month-olds. *Child Development, 58,* 750–767.

Heitmeyer, W., & Olk, T. (1995). The role of individualization theory in adolescence socialization. In G. Neubauer & H. Hurrelmann (Eds.), *Individualization in childhood and adolescence* (pp. 15–35). Berlin: de Gruyter.

Hentschel, E., & Keller, H. (2006). *Cultural concepts of parenting: A linguistic analysis.* Manuscript submitted for publication.

Hetherington, M., & Frankie, G. (1967). Effects of parental dominance, warmth, and conflict on imitation in children. *Journal of Personality and Social Psychology, 6,* 119–125.

Hewlett, B. S. (1991a). Demography and childcare in preindustrial societies. *Journal of Anthropological Research, 47,* 1–37.

Hewlett, B. S. (1991b). *Intimate fathers: The nature and context of Aka Pygmy paternal infant care.* Ann Arbor: University of Michigan Press.

Hewlett, B. S., & Lamb, M. E. (2002). Integrating evolution, culture and developmental psychology: Explaining caregiver–infant proximity and responsiveness in Central Africa and the United States of America. In H. Keller, Y. H. Poortinga, & A. Schölmerich (Eds.), *Between culture and biology* (pp. 241–269). London: Cambridge University Press.

Hewlett, B. S., Lamb, M. E., Leyendecker, B., & Schölmerich, A. (2000). Parental investment strategies among Aka foragers, Ngandu farmers, and Euro-American urban industrialists. In L. Cronk, N. Chagnon, & W. Irons (Eds.), *Adaptation and human behavior: An anthropological perspective* (pp. 155–178). New York: Aldine de Gruyter.

Hill, K., & Hurtado, A. M. (1996). *Ache life history: The ecology and demography of a foraging people.* New York: de Gruyter.

Hitchcock, J. T., & Minturn, L. (1963). The Rajput of Khalapur, India. In B. B. Whiting (Ed.), *Six cultures: Studies of child rearing* (pp. 203–362). New York: Wiley.

Ho, D. Y. F. (1986). Chinese pattern of socialization. In M. Bond (Ed.), *The psychology of Chinese people* (pp. 1–37). Hong Kong: Oxford University Press.

Hofer, J., & Chasiotis, A. (2003). Congruence of life goals and implicit motives as predictors of life satisfaction: Cross-cultural implications of a study of Zambian male adolescents. *Motivation and Emotion, 27,* 251–272.

Hofer, J., Chasiotis, A., & Campos, D. (2006). Congruence between social values and implicit motives: Effects on life satisfaction across three cultures. *European Journal of Personality, 20*(4), 305–324.

Hoff-Ginsberg, E., & Tardif, T. (1995). Socioeconomic status and parenting. In M. H. Bornstein (Ed.), *Handbook of parenting: Vol. 2. Biology and ecology of parenting* (pp. 161–188). Mahwah, NJ: Lawrence Erlbaum Associates, Inc.

Hollos, M., & Leis, P. E. (2002). Remodeling concepts of the self: An Ijo example. *Ethos, 29,* 371–387.

Howe, M. L., & Courage, M. L. (1993). On resolving the enigma of infantile amnesia. *Psychological Bulletin, 113,* 305–326.

Howe, M. L., & Courage, M. L. (1997). The emergence and early development of autobiographical memory. *Psychological Review, 104,* 499–523.

Hrdy, S. B. (1986). Sources of variation in the reproductive success of female primates. *Proceedings of the International Meeting on Variability and Behavioural Evolution, 259,* 191–203.

Hsu, F. L. K. (1971). *Under the ancestor's shadow: Kinship, personality, and social mobility in China.* Stanford, CA: Stanford University Press.

Hu, P., & Meng, Z. (1996, August). *An examination of infant–mother attachment in China.* Poster presented at the meeting of the International Society for the Study of Behavioral Development, Quebec City, Canada.

Hudson, J. A. (1990). The emergence of autobiographic memory in mother–child conversations. In R. Fivush & J. A. Hudson (Eds.), *Knowing and remembering in young children* (pp. 166–196). New York: Cambridge University Press.

Hulbert, A. (2003). *Raising America: Experts, parents, and a century of advice about children.* New York: Knopf.

Hunt, J. M. (1963). Motivation inherent in information processing and action. In O. J. Harvey (Ed.), *Motivation and social interaction: Cognitive determinants* (pp. 35–94). New York: Ronald.

Huttenlocher, J., Newcombe, N., & Sandberg, E. (1994). The coding of spatial location in young children. *Cognitive Psychology, 27,* 115–147.

Iacoboni, M. (2005). Understanding others: Imitation, language, empathy. In S. Hurley & N. Chater (Eds.), *Perspectives on imitation: From cognitive neuroscience to social science* (Vol 1, pp. 77–99). Cambridge, MA: MIT Press.

Jagenow, A., & Mittag, J. (1984). Weiblicher Kinderwunsch und Sexualität [Female wish to have children and sexuality]. *Psychosozial, 21,* 7–26.

James, W. (1890). *The principles of psychology* (Vol. 1). New York: Holt.

Jenkins, J. M., & Astington, J. W. (1996). Cognitive factors and family structure associated with "theory of mind" development in young children. *Developmental Psychology, 32,* 70–78.

Joerchel, A. C., & Valsiner, J. (2004). Making decisions about taking medicines: A social coordination process. *Forum: Qualitative Social Research (FQS), 5*(1), Art. 17. Retrieved October 19, 2005, from http://www.qualitative-research.net/fqs-texte/1-04/1-04joerchelvalsiner-e.htm

Johnson, T., Kulesa, P., Cho, Y. I., & Shavitt, S. (2005). The relation between culture and response styles. Evidence from 19 countries. *Journal of Cross-Cultural Psychology, 36,* 264–277.

Joshi, M. S., & MacLean, M. (1997). Maternal expectations of child development in India, Japan, and England. *Journal of Cross-Cultural Psychology, 28,* 219–234.

Jusczyk, P. (1997). *The discovery of spoken language.* Cambridge, MA: MIT Press.

Kağitçibaşi, C. (1990). Family and socialization in cross-cultural perspective: A model of change. In J. J. Berman (Ed.), *Cross-cultural perspectives: Nebraska Symposium on Motivation 1989* (pp. 135–200). Lincoln: University of Nebraska Press.

Kağitçibaşi, C. (1996a). The autonomous-relational self: A new synthesis. *European Psychologist, 1,* 180–186.

Kağitçibaşi, C. (1996b). *Family and human development across cultures: A view from the other side.* Mahwah, NJ: Lawrence Erlbaum Associates, Inc.

Kağitçibaşi, C. (1997). Individualism and collectivism. In J. W. Berry, M. H. Segall, & C. Kağitçibaşi (Eds.), *Handbook of cross-cultural psychology: Vol. 3. Social behavior and applications* (2nd ed., pp. 1–49). Boston: Allyn & Bacon.

Kağitçibaşi, C. (2005). Autonomy and relatedness in cultural context: Implications for self and family. *Journal of Cross-Cultural Psychology, 36,* 403–422.

Kağitçibaşi, C., Bekman, S., Özkök, U. S., & Kuscul, Ö. H. (1995). *Handbook of mother support program* (Mother–Child Education Foundation Publication No. 1). Istanbul, Turkey: Mother Education Foundation.

Kağitçibaşi, C., Bekman, S., & Sunar, D. (1991). *Handbook of mother enrichment program.* Ankara Turkey: UNICEF Publications.

Kail, R. V. (1997). Processing time, imagery, and spatial memory. *Journal of Experimental Child Psychology, 64,* 67–78.

Kakar, S. (1978). *The inner world: A psychoanalytic study of childhood and society in India.* New Delhi, India: Oxford University Press.

Kärtner, J., Keller, H., & Yovsi, R. D. (2005, April). *Self-recognition in different socio-cultural environments: A cross-sequential study.* Paper presented at the biennial meeting of the Society for Research in Child Development, Atlanta, GA.

Kärtner, J., Keller, H., Yovsi, R. D., Abels, M., & Lamm, B. (2006). *Manifestations of agency and interpersonal distance in verbal discourse across culture.* Manuscript submitted for publication.

Keller, H. (1979). Geschlechtsunterschiede in der Reaktion auf auditive Reize in den ersten drei Lebensmonaten [Gender differences in infant' s reactions to auditory stimuli during the first three months of life]. *Zeitschrift für Entwicklungspsychologie und Pädagogische Psychologie, 11,* 185–194.

Keller, H. (1991). A perspective on continuity in infant development. In M. E. Lamb & H. Keller (Eds.), *Infant development: Perspectives from German speaking countries* (pp. 135–150). Hillsdale, NJ: Lawrence Erlbaum Associates, Inc.

Keller, H. (1992). The development of exploratory behavior. *The German Journal of Psychology, 16,* 120–140.

Keller, H. (Ed.). (1997). *Handbuch der Kleinkindforschung* [Handbook of infant research] (2nd rev. ed.). Bern, Switzerland: Huber.

Keller, H. (2000a). Evolutionary approaches to the life span. In A. L. Comunian & U. P. Gielen (Eds.), *Cross-cultural perspectives on human development* (pp. 117–130). Padua, Italy: Cedam.

Keller, H. (2000b). Human parent–child relationships from an evolutionary perspective. *American Behavioral Scientist, 43,* 957–969.

Keller, H. (2001). Lifespan development: Evolutionary perspectives. In N. J. Smelser & P. B. Baltes (Eds.), *International encyclopedia of the social and behavioral sciences* (Vol. 13, pp. 8840–8844). Oxford, England: Elsevier Science.

Keller, H. (2002a). Development as the interface between biology and culture: A conceptualization of early ontogenetic experiences. In H. Keller, Y. Poortinga, & A. Schölmerich (Eds.), *Between culture and biology* (pp. 215–240). Cambridge, England: Cambridge University Press.

Keller, H. (2002b). Introduction: Developmental psychology and its application across cultures. *Cross-Cultural Psychology Bulletin, 35*(4), 6–9.

Keller, H. (2002c). The role of development for understanding the biological basis of cultural learning. In H. Keller, Y. Poortinga, & A. Schölmerich (Eds.), *Between culture and biology* (pp. 215–239). Cambridge, England: Cambridge University Press.

Keller, H. (2003a). Biologische Grundlagen und kulturelle Determinanten elterlichen Verhaltens [Biological basics and cultural determinants of parental behavior]. *Systeme, 17*, 22–35.

Keller, H. (2003b). Ontogeny as the interface between biology and culture: Evolutionary considerations. In T. S. Saraswathi (Ed.), *Cross-cultural perspectives in human development: Theory, research and applications* (pp. 102–127). New Delhi, India: Sage.

Keller, H. (2003c). Socialization for competence: Cultural models of infancy. *Human Development, 46*, 288–311.

Keller, H. (2004a). Kultur und Bindung [Culture and attachment]. In L. Ahnert (Ed.), *Frühe Bindung: Entstehung und Entwicklung* (pp. 110–124). Munich, Germant: Reinhardt Verlag.

Keller, H. (2004b, October). *Narrations about parenting and narrative styles during interactional episodes.* Invited lecture, Tartu University Psychology Department, Tartu, Estonia.

Keller, H. (2005, Feburary). *The bio-culture of parenting: The role of education on parental strategies.* Invited lecture presented at the advanced Study Institute, M.S. University of Baroda, Baroda, India.

Keller, H., Abels, M., Borke, J., Lamm, B., Lo, W., Su, Y., et al. (2006). *Socialization environments of Chinese and Euro-American middle-class babies: Parenting behaviors, verbal discourses and ethnotheories.* Manuscript submitted for publication.

Keller, H., Abels, M., Lamm, B., Yovsi, R. D., Voelker, S., & Lakhani, A. (2005). Ecocultural effects on early infant care: A study in Cameroon, India, and Germany. *Ethos, 33*(4), 512–541.

Keller, H., Borke, J., Staufenbiel, T., Yovsi, R. D., Abels, M., Papaligoura, Z., et al. (2006). *Distal and proximal parenting as two alternative parenting strategies during infant's early months of life: A cross-cultural study.* Manucript submitted for publication.

Keller, H., Borke, J., Yovsi, R. D., Lohaus, A., & Jensen, H. (2005). Cultural orientations and historical changes as predictors of parenting behavior. *International Journal of Behavioral Development, 29*, 229–237.

Keller, H., & Chasiotis, A. (2005). Zur natürlichen und geschlechtlichen Selektion der menschlichen Individualentwicklung [Natural and sexual selection of human individual development: Evolutionary and ethological approaches]. In W. Schneider & F. Wilkening (Eds.), *Enzyklopädie der Psychologie, Band 1: Theorien, Modelle und Methoden der Entwicklungspsychologie* (pp. 509–551). Göttingen, Germany: Hogrefe.

Keller, H., & Chasiotis, A. (2006a). Evolutionary perspectives on social engagement. In P. J. Marshall & N. A. Fox (Eds.), *The development of social engagement: Neurobiological perspectives* (pp. 275–303). Oxford, England: Oxford University Press.

Keller, H., & Chasiotis, A. (2006b). Zur natürlichen und geschlechtlichen Selektion der menschlichen Individualentwicklung [Natural and sexual selection of the human individual development: Evolutionary and ethological approaches]. In W. Schneider &

F. Wilkening (Eds.), *Enzyklopädie der Psychologie, Band 1: Theorien, Modelle und Methoden der Entwicklungspsychologie* (pp. 509–551). Göttingen, Germany: Hogrefe.

Keller, H., Chasiotis, A., & Runde, B. (1992). Intuitive parenting programs in German, American, and Greek parents of 3-month-old infants. *Journal of Cross-Cultural Psychology, 23,* 510–520.

Keller, H., & Demuth, C. (2005). Further explorations of the "Western mind": Mothers' and grandmothers' parental ethnotheories in Los Angels, California, and Berlin, Germany. *Forum Qualitative Social Research, 7(1), Art. 5.* Retrieved January 11, 2006, from http://www.qualitative-research.net/fqs-texte/1-06/06-1-5-e.htm

Keller, H., & Demuth, C. (in press). The discursive construction of selfhood in Chinese and Euro-American mother–infant interactions. In G. Zheng, K. Leung, & J. Adair (Eds), *Perspectives and progress in contemporary cross-cultural psychology.* Beijing: China Light Industry Press.

Keller, H., Demuth, C., & Yovsi, R. D. (2006). *The social construction of independence and interdependence of Cameroonian Nso women with varying degrees of formal education.* Manuscript submitted for publication.

Keller, H., & Gauda, G. (1987). Eye contact in the first months of life and its developmental consequences. In H. Rauh & H. C. Steinhausen (Eds.), *Psychobiology and early development* (pp. 129–143). Amsterdam: Elsevier.

Keller, H., Gauda, G., Miranda, D., & Schölmerich, A. (1985). Die Entwicklung des Blickverhaltens im ersten Lebensjahr [The development of eye-contact behavior during the first year of life]. *Zeitschrift für Entwicklungspsychologie und Pädagogische Psychologie, 17,* 258–269.

Keller, H., & Greenfield, P. M. (2000). History and future of development in cross-cultural psychology. *Journal of Cross-Cultural Psychology, 31,* 52–62.

Keller, H., Harwood, R. L., & Carlson, V. (2006). *Culture and developmental pathways of relationship formation.* Manuscript submitted for publication.

Keller, H., Hentschel, E., Yovsi, R. D., Abels, M., Lamm, B., & Haas, V. (2004). The psycho-linguistic embodiment of parental ethnotheories: A new avenue to understand cultural differences in parenting. *Culture & Psychology, 10,* 293–330.

Keller, H., Kärtner, J., Borke, J., Yovsi, R. D., & Kleis, A. (2005). Parenting styles and the development of the categorial self: A longitudinal study on mirror self recognition in Cameroonian Nso farming and German families. *International Journal of Behavioral Development, 29,* 496–504.

Keller, H., & Keller, W. (1981). Verbales und vokales Verhalten von Vätern und Müttern gegenüber ihren weiblichen und männlichen Säuglingen in einem dreieinhalbmonatigen Längsschnitt [Verbal and vocal behavior of mothers and fathers towards their male and female babies: A three-month longitudinal study]. *Zeitschrift für Entwicklungspsychologie und Pädagogische Psychologie, 13,* 116–126.

Keller, H., Kuensemueller, P., Abels, M., Voelker, S., Yovsi, R. D., Jensen, H., et al. (2005). *Parenting, culture, and development. A comparative study.* San José, CR: Universidad de Costa Rica, Instituto de Investigaciones Psychologicas.

Keller, H., & Lamm, B. (2005). Parenting as the expression of sociohistorical time: The case of German individualism. *International Journal of Behavioral Development, 29,* 238–246.

Keller, H., Lamm, B., Abels, M., Yovsi, R. D., Borke, J., Jensen, H., et al. (2006). Cultural models, socialization goals, and parenting ethnotheories: A multi-cultural analysis. *Journal of Cross-Cultural Psychology, 37(2),* 155–172 .

Keller, H., Loewer, M., & Runde, B. (1990). Analyse spontaner Sprache von Eltern in Interaktionssituationen mit ihren Säuglingen und Kleinkindern: Entwicklungsveränderungen und kulturspezifische Aspekte [The analysis of spontaneous speech of parents in interactional situations with their small children: Developmental changes and cultural specifics]. *Zeitschrift für Entwicklungspsychologie und Pädagogische Psychologie, 22,* 341–353.

Keller, H., Lohaus, A., Kuensemueller, P., Abels, M., Yovsi, R. D., Voelker, S., et al. (2004). The bio-culture of parenting: Evidence from five cultural communities. *Parenting: Science and Practice, 4,* 25–50.

Keller, H., Lohaus, A., Völker, S., Cappenberg, M., & Chasiotis, A. (1999). Temporal contingency as an independent component of parenting behavior. *Child Development, 70,* 474–485.

Keller, H., Miranda, D., & Gauda, G. (1984). The naive theory of the infant and some maternal attitudes: A two-country study. *Journal of Cross-Cultural Psychology, 15,* 165–179.

Keller, H., Otto, H., Yovsi, R. D., & Lohaus, A. (2006). *Contingency and synchrony in mother–infant vocal/verbal interactions.* Manuscript submitted for publication.

Keller, H., Poortinga, Y. H., & Schölmerich, A. (Eds.). (2002). *Between culture and biology.* Cambridge, England: Cambridge University Press.

Keller, H., Schneider, K., & Henderson, B. (Eds.). (1994). *Curiosity and exploration.* Heidelberg, Germany: Springer.

Keller, H., Schölmerich, A., & Eibl-Eibesfeldt, I. (1988). Communication patterns in adult–infant interactions in Western and non-Western cultures. *Journal of Cross-Cultural Psychology, 19,* 427–445.

Keller, H., Voelker, S., & Yovsi, R. D. (2005). Conceptions of parenting in different cultural communities. The case of West African Nso and Northern German women. *Social Development, 14,* 158–180.

Keller, H., Voelker, S., Yovsi, R. D., & Shastri, J. (2005). The representation of independent and interrelated conceptions of caretaking. In P. Mohite (Ed.), *Theoretical approaches to early development: Implications for interventions* (pp. 116–140). Baroda, India: M. S. University of Baroda, Centre of Advanced Studies, Department of HDFS.

Keller, H., Voelker, S., & Zach, U. (1997). Attachment in cultural context. *ISSBD Newsletter, 1*(31), 1–3.

Keller, H., Yovsi, R. D., Borke, J., Kärtner, J., Jensen, H., & Papaligoura, Z. (2004). Developmental consequences of early parenting experiences: Self regulation and self recognition in three cultural communities. *Child Development, 75,* 1745–1760.

Keller, H., Yovsi, R. D., Borke, J., Lohaus, A., & Lamm, B. (2006). *Developing patterns of parenting in two cultural communities.* Manuscript submitted for publication.

Keller, H., Yovsi, R. D., & Voelker, S. (2002). The role of motor stimulation in parental ethnotheories: The case of Cameroonian Nso and German women. *Journal of Cross-Cultural Psychology, 33,* 398–414.

Keller, H., & Zach, U. (2002). Gender and birth order as determinants of parental behaviour. *International Journal of Behavioral Psychology, 26,* 177–184.

Keller, H., Zach, U., & Abels, M. (2005). The German family: Families in Germany. In J. Roopnarine & U. Gielen (Eds.), *Families in global perspective* (pp. 242–258). Boston: Allyn & Bacon.

Keller, H., Zach, U., Völker, S., Chasiotis, A., Lohaus, A., & Cappenberg, M. (1994, June). *Parental responsivity from a cross-cultural perspective.* Paper presented at the 9th biennial International Conference for Infant Studies, Paris.

Kessen, W. (1979). The American child and other cultural inventions. *American Psychologist, 34,* 815–820.

Killen, M., McGlothlin, H., & Lee-Kim, J. (2002). Between individuals and culture: Individuals' evaluations of exclusion from social groups. In H. Keller, Y. H. Poortinga, & A. Schölmerich (Eds.), *Between culture and biology* (pp. 159–190). London: Cambridge University Press.

Killen, M., & Wainryb, C. (2000). Independence and interdependence in diverse cultural contexts. In S. Harkness, C. Raeff, & C. M. Super (Eds.), *Variability in the social construction of the child* (pp. 23–39). San Francisco: Jossey-Bass.

Knopf, M. (2003). Die Entwicklung des Gedächtnisses von Säuglingen [The development of memory in infancy]. In H. Keller (Ed.), *Handbuch der Kleinkindforschung* (3rd ed., pp. 895–926). Bern, Switzerland: Huber.

Kochanska, G., & Aksan, N. (1995). Mother–child mutually positive affect, the quality of child compliance to requests and prohibitions and maternal control as correlates of early internalization. *Child Development, 60,* 236–254.

Kochanska, G., & Thompson, R. A. (1997). The emergence and development of conscience in toddlerhood and early childhood. In J. E. Grusec & L. Kuczynski (Eds.), *Parenting and children's internalization of values: A handbook of contemporary theory* (pp. 53–77). New York: Wiley.

Koehler, L. (1986). Von der Biologie zur Phantasie: Forschungsbeiträge zum Verständnis der frühkindlichen Entwicklung aus den USA [From biology to phantasy: Research reports for the understanding of early child development in the USA]. In J. Stork (Ed.), *Zur Psychologie und Psychopathologie des Säuglings* (pp. 73–92). Stuttgart, Germany: Frommann-Holzboog.

Kohli, M. (1999). Private and public transfers between generations: Linking the family and the state. *European Societies, 1,* 81–104.

Kohli, M., Kuenemund, H., Motel, A., & Szydlik, M. (1997). Generationenkonstellationen, Haushaltsstrukturen und Wohnentfernungen in der zweiten Lebenshälfte: Erste Befunde des Alterssurveys [Generation constellations, household structures, and residence distances in the second half of life: First results of an aging-survey]. In R. Becker (Ed.), *Generationen und sozialer Wandel* (pp. 157–175). Opladen, Germany: Leske + Budrich.

Konner, M. (1991). *Childhood.* Boston: Little, Brown.

Kopp, C. B. (1982). Antecedents of self regulation: A developmental perspective. *Developmental Psychology, 18,* 199–214.

Kopp, C. B. (2001). Self-regulation in childhood. In N. J. Smelser & P. B. Baltes (Eds.), *International encyclopedia of the social and behavioral sciences* (pp. 13862–13866). Oxford, England: Elsevier Science.

Kopp, C. B., & Brownell, C. A. (Eds.). (1991). The development of the self: The first three years [Special issue]. *Developmental Review, 11*(3).

Kuczynski, L., & Kochanska, G. (1990). Development of children's noncompliance strategies from toddlerhood to age 5. *Develomental Psychology, 26,* 398–408.

Kuczynski, L., Zahn-Waxler, C., & Radke-Yarrow, M. (1987). Development and content of imitation in the second and third years of life: A socialization perspective. *Developmental Psychology, 23,* 276–282.

Kuhl, J. (2001). *Motivation und Persönlichkeit: Interaktionen psychischer Systeme* [Motivation and personality: Interactions of psychical systems]. Göttingen, Germany: Hogrefe.

Kurtz, S. N. (1992). *All the mothers are one.* New York: Columbia University Press.

Kusserow, A. S. (1999). De-homogenizing American individualism: Socializing hard and soft individualism in Manhattan and Queens. *Ethos, 27,* 210–234.

Lakhani, A., Ganju, S., & Mahale, P. (1997). *Reproductive and child health status in the Nandesari area*. New Delhi, India: Deepak Medical Foundation, Deepak Charitable Trust.

Lamb, M. E. (1981). The development of social expectations in the first year of life. In M. E. Lamb & L. R. Sherrod (Eds.), *Infant social cognition: Empirical and theoretical considerations* (pp. 155–175). Hillsdale, NJ: Lawrence Erlbaum Associates, Inc.

Lamb, M. E. (Ed.). (1997). *The role of the father in child development* (3rd ed.). New York: Wiley.

Lamb, M. E., Bornstein, M. H., & Teti, D. M. (2002). *Development in infancy* (4th ed.). Mahwah, NJ: Lawrence Erlbaum Associates, Inc.

Lamb, M. E., & Easterbrooks, M. A. (1981). Individual differences in parental sensitivity: Origins, components, and consequences. In M. E. Lamb & L. R. Sherrod (Eds.), *Infant social cognition: Empirical and theoretical considerations* (pp. 127–154). Hillsdale, NJ: Lawrence Erlbaum Associates, Inc.

Lamb, M. E., & Sternberg, K. J. (1992). Sociocultural perspectives on nonparental childcare. In M. E. Lamb, K. J. Sternberg, C.-P. Hwang, & A. Broberg (Eds.), *Child care in context: Cross-cultural perspectives* (pp. 1–23). Hillsdale, NJ: Lawrence Erlbaum Associates, Inc.

Lamb, M. E., Thompson, R. A., Gardner, W., Charnov, E. L., & Estes, D. (1984). Security of infantile attachment as assessed in the Strange Situation: Its study and biological interpretation. *Behavioral and Brain Sciences, 7,* 127–147.

Lamm, B., Borke, J., Eickhorst, A., & Keller, H. (2006). *Father–infant interaction, and paternal ideas about early child care and their consequences for the timing of children's self recognition*. Manuscript submitted for publication.

Lamm, B., & Keller, H. (2006). *Understanding cultural models of parenting: The role of intra-cultural variation and response style*. Manuscript submitted for publication.

Landers, C. (1989). A psychobiological study of infant development in South India. In J. K. Nugent, B. M. Lester & T. B. Brazelton (Eds.), *The cultural context of infancy* (pp. 169–207). Norwood, NJ: Ablex.

Laungani, P. (2005). Changing patterns of family life in India. In J. L. Roopnarine & U. P. Gielen (Eds.), *Families in global perspective* (pp. 85–103). Boston: Allyn & Bacon.

Lave, J., & Wenger, E. (1991). *Situated learning: Legitimate peripheral participation*. Cambridge, England: Cambridge University Press.

Lavelli, M., & Fogel, A. (2002). Developmental changes in mother–infant face-to-face communication: Birth to 3 months. *Developmental Psychology, 38,* 288–305.

Lay, C., Fairlie, P., Jackson, S., Ricci, T., Eisenberg, J., Sato, T., et al. (1998). Domain-specific allocentrism-idiocentrism. *Journal of Cross-Cultural Psychology, 29,* 434–460.

Legerstee, M. (1991). The role of person and object in eliciting early imitation. *Journal of Experimental Child Psychology, 51,* 423–433.

Leichtman, M. D., Wang, Q., & Pillemer, D. B. (2003). Cultural variations in interdependence and autobiographical memory: Lessons from Korea, China, India, and the United States. In R. Fivush & C. A. Haden (Eds.), *Autobiographical memory and the construction of a narrative self* (pp. 73–97). Mahwah, NJ: Lawrence Erlbaum Associates, Inc.

Lerner, R. M., & De Stefanis, I. (1999). The import of infancy to individual, family, and societal development. *Infant Behavior and Development, 22,* 475–482.

LeVine, R. A. (1974). Parental goals: A cross-cultural view. *Teachers College Record, 76,* 226–239.

LeVine, R. A. (1977). Child rearing as cultural adaptation. In P. H. Leiderman, S. R. Tulkin, & A. Rosenfeld (Eds.), *Culture and infancy: Variables in the human experience* (pp. 15–27). New York: Academic.

LeVine, R. A. (1988). Human parental care: Universal goals, cultural strategies, individual behavior. In R. A. LeVine, P. M. Miller, & M. M. West (Eds.), *Parental behavior in diverse societies* (pp. 3–12). San Francisco: Jossey-Bass.

LeVine, R. A. (1990). Infant environments in psychoanalysis: A cross-cultural view. In J. W. Stigler, R. A. Shweder, & G. Herdt (Eds.), *Cultural psychology: Essays on comparative human development* (pp. 454–474). Cambridge, England: Cambridge University Press.

LeVine, R. A. (1994). *Child care and culture: Lessons from Africa.* Cambridge, England: Cambridge University Press.

LeVine, R. A. (1999). An agenda for psychological anthropology. *Ethos, 27,* 15–24.

LeVine, R. A. (2002). Contexts and culture in psychological research. *New Directions for Child and Development, 96,* 101–106.

LeVine, R. A. (2004). Challenging expert knowledge: Findings from an African study of infant care and development. In U. P. Gielen & J. L. Roopnarine (Eds.), *Childhood and adolescence: Cross-cultural perspectives and applications* (pp. 149–165). Westport, CT: Greenwood.

LeVine, R. A., Dixon, S., LeVine, S., Richman, A., Leiderman, P. H., Keefer, C. H., et al. (1994). *Child care and culture: Lessons from Africa.* New York: Cambridge University Press.

LeVine, R. A., & Miller, P. M. (1988). *Parental behavior in diverse societies.* San Francisco: Jossey-Bass.

LeVine, R. A., Miller, P. M., Richman, A. L., & LeVine, S. (1996). Education and mother–infant interaction: A Mexican case study. In S. Harkness & C. M. Super (Eds.), *Parents' cultural belief systems* (pp. 254–288). New York: Guilford.

LeVine, R. A., Miller, P. M., & West, M. M. (Eds.). (1988). *Parental behavioral sciences series.* San Francisco: Jossey-Bass.

LeVine, R. A., & Norman, K. (2001). The infant's acquisition of culture: Early attachment reexamined in anthropological perspective. In C. C. Moore & H. F. Methews (Eds.), *The psychology of cultural experience* (pp. 83–104). Cambridge, England: Cambridge University Press.

Levy, R. L. (1984). Emotion, knowing, and culture. In R. A. Shweder & R. A. LeVine (Eds.), *Culture theory: Essays on mind, self, and emotion* (pp. 214–237). Cambridge, England: Cambridge University Press.

Lewis, M. (1994). Myself and me. In S. T. Parker, R. W. Mitchell, & M. L. Boccia (Eds.), *Self-awareness in animals and humans: Developmental perspectives* (pp. 20–34). New York: Cambridge University Press.

Lewis, M., & Brooks-Gunn, J. (1979). *Social cognition and the acquisition of self.* New York: Plenum.

Lewis, M., & Goldberg, S. (1969). Perceptual-cognitive development in infancy: A generalized expectancy model as a function of the mother–infant interaction. *Merrill-Palmer Quarterly, 15,* 81–100.

Lewis, M., Sullivan, M., Stranger, C., & Weiss, M. (1989). Self-development and self-conscious emotions. *Child Development, 60,* 146–156.

Leyendecker, B., Lamb, M. E., Fracasso, M. P., Schölmerich, A., & Larson, C. (1997). Playful interaction and the antecedents of attachment: A longitudinal study of Central American and Euro-American infants and mothers. *Merrill-Palmer Quarterly, 43,* 24–47.

Locke, J. L., & Bogin B. (in press). Language and life history: A new perspective on the development and evolution of human language. *Behavioral and Brain Sciences.*

Lohaus, A., Keller, H., Ball, J., Voelker, S., & Elben, C. (2004). Maternal sensitivity in interactions with three-and 12-month-old infants: Stability, structural compositions, and developmental consequences. *Infant and Child Development, 13,* 235–252.

Lohaus, A., Keller, H., Lissmann, I., Ball, J., Borke, J., & Lamm, B. (2005). Contingency experiences with three months of age and their relation to later developmental achievements. *Journal of Genetic Psychology, 166,* 365–383.

Lohaus, A., Keller, H., Voelker, S., Cappenberg, M., & Chasiotis, A. (1997). Intuitive parenting and infant behavior: Concepts, implications, and empirical validation. *The Journal of Genetic Psychology, 158,* 271–286.

Lohaus, A., Völker, S., Keller, H., Cappenberg, M., & Chasiotis, A. (1998). Wahrgenommene kindliche Problemlage und mütterliche Interaktionsqualität: Eine längsschnittliche Zusammenhangsanalyse [Perceived infant's problems and maternal interactional quality: A longitudinal analysis of relationships]. *Zeitschrift für Entwicklungspsychologie und Pädagogische Psychologie, 30,* 111–117.

Lorenz, K. (1969). Innate bases of learning. In K. H. Pribram (Ed.), *On the biology of learning* (pp. 13–93). New York: Harcourt.

Maccoby, E. E. (1984). Middle childhood in the context of the family. In W. A. Collins (Ed.), *Development during middle childhood: The years from 6–10* (pp. 184–239). Washington, DC: National Academy Press.

Maccoby, E. E., & Martin, J. A. (1983). Socialization in the context of the family: Parent–child interaction. In E. M. Hetherington (Vol. Ed.) & P. H. Mussen (Series Ed.), *Handbook of child psychology: Vol. 4. Socialization, personality, and social development* (4th ed., pp. 1–101). New York: Wiley.

MacDonald, K. B. (1988). *Social and personality development: An evolutionary synthesis.* New York: Plenum.

MacDonald, K. B. (1992). Warmth as a developmental construct: An evolutionary analysis. *Child Development, 63,* 753–773.

Main, M. (1990). Cross-cultural studies of attachment organization: Recent studies, changing methodologies, and the concept of conditional strategies. *Human Development, 33,* 48–61.

Maratou-Alipranti, L. (1999). *Greece: Contributions to social reporting: Institutions, activities, publications* (EuReporting Working Paper No. 8, Subproject European System of Social Indicators). Athens, Greece: National Centre for Social Research (EKKE).

Markus, H. R., & Kitayama, S. (1991). Culture and the self: Implications for cognition, emotion and motivation. *Psychological Review, 98,* 224–253.

Markus, H. R., & Kitayama, S. (1994). The cultural construction of self and emotion: Implications for social behavior. In S. Kitayama & H. R. Markus (Eds.), *Emotion and culture: Empirical studies of mutual influence* (pp. 89–130). Washington, DC: American Psychological Association.

Martin, J. A. (1989). Personal and interpersonal components of responsiveness. In M. H. Bornstein (Ed.), *Maternal responsiveness: Characteristics and consequences* (pp. 5–14). San Francisco: Jossey-Bass.

Martin, L., & Tesser, A. (Eds.). (1996). *Striving and feeling: Interactions between goals and affect.* Hillsdale, NJ: Lawrence Erlbaum Associates, Inc.

Martin, R. D. (1983). *Human brain evolution in an ecological context: Fifty-second James Arthur Lecture.* New York: American Museum of Natural History.

Mascolo, M. F., & Li, J. (Eds.). (2004). *Culture and developing selves: Beyond dichotomization.* San Francisco: Jossey-Bass.

Maynard, A. E. (2002). Cultural teaching: The development of teaching skills in Maya sibling interactions. *Child Development, 73,* 969–983.

Maynard, A. E., & Martini, M. I. (2005). *Learning in cultural context: Family, peers, and school.* New York: Kluwer Academic/Plenum.

Mayr, E. (1988). *Towards a new philosophy of biology.* Cambridge, MA: Harvard University Press.

Mbiti, J. S. (1990). *African religions and philosophy* (2nd ed.). Oxford, England: Heinemann Educational.

McCabe, A., & Peterson, C. (1991). Getting the story: A longitudinal study of parental styles in eliciting narratives and developing narrative skill. In A. McCabe & C. Peterson (Eds.), *Developing narrative structure* (pp. 217–253). Hillsdale, NJ: Lawrence Erlbaum Associates, Inc.

McClelland, D. C. (1987). *Human motivation.* Cambridge, MA: Harvard University Press.

McClelland, D. C., Koestner, R., & Weinberger, J. (1989). How do self-attributed and implicit motives differ? *Psychological Review, 96,* 690–702.

McClelland, D. C., & Pilon, D. A. (1983). Sources of adult motives in patterns of parent behavior in early childhood. *Journal of Personality and Social Psychology, 44,* 564–574.

McClosky, H., & Zaller, J. (1984). *The American ethos: Public attitudes towards capitalism and democracy.* Cambridge, MA: Harvard University Press.

McGillicuddy-deLisi, A. V. (1982). Parental beliefs about developmental processes. *Human Development, 25,* 192–200.

McGillicuddy-deLisi, A. V. (1985). The relationship between parental beliefs and children's cognitive level. In I. E. Sigel (Ed.), *Parental belief systems: The psychological consequences for children* (pp. 7–24). Hillsdale, NJ: Lawrence Erlbaum Associates, Inc.

McKenna, J. J. (1995). The potential benefits of infant parent co-sleeping in relation to SIDS prevention: Overview and critique of epidemiological bed sharing studies. In T. O. Rognum (Ed.), *Sudden infant death syndrome: New trends in the nineties* (pp. 256–265). Oslo, Norway: Scandinavian University Press.

McKenna, J. J. (2000). Cultural influences on infant and childhood sleep biology, and the science that studies it: Toward a more inclusive paradigm. In J. Loughlin, J. Carroll, & C. Marcus (Eds.), *Sleep and breathing in children: A developmental approach* (pp. 199–230). New York: Marcel Dekker.

Meltzoff, A. N. (1990). Towards a development cognitive science: The implications of cross-modal matching and imitation for the development of memory in infancy. In A. Diamond (Ed.), *The development and neural bases of higher cognitive functions* (Vol. 608, pp. 1–37). New York: Annals of New York Academy of Sciences.

Meltzoff, A. N. (1995). Infants' understanding of people and things: From body imitation to folk psychology. In J. L. Bermudez, A. Marcel, & N. Eilan (Eds.), *The body and the self* (pp. 43–69). Cambridge, MA: MIT Press.

Meltzoff, A. N., & Moore, M. K. (1977). Imitation of facial and manual gestures by human neonates. *Science, 198,* 75–78.

Meltzoff, A. N., & Moore, M. K. (1984). Newborn infants imitate adult gestures. *Child Development, 54,* 702–709.

Meltzoff, A. N., & Moore, M. K. (1992). Early imitation within a functional framework: The importance of person identity, movement, and development. *Infant Behavior and Development, 15,* 479–505.

Meltzoff, A. N., & Moore, M. K. (1994). Imitation, memory, and the representation of persons. *Infant Behavior and Development, 17,* 83–99.

Meltzoff, A. N., & Moore, M. K. (1997). Explaining facial imitation: A theoretical model. *Early Development and Parenting, 6,* 179–192.

Menon, P. (2003). Bollywood undressed. Retrieved December 20, 2005, from http://www.student.city.ac.uk/~ra831/group8/printer/prashprint.htm

Mey, G. (2000, June). Qualitative research and the analysis of processes: Considerations towards a qualitative developmental psychology. *Forum Qualitative Sozialforschung, 1*(1). Retrieved February 1, 2006, from http://www.qualitative-research.net/fqs-texte/1-00/1-00mey-e.htm

Middlemore, M. (1941). *The nursing couple.* Edinburgh, Scotland: Hamish Hamilton.

Millar, W. S. (1972). A study of operant conditioning under delayed reinforcement in early infancy. *Monographs of the Society for Research in Child Development, 37,* 1–44.

Miller, B. C., Leavitt, S. C., Merrill, J. K., & Park, K.-E. (2005). Marriages and families in the United States. In J. L. Roopnarine & U. P. Gielen (Eds.), *Families in global perspective* (pp. 293–310). Boston: Pearson.

Miller, P. J. (1996). Instantiating culture through discourse practices: Some personal reflections on socialization nd how to study it. In R. Jessor, A. Colby, & R. Shweder (Eds.), *Ethnography and human development. Context and meaning in social inquiry* (pp. 183–204). Chicago: University of Chicago Press.

Miller, P. J., Jung, H., & Mintz, J. (1996). Self construction through narrative practices: A Chinese and American comparison of early socialization. *Ethos, 24,* 237–280.

Miller, P. J., Potts, R., Fung, H., Hoogstra, L., & Mintz, J. (1990). Narrative practices and the social construction of self in childhood. *American Ethnologist, 17,* 292–311.

Miller, P. J., Wiley, A. R., Fung, H., & Liang, C. H. (1997). Personal storytelling as a medium of socialization in Chinese and American families. *Child Development, 68,* 557–568.

Minami, M. (2002). *Culture-specific language styles: The development of oral narrative and literacy.* Tonawanda, NY: Multilingual Matters.

Miranda, D., & Rosabal-Coto, M. (1997) *Patrones de Socialización Temprana: Reporte de Investigación, Instituto de Investigaciones Psicológicas* [Early socialization patterns: Research reports of the Institute of Psychological Studies]. San José, Costa Rica: Universidad de Costa Rica.

Mischel, W., Shoda, Y., & Rodriguez, M. L. (1989). Delay of gratification in children. *Science, 244,* 933–938.

Mize, J., & Pettit, G. S. (1997). Mothers' social coaching, mother–child relationships style and children's peer competence: Is the medium the message? *Child Development, 68,* 312–332.

Mondloch, C. J., Lewis, T. L., Budreau, D. R., Maurer, D., Dannemiller, J. L., Stephens, B. R., et al. (1999). Face perception during early infancy. *Psychological Science, 10,* 419–422.

Montagu, A. (1958). *Education and human relations.* New York: Grove.

Morelli, G. A., Rogoff, B. R., Oppenheim, D., & Goldsmith, D. (1992). Cultural variation in infants' sleeping arrangements: Questions of independence. *Developmental Psychology, 28,* 614–621.

Morelli, G. A., & Tronick, E. Z. (1991). Parenting and child developments in the Efe foragers and Lese farmers of Zaire. In M. H. Bornstein (Ed.), *Cultural approaches to parenting* (pp. 91–114). Hillsdale, NJ: Lawrence Erlbaum Associates, Inc.

Morton, J., & Johnson, M. H. (1991). Conspec and Conlearn: A two-process theory of infant face recognition. *Psychological Review, 98,* 164–181.

Mosko, S., Richard, C., McKenna, J., Drummond, S., & Mukai, D. (1997). Maternal proximity and infant CO_2 environment during bedsharing and possible implications for SIDS research. *American Journal of Physical Anthropology, 103,* 315–328.

Mülhäusler, P., & Harré, R. (1990). *Pronouns and people: The linguistic construction of social and personal identity.* Worcester, England: Blackwell.

Mullen, M. K. (1994). Earliest recollections of childhood: A demographic analysis. *Cognition, 52,* 55–79.

Mullen, M. K., & Yi, S. (1995). The cultural context of talk about the past: Implications for the development of autobiographical memory. *Cognitive Development, 10,* 407–419.

Mundy-Castle, A. C. (1974). Social and technological intelligence in Western and non-Western cultures. *Universitas, 4,* 46–52.

Mundy-Castle, A. C. (1991, June–July). Commentary and discussion. In P. M. Greenfield & R. R. Cocking (Chairs), *Continuities and discontinuities in cognitive socialization of minority children.* Proceedings of a workshop at the Department of Health and Human Services, Public Health Service, Alcohol, Drug Abuse, and Mental Health Administration, Washington, DC.

Munroe, R. H., & Munroe, R. L. (1971). Household density and infant care in an East African society. *Journal of Social Psychology, 83,* 3–13.

Mussen, P. H., & Parker, A. L. (1965). Mother nurturance at girls' incidental imitative learning. *Journal of Personality and Social Psychology, 2,* 94–97.

Naito, M. (2003). The relationship between theory of mind and episodic memory: Evidence for the development of autonoetic consciousness. *Journal of Experimental Psychology, 85,* 312–336.

Naito, M. (2004). Is theory of mind a universal and unitary construct? *ISSBD Newsletter, 1*(45), 9–11.

Naito, M., & Koyama, K. (2005). *The development of false belief understanding in Japanese children: Delay and deviance?* Manuscript submitted for publication.

Nakagawa, M., Lamb, M. E., & Miyake, K. (1992). Antecedents and correlates of the Strange Situation behavior of Japanese infants. *Journal of Cross-Cultural Psychology, 23,* 300–310.

Nash, M. (1997, February 3). Fertile minds. *Time,* pp. 48–56.

Neff, K. (2003). Understanding how universal goals of independence and interdependence are manifested within particular cultural contexts: Commentary on Heidi Keller's paper. *Human Nature, 46,* 312–318.

Neisser, U. (1993). The self perceived. In U. Neisser (Ed.), *The perceived self: Ecological and interpersonal sources of self-knowledge* (pp. 3–21). New York: Cambridge University Press.

Nelson, C. A. (1999). Change and continuity in neurobehavioral development: Lessons from the study of neurobiology and neural plasticity. *Infant Behavior and Development, 22,* 415–429.

Nelson, C. A. (2005, September). *Neuroscience and developmental psychlogy: An arranged marriage or a marriage of love?* Paper presented at the 17th Congress of the Developmental Psychology of the German Society for Psychology, Bochum, Germany.

Nelson, K. (1993). The psychological and social origins of autobiographical memory. *Psychological Science, 4,* 7–14.

Nelson, K. (1996). *Language in cognitive development: Emergence of the mediated mind.* New York: Cambridge University Press.

Nelson, K. (2003). Narrative and self, myth and memory: Emergence of the cultural self. In R. Fivush & C. A. Haden (Eds.), *Autobiographical memory and the construction of a narrative self: Developmental and cultural perspectives* (pp. 3–28). Mahwah, NJ: Lawrence Erlbaum Associates, Inc.

Neubauer, G., & Hurrelmann, K. (1995). Introduction: Comments on the individualization theorem. In G. Neubauer & K. Hurrelmann (Eds.), *Individualization in childhood and adolescence* (pp. 1–12). Berlin: Walter de Gruyter.

Ninio, A. (1979). The naive theory of the infant and other maternal attitudes in two subgroups in Israel. *Child Development, 50,* 976–980.

Nsamenang, A. B. (1992). *Human development in cultural context: A third world perspective.* Newbury Park, CA: Sage.

Nsamenang, A. B. (2003). Conceptualizing human development and education in sub-Saharan Africa at the interface of indigenous and exogenous influences. In T. S. Saraswathi (Ed.), *Cross-cultural perspectives in human development: Theory, research and applications* (pp. 213–235). New Delhi, India: Sage.

Nsamenang, A. B., & Lamb, M. E. (1994). Socialization of Nso children in the Bamenda grassfields of northwest Cameroon. In P. M. Greenfield & R. R. Cocking (Eds.), *Cross-cultural roots of minority child development* (pp. 133–146). Hillsdale, NJ: Lawrence Erlbaum Associates, Inc.

Nsamenang, A. B., & Lamb, M. E. (1995). The force of beliefs: How the parental values of the Nso of northwest Cameroon shape children's progress toward adult models. *Journal of Applied Developmental Psychology, 16,* 613–627.

Ochs, E. (1988). *Culture and language development: Language acquisition and socialization in a Samoan village.* Cambridge, England: Cambridge University Press.

Ogunnaike, O. A., & Houser, R. F. (2002) Yoruba toddlers' engagement in errands and cognitive performance on the Yoruba Mental subscale. *International Journal of Behavioral Development, 26,* 145–153.

Oleson, M. D. (1998). *Adolescents' recollection of early physical contact: Implications for attachment and intimacy.* Parkland, FL: Dissertation.com.

Palacios, J., & Moreno, M. C. (1996). Parents' and adolescents' ideas on children: Origins and transmission of intracultural diversity. In S. Harkness & C. M. Super (Eds.), *Parents' cultural belief systems: Their origins, expressions, and consequences* (pp. 215–253). New York: Guilford.

Papoušek, H., & Papoušek, M. (1987). Intuitive parenting: A dialectic counterpart to the infant's integrative competence. In J. D. Osofsky (Ed.), *Handbook of infant development* (2nd ed., pp. 669–720). New York: Wiley.

Papoušek, H., & Papoušek, M. (1991). Innate and cultural guidance of infants' integrative competencies: China, the United States, and Germany. In M. H. Bornstein (Ed.), *Cultural approaches to parenting* (pp. 23–44). Hillsdale, NJ: Lawrence Erlbaum Associates, Inc.

Papoušek, M. (1994). *Vom ersten Schrei zum ersten Wort: Vorsprachliche Kommunikation zwischen Mutter und Kind als Schrittmacher der Sprachentwicklung* [From the first cry to the first word: Prelinguistic communication between mother and child as pacemaker of language development]. Bern, Switzerland: Huber.

Papoušek, M., & Papoušek, H. (1991). Early verbalizations as precursors of language development. In M. E. Lamb & H. Keller (Eds.), *Infant development. Perspectives from German-speaking countries* (pp. 299–328). Hillsdale, NJ: Lawrence Erlbaum Associates, Inc.

Papoušek, M., Papoušek, H., & Bornstein, M. H. (1985). The naturalistic vocal environment of young infants: On the significance of homogeneity and variability in parental speech. In T. M. Field & N. Fox (Eds.), *Social perception in infants* (pp. 269–297). Norwood, NJ: Ablex.

Pascalis, O., de Schonen, S., Morton, J., Deruelle, C., & Fabre-Grenet, M. (1995). Mother's face recognition by neonates: A replication and an extension. *Infant Behavior and Development, 18,* 79–85.

Pelto, P. J. (1968, April). The difference between "tight" and "loose" societies. *Transaction,* pp. 37–40.

Perner, J., Ruffman, T., & Leekham, S. R. (1994). Theory of mind is contagious: You catch it from your sibs. *Child Development, 65,* 1228–1238.

Perrez, M., Achermann, E., & Diethelm, K. (1983). Die Bedeutung der sozialen Kontingenzen fuer die Entwicklung des Kindes im ersten Lebensjahr [The meaning of social contingencies for the development of the infant during the first year of life]. *Verhaltensmodifikation, 4,* 114–129.

Piaget, J. (1953). *The origins of intelligence in children.* London: Routledge.

Pillemer, D. B., & White, S. H. (1989). Childhood events recalled by children and adults. In H. W. Reese (Ed.), *Advances in child development and behavior* (Vol. 21, pp. 297–340). Orlando, FL: Academic.

Pipp-Siegel, S., & Foltz, C. (1997). Toddlers' acquisition of self/other knowledge: Ecological and interpersonal aspects of self and other. *Child Development, 68,* 69–79.

Pirttilä-Backman, A.-M., Kassea, B. R., & Ikonen, T. (2004). Cameroonian forms of collectivism and individualism. *Journal of Cross-Cultural Psychology, 35,* 481–498.

Pomerleau, A., Malcuit, G., & Sabatier, C. (1991). Child-rearing practices and parental beliefs in three cultural groups of Montréal: Québécois, Vietnamese, Haitian. In M. H. Bornstein (Eds.), *Cultural approaches to parenting* (pp. 45–68). Hillsdale, NJ: Lawrence Erlbaum Associates, Inc.

Poortinga, Y. H. (1992). Towards a conceptualization of culture for psychology. In S. Iwawaki, Y. Kashima, & K. Leung (Eds.), *Innovations in cross-cultural psychology* (pp. 3–17). Lisse, the Netherlands: Swets & Zeitlinger.

Posada, G., Jacobs, A., Richmond, M. K., Carbonell, O. A., Alzate, G., Bustamante, M. R., et al. (2002). Maternal caregiving and infant security in two cultures. *Developmental Psychology, 38,* 67–78.

Potter, J., & Wetherell, M. (1987). *Discourse and social psychology.* London: Sage.

Power, T., & Chapieski, M. (1986). Child rearing and impulse control in toddlers: A naturalistic investigation. *Developmental Psychology, 2,* 271–275.

Prechtl, H. (1984). *Continuity of neural functions from prenatal to postnatal life.* London: Spastics International Medical Publications.

Priel, B., & de Schonen, S. (1986). Self recognition: A study of a population without mirrors. *Journal of Experimental Child Psychology, 41,* 237–250.

Quartz, S. R., & Sejnowski, T. J. (1997). The neural basis of cognitive development: A constructivist manifesto. *Behavioral and Brain Sciences, 20,* 537–596.

Quinn, N., & Holland, D. (1987). *Cultural models of language and thought.* New York: Cambridge University Press.

Rabain-Jamin, J. (1979). *L'enfant du lignage: Du sevrage à la classe d'âge chez les Wolof du Sénégal* [Infant of Lineage: From weaning until the coming of age with the Wolof from Senegal]. Paris: Payot.

Rabain-Jamin, J., Maynard, A. E., & Greenfield, P. M. (2003). Implications of sibling caregiving for sibling relations and teaching interactions in two cultures. *Ethos, 31,* 204–231.

Rabain-Jamin, J., & Sabeau-Jouannet, E. (1997). Maternal speech to 4-month-old infants in two cultures: Wolof and French. *International Journal of Behavioral Development, 20,* 425–451.

Rabinovich, E. P. (1998, August). *Comparative study of sleeping arrangements and breastfeeding in Brazilian children.* Paper presented at the 14th IACCP Congress, Bellingham, WA.

Radke-Yarrow, M., Zahn-Waxler, C., & Chapman, M. (1983). Children's prosocial disposition and behavior. In E. M. Hetherington (Ed.), *Handbook of child psychology* (Vol. 4, pp. 469–545). New York: Wiley.

Realo, A. (2003). Comparison of public and academic discourses: Estonian individualism and collectivism revisited. *Culture and Psychology, 9,* 47–77.

Reese, E., Haden, C. A., & Fivush, R. (1993). Mother–child conversations about the past: Relationships of style and memory over time. *Cognitive Development, 8,* 403–430.

Registrar General of India. (2003). *SRS based abridged life tables* (SRS Analytical Studies, Report No. 3, 2003). New Delhi, India: Registrar General of India. Retrieved December 12, 2005, from http://www.indiatogether.org/health/infofiles/life.htm

Richman, A. L., LeVine, R. A., Staples New, R., Howrigan, G. A., Welles-Nystron, B., & LeVine, S. E. (1988). Maternal behavior to infants in five cultures. In R. A. LeVine, P. M. Miller, & M. M. West (Eds.), *Parenting behavior in diverse societies* (pp. 81–98). San Francisco: Jossey-Bass.

Richman, A. L., Miller, P. M., & LeVine, R. A. (1992). Cultural and educational variations in maternal responsiveness. *Developmental Psychology, 28,* 614–621.

Rizzolatti, G., Fogassi, L., & Gallese, V. (2001). Neurophysiological mechanisms underlying the understanding and imitation of action. *Nature Reviews Neuroscience, 2,* 661–670.

Rizzolatti, G., Luppino, G., & Matelli, M. (1998). The organization of the cortical motor system: New concepts. *Electroencephalography and Clinical Neurophysiology, 106,* 283–296.

Rochat, P. (1997). Early development of the ecological self. In C. Dent-Read & P. Zukow-Goldring (Eds.), *Evolving explanations of development: Ecological approaches to organism–environment systems* (pp. 91–121). Washington, DC: American Psychological Association.

Rochat, P. (2004). Origins of self-concept. In G. Bremner & A. Fogel (Eds.), *Blackwell handbook of infant development* (2nd ed., pp. 191–212). Malden, MA: Blackwell.

Roggman, L., Boyce, L. K., Cook, G. A., Christiansen, K., & Jones, D. (2004, Winter). Playing with daddy: Social toy play, early head start and developmental outcomes. *Fathering, 2,* 83–108.

Rogoff, B. (1978). Spot observation: An introduction and examination. *Quarterly Newsletter of the Institute for Comparative Human Development, 2*(2), 21–26.

Rogoff, B. (2003). *The cultural nature of human development.* New York: Oxford University Press.

Rogoff, B., Mistry, J., Göncü, A., & Mosier, C. (1993). Guided participation in cultural activity by toddlers and caregivers. *Monographs of the Society for Research in Child Development, 58*(8).

Rogoff, B., Paradise, R., Mejfa Arauz, R., Correa-Chávez, M., & Angelillo, C. (2003). First-hand learning through intent participation. *Annual Review of Psychology, 54,* 175–203.

Rohner, R. P. (1986). *The warmth dimension: Foundations of psychological acceptance–rejection theory.* Beverly Hills, CA: Sage.

Rosabal-Coto, M. (2000, July). *Socialization goals and child rearing in Costa Rica.* Paper presented at Advanced Research and Training Seminars 2000: Pathways across development: Cross-cultural perspective, Stockholm, Sweden.

Rosabal-Coto, M. (2004). *Parental belief systems, conflict resolution strategies, and cultural orientation in the mother–child interactive context: A comparative study of two Costa Rican samples.* Unpublished doctoral dissertation, University of Osnabrück, Faculty of Human Sciences, Osnabrück, Germany.

Ross, M. (1989). Relation of implicit theories to the construction of personal histories. *Psychological Review, 96,* 341–357.

Rothbaum, F., Pott, M., Azuma, H., Miyake, K., & Weisz, J. (2000). The development of close relationships in Japan and the United States: Paths of symbiotic harmony and generative tension. *Child Development, 71,* 1121–1142.

Rothbaum, F., Weisz, J., Pott, M., Miyake, K., & Morelli, G. (2000). Attachment and culture: Security in the United States and Japan. *American Psychologist, 55,* 1093–1104.

Rovee-Collier, C. (1997). Dissociations in infant memory: Rethinking the development of implicit and explicit memory. *Psychological Review, 104,* 467–489.

Rovee-Collier, C., & Shye, C. W. G. (1992). A functional and cognitive analysis of infant longterm memory retention. In M. L. Howe, C. J. Brainerd, & V. F. Reyna (Eds.), *Development of longterm retention* (pp. 3–55). New York: Springer.

Ruffman, T., Perner, J., Naito, M., Parkin, L., & Clements, W. (1998). Older (but not younger) siblings facilitate false belief understanding. *Developmental Psychology, 34,* 161–174.

Ruffman, T., Perner, J., & Parkin, L. (1999). How parenting style affects false belief understanding. *Social Development, 8,* 395–411.

Ruffman, T., Slade, L., & Crowe, E. (2002). The relation between children's and mothers' mental state language and theory of mind understanding. *Child Development, 73,* 734–751.

Russel, A. (1997). On contingency as the precursor of secure attachment. *ISSBD Newsletter, 31*(1), 5–7.

Salapatek, P. (1975). Pattern perception in early infancy. In L. Cohen & P. Salapatek (Eds.), *Infant perception: From sensation to cognition: Vol. 1. Basic visual processes* (pp. 133–248). New York: Academic.

Saraswathi, T. S. (1994). Women in poverty context: Balancing economic and child care needs. In R. Borooah, K. Cloud, S. Seshadri, T. S. Saraswathi, J. T. Peterson, & A. Verma (Eds.), *Capturing complexity. An interdisciplinary look at women, households and development* (pp. 162–178). New Delhi, India: Sage.

Saraswathi, T. S. (2004, August). *Beyond the two and three dimensional models of "self-ways."* Paper presented at the 28th International Congress of Psychology, Beijing, China.

Saraswathi, T. S., & Ganapathy, H. (2002). Indian parents' ethnotheories as reflections of the Hindu scheme of child and human development. In H. Keller, Y. Poortinga, & A. Schölmerich (Eds.), *Between culture and biology* (pp. 79–88). Cambridge, England: Cambridge University Press.

Saraswathi, T. S., & Pai, S. (1997). Socialization in the Indian context. In H. S. R. Kao & D. Sinha (Eds.), *Asian perspectives on psychology* (pp. 74–92). New Delhi, India: Sage.

Schaefer, E. S. (1959). A circumflex model for maternal behavior. *Journal of Abnormal and Social Psychology, 59,* 226–235.

Schneider-Rosen, K., & Rothbaum, F. (1993). Quality of parental caregiving and security of attachment. *Developmental Psychology, 29,* 358–367.

Schölmerich, A., Keller, H., & Leyendecker, B. (1991). The study of early interaction in a contextual perspective: Culture, communications, and eye contact. In J. Valsiner (Ed.), *Child development within culturally structured environments: Vol. 3. Comparative-cultural and constructivist perspectives* (pp. 29–50). Norwood, NJ: Ablex.

Schölmerich, A., & Weßels, H. (1998). Beobachtungsmethoden und Auswertungsverfahren in der Entwicklungspsychologie [Observational methods and evaluation procedures in developmental psychology]. In H. Keller (Ed.), *Lehrbuch Entwicklungspsychologie* (pp. 243–260). Bern, Switzerland: Huber.

Schore, A. N. (1994). *Affect regulation and the origin of the self: The neurobiology of emotional development.* Hillsdale, NJ: Lawrence Erlbaum Associates, Inc.

Schore, A. N. (2000). Attachment and the regulation of the right brain. *Attachment and Human Development, 2,* 23–47.

Schore, A. N. (2001). The effects of a secure attachment relationship on right brain development, affect regulation, and infant mental health. *Infant Mental Health Journal, 22,* 7–66.

Schütz, A., &. Luckmann, T. (1984). *Strukturen der Lebenswelt. Band 1 und 2* [Structure of the life world: Vols. 1 & 2]. Frankfurt, Germany: Suhrkamp.

Seidel, J. V. (1998). Qualitative data analysis. *The Ethnograph, 5, Appendix E.* Retrieved February 2, 2006, from http://www.qualisresearch.com

Seligman, M. E. P. (1975). *Learned helplessness: Depression, development and death.* New York: Freeman.

Serpell, R., & Hatano, G. (1996). Education, schooling, and literacy. In J. W. Berry, P. R. Dasen, & T. S. Saraswathi (Eds.), *Handbook of cross-cultural psychology: Vol. 2. Basic processes and human development* (2nd ed., pp. 339–376). Boston: Allyn & Bacon.

Seymour, S. (1999). *Women, family, and child care in India: A world in transition.* Cambridge, England: Cambridge University Press.

Sheingold, I. C., & Tenney, Y. J. (1982). Memory for a salient childhood event. In U. Neisser (Ed.), *Memory observed: Remembering in natural context* (pp. 201–212). San Francisco: Freeman.

Shimizu, H. (2001). Beyond individualism and sociocentrism: An ontological analysis of the opposing elements in personal experiences of Japanese adolescents. In H. Shimizu & R. A. LeVine (Eds.), *Japanese frames of mind: Cultural perspectives on human development* (pp. 205–227). New York: Cambridge University Press.

Shonkoff, J., & Phillips, D. (2000). *From neurons to neighborhoods: The science of early childhood development.* Washington, DC: National Academy Press.

Shostak, M. (1981). *Nisa. The life and Words of a !Kung woman.* Cambridge, MA: Harvard University Press.

Shotter, J. (1989). Social accountability and the social construction of "you." In J. Shotter & K. J. Gergen (Eds.), *Texts of identity* (pp. 133–151). London: Sage.

Shweder, R. A., & Bourne, E. J. (1984). Does the concept of a person vary cross-culturally? In R. A. Shweder & R. A. LeVine (Eds.), *Culture theory: Essays on mind, self and emotion* (pp. 158–199). Cambridge, England: Cambridge University Press.

Shweder, R. A., Goodnow, J., Hatano, G., LeVine, R. A., Markus, H., & Miller, P. (1998). The cultural psychology of development: One mind, many mentalities. In R. M. Lerner (Ed.), *Handbook of child psychology: Vol. 1. Theoretical models of human development* (5th ed., pp. 865–937). New York: Wiley.

Shweder, R. A., Jensen, L. A., & Goldstein, W. M. (1995). Who sleeps by whom revisited: A method for extracting the moral goods implicit in practice. In J. Goodnow, P. Miller, & F. Kessel (Eds.), *Cultural practices as contexts for development* (pp. 21–39). San Francisco: Jossey-Bass.

Siegel, D. J. (1999). *The developing mind: Toward a neurobiology of interpersonal experience.* New York: Guilford.

Siegler, R., Deloache, J., & Eisenberg, N. (2003). *How children develop.* New York: Worth.

Sigel, I. E. (Ed.). (1985). *Parental belief systems: The psychological consequences for children.* Hillsdale, NJ: Lawrence Erlbaum Associates, Inc.

Simion, F., Valenza, E., & Umilta, C. (1998). Mechanisms underlying face preference at birth. In F. Simion & G. Butterworth (Eds.), *The development of sensory, motor and cognitive capacities in early infancy: From perception to cognition* (pp. 87–101). Hove, England: Psychology Press.

Simmons, G. B., & Bernstein, S. (1982). The educational status of parents, and infant and child mortality in rural North India. *Health Policy Education, 2*(3–4), 349–367.

Singh, R. L. (1971). Gujarat region. In R. L. Singh (Ed.), *India: A regional geography* (pp. 879–906). Varanasi, India: National Geographic Society of India.

Sinha, D. (1988, February). *Indicators of psycho-social development of children in India.* Keynote address at the Workshop on Developmental Norms of Children, National Institute of Public Cooperation and Child Development, New Delhi, India.

Skinner, E. A. (1985). Determinants of mother sensitive and contingent responsive behavior: The role of child rearing beliefs and socioeconomic status. In I. E. Sigel (Ed.), *Parental belief systems: The psychological consequences for children* (pp. 51–82). Hillsdale, NJ: Lawrence Erlbaum Associates, Inc.

Slater, A. (2004). Visual perception. In G. Bremner & A. Fogel (Eds.), *Blackwell handbook of infant development* (2nd ed., pp. 5–34). Malden, MA: Blackwell.

Spock, B., & Rothenberg, M. B. (1992). *Dr. Spock's baby and child care* (6th rev. ed.). New York: Dutton.

Sroufe, L. A. (1988). The role of infant–caregiver attachment in development. In J. Belsky & T. Nezworski (Eds.), *Clinical implications of attachment* (pp. 18–40). Hillsdale, NJ: Lawrence Erlbaum Associates, Inc.

Stack, D. M. (2004). The salience of touch and physical contact during infancy: Unraveling some of the mysteries of the somesthetic sense. In G. Bremner & A. Fogel (Eds.), *Blackwell handbook of infant development* (2nd ed., pp. 351–378). Malden, MA: Blackwell.

Stang, W. (1989). *Lernen visueller Kontingenzen bei dreimonatigen Säuglingen* [Learning of visual contingencies in three-month-old infants]. Unpublished doctoral dissertation, Free University, Berlin.

Staub, E. (1979). *Positive behavior and morality: Socialization and development* (Vol. 2). New York: Academic.

Stern, D. N. (1985). Affect attunement. In J. D. Call, E. Galenson, & R. L. Tyson (Eds.), *Frontiers of infant psychiatry* (pp. 3–14). New York: Basic Books.

Stern, D. N. (1985). *The interpersonal world of the infant: A view from psychoanalysis and developmental psychology.* New York: Basic Books.

Stern, W. (1923). *Psychologie der frühen Kindheit.* Leipzig, Germany: Quelle & Meyer. (Original work published 1914)

Stocking, G. (1974). *A Franz Boas reader: The shaping of American anthropology, 1883–1911.* New York: Basic Books.

Stone, J., Smith, H., & Murphy, L. (Eds.). (1973). *The competent infant.* New York: Basic Books.

Storfer, M. (1999). Myopia, intelligence, and the expanding human neocortex: Behavioral influences and evolutionary implications. *International Journal of Neuroscience, 98,* 153–276.

Strauss, A., & Corbin, J. (1990). *Basics of qualitative research—Grounded theory procedures and techniques.* Newbury Park, CA: Sage.

Sünker, H. (1995). Childhood between individualization and institutionalization. In G. Neubauer & H. Hurrelmann (Eds.), *Individualization in childhood and adolescence* (pp. 37–51). Berlin: de Gruyter.

Suomi, S. J. (1999). Attachment in Rhesus monkeys. In J. Cassidy & P. R. Shaver (Eds.), *Handbook of attachment: Theory, research, and clinical applications* (pp. 181–197). New York: Guilford.

Super, C. M. (1976). Environmental effects on motor development: A case of African infant precocity. *Developmental Medicine and Child Neurology, 18,* 561–567.

Super, C. M. (1981). Behavioral development in infancy. In R. H. Munroe, R. L. Munroe, & B. B. Whiting (Eds.), *Handbook of cross-cultural human development* (pp. 181–270). New York: Garland.

Super, C. M., & Harkness, S. (1981). Figure, ground, and gestalt: The cultural context of the active individual. In R. M. Lerner & N. A. Busch-Rossnagel (Eds.), *Individuals as producers of their development: A life-span perspective* (pp. 69–86). New York: Academic.

Super, C. M., & Harkness, S. (1982). The infant's niche in rural Kenya and metropolitan American. In L. L. Adler (Ed.), *Cross-cultural research at issue* (pp. 47–55). New York: Academic.

Super, C. M., & Harkness, S. (1996). The cultural structuring of child development. In J. W. Berry, P. R. Dasen, & T. S. Saraswathi (Eds.), *Handbook of cross-cultural psychology: Vol. 2. Basic processes and human development* (2nd ed., pp. 1–39). Boston: Allyn & Bacon.

Symons, D. K., & Moran, G. (1994). Responsiveness and dependency are different aspects of social contingencies: An example from mother and infant smiles. *Infant Behavior and Development, 17,* 209–214.

Tamis-LeMonda, C. S., Bornstein, M. H., Cyphers, L., Toda, S., & Ogino, M. (1992). Language and play at one year. *International Journal of Behavioral Development, 15,* 19–42.

Tanner, J. (1978). *From fetus into man: Physical growth from conception to maturity.* Cambridge, MA: Harvard University Press.

Tapia Uribe, F. M., LeVine, R. A., & LeVine, S. E. (1994). Maternal behavior in a Mexican community: The changing environments of children. In P. M. Greenfield & R. R. Cocking (Eds.), *Cross-cultural roots of minority child development* (pp. 41–54). Hillsdale, NJ: Lawrence Erlbaum Associates, Inc.

Tarabulsy, G. M., Tessier, R., & Kappas, A. (1996). Contingency detection and the contingent organization of behavior in interactions: Implications for socioemotional development in infancy. *Psychological Bulletin, 120,* 25–41.

Taubman, B. (1990). *Curing infant colic: The 7 minute program for soothing the fussy baby.* New York: Bantam.

Tchombe, T. (1997). Mütterliches Sozialisationsverhalten in Kamerun: Kontinuität und Veränderung [Maternal socialisatory behaviors in Cameroon: Continuity and change]. In B. Nauck & U. Schönpflug (Eds.), *Familien in verschiedenen Kulturen* (pp. 125–141). Stuttgart, Germany: Enke Verlag.

Teachman, J. D., Tedrow, L. M., & Crowder, K. D. (2000). The changing demography of America's families. *Journal of Marriage and the Family, 62,* 1234–1246.

Tessler, M., & Nelson, K. (1994). Making memories: The influence of joint encoding on later recall by young children. *Consciousness and Cognition, 3,* 307–326.

Thomas, D. G., Whitaker, E., Crow, C. D., Little, V., Love, L., Lykins, M. S., et al. (1997). Event-related potential variability as a measure of information storage in infant development. *Developmental Neuropsychology, 13,* 205–232.

Tiedemann, D. (1787). Beobachtungen über die Entwicklung der Seelentätigkeit bei Kindern [Observations about the development of children's mental activities]. *Hessische Beiträge zur Gelehrsamkeit und Kunst, Band II*(2–3).

Tobin, J. J., Wu, D. Y. H., & Davidson, D. H. (1989). *Preschool in three cultures: Japan, China and the United States.* New Haven, CT: Yale University Press.

Tomasello, M., Kruger, A. C., & Ratner, H. H. (1993). Cultural learning. *Behavioral and Brain Sciences, 16,* 495–552.

Tooby, J., & Cosmides, L. (1990). The past explains the present: Emotional adaptations and the structure of ancestral environments. *Ethology and Sociobiology, 11,* 375–424.

Triandis, H. C. (1995). *Individualism and collectivism.* Boulder, CO: Westview.

Trivers, R. L. (1985). *Social evolution.* Menlo Park, CA: Benjamin/Cummings.

Tulviste, T. (2003). Contextual variability in interactions between mothers and 2 years olds. *First Language, 23,* 311–325.

Tzourio-Mazoyer, N., Landeau, B., Papathanassiou, D., Crivello, F., Etard, O., Delcroix, N., et al. (2002). Automated anatomical labeling of activations in SPM using a macroscopic anatomical parcellation of the MNI MRI single-subject brain. *NeuroImage, 15,* 273–289.

Uberoi, P. (Ed.). (2005). *Family, kinship and marriage in India.* New Delhi, India: Oxford University Press.

U.S. Department of Health and Human Services, Health Resources and Services Administration. (2005). *Women's health USA 2005.* Rockville, MD: Author.

Van de Vijver, F., & Leung, K. (1997). *Methods and data analyisis for cross-cultural research.* Thousand Oaks, CA: Sage.

van Egeren, L. A., Barratt, M. S., & Roach, M. A. (2001). Mother–infant responsiveness: Timing, mutual regulation, and interactional context. *Developmental Psychology, 37,* 684–697.

van IJzendoorn, M. H., & Sagi, A. (1999). Cross-cultural patterns of attachment: Universal and contextual dimensions. In J. Cassidy & P. R. Shaver (Eds.), *Handbook of attachment: Theory, research, and clinical applications* (pp. 713–734). New York: Guilford.

Vaskovics, L. A. (Ed.). (1999). *Gewalt in der Familie und gesellschaftlicher Handlungsbedarf* [Violence in the family and the necessity for societal intervention]. Bamberg, Germany: Universität, Staatsinstitut für Familienforschung.

Vega-Robles, I. (2001). Las familias costarricenses en el contexto del nuevo milenio [Costa Rican families in the context of the new millennium]. In I. Vega-Robles & A. Cordero (Eds.), *Realidad familiar en Costa Rica.* San José, Costa Rica: FLACSO.

Vinden, P. G. (2001). Parenting attitudes and children's understanding of mind: A comparison of Korean American and Anglo-American families. *Cognitive Development, 16,* 793–809.

Voelker, S. (2000). *Eine Analyse von Interaktionsmustern zwischen Mutter und Kind im dritten Lebensmonat: Die Bedeutung von Wärme und Kontingenz* [An analysis of interactional patterns between mother and three-month-old infants]. Unpublished doctoral dissertation, University of Osnabrück, Department of Psychology and Health Sciences, Osnabrück, Germany.

Voelker, S., Yovsi, R. D., & Keller, H. (1998, July). *Maternal interactional quality as assessed by non-trained raters from different cultural backgrounds.* Poster presented at the 15th biennial ISSBD meetings, Bern, Switzerland.

Voland, E., Dunbar, R., Engel, C., & Stephan, P. (1997). Population increase and sex biased parental investment in humans: Evidence from 18th and 19th century Germany. *Current Anthropology, 38,* 129–135.

Wahler, R. G. (1994). Child conduct problems: Disorders in conduct or social continuity? *Journal of Child and Family Studies, 3,* 143–156.

Walsh Escarce, M. E. (1989). A cross-cultural study of Nepalese neonatal behavior. In J. K. Nugent, B. M. Lester, & T. B. Brazelton (Eds.), *The cultural context of infancy: Vol. 1. Biology, culture, and infant development* (pp. 65– 86). Norwood, NJ: Ablex.

Wang, Q. (2001). Cultural effects on adults' earliest childhood recollection and self description: Implications for the relation between memory and the self. *Journal of Personality and Social Psychology, 81,* 220–233.

Wang, Q. (2004). The emergence of cultural self-constructs: Autobiographical memory and self-description in European American and Chinese children. *Developmental Psychology, 40,* 3–15.

Wang, Q., Leichtman, M. D., & Davies, K. I. (2000). Sharing memories and telling stories: American and Chinese mothers and their three-year-olds. *Memory, 8,* 159–177.

Washburn, S. L. (1960). Tools and human evolution. *Scientific American, 203,* 63–75.

Watson, J. S. (1967). Memory and "contingency analysis" in infant learning. *Merrill-Palmer Quarterly, 13,* 55–76.

Watson, J. S. (1971). Cognitive-perceptual development in infancy: Setting for the seventies. *Merrill-Palmer Quarterly, 17,* 139–152.

Watson, J. S. (1972). Smiling, cooing, and "the game". *Merrill-Palmer Quarterly, 18,* 323–340.

Watson, J. S. (1979). Perception of contingency as a determinant of social responsiveness. In E. B. Thomas (Ed.), *Origins of the infants social responsiveness* (pp. 33–64). Hillsdale, NJ: Lawrence Erlbaum Associates, Inc.

Watson, J. S. (1985). Contingency perception in early social development. In T. M. Field & N. A. Fox (Eds.), *Social perception in infants* (pp. 157–176). Norwood, NJ: Ablex.

Watson, J. S. (2001). Contingency perception and misperception in infancy: Some potential implications for attachment. *Bulletin of the Menninger Clinic, 65,* 296–320.

Watson, M. W. (1994). The relation between anxiety and pretend play. In A. Slade & D. P. Wolf (Eds.), *Children at play: Clinical and developmental approaches to meaning and representation* (pp. 33–47). New York: Oxford University Press.

Weisner, T. S. (1987). Socialization for parenthood in sibling caretaking societies. In J. B. Lancaster, J. Altmann, A. S. Rossi, & L. Sherrod (Eds.), *Parenting across the life span: Biosocial dimensions* (pp. 237–270). New York: Aldine.

Weisner, T. S. (1989). Social support for children among the Abaluyia of Kenya. In D. Belle (Ed.), *Children's social networks and social supports* (pp. 70–90). New York: Wiley.

Weisner, T. S. (2000). Culture, childhood, and progress in Sub-Saharan Africa. In L. E. Harrison & S. P. Huntington (Eds.), *Culture matters: How values shape human progress* (pp. 141–157). New York: Basic Books.

Weisner, T. S. (2002). Ecocultural understanding of children's developmental pathways. *Human Development, 45,* 275–281.

Welch-Ross, M. K. (1997). Mother–child participation in conversation about the past: Relationships to preschoolers' theory of mind. *Developmental Psychology, 33,* 618–629.

Welch-Ross, M. K. (2001). Personalizing the temporally extended self: Evaluative self-awareness and the development of autobiographical memory. In C. Moor & K. Lemmon (Eds.), *The self in time: Developmental perspectives* (pp. 97–120). Mahwah, NJ: Lawrence Erlbaum Associates, Inc.

Wellman, H. M., Cross, D., & Watson, J. S. (2001). Meta-analysis of theory-of-mind development: The truth about false belief. *Child Development, 72,* 655–684.

Wellman, H. M., & Miller, J. G. (2005). *Including deontic reasoning as fundamental to theory of mind.* Manuscript submitted for publication.

Whiting, B. B. (1963). *Six cultures: Studies of child rearing.* New York: Wiley.

Whiting, B. B., & Edwards, C. (1988). *Children of different worlds: The formation of social behavior.* Cambridge, MA: Harvard University Press.

Whiting, J. W. M. (1981). Environmental constraints on infant care practices. In R. H. Munroe, R. L. Munroe, & B. B. Whiting (Eds.), *Handbook of cross-cultural human development* (pp. 155–179). New York: Garland.

Whiting, J. W. M., & Child, L. (1953). *Child training and personality.* New Haven, CT: Yale University Press.

Wilson, E. O. (1975). *Sociobiology: A new synthesis.* Cambridge, MA: Harvard University Press.

Wilson, M., & Daly, M. (1997). Life expectancy, economic inequality, homicide, and reproductive timing in Chicago neighbourhoods. *British Medical Journal, 314,* 1271–1278.

Woike, B. A., Gershkovich, I., Piorkowski, R., & Polo, M. (1999). The role of motives in the content and structure of autobiographical memory. *Journal of Personality and Social Psychology, 76,* 600–612.

Wolf, A. W., Lozoff, B., Latz, S., & Paludetto, R. (1996). Parental theories in the management of young children's sleep in Japan, Italy, and the United States. In S. Harkness & C. M. Super (Eds.), *Parent's cultural belief systems: Their origin, expression, and consequences* (pp. 364–384). New York: Guilford.

Wu, D. (1985). Child training in Chinese culture. In W. S. Tseng & D. Wu (Eds.), *Chinese culture and mental health* (pp. 113–134). Orlando, FL: Academic.

Xiao, H. (2000). Structure of childrearing values in urban China. *Sociological Perspectives, 43,* 457–471.

Yarrow, L. J., Pedersen, F. A., & Rubenstein, J. (1977). Mother–infant interaction and development in infancy. In P. H. Leiderman, S. R. Tulkin, & A. Rosenfeld (Eds.), *Culture and infancy: Variations in the human experience* (pp. 539–564). New York: Academic.

Yogman, M. W. (1982). Development of the father–infant relationship. In H. E. Fitzgerald, B. M. Lester, & M. W. Yogman (Eds.), *Theory and research in behavioral pediatrics* (pp. 221–279). New York: Plenum.

Yovsi, R. D. (2001). *Ethnotheories about breastfeeding and mother–infant interaction: The case of sedentary Nso farmers and nomadic Fulani pastorals with their infants 3–6 months of age in Mbvem subdivision of the Northwest providence of Cameroon, Africa.* Unpublished doctoral dissertation, University of Osnabrück, Faculty of Human Sciences, Osnabrück, Germany.

Yovsi, R. D. (2003). *An investigation of breastfeeding and mother–infant interactions in the face of cultural taboos and belief systems: The case of Nso and Fulani mothers and their infants of 3–5 months of age in Mbvem subdivision of the northwest province of Cameroon.* Münster, Germany: Lit.

Yovsi, R. D. (2004). *The Yovsi Scale of Nso parenting quality.* Unpublished manual, University of Osnabrück, Faculty of Human Sciences, Department of Culture and Development, Osnabrück, Germany.

Yovsi, R. D., & Keller, H. (2003). Breastfeeding: An adaptive process. *Ethos, 31,* 147–171.

Yovsi, R. D., & Keller, H. (2006). *The architecture of co-sleeping: The case of the Cameroonian Nso.* Manuscript submitted for publication.

Yovsi, R. D., Keller, H., Kärtner, J., & Lohaus, A. (2006). *Maternal interactional quality in two cultural environments: German middle-class and Cameroonian Nso rural mothers.* Manuscript submitted for publication.

Zimba, R. F. (2001). Development applied: The impact of adversity of childhood and youth development in Southern Africa. *Cross-Cultural Psychology Bulletin, 35*(4), 10–16.

Zukow-Goldring, P. (1995). Sibling caregiving. In M. Bornstein (Ed.), *Handbook of parenting: Vol. 3. Status and social conditions of parenting* (pp. 177–208). Hillsdale, NJ: Lawrence Erlbaum Associates, Inc.

Author Index

Subject Index